THE CLERICAL
ORGANIZATION OF THE
HOUSE OF COMMONS
1661–1850

BY

ORLO CYPRIAN WILLIAMS
C.B., M.C., D.C.L.

OXFORD
AT THE CLARENDON PRESS
1954

PRINTED IN GREAT BRITAIN

TO MY OLD FRIEND

GILBERT, LORD CAMPION

WITH GREAT AFFECTION

Oxford University Press, Amen House, London E.C. 4
GLASGOW NEW YORK TORONTO MELBOURNE WELLINGTON
BOMBAY CALCUTTA MADRAS KARACHI CAPE TOWN IBADAN
Geoffrey Cumberlege, Publisher to the University

PREFACE

I WISH to record my gratitude to the Trustees of the Lever-
hulme Research Fund for the award of a grant for one year
which was of material assistance at the beginning of my
researches.

I am particularly grateful to Mr. J. B. Whitmore, F.S.A., for
his very generous assistance in furnishing me with genealogical
information regarding John Hatsell, the Ley family, and the White
family; also to Mr. M. F. Bond, Records Officer of the House of
Lords, for his help and for his discovery to me of a hitherto lost
record of the House of Commons. And I express my warm
thanks to the following for courteous and valuable response to
inquiries:—Miss Gladys Scott Thomson; Mrs. Henry Ley; Mr.
John Henry Hansard who allowed me to consult Luke Hansard's
ledger; the Librarians and assistant Librarians of King's College,
Cambridge, Balliol College, Oxford, and All Souls College,
Oxford; the Librarians of the four Inns of Court; the Archivists
of the City of Westminster, of the Lancashire Record Office, and of
the City of Bristol; the Deputy Keeper of the Records, City of
London Corporation; the City Treasurer of Liverpool, the Town
Clerk of Worcester, and the City Librarians of Sheffield and
Nottingham; and Mr. D. C. L. Holland of the House of Com-
mons Library.

I also thank the present Speaker of the House of Commons,
the Rt. Hon. W. S. Morrison, for permission to make reference in
my last chapter to the manuscript minutes of the Commissioners
for the House of Commons Offices; and Sir David Keir, the
Master of Balliol, for permission to quote a passage from his
Constitutional History of Modern Britain.

Finally, I must record my deep regret for the premature death,
through a most unlucky accident, of the late Mr. C. John Brooke,
of Trehill, Devonshire, who placed at my disposal the Ley
manuscripts. Nor can I forget the immense debt which anybody
who embarks on researches of this kind owes to the incomparable
collection of records at the Public Record Office and to the
collection of manuscripts in the British Museum.

O. W.

THE ATHENÆUM *27 March 1954*

CONTENTS

ABBREVIATIONS

Addl. MSS.	The Additional Manuscripts in the British Museum.
Brit. Mus.	British Museum, London.
Bull. I.H.R.	*Bulletin of the Institute of Historical Research*, London.
Burton	*Diary of Thomas Burton, esquire, member in the parliaments of Oliver and Richard Cromwell*, 4 vols. 1828.
Cal. Pat. Rolls	*Calendar of Patent Rolls* (Public Record Office).
Cal. S.P. Dom.	*Calendar of State Papers (Domestic)* (Public Record Office).
Cal. T.P.	*Calendar of Treasury Papers* (Public Record Office). The volumes of the older series are marked with the years between which the records are calendared. The later and more complete series is numbered by volumes in roman figures.
C.L. Accts.	The Civil List Accounts in the P.R.O., Treasury series T. 38/-.
Colchester	*Diary and Correspondence of Charles Abbot, Lord Colchester*, 3 vols., 1861. The manuscript of the diary contains much that was omitted from this publication, for quotations from which source reference is made to 'Abbot's MS. diary' and the number of the volume in the P.R.O.
C.J.	*Journals* of the House of Commons, preceded by the volume-number and followed by the page-number in that volume.
Courthope	*The Minute Book of James Courthope*, ed. O. C. Williams, in *Camden Miscellany*, vol. xx (Royal Historical Society, London, 1953).
D.N.B.	*The Dictionary of National Biography.*
Eng. Hist. Rev.	*English Historical Review.*
Harl. MSS.	The Harleian MSS. in the British Museum.
Hatsell	John Hatsell, *Precedents of Proceedings in the House of Commons*, 4 vols., 1776–96.
H.C. (or H.L.)	House of Commons (or House of Lords), followed by year in brackets and numeral, parliamentary paper printed by order of the House.
H.L. MSS. New Series	The volumes of *House of Lords Manuscripts New Series* (H.M. Stationery Office).
Ley MSS.	Manuscript correspondence in the possession of the descendants of John Henry Ley, Clerk of the House; see Introduction.
L.J.	*Journals* of the House of Lords, preceded by the volume number and followed by the page number in that volume.

L.P.	The Registers of Letters Patent in the Public Record Office.
Min. Comm. H.C.O.	The manuscript minutes of the Commissioners for the House of Commons Offices in the possession of the Speaker.
Parl. Hist.	*Parliamentary History of England from the Earliest Period to the Year 1803*, ed. Cobbett and Hansard.
P.R.O.	Public Record Office, London, often followed by a reference to a volume of records as there catalogued, e.g. Works 3/1, fol. 8. To save space this prefix is omitted from very numerous references to the Treasury books and papers in the P.R.O.; see below.
Rep.	Repertories of the Court of Aldermen, in the City of London Record Office.
Rot. Parl.	*Rotuli Parliamentorum.*
R. Comm. Hist. MSS.	The publications of the Royal Commission on Historical Manuscripts (H.M. Stationery Office).
S.P. Dom.	The State Papers (Domestic) in the P.R.O.
Trans. R. Hist. Soc.	*Transactions of the Royal Historical Society*, London.
T.	followed by a numeral, stroke, and another numeral, one of the series of Treasury books in the P.R.O., the first numeral indicating the series and the second the volume in that series: the folio number often follows. The series principally referred to are Treasury out-letters (T. 27/–), Treasury Board Minutes (T. 29/–), King's Warrants (T. 52/–), and Money Warrants (T. 53/–).
Williams	O. C. Williams, *The Historical Development of Private Bill Procedure and Standing Orders in the House of Commons*, 2 vols. (London, H.M. Stationery Office, 1948–9).

INTRODUCTION

NOT long after I had been appointed a clerk in the House of Commons, Sir Courtenay Ilbert, the Clerk of the House, suggested that I should see what I could discover about the history of the clerks and put it together in a consecutive account. The result of my endeavours was a document entitled *The Officials of the House of Commons* (J. B. Nichols, 1909). This folio monograph was never published in the sense of being on sale to the public, but copies of it have found their way into various libraries, and references to it have frequently been made in other publications. I am not ashamed of this youthful effort, although it relied only on fairly accessible printed sources: and these were not then so numerous as they are today. It led, among other things, to my *Life and Letters of John Rickman*. Its shortcomings are those of omission rather than of inaccuracy, although it is not free from error, and of failure then to realize how much more there was to be found if one looked beyond the printed page. When I retired after forty-one years' service in the House of Commons, I felt an obligation to undertake the research which would enable me to redeem these shortcomings and to replace my early monograph by an authoritative account[1] based upon all available information as well as on a long familiarity with the practice, procedure, and machinery of the House which I had not acquired in 1909.

As regards the period covered by my researches, I considered it unnecessary to do again the work on the medieval and Tudor periods so admirably done by the late Professor A. F. Pollard and by Professor J. E. Neale. I draw freely on their contributions to knowledge, especially in my first chapter, which I conceived as a retrospect such as William Goldesbrough, the first Clerk of the Restoration, might have framed on assuming his office. It is from

---

[1] I have been obliged, however, to restrict my attention to the history of the Clerk and his department, and to neglect the departments of the Speaker and the Serjeant at Arms which were, to some extent, included in my original survey.

the Restoration that my study begins, for I soon became convinced, as I delved among the records, that the development of the Clerk's Office into a department of several branches only became possible after 1660, and had proceeded very little way before the Revolution and the long Clerkship of Paul Jodrell, which was of prime importance. From his time onwards the development can be clearly traced, though with some lamentable gaps in the available material, right up to 1833, at which date the evidence taken before the Select Committee on the House of Commons Offices provides a comprehensive picture of the establishment, its methods of work, and its extremely complicated system of emoluments. By 1850 the transformation from the archaic to the modern system was completed: and with this year, in which John Henry Ley, the last Clerk of the House nurtured in the old tradition, retired and died, I have brought my account to a close, for reasons which I give in my 'Epilogue'.

In the present work are contained, for the first time, not only an account, functional and biographical, of the successive Clerks of the House, but also—what is really more important—a tracing of the gradual development of the Clerk's department from zero to a high state of organization. In following the stages of this growth, the reader will perhaps gain a clearer idea of the clerks' activities and functions than he would get from a merely factual survey of modern practice. Indeed, I think that my central chapters may claim to throw a new light upon such matters as the emoluments of the Clerk of the House and his subordinates, on the committee machinery, on the relations of the Treasury in the eighteenth century with certain clerks who became its agents, on the methods of producing the *Journals* and the *Votes*, on the proceedings of the House as regards controverted elections, and upon the origins of professional parliamentary agency, as to which last I put forward a view differing from that hitherto accepted. My footnotes are unavoidably numerous (for the purpose of accurate reference) and some of them, though they condense necessary information, are long: similarly, the appendixes are long, but they are important, for they assemble and bring into print for the first time many documents and facts hitherto buried in manuscript records.

It may not be out of place briefly to call attention to certain of these and other documents to the discovery and consideration of which I was led, apart from all that was to be found in volume after volume of the Treasury books. Firstly, there is the minute-book of James Courthope, one of the first quartet of under-clerks without doors, in which he kept the minutes of the many select committees which he attended during the sessions 1697–8 and 1698–9. This quite unique survival (Bodleian MS. Rawlinson A. 86) provides most illuminating evidence as to the committee system in those comparatively early days. My edition, with notes, of this document has been published in *Camden Miscellany*, vol. xx (1953), by the Royal Historical Society: and I refer to it in the present work so far as is necessary. Secondly, a find of great interest and some importance was the collection of unpublished letters, here referred to as the Ley MSS., which passed between John Hatsell, Clerk of the House from 1768 to 1820, and John Ley, his Clerk Assistant and, after 1797, Deputy Clerk. These were kindly placed at my disposal by their owner, the late Mr. C. John Brooke, a descendant of the Ley family. This correspondence totals ninety-six letters from Hatsell, drafts of ten letters from Ley, and some other letters exchanged by Ley with his colleagues. A few of the letters, notably those exchanged in 1772 and 1801, throw a definite light upon the clerks and their work at the time, and I have natu-rally quoted from them: but the bulk of the letters were concerned more with Hatsell's social life and his views of events, and are therefore irrelevant to my subject. However, since there are more than sixty unpublished letters from Hatsell among the Auckland papers in the British Museum, and others among the Liverpool papers, the Harrowby papers, the Chatham correspondence in the Public Record Office and, in all probability, among the Sidmouth papers, I cannot help hoping that, at some future time, it may be possible to produce an edition of Hatsell's letters.

Thirdly, although the details are fully given in the respective Appendixes in which they are reproduced, I mention as hitherto unpublished documents the long memorial of the clerks of 1709–11 (Appendix II), the lost report of the Select Committee on Fees and Salaries of 1731/32 which was not printed in the *Journal* but was luckily copied into a small vellum-covered notebook by some clerk in the House of Lords and is therefore preserved among the House of Lords records (Appendix IV), and the transcript of the proceedings of the Select Committee on the State of the Gaols when they were inquiring into the charges against Sir Robert Eyre, Lord Chief Justice of Common Pleas, in 1730, made by the shorthand clerk Lucas Kenn and now reposing among the Stowe manuscripts in the British Museum (Appendix VIII). All of these provide important, new information.

Fourthly, in my researches into the history of agency for private bills, I was fortunate in collecting several solicitors' accounts, including a perfect example of 1695 from my own college of Balliol, from a few among the many archivists to whom I addressed inquiries: extracts from these and from the bills of City Remembrancers among the City of London records are given in Appendix V. Fifthly, in the later chapters and in Appendix IX I make use of certain extremely interesting entries, which have a remarkably human side, in Speaker Abbot's manuscript diary, now in the Public Record Office. They reveal, among other things, that in 1799 William Pitt, in spite of heavy public anxieties, keenly interested himself in the domestic troubles of an impoverished committee clerk; also that John Ley, at the end of his life, had a violent difference with Hatsell, in which Abbot decisively took Hatsell's side.

Finally, I must refer to another by-product of my researches which has been reproduced in a limited form. This is my monograph *The Topography of the Old House of Commons*, with its twenty-nine reproductions of plans and drawings, which has been generously placed on record (the text in typescript with photographed illustrations and the whole bound, 16 by 20 in.) by the Ministry of Works in three copies, one of which can be consulted at the Ministry's Library at Lambeth Bridge House, London, S.E. 1. Another has been presented to the Library of the House of Commons for the use of members. The placing on record of this piece of research, which I found myself obliged to undertake owing to the complete absence of any accurate information on the subject, enables me to renounce my original purpose of including a topographical chapter in the present work, to explain the location at various times of offices, committee rooms, and official residences. Certain topographical details will be found in my text or notes, but any reader who might be interested in learning how the House of Commons, at first only in possession of St. Stephen's (i.e. the Chamber and the lobby), gradually spread its hold over half the Palace of Westminster and the 'stone building in St Margaret's Lane', of which my monograph gives the first accurate account, must be referred to that monograph and its accompanying plans. The fire of 1834 completely disorganized the House of Commons' offices, besides destroying a mass of documents whose loss was a far greater calamity than that of the incommodious building.

I

RETROSPECT
1363–1661

(1)

WHEN William Goldesbrough senior was appointed Clerk of the House of Commons, not by the House as had been his predecessors since 1649, but by letters patent under the seal of a restored king, a fresh page in the history of the Clerk's Office was begun. Its novelty, at first, was not striking, and the successful Revolution had to ensue before the latent germs of a new development could become apparent. Then, during the eighteenth century, slowly for a time but in ever quickening *tempo*, the massive apparatus of modern parliamentary government took its shape, transforming many relations, notably those between Westminster and Whitehall, and necessitating the creation of much new machinery, both in Parliament and without. In this movement the Clerk's Office was inevitably involved as part of the House of Commons' machinery—to put it no higher—and there began for it a process of transition from the still lingering medieval conception of the *sub-clericus parliamenti*, employing one or two men to drive a quill, to that of the whole-time servant, not only of the House but of the State, the highest authority on a vastly intricate *corpus* of procedure, and the administrative head of an active department. The process could hardly have begun till the struggle between King and Parliament had been decided by the victory of the latter, and—ironical fact—it could only continue when a king had been restored.

A modern constitutional historian has well summed up the conflict of 1604–60 in these words:

Successive ill-founded and unfortunate experiments at length drove the nation back upon its own constitutional tradition, and led it in 1660 to piece together what could be salved of the delicately adjusted system which had broken down between 1603 and 1642. A Crown reinvested at least in its essential prerogatives, a Parliament confirmed in its sovereignty and its essential privileges, once more appeared as the indelible marks of the English governmental system.[1]

A small but curious feature of this conjuncture was that the King reassumed the prerogative, and the Commons did not reassert the privilege, of appointing the Clerk of the House. It was an anomaly that the House of Commons, having appointed its own Clerk when it had disposed of the King, and having expressed its dislike of patents in this connexion,[2] acquiesced in the Crown's appointment of its principal officer (after the Speaker) when there was again a king. To explain the continuation of an old anomaly, under the conventions of modern parliamentary government, is simple enough: to explain the anomaly away is impossible.

Be that as it may, from the date of that anomaly my main story begins, 300 years after the issue of the first patent granting a yearly salary to an 'under-clerk of Parliament'. This is a considerable stretch of time; and of the Clerks who filled it, of their status and activities, something must be said. Let us imagine William Goldesbrough, with greater knowledge than he in fact possessed, looking backwards over the line of his predecessors so as to form a conception of the position at which he had arrived, and surveying the duties and advantages appertaining to his seat at the table of the House. What he would have found and what concluded the remainder of this chapter will attempt, briefly, to describe.[3]

---

[1] Sir David L. Keir, *The Constitutional History of Modern Britain*, 5th ed. (London, 1953), p. 162.

[2] In Scobell's case, see Burton, i. xx.

[3] As regards the medieval Clerks I here acknowledge my indebtedness to the work of the late A. F. Pollard, viz. 'The Medieval Under-Clerks of Parliament', *Bull. I.H.R.* xvi. 65–87; 'The Under-Clerks and the Commons Journals (1509–1558)', ibid., pp. 144–67; and three articles on 'The Clerical Organisation of Parliament' in *Eng. Hist. Rev.*, vol. cvii. These studies, with certain shorter notes by Pollard in *Bull. I.H.R.* xvii. 1–5, 49–51, are particularly valuable for biographical details of the early Clerks, including the references to the patent rolls or Chancery warrants which date their appointments. For the Elizabethan period Professor J. E. Neale's *The Elizabethan House of Commons* (London, 1949) is exhaustive.

(2)

The list of Clerks of the Commons up to the resignation of Elsyng in 1648 is as follows (the year in each case being that in which the patent was granted):

1363   Robert de Melton.[1]
1385   John de Scardeburgh.
1414   Thomas Haseley.
1440   John Dale.
1461   Thomas Bayen.
1503?   Thomas Hylton.
1510   William Underhill.
1515   Richard Urmeston, or Ormeston.
1548   John Seymour.
1567   Fulk Onslow.
1603   Ralph Ewens (d. 1611).
1613   John Wright.
1640   Henry Elsyng.

Clerks Assistant[2]

1640   John Rushworth.
1648   Ralph Darnall.

Down to and including Thomas Bayen these under-clerks of Parliament were all clerks in Chancery; Richard Urmeston, who was a fellow of Gray's Inn, began the long connexion of the Clerks of the House with the Inns of Court. William Underhill was the first to be designated 'Clerk of the Parliament of Our Lower House'. Haseley, Bayen, and Seymour were, for a short time, members of Parliament before their appointments. Urmeston was the first to be formally authorized to exercise his office by sufficient

---

[1] In the patent granting him 100 shillings a year for life (*Cal. Pat. Rolls, 1361–4,* p. 323) he was not designated *sub-clericus parliamenti,* but John de Scardeburgh in his patent of 1385 (*Cal. Pat. Rolls, 1381–5,* p. 535) was appointed in succession to Robert de Melton *defuncto nuper sub-clerico parliamenti.*

[2] Rushworth (2 C.J. 12) and Darnall (5 C.J. 466) were the first two Clerks Assistant formally admitted as such: but, Rushworth being permanently absent in the field after 1645, John Smythe (4 C.J. 90) in 1645 and Robert Robinson, 'Servant to the Clerk of the House' (5 C.J. 261), in 1647 were temporarily admitted to assist the Clerk in the House. For such assistance previous to 1640, see below, pp. 14–15.

deputy,[1] a power granted to all subsequent Clerks up to John Hatsell, who exercised it for twenty-three years. The most interesting of the pre-Elizabethan Clerks were John de Scardeburgh and Thomas Haseley. The former occasioned one of the very rare references to the Commons Clerk in the Rolls of Parliament, to keep which was the exclusive function of the then more important and highly paid Clerk of the Parliament. This was on the occasion when Richard II granted him an aid in 1388.[2] He was in favour with the King, who granted him lands and other offices at various times, including the coronership of London. He seems to have debarred himself from ecclesiastical preferment after 1388 by committing some irregularity, probably marriage, which was still forbidden to a clerk. Even more interesting is the probability that he was the author of the lively account of the Good Parliament of 1376 in the 'Anonimale' Chronicle of St. Mary's, York.[3]

Thomas Haseley[4] had no parliamentary history: indeed, he ceased to attend the Commons after 1425, John Dale acting as his deputy. He was a financial adventurer who made the most of his opportunities in confused times. He was deputy-butler, i.e. senior revenue officer, at Chichester and Shoreham, he arrested contrabanders and divers men impeached for high treason, got £40 a year of the wool dues of Bristol, £10 from the hanaper as Clerk of the Crown, and 6*d.* a day from the issues of Oxford and Berkshire. Though imprisoned for a time in the Fleet, he was released in 1439 and granted a general pardon. In 1445 he was knighted.

Haseley brought the era of clerkly adventure to an end: the

---

[1] But the power was exercised in practice by Haseley, for whom John Dale deputized without fee for thirteen years before he succeeded to the Clerkship.

[2] *Rot. Parl.*, 1388: 'le roi . . . granta auxint a la request des communes d'aider John de Scardesburgh, lour commune clerk.'

[3] See A. F. Pollard, 'The Authorship and Value of the Anonimale Chronicle', *Eng. Hist. Rev.* liii (1938), 578–605. The connexion depends on the identification of J. de S., the under-clerk of Parliament, with the J. de S. who was a protonotary at York, became clerk of the diocese of York in 1376, and from 1380 onwards held a prebend in the chapel of St. Mary. Pollard, to surmount the difficulty that J. de S. was not under-clerk in 1376, supposes that, as a clerk in Chancery, he was temporarily employed in parliamentary duties under Robert de Melton.

[4] See *D.N.B.* and A. F. Pollard's articles mentioned on p. 2, n. 3 above, in which Haseley is styled 'the most enterprising and flamboyant clerk of the Commons in the middle ages'.

office of Clerk of the Commons House was coming to need more serious application. Urmeston held it for over thirty years, attending Henry VIII's many Parliaments from 1515 till the end of the reign, but he derived nothing more from his assiduity than the doubling in 1534 of his salary and the post of weigher of wool in the port of London.

Seymour and Onslow,[1] the Elizabethan Clerks, both came from the ranks of the country gentlemen. The former sat in Henry VIII's last Parliament as member for West Bedwin; and the latter was the brother of Richard Onslow who was elected Speaker in 1566. Their inception and development of the Commons *Journal*, of which the first two books originally bore their respective names, imposed thereafter on the Clerk one of his most important duties. Onslow died on 8 August 1602, and Ralph Ewens, who succeeded him the following January,[2] died in 1611 without making any particular mark upon history. One William Pynches was directed on 30 August 1611 to take charge of books and papers of the Lower House, but did not become Clerk, the next appointment being that of John Wright,[3] who remained Clerk till 1640, though there were no Parliaments for him to attend after 1629. He favoured the country party and was accordingly ill regarded by the Court. He was, in fact, arrested with others in 1621, but was able to return to his office after 1624, during part of which year his son deputized for him in the House and was rewarded for his pains.

Henry Elsyng[4] was the son of the Henry Elsyng who was Clerk of the Parliaments[5] and author of the treatise *On the Manner and*

---

[1] Seymour's patent (*Cal. Pat. Rolls*, Edw. VI, ii. 3) was dated 26 May 1548, but he discharged the duties of the office from the beginning of Edward VI's first Parliament (see A. F. Pollard in *Bull. I.H.R.* xvii. 1–5).

[2] L.P. 45 Eliz., pt. viii.

[3] L.P. 10 Jac. I, pt. viii, 19 Nov. 1613. See introduction to *Commons Debates of 1629*, ed. Notestein and Relf (Univ. of Minnesota, 1921).

[4] L.P. 15 Car. I, pt. xxii; see *D.N.B.*

[5] *The Knyvett Letters, 1620–44*, ed. Bertram Schofield (Norfolk Record Society, xx), show that he was a cousin of Thomas Knyvett of Norfolk with whom he was on intimate terms, sending him parliamentary news and once intervening with the authorities on his behalf. An interesting note (p. 92) in this volume shows that Henry Elsyng jun. in 1637 petitioned the King for the reversion of the office of Clerk of the Parliaments after Daniel Bedingfield. The petition was unsuccessful,

Form of holding a Parliament in England, which the son edited. He resigned, for conscience' sake, on the death of the King, and died in 1654 in such poor circumstances that he was buried at the expense of his friends;[1] in 1660 the House of Commons voted £500 to his children who were in poverty. In the eight stormy years of his attendance upon the Commons, he won golden opinions for his grasp of business and assistance to the House.[2]

William Goldesbrough, his backward glance having come near the present, would have been aware of all that had been said and thought, not only of Elsyng, but of John Rushworth, once Clerk Assistant and a distinguished servant of the Commonwealth during the Civil War, but now in 1661 member for Berwick and Secretary to the Council of State. Goldesbrough, being a King's man, could hardly have approved of Rushworth's employment, not so much in the capacity of Clerk Assistant, as in that of emissary and general intelligencer with the armies of the militant Commons; but he might have admired the readiness with which Rushworth performed his historically famous parliamentary exploit, that of taking down in shorthand the King's words when he came to the House to arrest the five members on 4 January 1642.[3]

but possibly led to Elsyng's appointment to the Commons in 1640. Hatsell says that Laud was responsible for his appointment (Hatsell, ii. 259 n.).

[1] See A. I. Dasent, *The Speakers of the House of Commons* (London, 1911), p. 204. William Lenthall quoted this fact in his self-defence against the charge of taking exorbitant fees as Speaker.

[2] The rather florid encomium in Wood's *Athenae Oxonienses*, quoted by Hatsell, is well known, especially for the assertion that 'more reverence was paid to his (Elsyng's) stool than to the Speaker's chair'. But in my monograph, *The Officials of the House of Commons* (J. B. Nichols, 1909), p. 4, there is a note for which I remember I was indebted to Sir Courtenay Ilbert: 'Professor C. H. Firth thinks that the authority for Elsyng's services as clerk ultimately rests upon the passage in Whitelock's *Memorials* (ed. 1832), ii. 364', which is then quoted. Whitelock, who was a great friend of Elsyng, called him 'the most excellent Clerk, both to take and express the sense of the House, that I believe ever sat there'.

[3] See *D.N.B.* for a full account of Rushworth's life and services to the Commonwealth and State which have little bearing on the functions of a Clerk Assistant. Rushworth outlived Goldesbrough sen. by twelve years before he died wretchedly in 1690 as a debtor and drunkard in the King's Bench prison; see Anthony Powell, *John Aubrey and his Times* (London, 1948), pp. 209, 213. The first of these two references, from Aubrey's letter to Wood, the biographer, is dated 29 June 1689: 'Yesterday I saw Mr. Rushworth which was a great mortification. He hath quite

(3)

Nicholas Hardinge, Clerk of the House in 1742, in his report on the state of the *Journals*,[1] said that the *Journals* from 1642 to the Restoration were kept separate from the rest, there being a doubt whether they had not been razed or expunged at the Restoration— a doubt which he did not himself entertain. Goldesbrough in 1661, with whatever abhorrence he may have regarded these records of a regicide Parliament, had them in his custody, and from them would have compiled the following list of Clerks and Clerks Assistant:

Clerks		Clerks Assistant	
1649	Henry Scobell	1649	John Phelpes[2]
1658	John Smythe	1649	Ralph Darnall
1658	Thomas St. Nicholas	1653	Davey
1660	William Jessop	1654	Ralph Darnall
		1660	,, ,,

Scobell, who was appointed Clerk on 5 January 1649, when Elsyng's patent was called in, figured in one or two picturesque parliamentary events during the interregnum, as recorded by Burton. On his entering and taking his place at the opening of the 1654 Parliament objection was taken, and he was informed that the House had no liking for patents: he withdrew, and was then chosen as Clerk. The House of Lords having been temporarily abolished, he was made Clerk of the Parliament by a special Act. This led to trouble when in 1658 the House of Lords was revived and Scobell, by virtue of his office, became its Clerk, while retaining all the records of the House of Commons by virtue of his Act. At first he refused to surrender them, but eventually agreed to sur-

lost his memory with drinking Brandy. Remembered nothing of you etc. His landlady wiped his nose like a child.'

[1] 24 C.J. 262–6.

[2] For a very short time before Darnall's appointment John Phelpes, whom Elsyng had appointed his deputy on 26 Dec. 1648, held the post of Clerk Assistant, being succeeded by Darnall on 5 Jan. 1649. He was one of the two clerks to the High Court which tried Charles I and clerk to the committee of Parliament chosen to confer with deputies of Scotland on the question of the Union. In 1659 he was temporarily Clerk of the House during the absence of Thomas St. Nicholas. At the Restoration he was included among the regicides and attainted; but he evaded arrest and fled to Lausanne.

render the Commons *Journals* and other records on receipt of a specific order. This was made on 25 January 1658, and John Smythe, who had meanwhile been appointed Clerk of the House of Commons, took them over. Finally, on 7 January 1659, Scobell was brought to the bar of the House for having entered in the *Journal*: '20th April 1653, This day his Excellency the Lord General dissolved this Parliament.' The entry was ordered to be expunged as a forgery, but Scobell, though threatened with penalties, did not suffer.[1] He was the author of a treatise on procedure based on precedents up to about 1640.[2]

John Smythe had been admitted in 1645 to assist Elsyng, but in this capacity of temporary Clerk Assistant he was succeeded in 1647 by Robert Robinson, one of the Clerk's 'servants', about whom history is otherwise silent. Smythe was appointed Clerk on 20 January 1658, but only remained as such till the dissolution in April 1659. His expenses in storing the House's records till he was ordered to hand them over to Darnall in May of that year were repaid by a vote of £20.[3] Thomas St. Nicholas, M.P. for York in 1643 and for Canterbury in 1656 and 1658–9, was added to the Council of State in 1653, and when chosen Clerk of the House in the Rump Parliament he was absent from London, his place being taken temporarily by John Phelpes to whom £50 was voted for his services.[4]

William Jessop, M.P. for Stafford in 1658–9, was only Clerk of the House during the Convention Parliament, which recommended that the King should grant him the office by patent. It was Goldesbrough who got the patent, and Jessop subsequently became Secretary to the Commissioners of Accounts.[5] With him

---

[1] For the objection taken to Scobell's entry in 1654, see 7 C.J. 365, Burton, i. xx; for the dispute over the custody of the Commons *Journals*, Burton, ii. 336–7, 349–50, 403, 404; 7 C.J. 581; see also *D.N.B.* Scobell was deputy register of Chancery from 1635 till at least 1645 (see Thomas Duffin Hardy's catalogue (1843) of the principal officers of Chancery) and was assistant secretary to the Council of State in 1653.

[2] *Memorials of the Method and Manner of Proceedings in Parliament in passing Bills*, by H.S.E.C.P. (1656). He also published collections of Statutes.

[3] See 4 C.J. 90; 7 C.J. 578, 650, 652; and Burton, ii. 316–18.

[4] See 7 C.J. 285, 644, 650, 853, 879.

[5] See Pepys's *Diary*, ed. H. B. Wheatley (London, 1893), vii. 286, 298. The

Ralph Darnall,[1] who had been Clerk Assistant for all but one session during the interregnum, disappeared from the table of the House.

(4)

William Goldesbrough is unlikely to have troubled his head about the functions of his medieval predecessors; and if he had, there would have been little enough material to satisfy his curiosity. Being himself deputy register of Chancery, he would have realized the qualifications of the Chancery clerks whom the kings had kindly placed at the service of the partly illiterate and somewhat reluctant body of local representatives obliged to comply with their summons to attend their Parliaments, wherever they might be held. These clerks could read and write in Latin, French, and English, in which they knew the correct legal turns of phrase. In their service of the Commons reading aloud was doubtless the most important of their functions, since it was only orally that the knights of the shire and burgesses could be informed what was the business in hand. They made copies of documents, chiefly petitions, for those who desired them and paid the necessary fee, they wrote superscriptions and endorsements on bills, and possibly they assisted, during the linguistically transitional fifteenth century, in turning into English petitions drafted in French. They may have registered attendances, though that was not made compulsory till 1514, when by Act of Parliament members were forbidden to depart without leave before the end of the session, such leave to be

second of these entries, 31 Jan. 1668, tells of a visit by Pepys to the Commissioners of Accounts: 'They have Mr. Jessop their Secretary: and it is pretty to see that they are fain to find out an old-fashioned man of Cromwell's to do their business for them.'

[1] Darnall had been an Attorney of the Court of Wards and Liveries, and on the abolition of that Court by Ordinance, he was paid £3,400 for his loss of office (5 C.J. 655). He appears to have been a satisfactory Clerk Assistant all through the interregnum, but, except for various references to his salary and arrears of it in the *Journal*, his history is slight. In 1650 (6 C.J. 393) he was appointed register to the Trustees for the sale of delinquent lands. Why the Little Parliament of 1653 preferred Mr. Davey, who Mr. Davey was, and who the Mr. Blanchford whose proposed appointment as Clerk Assistant was negatived after a division before Davey was appointed (7 C.J. 298–9), I have no knowledge.

entered of record in the Clerk's book.[1] It has been suggested that the early Clerks drafted petitions,[2] but for this conjecture Goldesbrough would have found no evidence: on the contrary, such treatises as he might have read on parliamentary procedure, if they mentioned drafting of bills at all, stated that it was regularly performed, as regards Commons bills, by members of the House, usually lawyers.[3]

Even for the Elizabethan period, of which we today know so much from the parliamentary diaries and tracts of that efflorescent age, Goldesbrough, who knew much less, would not have found the history of the Clerks particularly impressive or (apart from the modest inception of the Commons *Journal*) rich in new developments. Before these could occur, the House itself had to develop a new spirit of unity and independence. Henry VIII found it docile to fulfil his purposes: Elizabeth, though she dominated it and used unfailing astuteness in dealing with it, trained it to become a scourge of princes. During her reign the House of Commons grew portentously in power, in self-consciousness, and in factiousness; it became the set political arena; it was obliged to frame settled forms for its debates and processes for its enactments; unwilling attendance at Westminster gave way to fierce competition for a seat in the House, local worthies being ousted by able and ambi-

[1] 6 Hen. VIII, c. 16. The Clerk's book there referred to, as is now generally agreed, was not an embryo *Journal*, but the list of members returned which the Clerk of the Crown delivered to the Clerk of the House. It was not till Stuart times that 'the clerk's book', in a *Journal* entry, meant the *Journal*, or the rough notes for the *Journal*.

[2] e.g. A. F. Pollard, 'The Clerical Organization of Parliament', *Eng. Hist. Rev.*, vol. vii, and *The Evolution of Parliament* (2nd ed. 1934), p. 125; Howard L. Gray, *The Influence of the Commons on Early Legislation* (Harvard Historical Studies) (Cambridge, Mass., 1932), pp. 229 ff.; Sir David L. Keir, *The Constitutional History of Modern Britain*, 5th ed. (London, 1953), p. 40.

[3] See W. Hakewil, *The Manner how Statutes are enacted in Parliament by passing of Bills* (1641). Addl. MSS. 36856, which Professor J. E. Neale frequently quotes in *The Elizabethan House of Commons* as an early Stuart tract on procedure, and which Mr. Howard L. Gray, op. cit., in preceding note, attributes to Sir Thomas Richardson, Speaker in 1620, seems to be more or less identical with Hakewil's printed treatise, and it contains the same passage on drafting. Probably it was one of the unauthorized copies of his work of which Hakewil complained in his introduction. Hatsell makes no mention of any tradition of drafting by the Clerk. See, however, chapter 8 on the connexion of the clerks with money bills and the Treasury.

tious graduates from the Inns of Court. It was a great period of parliamentary life,[1] in which the Clerk's office was inevitably enhanced as the prestige, vigour, and experience of the House itself increased; though, possibly, the increasing knowledge, ability, and self-reliance of members diminished their reliance on the Clerk, who could only come into his own as the professional adviser of House and Speaker on parliamentary practice when that had accumulated into a *corpus*. Indeed, the table of the House had hardly achieved much dignity when John Seymour sat there, and Hooker described it as 'a little board before him (the Clerk) to write and lay his books upon'.[2]

Besides noting attendances and licences to depart, the Clerk read the Litany and also other prayers at the opening of a sitting, until in 1597 a preacher was appointed for this purpose;[3] he read all such documents as he was directed to read, and in this respect the gradual adoption of the regular stages (including the three readings) in the passing of bills formalized his duties until his functions at each reading of a bill, at its committal (when he took down the names of members nominated), at the committee's report (reading out twice amendments and interlinings), as to ingrossment and amendment after ingrossment (written in by the Clerk's 'man' at the table of the House), could be described with precision in the treatises on procedure.[4] When the committees of the whole House

---

[1] Of which Professor Neale has drawn a fascinating picture in the work mentioned in the preceding note. His chapter on 'The Officers of the House' contains all there is to be known about the Clerk's functions and emoluments in Elizabeth's reign.

[2] Hooker (alias Vowell), 'The Order of Kepinge of a Parliament' (Exeter City Records), also incorporated in Mountmorres's *Irish Parliament*.

[3] See J. E. Neale, op. cit., p. 368. Nevertheless in 1603 on 23 Mar. the *Journal* records that the customary prayers were read by the Clerk of the House 'to whose place the service anciently appertains'. It looks as though the then Clerk was attempting to oust the preacher. The first regular Chaplain was appointed at the Restoration.

[4] The earliest tracts on procedure—those of Hooker (see n. 2 above) and Lambarde (Addl. MSS. 5123)—are mid-Elizabethan. Those of Hakewil, Elsyng sen., and Scobell belong to the first half of the ensuing century. The introduction to *The Liverpool Tractate*, ed. Catherine Strateman (Columbia University Press, 1937), gives a very full summary of the various early tracts on procedure from Lambarde onwards. Hakewil describes the Clerk's duties on each stage of a bill very clearly.

developed at the end of the sixteenth century, it seems doubtful whether the Clerk attended them. Scobell in his treatise says that 'the chairman of the Grand Committee is to sit in the Clerk's place at the table, and to write the Votes of the Committee', which he would not have done had the Clerk been there. Townshend, it is true, records that in 1601, the Clerk Onslow being absent, Anthony Maynard, a member of the House, sat in the chair as Clerk 'to register the order' of a large committee on the subsidy and was allowed to wear his hat (which the Clerk never did); but this suggests that he was acting as chairman.[1]

John Seymour, however, sitting at his 'little board' made a momentous innovation: he began to keep a consecutive diary. 'Seymour' was the name of the first volume (1547–66) of the Commons *Journals*, and 'Onslow' the name of the second (1571–81). At first it was only a primitive record and little more than a register of bills such as previous Clerks had kept;[2] but Seymour's innovation—a synthesis of isolated notes into a single diary—was seminal; and when Onslow in 1571 introduced

A new technique in compiling his Journal, writing a second or fair copy from the rough notes scribbled in the House, and at the same time changing its format from a small dishevelled quarto, 6″ × 8″, to a neat and orderly folio, 8″ × 13″, there was scope for the Clerk's private diary or notebook to become the official Journal of the House.[3]

It was not, however, till James I's reign that the Commons be-

---

[1] Scobell, op. cit., on p. 8, n. 2 above (ed. 1670), p. 37; Townshend, *Historical Collections*, p. 200. When a Clerk Assistant was regularly appointed, it became the practice, which still continues, that he attended all committees of the whole House, the Chairman sitting in the Clerk's seat. There was no inherent reason why this practice should have arisen, or why the Clerk should not have attended committees of the whole House, unless it was that, originally, the Clerk like the Speaker was regarded as a 'King's man' (see below, pp. 51–52, for this probability).

[2] See J. E. Neale, 'The Commons Journals of the Tudor Period', *Trans. R. Hist. Soc.*, 4th ser. iii (1920), an authoritative account part of which is incorporated in his *Elizabethan House of Commons*. The first session recorded in 1 C.J. is, as he says, a rewriting of Urmeston's register of bills in Seymour's hand. When Hooker (*circ.* 1572) wrote that among the Clerk's duties was 'to enter and make true records and truly to write all such orders as be taken in that House' he was clearly thinking of such a formal note as the clerk might take of a Court's proceedings, not of an official chronicle.

[3] J. E. Neale, *The Elizabethan House of Commons*, p. 369.

came aware of the importance of keeping a record which truly represented their proceedings in their contest with the Crown, and definitely assumed, and long continued, control of what the Clerk entered in his book.[1] Goldesbrough, at all events, would have been well aware how this register had developed into an official *Journal*, and that *Journal* into a full though formal narrative, diversified at first by the entry (at the House's direction) of particular arguments and (without the House's direction) of summaries of speeches until the entry of particular members' speeches was forbidden in 1628.[2] He would also have realized that the fair copying of rough notes begun by Onslow had sadly lapsed, and that most of the *Journals* after 1604 were nothing but the rough notes,[3] often confused and full of omissions. Moreover, he would have been sadly aware that the *Journals* for the years 1584–1601 had completely disappeared, both the finished copy and the Clerk's rough book of notes having been lost.[4] Such losses were due to

[1] In 1604 (see 1 C.J. 215), when the House made its first attempt to get a place for keeping its records, the reference was to 'the register and records and papers of the House', and to the order 'that all acts, resolutions, and judgments of the House, which are there entered and registered by their common Servant, the Clerk, should be written and ingrossed in one fair Register Book, and that to be kept by the Clerk for the use and direction of the said House'. From 1 C.J. 215, onwards to the 9th volume of the *Journals*, resolutions or orders as to supervision of what the Clerk had entered in his book are frequent.

[2] See 1 C.J. 885, 17 Apr. Owing to the desire expressed by the House of Lords to see a speech as entered in the *Journal*, the House expressly stated that the entry of particular men's speeches was without warrant at all times. Directions to this effect were given to Rushworth on his appointment as Clerk Assistant, 25 Apr. 1640, and again in Dec. 1640.

[3] See the Clerk Hardinge's report on the *Journals* in 1742 (24 C.J. 262–6) and introduction to *The Commons Debates of 1629*, ed. Notestein and Relf (University of Minnesota, 1921).

[4] Professor Neale, in the article referred to on p. 12, n. 2 above, thoroughly discusses this matter, proving by detailed examination that the official manuscripts, lent to him by the Clerk John Wright, from which Sir Simonds D'Ewes compiled his parliamentary diaries, were the rough notes, not the finished *Journal*. He conjectures that the finished *Journal* was among the papers lost after the death of Ralph Ewens in 1611 (cf. 1 C.J. 491) and that the rough notes, which D'Ewes said he had returned but which were known to be lost when Bowes published D'Ewes's diaries after the Restoration, probably disappeared between the end of the Convention Parliament in 1660 and the meeting of Charles II's first Parliament, i.e. in the gap between William Jessop and William Goldesbrough. 'A list of Journal books of the House of Commons as now found in Mr. Goldesborough's keeping,

the fact that, despite repeated efforts of the House to obtain a place for the safe preservation of its records[1] no such place had been permanently provided; so that the *Journals* and other papers of the House were still part of a Clerk's luggage, kept in his private residence or lodging, and apt to be dispersed by carelessness of executors or other negligence.[2] This *Journal*, at all events, of which the existing volumes now reposed in Goldesbrough's lodgings, he would continue to keep, and perhaps acquire from his study of them the quality, so much admired by Whitelock in Elsyng, of 'helping to state the questions and to draw the orders free from exceptions'. After the confused proceedings of the last twelve years, it was time that the Commons again had Clerks of certain tenure whose accumulated experience would fit them for the highest of their duties—that of advising the Speaker and other members of the House.

A Clerk Assistant had been formally appointed ever since Rushworth, traditionally the first Clerk Assistant, was appointed, at the Clerk's request, in 1640. His chief business was to assist the Clerk at the table, not only in noting the proceedings for the *Journal*, but in taking charge of papers and bills, dealing with inquiries from members, and arranging for copies of documents to be made for them. As D'Ewes observed,[3] there was in 1641 incredible confusion about the Clerk's table, with excited members snatching papers off the table or clamouring for copies in haste. It is certain that the Clerk needed similar assistance before that date. A print of 1624[4] shows two clerks seated at the table, and Professor Wallace

July 20, 1678' (S.P. Dom. Car. II 405, fol. 112) shows that these volumes of the *Journal* were then missing.

[1] See 1 C.J. 215 (1604), 491 (1614); 2 C.J. 21, 42 (1640), 273 (1645); 6 C.J. 333 (1649), 350 (1650), 542 (1651); 7 C.J. 588, 590 (1658). The records of the House were only safe during the years 1654–8 when Scobell, as Clerk of the Parliament, kept them in the stone tower which was part of his official residence. After the dispute in 1658 (see pp. 7, 8 above) Scobell handed them over to John Smythe, who seems to have taken good care of them till he handed them over to Darnall, the Clerk Assistant, in 1659 (7 C.J. 652).

[2] For the subsequent history of this matter, see below, pp. 37–40 and chapter 9.

[3] Harl. MSS. 163, fol. 97, quoted by Professor Notestein in *The Commons Debates of 1629*, introd.

[4] See J. E. Neale, *The Elizabethan House of Commons*, p. 9, and reproduction facing p. 364. It was made for the Parliament which met in Feb. 1624. A print of

Notestein has remarked that the *Journal* for 1629 is written in two different hands. Even in 1604 there is a marginal note in the *Journal*[1] to the effect that the Clerk's deputy, Mr. Cadwallader Tydder, had been sick and absent for two days—an entry which could hardly have been made except to explain the deputy's absence from the House itself. The truth, no doubt, is that the chief of the minor clerks, known as the Clerk's 'servants' or 'men', was called in, not only to ingross amendments made to an ingrossed bill, but to give other assistance at the table when his master required it, and not necessarily as the Clerk's deputy.

As regards the Clerk's servants, men, or under-clerks in general, how many there were and what their precise functions, William Goldesbrough in 1661 must have known more than we know today. The scattered pieces of evidence do not help us to form any clear picture. Hooker's account says that outside the House was another (room) in which the under-clerks sat; in 1588–9 the House, on the Speaker's motion, agreed in Fulk Onslow's absence to accept the attendance of such of his clerks and servants as had previously taken the oath administered to members;[2] and names of Clerk's servants crop up from time to time.[3] Moreover, nothing much can be gathered as to their number or duties from allusions to their payment or receipts from fees, of which more will be said

---

it is in Harl. MSS. 159, fol. 2, and it has been reproduced in several books of modern date. According to Hatsell, i. 263 and note, Speaker Onslow said Rushworth was not the first Clerk Assistant, since he had seen a print of the House of Commons in 1620 in which were two clerks sitting at the table. Hooker and the other authors of early tracts on procedure only mention one Clerk. We can conclude that Rushworth was the first *official* Clerk Assistant.

[1] 1 C.J. 232; cf. also 1 C.J. 275 (26 Feb. 1606): 'The Bill against Heads of Colleges read; and (by a mistaking of my Man, of putting Cambridge before Oxford) Question, whether Cambridge should be set first upon the title. Great dispute, much time spent and resolved with much odds, that Oxford.' The Clerk's man must have been at the table to write the title of the bill wrong. Cadwallader Tydder, Fulk Onslow's 'Servant', had been appointed his deputy in 1601, and Ewens had presumably retained him in that position.

[2] Sir Simonds D'Ewes, *Journals of all the Parliaments during the reign of Queen Elizabeth* (1682), p. 430.

[3] Besides Cadwallader Tydder and Robert Robinson already mentioned, one Seyre, or Sayres, 'servant and bag-bearer to the Clerk', occurs in 1606 (1 C.J. 295, 305).

in the ensuing section. However, in 1607, in the distribution of the benevolence of the House among its officers, we learn from the *Journal* that four of Mr. Ewens's servants received 20*s*. a piece;[1] but we then have to wait till 1660 for a similar piece of evidence, viz. that the Convention Parliament authorized the payment of £25 to the under-clerks, from which it may be conjectured that those who received this sum were not more than four in number.[2] But, since the Clerk of the House, in general, engaged and paid his underlings, he may, from early days, have had an indeterminate number of casual scribes at his beck and call, who picked up fees for copying and so forth as opportunity offered.[3] The main function of these 'servants' or under-clerks must, at all events up to the Restoration, have consisted almost wholly in copying and ingrossing, for which services fees were paid to the Clerk from the earliest times: and these fees were for the first time stabilized in the Table of Fees agreed to by the House in 1649. In this table (given in App. III) the only fee which directly accrued to the under-clerks was 10*s*. for every private bill: there were no fees for their attendance on committees, and it may be safely assumed that such attendance was not part of their duties. It is more likely that the administrative parliamentary committees of the Commonwealth employed clerks on their own initiative, and paid them,[4] while the innumerable select committees of the House on public matters and bills and on private bills proceeded without a clerk, the chairman himself preparing the report.[5] Nevertheless, one would very much like to know what staff William Goldesbrough contemplated, on the

---

[1] 1 C.J. 391.

[2] 8 C.J. 229. On the same occasion John Tench, clerk to the committee on public debts, and J. Vine, clerk to the committee for Customs, Excise, Trade and Navigation, got £10 each. Whether these men were also under-clerks of the House cannot be determined. Probably they were not.

[3] See J. E. Neale, op. cit., pp. 342–3.

[4] Cf. 3 C.J. 115–16. The Committee of Accounts then appointed (5 June 1643) had power to employ and pay agents, accountants, clerks, and messengers.

[5] An order of the House (8 C.J. 325) of 1661 referring to the custody by the chairman of a committee of papers and evidence and ordering him to permit parties to take copies of them, and another order of 1663 (ibid., p. 488) that, when any bill is committed, no private member ought to take it away, but the Clerk of the House or his deputy is to attend with the bill and order at the time and place appointed for the first meeting of the committee, and deliver the same in at the

basis of precedent, when he was appointed in 1661, whether he took over any under-clerks already employed or whether he entirely recruited his own.

(5)

It would be no less interesting to know how William Goldesbrough regarded the financial prospects of his new office, all the more since, as we shall see, he had considerable difficulty in getting his dues. Since the resignation of Elsyng there had been a departure from long precedent, in that a fixed salary had been voted by the House to Clerk and Clerk Assistant, over and above any fees that he might collect. In 1649 Scobell and Darnall were given £500 and £200 a year respectively, the salary to Scobell being voted for life.[1] The Little Parliament of 1653 was more niggardly: it cut the Clerk's salary to £400, out of which he was to pay his under-clerks except the Clerk Assistant, and when a salary of £150 was proposed for the latter, this was negatived on a division and the salary was fixed at £100, while the scale of fees was appreciably reduced.[2] Subsequent Parliaments had awarded the higher salaries of £500 and £200; and the Convention Parliament of 1660 had, at the end of its first sitting, voted £500 for the use of the Clerk, Serjeant at Arms, under-clerks, and other officers (Darnall to have £200 for service since 24 February 1659), and at the end of its second sitting an itemized sum, amounting in all to £731. 10s., for the officers of the House, the printers, the stationer, and the provost-marshal of Westminster, out of which Jessop the Clerk was to have £72. 10s. salary and £50 for ingrossing public bills, Darnall £100, and the under-clerks £25.[3] But now the King was restored, and Goldesbrough would only receive letters patent appointing him for life at a yearly salary of £10 together with the right to 'all rewards, dues, rights, profits, commodities, advantages and emoluments whatsoever to the said office . . . appertaining'.

committee, after the chairman is chosen, both point to there being no regular committee clerks in Goldesbrough's day.

[1] 6 C.J. 287.
[2] 7 C.J. 291–2, and see Appendix III.
[3] 7 C.J. 476, 767, 853, 879; 8 C.J. 165–6, 169, 229.

Surveying the past, as a deputy register of Chancery having access to the patent rolls could easily do, Goldesbrough would have known that the original salary of the Clerk was 100s., that it was first raised to £10 for Urmeston, and that this higher salary, except for a reversion to £5 under Mary, had been maintained in all subsequent patents to the Clerk. Besides this salary, individual clerks had been rewarded with benefices, grants of land, and lucrative offices, while Elizabethan Clerks had received gratuities from the Crown at the end of each session. These, starting at £10 in 1534, had reached fifty marks (£33. 6s. 8d.) by 1550.[1] The early Stuarts had not continued this gratuity; but the House itself had come to the rescue by making a sessional collection for the Clerk and other officers of the House: thus, whereas in the distribution of this benevolence in 1601 the Clerk got nothing,[2] he got £10 in 1607, was recommended for 'some extraordinary reward' in 1610, got £30, and his son £10, in 1623, and £100 in 1626.[3] Later figures are not given in the *Journal*, but by 1649 in the table of fees the sessional payment of 5s. for a knight of the shire and 2s. 6d. for a burgess—formerly a benevolence, partly for the poor—had been entirely appropriated to the Clerk. Moreover, the Clerk had been accustomed to receive, no doubt from earliest days, gratuities from those outside persons or corporations who were petitioning Parliament, in particular for private bills: some interesting researches by Professor J. E. Neale and his assistants show the extent and the value (to the Clerk and his 'man') of this practice in Elizabethan Parliaments.[4]

However, until the fees, mainly on private bills, were fixed and publicly announced, as they were for the first time in 1649, the line between accustomed fees and extraordinary gratuities would

[1] See A. F. Pollard in *Bull. I.H.R.* xvi. 147–8.

[2] 1 C.J. 249. He was then wealthy enough to present the parliamentary feast held at Merchant Taylors' Hall with a march-pane representing the Commons House sitting (ibid., p. 251).

[3] 1 C.J. 391, 452, 715, 871, 898.

[4] J. E. Neale, op. cit., pp. 340–2. The City of London was particularly generous in this respect. Later entries in the Repertories of the Court of Aldermen than those quoted by Professor Neale show that this generosity continued beyond Elizabeth's reign. Ewens had a gift of £10 in 1604 (Rep. 26.2, fol. 418 b) and Goldesbrough (see p. 22 below) did even better out of the City.

have been hard to draw. Some of the fees were very ancient. For instance, Hooker mentions that the charge for copying bills was one penny for ten lines; and this is the charge given in the *Modus Tenendi Parliamentum* to be made by the two clerks of Parliament for the transcript of a person's suit.[1] Indeed, research into the fees charged in Chancery and other Courts of law from their origins could probably show that they contained parallels for every fee mentioned in the 1649 table of fees sanctioned by the House. The question is what the Clerk's revenue from fees, part of which went to his subordinates, was worth at various periods. Until the House of Commons sat annually for an appreciable time, it can only have been occasional, and it depended mainly on the number of private bills promoted, the number and length of bills to be ingrossed, and the amount of copying required. The fact that all the early Clerks had additional revenues as clerks in Chancery, and that Elsyng died in dire poverty, shows that the Clerk's parliamentary income cannot have been considerable up to the middle of the seventeenth century; and that it remained comparatively small even at the beginning of the eighteenth will appear in a later chapter. Goldesbrough cannot have looked forward to more than a modest income from his Clerkship, and wisely remained what he already was, a deputy register of Chancery, while officiating at the table of the House. Moreover, if his income was modest, that of the Clerk Assistant and under-clerks was likely to be still more so: and they only held office at the Clerk's pleasure, while he, under medieval common law, held his office as property—a freehold for life[2]—and this tenure was the source of his right to all advantages, &c., appertaining to his office.

[1] 'non negabunt cuiquam transcriptum processus sui, sed liberabunt illud cuilibet qui hoc petierit, et capient semper pro decem lineis unum denarium, nisi forte facta fide de impotentia, in quo casu nihil capient'. The *Modus Tenendi Parliamentum*, written in mid-fourteenth century, described what a Chancery clerk considered proper clerical organization for Parliament; see William A. Morris in *Eng. Hist. Rev.* xlix. 407.

[2] See Sir William Holdsworth, *History of English Law* (3rd ed. 1945), i. 248, 257, 262.

2

THE CLERKS
1661-83

(1)

WILLIAM GOLDESBROUGH senior was appointed to the office of Under-clerk of Parliament by letters patent dated 13 April 1661.[1] He claimed—in one of his subsequent petitions for the payment of his salary[2] —that from the beginning of the rebellion he had served the Crown, 'not without loss, hazards, and considerable expense'. No doubt his sympathies had been royalist, but it is difficult to believe that he had suffered very severely, since he had been a deputy register of the Court of Chancery since 1650, even acting as register in 1658.[3] His only hazard, so far as we know, was connected with that office, and not with the constitutional struggle. It was perhaps the most lively episode in his life, and it occurred a year before he was appointed Clerk of the House. As deputy register in 1660 he was involved in the dispute between Walter Long, M.P., and Lady Jermyn as to the right, which both claimed, to the office of chief register of Chancery. The dispute, which had been referred by the House of Commons in 1659 to the arbitration of Denzil Holles and Sir Harbottle Grimston, apparently without

[1] L.P. 13 Car. II, pt. xliv, no. 7. There was an unsuccessful petitioner for the post, one Noah Bridges, B.C.L. He averred in one petition that the late King had granted him the place on the revocation of a former grant to Elsyng, but the grant failed to pass the Great Seal owing to the surrender of Oxford (*Cal. S.P. Dom. Car. II, 1660–61*, p. 347). He petitioned again, after Goldesbrough's appointment, for the office of Teller and Weigher of the Mint (*Cal. S.P. Dom. Car. II, 1661–62*, p. 219). Presumably Bridges acted as clerk to the short-lived 'Oxford' Parliament of Charles I in 1643.

[2] P.R.O. 30/32, vol. 36, p. 6.

[3] See Thomas Duffins Hardy, *A Catalogue of Lords Chancellors, Keepers of the Great Seal, Masters of the Rolls, and Principal Officers of the High Court of Chancery* (1843).

success, came before the House of Lords in 1660 and was settled in Lady Jermyn's favour, is set out in the Lords *Journals* and the records of the House of Lords.[1] All that concerns us, so far as Goldesbrough is concerned, is that, on Walter Long's own showing, Oliver Cromwell had put Goldesbrough and others into the office in 1654, and that, when Long returned from military service and endeavoured, by means both legal and illegal, to regain the registership, Goldesbrough, acting on Lady Jermyn's side, resisted high-handed action on his part by preventing his coming into the Chancery registry. When Long succeeded in getting into the office, assaulted Goldesbrough's clerk, and by force abstracted some of the records, Goldesbrough and others complained to the Commissioners for the Great Seal, and, so Long alleged, broke open a room and recovered some of the records which Long had seized. The affidavits made after this violent scene by William Brerewood, Goldesbrough's clerk, and by two other witnesses gave a most lively description of Long's incursion accompanied by four or five armed companions, one of whom dragged Brerewood from the inner to the outer office by the hair of his head, after which Long gave him into the custody of some bailiffs who refused to release him till he had given a bond of £500 for his appearance, with two sufficient sureties.[2]

Eventually the House of Lords ordered Long to restore the purloined books and decided that the Jermyn interest, under a patent granted by Charles I to Lord Jermyn, had not been voided by any delinquency of the latter. Accordingly, we find that in 1689 T. L. Jermyn was register of the Court of Chancery and Edward Goldesbrough, one of William's sons, was a deputy register.[3] Moreover, it is fairly certain that William Goldesbrough continued to be a

[1] See 11 L.J. 8, 9, 13, 26; *R. Comm. Hist. MSS. 7. H.L. MSS.*, Appendix, pp. 79, 80, 85. Long's contention was that Lord Jermyn had forfeited the patent of the office granted to him by Charles II as a delinquent, and that his own appointment as register in 1644 remained valid.

[2] See ibid., Appendix, p. 85a, entry for 18 May 1660, which mentions ten documents annexed to the petition of Lady Jermyn. Three of these are the affidavits, which I transcribed myself from the originals in the Lords Record Office, as they are not printed elsewhere; but they are too long for inclusion here.

[3] *R. Comm. Hist. MSS.* 12, p. 327.

deputy register of Chancery after his appointment to the Clerk-ship of the House of Commons. This would explain the curious entry in the *Journal* for 18 November 1667:[1]

'*Order*, Mr Devenish to be taken into the custody of the Serjeant at Arms for his abuse and breach of privilege in taking away by force and detaining the Book of Causes in Chancery, from the servant of Mr. Goldesbrough, Clerk of this House, in the Register's Office, and re-fusing to restore it, contrary to the Order and Direction of the Lord Keeper.

One would naturally inquire with some surprise what the Clerk's servant was doing in the Chancery registry with a book of Chan-cery Causes: but the answer is fairly simple when one knows that Mr. Devenish was also a deputy register in Chancery, and that Goldesbrough's servant was the William Brerewood whom Walter Long assaulted in 1660, and who had since become an under-clerk of the House.[2]

Thus, in William Goldesbrough's appointment, there was re-sumed the long traditional connexion between the Clerks of the lower House and the clerks of Chancery, from among whom all the medieval Clerks of the House were appointed. Goldesbrough senior was a member of the Glass-sellers' Company and seems to have earned the gratitude of the City. On 28 March 1672 the City Chamberlain was ordered by the Court of Aldermen to present him with 30 guineas 'as the gift of this Court for his many favours and respects to this City', and on 25 May 1677 he was ordered to be given 20 guineas.[3] His will,[4] dated 20 November 1678, shows that, if not nearly so wealthy as Paul Jodrell became, he died a man of substance, for he left £1,000 to his daughter Grace, other sub-stantial money legacies to his sons, and to his wife, jointly with his eldest son, he left all his mortgages, acts, and titles in the parish of St. Giles's in the Fields. He died in 1678, as is proved by the Trea-sury warrant[5] to Sir R. Howard, the Auditor of the Exchequer,

[1] 9 C.J. 21. [2] See below, pp. 32–34.
[3] Rep. 78, fol. 124; 82, fol. 171. Cf. J. E. Neale, *The Elizabethan House of Commons* (London, 1949), p. 341 n., for earlier donations by the City to the Clerk.
[4] Commissary Court of London, Reg. 36, Dec. 1678.
[5] T. 53/2, fol. 114.

dated 7 June 1680, wherein it is stated there was due to his executors the sum of £170 for arrears of salary (£10 a year) for seventeen years to midsummer 1678. He was succeeded as Clerk of the House by his son William, who had been granted the reversion of the office during his father's lifetime, in 1673.[1] He lived in Lincoln's Inn, of which he was a member, the year of his call being 1676, and died intestate at Acton in 1683. Probate was granted to his brother Robert on 4 September of that year, and on 2 November a Treasury warrant was issued to pay his executors £50 due for five years' arrears of salary ended midsummer 1683.[2]

All that we know of the elder Goldesbrough's activities during his tenure of the Clerkship is derived from his own references to them in his various petitions for payment of money due to him. It is, therefore, necessary to enter into the rather complex details of his not very successful efforts to obtain his dues from the Crown. For the first session of Charles II's first Parliament there was no difficulty, since the precedent[3] set in the Convention Parliament of the previous year was almost exactly followed. On 24 July 1661, after several petitions from officers of the House had been read, the House ordered that it be recommended to the Lord High Treasurer to give directions for the satisfaction of what was ordered by the last Assembly for the Clerk and other officers, and that his Lordship be desired to give a proportionable recompense to them (*sc.* for the current session) and to give order for the satisfaction of the stationer's bills. It was further ordered that a committee of sixteen members should 'consider what fees have been anciently due to the several clerks and officers of the House; and the number of the said officers, and how they were paid, and whence their satisfaction did arise, and how, for the future, they may have and receive a recompense suitable to their pains and attendance'.[4] The committee's report, if made, was not recorded in the *Journal*: but

---

[1] Two dockets of this grant exist in the Osborn–Godolphin papers in the British Museum: Addl. MSS. 28074, fol. 122, dated June 1673 acknowledged by Latimer on 17 Oct., and Addl. MSS. 28075, fol. 12, dated Nov. 1673 and acknowledged by Latimer on 3 Dec. 1673. See also *Cal. S.P. Dom. 1673*, p. 590.

[2] P.C.C.-Act. Book, 1683 (Sept.), and T. 53/2, fol. 165.

[3] See above, p. 17.

[4] 8 C.J. 309.

the recommendation had an effect in the Treasury. On 9 November 1661 Southampton signed a warrant to the Clerk of the Signet for a privy seal for the payment of £731 to William Goldesbrough for the allowances for the officers of the House of Commons for the Parliament begun 8 May and adjourned 30 July 1661, 'His Majesty having been pleased to be, upon the desire of the House of Commons, at this charge for this time only, hereafter the same to be defraied by the Members of the House themselves, which was the old practice to discharge their own officers'.[1] The detail[2] shows that the payments followed the precedent of the year before. Goldesbrough got £72. 10s. for himself and £30 for ingrossing public bills, Sharpe the Clerk Assistant £72. 10s., and the under-clerks again £25. The remainder went to the Serjeant at Arms and his servants, the chaplain, the provost-marshal and his men, the stationer, and for firing (£50). In none of his subsequent petitions for payment of arrears did Goldesbrough make any allusion to this one prompt payment. He petitioned in 1668,[3] and twice in other years, but according to one of the later petitions[4] he received nothing on account of his salary, or for 'his labour, care and charge of money bills and other public matters', but £100 in Lord Clifford's time and what he had received from Mr. Lowndes for bills copied in the session of 1677.[5] In the second he said that there was due to him £420 for arrears of salary, for ingrossment of bills and making copies of orders and transactions of public concern, of which arrears he had received £20. A warrant for £20 was certainly made out to him in 1669, and a privy seal and Treasury warrant for £100 were issued on 13 February 1770-1;[6] and on 13 July 1671 there was issued a privy seal for £319. 15s. 4d. to William Goldesbrough, Clerk in the Commons House of Parlia-

---

[1] *Cal. T.P.* i. 302, 310, 347.

[2] Given in P.R.O. Treasury Early Entry Book iii, fol. 31.

[3] *Cal. T.P.* vii. 287, for his salary and for £150 due to him from Nicholas Veile.

[4] *Cal. T.P.* v. 1342 (given in Appendix II, p. 284).

[5] See *Cal. T.P.* v. 614, Order dated 4 May 1677 to pay Lowndes £49. 6s. 8d. of which £34. 6s. 8d. was for his disbursements to the Clerks of the two Houses: and ibid., pp. 955, 1056, a similar order to repay Lowndes £26. 18s. 6d. disbursed to the Clerk of the House of Commons and others for the Parliament from 25 Mar. 1677 to 27 Mar. 1678.

[6] See *Cal. T.P.* v. 1384, and iii. 131, 203, 730, 731, 894.

ment 'for his pains in all those large bills on public concernments in that House, which he has attended, prepared and ingrossed from 1666, September 18th till March 6th last: also for many copies of bills, reports, narrations and other proceedings made out by him by direction of the Treasury Lords from 1666–67 January to 1670 March, for which he has yet had no allowances'. The money warrant for this sum was issued on 4 October: but the money was not then paid, nor was it ever paid in full. Nobody would ever have known what William Goldesbrough senior actually received at the Receipt of the Exchequer, had not Paul Jodrell, when petitioning in 1723 for payment of arrears due to himself, attached to his petition, as a precedent for the payment of arrears, a copy of a certificate from Sir Robert Howard, Auditor of the Exchequer, stating exactly what sums had been paid to Goldesbrough, or rather to the Goldesbroughs, father and son, between whom Sir R. Howard's certificate makes no distinction, or to their executors.

Sir Robert Howard's certificate,[1] dated 28 June 1686, mentions four separate sums, totalling £878. 12s., as having been paid out of the Exchequer, viz. £450 paid on 6 October 1666 (to the receipt of which Goldesbrough did not allude), £100 paid on 10 October 1673 to be distributed amongst the under-clerks, £200 paid on 12 November 1677 as part of £319. 15s. 4d. due to Goldesbrough for divers services between 1660 and 1670, and £128. 12s. paid on 21 November 1685 to 'his executors' for services in the Parliament begun on 6 March 1678–9. Comparing these figures with others stated either by Goldesbrough himself or in other Treasury records, it seems clear (*a*) that the warrant for £20 of 1669 did not result in a cash issue; (*b*) that the £100 issued 'in Lord Clifford's time' was for the under-clerks; (*c*) that of the privy seal for £319. 15s. 4d. issued in 1671 only £200 was paid, and that six years later; (*d*) that the £128. 12s. paid on 21 November 1685 went to the executors of the younger, not the elder, Goldesbrough; (*e*) that the Treasury warrant of 1680[2] for payment of seventeen years' arrears of his salary of £10 a year did not result in a cash issue; and (*f*) that a

---

[1] Given in full in Appendix II, p. 297.
[2] T. 53/2, fol. 114.

Treasury warrant of 2 November 1685[1] for the payment of £50—
five years' salary—to the executors of the younger Goldesbrough
also never reached the stage of payment at the Exchequer. The
result is that, whatever errors and omissions there may be in the
statements as to money received made by the elder Goldesbrough
in his petitions, the Treasury, on the showing of its own books,
owed the elder Goldesbrough on his death £289. 15s. 4d. and the
younger £50. It looks, in fact, as if the younger Goldesbrough received no payment at all—which is hardly surprising seeing that
he held office during the later years of Charles II's reign—for his
salary was wholly in arrear when he died, and the money due for
work done was only issued to his executors. His father must have
done fairly well out of fees on private bills and other proceedings[2]
during his term of office, during which Parliament sat annually:
but the junior only saw three sessions, one of which was the short-
lived Oxford Parliament of 1680, and there was very little private
legislation during that period. As he died intestate, there is no
means of knowing how he thrived.

Financial details apart, the records of Goldesbrough's petitions,
of the Treasury warrants issued to him and of the payments made
to him at the Exchequer, are highly interesting as evidence of the
entry of a wholly new element into the functions of the Clerk of
the House. As the servant of the House William Goldesbrough
doubtless carried out all the formal duties at the table which his
predecessors had performed; he was also responsible for the ingrossment of bills and for providing (on payment of fees) copies
of orders of the House, *Journal* entries, and so forth to those who
required them. He was not the first Clerk to receive specific payment for the ingrossment of public bills, nor is there any novelty
in the fact that the Treasury paid, or owed, him for copies of

---

[1] *Cal. T.P.* viii. 434: it was issued on the same date as the warrant for the
£128. 12s. which was paid out on 21 Nov. 1685.

[2] e.g. copies of orders and *Journal* entries. One such must be the copy signed
'William Goldesbrough Clerk. Dom. Com.' and dated 'die Jovis primi Feb. 1643'
of an order of the Committee of Sequestrations to sequester the profits of Mr.
Henley of the King's Bench (Addl. MSS. Egerton 2978, fol. 135). Goldesbrough
was not Clerk in 1643. For the list of stationery supplied to him in 1673 see Appendix IV, p. 311, n. 1.

various parliamentary documents. The novelty was that the Treasury—itself a new element of growing power in the machinery of government—employed the Clerk as a kind of outlying functionary of its own, to whom definite and peremptory orders could be directly issued. Such an order was made, for instance, to the younger Goldesbrough in 1680–1, when the Treasury required him by letter to make out exact copies of the lists of papists handed in by members under the Act for banishing papists, and to deliver the same to the judges appointed to go on circuit, taking care that each judge received copies for the counties in his circuit;[1] and it was the Treasury Lords who, before reporting to the King as to the moving of records from Westminster to Oxford for the Oxford Parliament of the same year, 'discoursed with William Goldesbrough' as to the amount of such records, books, and papers which it would be necessary to take.[2] However, the significant phrases are those used in one of the elder Goldesbrough's petitions and in the Treasury books to describe certain services performed by him. Goldesbrough complained on one occasion[3] that he had received nothing on account of his salary or 'for his labour, care and charge of money bills and other public matters': and the Treasury, in respect of two out of the four sums certified by Sir R. Howard as having been paid, described Goldesbrough's services as 'attending, preparing and ingrossing of divers large bills upon public concern', or specified that a payment to him was ordered 'for divers large bills on public concernments passed in that House which he attended, prepared and ingrossed'.[4] The important word in the Treasury entry is 'prepared', and in Goldesbrough's petition the phrase 'charge of money bills'. We shall find an extension of this kind of terminology in the records of Jodrell's relations with the

---

[1] *Cal. T.P.* vii. 442.

[2] Ibid., p. 60. It was decided that, though more of such documents (owing to the Popish Plot) would be necessary than in 1665, one close carriage would suffice. There is no extant bill of expenses for the carriage to Oxford and back of the Commons records: but that for the carriage of the Lords records on the same occasion by Mr. Parwater, four men, and six horses, is to be found in the British Museum (Addl. MSS. 5756, fol. 8). The total cost, for lodging, food, and horse meat, was £7. 16s. with £5 to Mr. Parwater for his trouble.

[3] See Appendix II, p. 284.

[4] Ibid., p. 297.

Treasury, and later, from the middle of the eighteenth century onwards, a new development by which, not the Clerk of the House but one of the under-clerks, was employed and paid by the Treasury for conducting some of its parliamentary business. It will be more convenient to deal with this important development in parliamentary machinery at a later stage: but it seems unquestionable that the process by which the Treasury employed a servant of the House in some sort as its 'parliamentary agent', particularly in the preparation and passing of money bills, began soon after the Restoration under the Lord High Treasurer Southampton and the Lords Commissioners of the Treasury who succeeded him. It is, unfortunately, impossible to say precisely what was meant by Goldesbrough's 'charge' of money bills, or by his 'preparing' bills of public concernment, all the more since the preparing of a money bill was always officially entrusted to certain members of the House, the law officers usually being among them, as is shown by innumerable entries in the *Journals*. Nevertheless, these phrases seem to point to the conclusion that Goldesbrough assisted, at all events, in drafting bills based upon resolutions in the Committee of Supply, and that he was made responsible for seeing such bills through all their stages and generally assisting whatever member of the administration was officially in charge.

(2)

A Mr. Sharpe was appointed Clerk Assistant in 1661 when the elder Goldesbrough became Clerk. He was still holding the office in May 1662, when the House ordered the members' contributions for the servants of the House to be paid to Mr. Sharpe, 'deputy to the Clerk of this House' and to be distributed amongst the servants of the House by Mr. Speaker.[1] Presumably Sharpe was appointed by Goldesbrough, since his letters patent gave him that power: but there is no record in the *Journals* of any formal introduction to the House of him or of his successor. I have been unable to find any information about this shadowy figure—not even his Christian name or the reason for his short term of office.

[1] 8 C.J. 432.

Sharpe was succeeded by Thomas Marsh, son of a Royalist Colonel Marsh. The collection for the servants of the House was ordered to be paid to him in 1663, 1664, 1666, 1670, and 1673.[1] It is impossible to say if he was identical with the Mr. Marsh to whom payment (jointly with Mr. Frensham) was ordered to be paid as under-clerk in the Rump Parliament:[2] but on his death in 1673 his widow, in a petition[3] for relief, represented that her husband had served as Clerk Assistant to Parliament for thirteen years since the Restoration. Since Sharpe was Clerk Assistant for the first two sessions of Charles II's Long Parliament, this statement cannot have been true. Also, Pepys's reference to Marsh in his diary leads to the inference that the latter was newly appointed at the date of the entry, 19 August 1663:[4]

Thence homewards . . . and met Tom Marsh, my old acquaintance at Westminster, who talks mightily of the honour of his place being Clerks Assistant to the Clerks of the House of Commons, and I take him to be a Coxcombe, and so did give him half a pint of wine, but drink none myself, and so got shut of him.

Probably Marsh had some subordinate post at Westminster as an under-clerk from 1660–3. In 1668 or 1669 the Commissioners chosen by the loyal officers of London and Westminster to manage the plate lottery granted to them by the King for six years appointed Marsh to receive offers for farming out the lottery for the several counties at the Great Almonry, Westminster Abbey.[5] A more interesting reference to Marsh in the public records is connected with the reward bestowed on him for his services in the shape of a place in the Customs—a common form of reward in those days. On 23 February 1670–1 a Treasury fiat was issued for letters patent to create Thomas Marsh comptroller of customs for Chichester[6] in place of John Martin deceased. He did not hold this place long, for some time in 1671 he petitioned for leave to surrender to Richard Quarry and William Broman his patent of the controllership of customs at Chichester, to which he had been

---

[1] 8 C.J., pp. 510, 562, 670; 9 C.J. 149, 274.
[2] 8 C.J. 16. [3] *Cal. T.P.* v. 1353.
[4] Ed. Wheatley (1893), iii. 255.
[5] *Cal. S.P. Dom. Car. II, 1668–69*, p. 124. [6] *Cal. T.P.* iii. 789.

appointed by the Lords Commissioners of the Treasury 'for his diligence as Clerk Assistant of the House of Commons', since he was unable to attend to both services, and had to discharge several bonds incurred by his father, Colonel John Marsh, for his loyalty.[1] In the list of Patent Officers of the Outports,[2] 1672, Marsh is entered as customer for Chichester at a salary of £13. 0s. 10d., but the Treasury fiat to make Quarry comptroller of customs there was dated 18 December 1671,[3] so that Marsh enjoyed his patent for less than a year. It is therefore not surprising that he left little money for his widow and four children, since he had no salary as Clerk Assistant, but only a share in the annual collection of 10s. from every knight of the shire and 5s. from every other member, besides such fees as fell to him on private bill proceedings or what he could earn by making copies of bills and other parliamentary matter.

The name of Marsh's successor as Clerk Assistant in 1673 cannot be stated with certainty, since it was only on the opening of a new Parliament that the name of the Clerk Assistant was given in the *Journal* as assisting to administer the oath. There was no new Parliament till 1679, and no Clerk Assistant is mentioned in the *Journal* as having attended at the opening of the Parliaments of 1679, 1680, or 1681. However, seeing that the reversion of the Clerk's Office was granted to William Goldesbrough junior in 1673 and on his accession in 1678 the reversion was granted to Paul Jodrell,[4] it is, perhaps, not unsafe to presume that William Goldesbrough junior was appointed Clerk Assistant by his father in 1673, and that he, when Clerk in 1678, appointed Paul Jodrell, there being no reason why the Clerk Assistant's post should have been left vacant for ten years. Indeed, there must have been a Clerk Assistant to attend committees of the whole House, and the committee of privileges and elections, which latter was occasionally very full.[5]

[1] *Cal. S.P. Dom. Car. II, 1670, Addenda 1660–70*, p. 622. The date given in the margin of the Calendar is '? 1670', but it cannot have been before 1671 or after the end of that year.

[2] Addl. MSS. (Godolphin) 28080, fol. 6.

[3] *Cal. T.P.* iii. 1162.   [4] *Cal. T.P.* v. 1303.

[5] *R. Comm. Hist. MSS. Ormonde. New Series*, vol. 14, p. 429. Sir Robert South-

(3)

Since the Clerk of the House had entire discretion in his appointment of under-clerks, there was no fixed 'establishment' in the modern sense; and it is not until late in the eighteenth century that the Clerk of the House can be seen to have adhered to a more or less fixed establishment of his own. The emergence of definite and publicly known offices under the Clerk of the House began in Jodrell's day. Previous to that, apart from the Clerk Assistant, who was first publicly recognized in 1640 on Rushworth's appointment, other persons employed in clerkly offices in the House of Commons were looked on merely as the Clerk's employees—as his 'servants' or 'men' in the Tudor phraseology. The table of fees of 1649 authorized a fee of 10s. on every private bill for the under-clerks. In 1660 and 1661, as has been mentioned, payments to under-clerks, named on one occasion, unnamed on another, were authorized by the House, and they were generically included among the 'servants of the House', for whom a collection was made at the end of the session. There is no evidence, however, to show that any such under-clerk was regarded as holding a definite position. In 1673 Goldesbrough received £100 to be distributed among the under-clerks, but one cannot say how many there were, or what were their duties or conditions of employment. Names otherwise unknown crop up here and there. One Bentley Phillips, for instance, sewer of the chamber without fee to the King, petitioned for a recommendation to a clerkship under the Commissioners for the duty on wine and spirits, pleading that he and his family suffered in the royal interest, 'so that he has lately been a clerk in the House of Commons'.[1] Again, there is a letter from Samuel Pepys to William Goldesbrough junior dated 8 September 1680, in which he recommends a Mr. Salisbury to succeed 'poor Mr. Hayes in the Employment wherein he has heretofore

---

well to the duke of Ormonde, 8 June 1678: 'On Thursday the Committee of Privileges were as numerous as at a full house' (Grantham election); and *R. Comm. Hist. MSS. Various MSS.* ii. 395. Sir Godfrey Copley writes on 8 May 1679: 'By this time Sir Thomas Meres was got into the chair, and it began to be a fuller house than hath been seen at a Committee this great while' (Aldborough election).

[1] *Cal. S.P. Dom. Car. II, 1667–68*, p. 368.

served ye House of Commons and you'.[1] I have no further knowledge of 'poor Mr. Hayes' or of Mr. Salisbury.

There is only one person employed as an under-clerk by the
Goldesbroughs about whom there are any facts to be found—and
he is William Brerewood, son of Sir Robert Brerewood of Chester,
Justice of the King's Bench at Oxford under Charles I.[2] William
Brerewood was admitted to the Middle Temple on 27 November
1657 and became a clerk to William Goldesbrough senior in the
registry of the Court of Chancery, where in 1660 he was assaulted
and dragged by his hair into the outer office by one William Smith,
so that Walter Long could seize some Chancery records, as already
related. Doubtless Goldesbrough, whose clerk he was, took him
under his wing to the House of Commons, when he himself was
appointed Clerk of the House, both of them retaining their positions in the Chancery registry. Hence, it is most likely that he was
the Clerk's servant, from whom Henry Devenish snatched a book
of Chancery records in 1666.[3] We hear of him next in 1671 when
John Evelyn, who then had the idea of writing a history of the
Dutch War, wished to borrow some of the Commons *Journals*.
There is among the State papers a memo dated 15 September 1671
by Joseph Williamson, then secretary to Lord Arlington, 'to inquire at the House of Commons where Mr. Hughs, the Keeper of
the Speaker's Chambers, etc. dwells, and to inquire of him who
keeps the House of Commons Journals now that Mr. Goldesbrough is out of town, and where they are kept'. At the foot is
written in a different hand: 'Mr. Brewood in Cursitor's Alley in
Chancery Lane, near the Rose Tavern on that side of the way,
between two barber's poles.'[4] That this homely sidelight on Brerewood's dwelling was in Evelyn's interest is proved by the entry in
his diary for 22 September of the same year, which records that
the Treasurer took him after dinner 'to Lincoln's Inn to one of the
Parliament Clearkes, to obtaine of him, that I might carry home
and peruse, some of the Journals, which were accordingly delivered to me to examine about the late Dutch war'.

---

[1] Bodleian, MSS. Rawl. A. 194, fols. 196–7.
[2] See *D.N.B.*   [3] See above, pp. 21–22.
[4] *Cal. S.P. Dom. Car. II, 1671*, p. 483.

In 1674 Brerewood petitioned the King for a grant of the reversion of the place of register of seizures after William Culliford, the existing holder. A report on this petition was ordered on 16 October,[1] and it is from Treasurer Danby's report[2] dated 4 November of the same year that we learn the details of the petition. These throw some light on Brerewood's work. The petitioner represented that he had for some time been employed as register to the late Commissioners for examining the accounts of the £60,000 granted for loyal and indigent officers,[3] and had therein behaved with much diligence and faithfulness, and never received any reward or payment for several necessaries provided for the said service: he had also been employed for some years past as a clerk under the Clerk of the House of Commons. It is to be observed that he does not style himself 'an under-clerk' of the House. It does not appear that he got this reversion, but he was very soon rewarded, as Thomas Marsh had been, by the grant of a place in the Customs. In February 1674–5 he was granted the post of controller of customs, 'Customer Inward' at Southampton.[4] He appears to have held this post jointly with William Andrews until 1676, when they jointly surrendered it.[5] Brerewood's reason for this surrender was simple enough: he had got the reversion of a better place in the Customs after presenting another petition. He had petitioned the King for the grant in reversion after Paul Barrett of the place of water bailiff and keeper of the prison at Dover, and the patent for the grant of this reversion is dated August 1675.[6]

This petition is also interesting for the light it throws on Brerewood's functions as a clerk in the House of Commons, its ground

---

[1] *Cal. T.P.* iv. 255.   [2] Ibid., p. 603.

[3] Under the Act of 1662 (13 and 14 Car. II, c. 8).

[4] P.R.O. Signet Docket Book 17, p. 134. The grant as given there is direct and not in reversion: but in Addl. MSS. 28075, fol. 150, the docket signed 'J. Mathew' and dated Feb. 1674 is in reversion after William Andrews. The Treasury fiat (*Cal. T.P.* iv. 668) for a Great Seal for the grant dated 3 Feb. 1674/5 was also for a grant in reversion after Andrews.

[5] *Cal. T.P.* v. 412, 525.

[6] P.R.O. Signet Docket Book 17, p. 192. Brerewood's petition as set out in *Cal. S.P. Dom. Car. II, 1678*, p. 601, is dated in the margin '? 1678'; but I have pointed out to the Deputy Keeper of the Records that it must be earlier than the docket.

being: 'his father, the late Sir Robert Brerewood of Chester, having served the late King as Justice of the King's Bench at Oxford,
and having been sequestered as a delinquent, and he himself having
served without allowance as under clerk of the House of Commons and being at great charge in paying for copies of bills etc.
for the late Lord Commissioners of the Treasury and the late and
now Lord Treasurer.' This allegation seems to have moved the
Treasury to inquire 'what Mr. Brerewood or any other person
have been allowed for sending copies of Parliament Bills to the
Lord Treasurer and Lord Keeper'.[1] Apparently this inquiry opened
no purse-strings, for on 2 May 1676 a petition was read in
the Treasury from William Brerewood and one Petty[2] for an
allowance for supplying the Treasury with copies of bills. On
29 August a money warrant to pay William Brerewood £150 for
copies of bills was issued, and instructions to pay followed on
2 October.[3] After this date, so far as can be ascertained, William
Brerewood disappears from history.[4] There is no further reference
to him in the Treasury papers, nor have I been able to discover if
he ever held the post of water bailiff and keeper of the prison at
Dover.

[1] *Cal. T.P.* iv. 337, Treasury minute to this effect, dated 1 Oct. 1675.
[2] Another *nominis umbra*.
[3] *Cal. T.P.* v. 318, 339.
[4] But his nephew, Thomas Brerewood, a clothier, was involved with Pitkin in
fraudulent dealings at a later date; see *H.L. MSS. New Series*, vii. 74–78.

3

PAUL JODRELL
1683–1726

(1)

Two Jodrells find places in the *Dictionary of National Biography*—Sir Paul Jodrell, the physician, and Richard Paul Jodrell, scholar, poet, and dramatist, his elder brother—but no mention is made of the fact that both were great-grandsons of Paul Jodrell, Clerk of the House of Commons from 1683 to 1726. A. I. Dasent in his *Speakers of the House of Commons* says of Jodrell:[1] 'some would have preferred him as Speaker in 1708 to Sir Richard Onslow': but Jodrell did not desert his seat at the table for a seat in the House, nor did he in any other direction court fame, who turned her back on him. Fortune, however, he courted not indifferently: he did pretty well for himself and for his descendants, in a most honourable way, and it is fitting that the Jodrell pedigree should begin with him.[2] He purchased the manor of Duffield and Belper in Derbyshire, that of Lewknor[3] in Oxfordshire came to him through his wife, and he left considerable wealth besides in money and plate, as his elaborate will and its codicil show.[4] At no time during his tenure of the Clerkship were its emoluments enough to make a man rich, although as will be seen, he received some very handsome grants in the way of fee-farm rents from William III. But Paul Jodrell the Older, as he styles himself in his will, of Chancery Lane, and of Syon Hill, Isleworth, had another profession. He was a solicitor to the Court of Chan-

---

[1] Op. cit., p. 242. He does not give his authority for this statement.

[2] The pedigree is in Addl. MSS. 6670, fols. 364, 366. His wife was eldest daughter of Thomas Rolles of Lewknor, Oxon.

[3] Where he was buried. The church has a mortuary chapel of the Jodrell family, in which there is a memorial tablet bearing a long Latin inscription setting forth all Paul Jodrell's services and merits.

[4] P.C.C. Brook, 1728, fol. 135.

cery—the only practising solicitor who ever became Clerk of the House—and retained his practice till the end, leaving £10 apiece for mourning to the clerks 'in my Chancery business', and enjoining certain other gentlemen to make up all arrears with clients, and to be diligent in that purpose, in making accounts up to date and 'in getting the money out', for which his eldest son was to reward them liberally. Evidence of his practice as a solicitor is to be found in certain letters[1] written by him in that capacity to Lord Hatton or his agent between 1687 and 1706, the earliest of which, dated 20 December 1687, informs his client that letters may be directed to him at Symond's Yard, Chancery Lane. Jodrell's interest in Lincoln's Inn, of which his son, Paul, became Treasurer in 1742, was that he was joint lessee, with John Clements, of the Inn in 1687:[2] and one may conjecture that it was through his connexion with Lincoln's Inn and the Court of Chancery that he recommended himself to William Goldesbrough senior and junior, whom he succeeded as Clerk of the House. It is hardly conceivable that he would have been granted the reversion[3] of this office after William Goldesbrough in 1678, when the younger Goldesbrough succeeded his father, except by their recommendation, the senior Goldesbrough having been deputy register of Chancery, and his son being a member of Lincoln's Inn.

On the death of William Goldesbrough junior in 1683, although there was no Parliament sitting at the time, Paul Jodrell, who had presumably been Clerk Assistant since 1678[4], succeeded immediately to the Clerkship of the House of Commons under the terms of his reversion. That he did so is proved by his petition to the King as Clerk of the House of Commons dated 16 November 1683,[5] and the matter of his petition shows the state of confusion

[1] Addl. MSS. (Hatton papers) 29562, fol. 458; 29568, fols. 21, 23, 24, 31, 32, 203, 204, 218. See also *H.L. MSS. New Series*, iii, *1697–99*, p. 299, showing Jodrell as acting for the earl of Meath as his agent in England in an action before the House of Lords in 1699. The inscription referred to on p. 35, n. 3, styles him 'in alta Curia Cancellarii per multos annos fidelis et insignis sollicitator'.

[2] *H.L. MSS. New Series*, iii, *1697–99*, no. 1201. Bishop of Chichester's Estate (Chancery Lane Act), p. 89 (b), affidavit of John Clements.

[3] *Cal. T.P.* v. 1303. Treasurer Danby's subscription of a Great Seal for this purpose. [4] See above, p. 30.

[5] *Cal. S.P. Dom. Car. II, 1683–84*, p. 92. Hatsell in his *Precedents of Proceedings*

in which the records, *Journals*, and papers of the House were still kept.[1] He states that

the petitioner on his admission to the said Office being informed that many books and papers belonging to the same were wanting and were in several persons' hands, His Majesty ordered in Council that all persons should forthwith deliver them to the petitioner, who finds that William Henchman and Thomas Fox, booksellers of Westminster, and others have by some indirect means got some books which they pretend to be a copy of the Journals and design to print the same, and therefore praying a further order for hindering the printing of the said books by ordering them to be seized or otherwise.

The Order in Council prayed for was made the same day.

Jodrell's earliest acts as Clerk, even before the meeting of James II's only Parliament, were directed towards the preservation of his records. The first was to get back certain folios of the Commons *Journal* relating to the Navy and to the accusation and commitment of Sir Anthony Deane and Samuel Pepys in 1679, which the latter had borrowed and kept overlong. Mr. Arthur Bryant[2] is a little unfair to Pepys in saying that Jodrell had 'quite a struggle' to get them back, for the correspondence[3] shows no reluctance on Pepys's part to send back the borrowed papers, but only an anxiety to safeguard himself. Jodrell, in February 1684/5 wrote:

I begg you to let the Bearer have that Jornall you have, for I have occasion for it. I hope your great Businesse has given you leave to lett it bee looked out. If you desire any further Use of it, It shall bee at y^r Service at any tyme.

Pepys replied next day from the Admiralty:

I have found time since I saw you last, to looke over my Books and Papers, as they were confusedly throwne together, upon Occasion of the late Fire in Our Neighbourhood, and have found the Journall you Desire, & shall have delivered to your owne hand, when ever you'l

wrongly dates Jodrell's Clerkship from 1684: but Hatsell was also unaware that there were two Goldesbroughs.

[1] For similar confusion in earlier times cf. J. E. Neale, 'The Commons Journals of the Tudor Period', in *Trans. R. Hist. Soc.*, 4th ser. iii (1920).
[2] *Samuel Pepys: The Saviour of the Navy* (London, 1942), p. 119.
[3] Bodleian, MSS. Rawl. A. 193, fols. 232–40.

please to give yourselfe the trouble of calling for it, in your way to or from Westminster-Hall. For, it coming into my hand in the manner it did, and haveing laine soe long there, I shall not think myselfe well Discharged of it, without a Receipt for it under yours; as being soe nearly concerned in some part of it myselfe. Which Caution, not doubting your holding me excused for, I remaine

> Your very humble
> Servant
> S. Pepys.

In consequence of the same Caution, Pray pardon mee in desiring only a sight of the Instrument by which I am to be Warranted in Delivering the Book to you.

It is understandable that Pepys should want, not only a receipt, but, since Jodrell had not yet sat as Clerk in the House, an assurance that he in fact held the office. The formal receipt is dated 12 March 1684/5, and it shows that Pepys had borrowed

A Journall Booke of the House of Commons, beginning Fol. 14; being Tuesday March the 18th 1678, (1679 new style) and ending Folio 188, being Tuesday the 27th of May following the day of that Parliament's Prorogation.

Since this is the last known instance of the lending of the original *Journal* to anybody, it seems probable that Jodrell, cautious solicitor that he was, determined to put an end to any such practices.

Almost at the same time as this exchange took place, Jodrell had taken a second step. He presented a petition to the King in which he set forth[1] that he had lately come into the office of Clerk of the House of Commons,

and has endeavoured his utmost for the preservation of the books and other things belonging thereto, for future service, he finding the same in a very disordered manner: that he apprehends such disorders have happened by reason there hath not been for many years any place of habitation appointed for the Clerk of the Commons (as the Clerk of

---

[1] *Cal. T.P.* viii. 91. The petition was considered by the Treasury Lords on 30 Mar. 1685. The house and premises therein mentioned were situated in Westminster next adjoining the Court of Wards at the west end of Westminster Hall between Old Palace Yard and the Fishyard, and were formerly enjoyed by the Usher of the Court of Wards.

the House of Lords has had, which is annexed to his office) for the more convenient execution of the said office.

It went on to say he had discovered that the King had a title to an old ruinous house and a little garden plot and some decayed rooms and appurtenances near the place where his office was executed, and offered at his own expense to assert the King's right thereto, and prayed a grant thereof for the better preservation and more convenient execution of his office. This petition was referred by Rochester to Sir Robert Howard, Mr. Harbord the Surveyor-General, Sir Christopher Wren, and William Wardour, Clerk of the Pells, as was Jodrell's answer to their first report. However, this attempt to obtain land on which to build a house for the Clerk and a repository for the *Journals* and papers was unsuccessful. It was not till 1760 that the dwelling house in Cotton Garden was built for the Clerk, and the *Journals* continued to be kept in part of the Court of Wards which had become the Clerk's office-room under the Goldesbroughs.[1] Jodrell himself continued to live in Chancery Lane, where he had his solicitor's office, until at some date unknown to me he moved to Syon Hill, Isleworth. But he seems to have had a garden at Westminster, since Christopher Wren's estimate for charges at the coronation of William and Mary—kitchens in St. Stephen's Court and other provision for the banquet in Westminster Hall—included fitting up some sheds for a scalding house in 'Mr. Jodrell's garden'.[2]

It must be added—to complete the story of Jodrell's reforms in the keeping of the House's records—that a few years later he took on a clerk especially for the purpose, maintained him in his own house, and paid him a salary at a total cost of £40 a year. This appears from the clerks' memorial of 1709–11, in which the relevant passage[3] runs as follows:

5thly. The Clerk of the House hath had a Clerk under him ever since the Revolution, Publick Business so much increasing, who hath the

[1] For further details of this matter, and discussion of the use eventually made of the Court of Wards, see my monograph *The Topography of the Old House of Commons* described in my introduction, pp. xvi–xvii.

[2] P.R.O. Works 3/1, fols. 8, 9.

[3] Appendix II, p. 291.

Charge and Custody (under his Master) of the Journals, and Bills and proceedings thereon, with other papers laid before the house, whereby the same are kept in order and from Confusion, and he is obliged to attend Constantly whilest the House is sitting, and at all times on Members of the House upon Searches, & otherwise when required; Hath not any Sallary from Her Majesty & very little (if any) perquisites for so doing the same, But the Clerk is necessitated to maintain him in his house to be constantly at hand and allow him a Considerable Sallary yearly whereby the Business of the House is much better dispatch't.

This statement was confirmed in the Speaker's report on the memorial. In 1709 the clerk in question was Zachary Hamlyn, who witnessed Jodrell's will, under which he was appointed a trustee, and who was probably living with Jodrell till the latter's death.[1] Thus Paul Jodrell, by engaging and maintaining Zachary Hamlyn, who remained his personal clerk,[2] laid the foundations of what became the Journal Office under the clerk of the journals and papers. Jodrell, indeed, paid assiduous attention to the *Journals* of the House, not only as regards their safe custody, but also as regards their form and accuracy. When, near the end of his career, in 1723 he petitioned the Lords Commissioners of the Treasury to pay him what they owed for ingrossments of public bills and copies of bills, accounts, and other papers for the last eight years, the total amounting to £1,807. 10s. 8d., Speaker Spencer Compton, to whom the Treasury referred the petition, recommended that it would not be unreasonable to allow him £1,500 in consideration of the services mentioned,

and also of his keeping the Journals of the House in a better manner than ever had been done by any of his Predecessors.[3]

[1] Jodrell left Hamlyn £10 for mourning if still living with him at the time of his (Jodrell's) death. If he was the original holder of this post, Hamlyn must have served the House for over fifty years, for he was still there in 1742 when Nicholas Hardinge made his report on the state of the *Journals* (24 C.J. 263).

[2] He seems often to have received Jodrell's fees. The Treasury Solicitor entered a payment of £50. 2s. 10d., on 23 July 1717, to Zachary Hamlyn for Mr. Jodrell for ingrossing documents relating to the trial of the earl of Oxford and for attending the trial (T. 53/26, fols. 200–3). And the Librarian of All Souls College informs me of an entry of the payment in 1715 of fees for the All Souls College Act of that year amounting to £188. 7s. 7d. 'as appears by Mr. Hamlyn's acquittance'.

[3] The deplorable state of the post-Restoration *Journals* up to 1685 was com-

Though not named in the *Journals* at the opening of the 1685 Parliament, Jodrell was undoubtedly the Clerk of the House who attended.[1] The Convention Parliament of 1688/9 resolved that he should be Clerk of the House, and he continued to hold that office through William III's reign, and through the stormy times of Queen Anne into the comparatively calmer days of Walpole's ascendancy. In March 1726 he pleaded old age and indisposition to excuse his absence from the House, and he must have retired in that year, having been Clerk of the House for forty-three years, as his memorial inscription in Lewknor church records.[2] His general conception of his duties may be judged from the opening of the clerks' memorial of 1709–11 in which it was represented that the office of Clerk of the House:

is a place of great trust and attendance in respect of the various public business there transacted, and of the many money and other public bills begun and carried on there and of the public papers delivered into the said House which are committed to his custody and care, and that owing to the increase of business in late years, the Clerk was obliged to spend a great deal of time after the House had risen in putting the papers in regular order, so that during the Session almost his whole time was spent in attending the duty of the House.

Although the plaint of the Clerk—which echoed a similar plaint already made by the under-clerks[3]—that the work of the House during the session took up all his time may sound odd in modern ears, it marks the important fact that, early in Jodrell's tenure of the Clerkship, the House of Commons after a long interval

mented on by Nicholas Hardinge in his report on the *Journals* in 1742 (24 C.J. 263, sqq.). Their improved state after 1685 was largely due to the printing of the *Votes* which was regularly ordered, under the supervision of Speaker and Clerk, after 1682, as Hardinge pointed out. But, as he also remarked, the new transcription of the *Journals* up to 1685 which was ordered in 1698 (12 C.J. 255–6) on the recommendation of a select committee, was not at all competently done by Jodrell's clerks. The copies were very inaccurate and no index was made, they were eventually lost in the fire of 1834. For this transcription, Jodrell received £200 in 1700 and £150 in 1701 (*Cal. T.P.* xv. 253, xvii. 105).

[1] Hatsell, ii. 263 n., says that Jodrell's name appeared in the minute book, though not in the *Journal*, as Clerk in this Parliament.

[2] The patent of his successor, Edward Stables (L.P. 13 Geo. 1, pt. 4, no. 6), was dated 11 Jan. 1726/7.

[3] See App. II, p. 285.

resumed annual sittings. For reasons familiar to students of our political history, never again would a year pass without a session of Parliament. An annual session lasting about five months, with an ever-increasing amount of business, undoubtedly added to the Clerk's duties, making his office as onerous as it was in Elsyng's day and likely to become more so. No doubt, during the session, Jodrell chafed at being detained from personally attending to his business of solicitor, particularly by the troublesome task of preserving, entering, and ranging the mass of papers laid upon the table of the House, and all too often mislaid, as the *Journals* of that time reveal, before they could be copied in, or annexed to, that official record. The difficulty of preserving and of arranging for future reference these papers clearly exercised his orderly legal mind and moved him to the original step of appointing and maintaining at his own charges, and in his own house, a subordinate clerk, to assist him in this part of his duties. Moreover, as will be seen, this personal clerk to deal with papers was not his only innovation in the matter of staff. The four 'under-clerks without doors' were first officially appointed under his régime; and the senior of these was made the collector of the fees on private bills, of which the official table was newly drawn up in the last decade of the seventeenth century. Paul Jodrell, in fine, as soon as Parliament assumed stability and regularity under William III, became the first of the modern Clerks of the House.

In one respect, however, he was the last of the ancient line of Clerks, in that he was the last to receive particular bounty from the Sovereign, to which he made allusion in his petition of 1723.[1] His salary of £10 a year under his patent remained unchanged, and was in arrear for the first ten years of his tenure. In 1693 £100 was paid him[2] to make up those arrears, and the Treasury books show that thereafter it was paid with fair regularity. Also, from time to time in the reigns of William III and George I, the same books show that during the session he was paid 8s. a week for supplying *Votes* for the use of his Majesty.[3] However, the bounty

---

[1] Appendix II, p. 296.   [2] T. 53/12, fol. 155.
[3] See *Cal. T.P.* x. 1263, xv. 202, and T. 53/24, fol. 432, the respective sums therein shown as issued being £14. 15s. 0d. (1695), £38. 16s. 0d. (1699), and

to which he referred took the old form of grants of property, all from William III to whom his services must have much commended themselves. In 1695, under letters patent, the King made a grant to Jodrell and his heirs to hold four fairs each year at Duffield in Derbyshire,[1] and then, on 17 April 1697, Jodrell was granted in reversion after the Queen Dowager's death for ninety-nine years at a reserved rent of only £13. 6s. 8d. various lands and rents in the counties of Norfolk, Stafford, Derby, and Wilts., also for thirty years the fishing of the rivers Derwent and Eccleston in Derbyshire.[2] To this not inconsiderable bounty, Queen Anne added a grant of the reversion of the Clerkship of the House to Jodrell's eldest son.[3]

In making his report to the Lord High Treasurer upon the clerks' memorial of 1709–11, Speaker Bromley, in the paragraph relating to Jodrell, said:

> He farther acquaints me that he used to have every session a gratuity of £50 on account of public business which for several years has been discontinued.

This type of payment might seem to go back to the end-of-session gratuity which the Tudor sovereigns habitually bestowed on the Commons Clerk, but the entries with regard to it in the Treasury books show that it was something more than an act of royal bounty; indeed, like similar payments to William Goldesbrough,[4] it was a payment authorized by the King's ministers for the Clerk's diligence in prosecuting their business, particularly their money bills, in the House. It began with a payment of £10 in 1689 from the Secret Service fund 'as royal bounty for his pains and care in soliciting the present Poll Bill[5] and passing the same in the House

---

£13. 16s. 0d. (1714–15). This payment continued, though possibly not continuously, throughout the eighteenth century. Its specific entry in the Treasury books is very capricious.

[1] L.P. 7 Will. III, pt. 3, no. 14, 26 Feb. 1694/5.

[2] The long list of these fee-farm rents on the Queen Dowager's estate is given in the return of grants of Crown property made (by order of the House) by the Auditor of the Duchy of Lancaster (12 C.J. 66).

[3] L.P. 2 Anne, no. 32. Paul Jodrell jun., however, remained at the Bar and became a successful counsel.

[4] See above, pp. 24–28.   [5] 1 Wm. and Mary, c. 13.

of Commons'. Next year Jodrell received £50 from the Secret
Service 'for his extraordinary pains in and about the two Money
Bills passed last session'. In 1692 he got £100 or 100 guineas from
the same fund for the dispatch of several money bills in the last
two sessions, in 1694/5 the same sum for the same services, and on
2 February in 1698/9 he was paid £200 from the Civil List,[1] i.e.
£50 per session for four sessions. After that date I find no references to any further payments of the kind in the Treasury books,
and we know from the clerks' memorial that they had been discontinued for some years before 1711.

It is curious that in neither of his petitions did Jodrell make any
complaint at the loss of this sessional payment, so that it is impossible to say whether, owing to some change in Treasury arrangements, Jodrell ceased to do certain work for them which he had
previously done in connexion with money bills. Yet these payments made by the Treasury to Goldesbrough and Jodrell, and the
terms in which the Treasury recorded them, are of considerable
historical interest. They were the beginning of the employment
for definite recompense from public funds of a House of Commons
Clerk to attend to Treasury business. This could not have occurred
before the rise of the Treasury after the Restoration. I shall deal
with this development in a later chapter, and only call attention
here to its constitutional aspect.

Today the Clerk of the House, though appointed by the Crown,
and his department are not part of the Civil Service: no minister
or civil department has any jurisdiction over them. The same is
true of the Clerk of the Parliaments and his department. The
maintenance of this position is essential for preserving the proper
relations of either House and its servants with the multifarious
public departments whose activities and expenditure are subject
to parliamentary criticism. The Goldesbroughs and Jodrell were
far from having reached this position of independence, just as the
House of Commons was far from having attained control of the
executive. The Treasury Lords of their day, at all events, took
the view that the Clerk of the House was to receive and comply
with their directions, and even to attend them when peremptorily

---

[1] See *Cal. T.P.* xvii. 519, 556, 670, 674, 751; xv. 43, 264.

summoned to do so:[1] and their hold was strengthened when they directly paid the Clerk, and later one of his subordinates, for seeing their business through the Commons. Jodrell was a servant of the Crown no less truly than he was servant of the House.

To return, however, to Jodrell's emoluments, his salary of £10 a year and the short-lived payment of £50 a year from the Treasury were but a small part of these in comparison with the revenue from fees which, as the eighteenth century unfolded, became ever larger until Hatsell's annual revenue, by the end of the century, reached a sum between £9,000 and £10,000 and was still increasing. In comparison, Jodrell's income from what he called in his will his 'parliamentary business' was humble enough, as was that of his subordinates, and the House's recommendation of 1700[2] that he and the other officers of the House should have competent salaries had borne no fruit. In 1713 Speaker Bromley, in his report to the Lord High Treasurer on the clerks' memorial of 1709–11 already referred to, stated that Jodrell received between three and four hundred pounds per annum, out of which he maintained Hamlyn. The object of this memorial having been to set forth the losses in fees to all the clerks caused by the passing of the General Nationalization Act of 1709 and the enactment of a certain standing order in the Lords, and Jodrell's annual loss on these accounts having been computed at £308 per annum,[3] it is clear that the Clerk of the House was then but modestly paid in money, even if, like other Clerks before him, he received occasional handsome gratuities from wealthy corporations for assisting them in getting private bills through the House.[4] The table of fees payable to

[1] See, for instance, orders from the Treasury to Jodrell to bring certain documents laid on the table of the House to a meeting of the Treasury Lords in 1689 and 1692 (*Cal. T.P.* ix. 276, 1576); ditto in 1693 (*Cal. T.P.* x. 273) and an order for copies of Commons documents in 1701 (*Cal. T.P.* xvi. 90). See also chapter 2, p. 27.

[2] 13 C.J. 316: see Appendix II, p. 285.

[3] Ibid., p. 291. He asked for a yearly payment of £260 in compensation, but, alone of the memorialists, received nothing.

[4] Thus, in 1694, Jodrell was paid by the Corporation of London 100 guineas for his pains and service in assisting to pass the City's act to satisfy debts due to orphans, plus his bill of £60. The Speaker, Sir John Trevor, and the chairman of the committee on the bill were subsequently expelled for accepting presents, for the same services, of 1,000 guineas and 20 guineas respectively (11 C.J. 270–83).

officers of the House was revised three times in the last decade of the seventeenth century, in 1690, 1695, and 1701: and the table of 1701 which was entered in the *Journal* remained in force, with very little alteration except by way of addition, until the whole basis of fees on private bills was altered in 1847.[1] From this table the chief items in the Clerk's income from fees can be seen, and, where total figures of income are available they afford some clue to the amount of business attracting fees which was done in a particular session. So far as Jodrell himself is concerned, a glance at the 1701 table of fees shows that the Clerk's fees on a single-fee private bill amounted to £5. 5s. and that the other principal items of profit would be the ingrossment fee of 12s. 6d. a press, of which the Clerk himself took a large proportion, the fees for copies of petitions, reports, papers, and *Journal*-entries (none of these being available in print) and, at this particular period, the fee for swearing persons to be naturalized. Taking into account the fact that many private bills paid double fees, and the variety of proceedings attracting fees, Jodrell's estimate of his income in 1709–11 as given by Speaker Bromley at between £300 and £400 would only be compatible with a very moderate amount of private legislation, excluding naturalization bills. The Statute Book confirms that private legislation was, in fact, moderate in amount, and remained so until the middle of the eighteenth century when a tremendous increase began. The figures relating to fees for naturalization 1698–1708 given in the clerk's memorial 1709–11 are interesting, but they afford no clue to Jodrell's total revenue from private bill fees, including ingrossments. On the other hand, the sums which he claimed in 1723 as due to him for ingrossments of public bills 1714–23[2] give a clue to the length and extent of the money bills passed in those sessions. Jodrell claimed that these were out of pocket expenses, but I cannot avoid the suspicion that he was charging the whole legitimate fee of 12s. 6d. a press of 72 words, of which, as late as 1833, only 9d. went to the actual ingrosser. There is no sign, however, in the Treasury books that Jodrell or his executors received the £1,500 for which the Speaker recommended the Treasury to compound.

[1] 13 C.J. 356–7; see Appendix III, pp. 300–3, and Williams, ii. 273–5.
[2] Appendix II, p. 296.

Probably it was this debt that Jodrell had in mind when in his will he expressed the hope that Stables, his successor, and Hamlyn, his personal clerk, would use their best endeavour, business, and concern in getting the money due to him in his 'parliamentary business'.

(2)

When Jodrell succeeded in 1683 to the Clerkship of the House under his grant of the reversion of that office, presumably no Clerk Assistant was appointed, since Parliament was not sitting. We do not hear of a Clerk Assistant until the opening of the Convention Parliament of 1689. On 22 January of that year the House of Commons resolved that Jodrell should be Clerk of the House and that Samuel Gwillym should be Clerk Assistant. Two months later the Speaker acquainted the House that Gwillym wished to quit their service, and return to his former employment, to which the House agreed.[1] He was immediately succeeded as Clerk Assistant by Culverwell Needler, who held the office till the end of 1710 and then retired because of ill health. Although no entry of his appointment appears in the *Journal*, its date is fixed by Needler's statement made in 1710 that he had served as Clerk Assistant for twenty-two years. This statement was made in an application to the Treasury for leave to surrender his other office—that of solicitor to the Commissioners for licensing hawkers and pedlars, which he had held between thirteen and fourteen years—to William Milward, his clerk.[2] Culverwell Needler was the son of Benjamin Needler and Marie Culverwell, sister of Nathaniel Culverwell, the Puritan divine. His father, also a divine, was ejected from his rectory of St. Margaret Moses in Friday Street, London, in 1662 and retired to North Warnborough in Hampshire where he preached privately till his death in 1682.[3]

[1] 10 C.J. 8, 43. In 1676 Gwillym had drafted two bills for the Solicitor General and petitioned for payment the following year (*Cal. T.P.* v. 1337): it was presumably legal work to which he returned.

[2] *Cal. T.P. 1708–14*, pp. 188–89. The Treasury money books show that his salary in respect of this office was £50 a year from 1698 to midsummer 1715 when he is referred to as 'the late solicitor'. These payments appear half-yearly in the warrants for payment of the Commissioners for licensing hawkers and pedlars.

[3] These and other details relating to Benjamin Needler are given in the *D.N.B.*

The future Clerk Assistant was baptized in March 1656. He was admitted by certificate of Clifford's Inn in October 1684 and of the Inner Temple in June 1692. His first employment of which there is any record was as a temporary writing clerk attending the Lords committee examining matters relating to the Popish Plot. He attended for a month and, after petition for compensation, was awarded £5 for his services in November 1680.[1] His will,[2] dated 4 July 1713, shows that he had messuages, tenements, and rents in St. Giles, Cripplegate, and St. Clement Danes, also some land in Suffolk, besides money in Exchequer annuities, the East India Company, and the Bank of England. Edward Stables, his successor, in a letter quoted below, said that Needler in 1710 was 'disabled by palsie', but he apparently lived on till the end of 1714, 'weak in body but of sound mind and memory' as he wrote in his will.[3] He was associated with the clerks' petitions for increased allowances from the Crown in 1701 and 1709–11, and he was the first Clerk Assistant to receive an annual salary from public funds, at first from the Secret Service fund and in Queen Anne's reign from the Civil List. This salary was 50 guineas, or £55 at the value of the guinea before 1700 and £53. 15s. thereafter. It appears to have begun, or at least to have been left on record, first in 1696; and its continuation can be traced through the Treasury books from that year until, as the result of the petition of Needler and the underclerks in 1701, the Clerk Assistant's salary was increased to £100 a year,[4] at which rate it remained till the middle of the eighteenth

---

[1] See 13 L.J. 478, and *R. Comm. Hist. MSS. 11th Report*, Appendix, pt. 2, House of Lords, p. 172. [2] Reg. Book 'Aston' 1714, fol. 85.

[3] That he retired at the end of 1710 is proved by Stables's letter and by the Treasury money books: but in the year of his retirement he had sat with Jodrell, the Clerk of the House, behind the Managers at the trial of Dr. Sacheverell (16 C.J. 340). He also produced a book *Debates of the House of Commons in January 1704 upon the Great Question, whether an action lies at Common Law for an Elector, who is denied his Vote for Members of Parliament.* The main part of the book is occupied by a report of the speeches made in committee of the whole House on 25 Jan. 1704 with regard to the case of *Ashby* v. *White* and the Aylesbury election. The volume in the British Museum is the 2nd edition, dated 1721, and it is stated, on the title-page, to be 'by Culverwell Needler, Gent., formerly Clerk Assistant to the Honourable House of Commons'. Needler must, therefore, have compiled the book between his retirement in 1710 and his death in 1714.

[4] The first payment to Needler that I have traced was dated 4 Sept. 1696, when

century. The Clerk Assistant's allegation in this petition was that he had been 'obliged to lay aside most of his other business', which statement would probably not have borne very careful scrutiny, since Needler was then solicitor to the Commissioners for licensing hawkers and pedlars at £50 a year. As for the memorial of 1709–11, which was clearly drafted in the earlier year while Needler was still Clerk Assistant, the allegations relating to the Clerk Assistant were that he was a loser by the diminution in naturalization bills and other private bills, and also 'by the new method the House hath taken to hear elections at the bar'[1]. He claimed another £50 a year salary, having computed his losses in fees on bills at £67 a year. The Speaker, reporting on this memorial in 1713, by which time Edward Stables was Clerk Assistant, gave the latter's estimate of the profits of his place as £120 including his salary, which would mean no more than £20 in fees. The upshot was that in 1713 an extra year's salary was awarded to all the officers who received yearly salaries from the Civil List, in compensation for their losses during the three years during which the General Naturalization Act of 1709 was in force: but the £100 for the Clerk Assistant was to be divided between Culverwell and Stables in proportion to their services. The contents of Needler's will and the fact that, as we shall see, Edward Stables was able to lend the King £4,200 while he was still Clerk Assistant, somewhat belie the pleas *ad misericordiam* of these clerks' petitions.

The interesting point, however, is that by 1696, for some unrecorded reason, the Treasury began paying clerks in the House of Commons, other than the Clerk of the House, an annual sum for services rendered. I have been unable to find any record of official decisions in this respect, or of any reason why the public purse, formerly closed to the Clerk's subordinates, should have been opened to them, albeit not profusely, in 1696. So far as the four

---

Cal. T.P. xvii. 784 gives his receipt for £55 from the Secret Service 'fund for services performed'. The following year (ibid., p. 809) the receipt is 'for £55, as of His Majesty's bounty and in reward for my pains and service relating to the public acts which passed last session'. For the increase awarded after the 1701 petition, see Appendix II, p. 286.

[1] See below, chapter 10, pp. 216–17, on the clerk to the Committee of Privileges and Elections, for the consideration of this statement.

under-clerks without doors were concerned, the reason may well be that the appointments were new,[1] and it would have been difficult to pay them salaries without similarly paying the Clerk Assistant. Jodrell himself, who received much bounty from William III, must have been instrumental in carrying these new arrangements through; and it is therefore a little ironical that the payments which he helped to secure in his subordinates in respect of public business continued while his £50 a year for similar services ceased on, or before, Queen Anne's accession.

Edward Stables succeeded Culverwell Needler as Clerk Assistant at the end of 1710. His antecedents, in spite of assiduous inquiry, remain obscure: in fact, as Clerk Assistant and, later, as Clerk he seems to have left no marks behind him but a long epitaph which was never cut in stone or brass.[2] Nevertheless, one letter from his hand of remarkable interest is extant. It was written by him on 23 January 1725/6 to the Speaker, Spencer Compton, to describe the manner of his succession to the post of Clerk Assistant. It is among the Townshend papers,[3] and I give it in full. The first and last paragraphs refer to Stables's illness in this month, during which Michael Aiskew was allowed to take his place at the table of the House.[4] The letter runs as follows:

Sir—I beg leave with a heart filled with the deepest sense of duty and gratitude, to return my most humble thanks for your honors great goodness, by again interposing between me and death, by overmuch fatigue in the service of the publick; as these are beyond expression, I humbly hope you will be pleased to accept, on all occasions, the utmost returns of gratitude in my power, long since a duty upon me, far above any ability of mine to answer, and will ever be so, tho' alwaies attempting to be acknowledged, and repaid, with the greatest pleasure.

Upon my present recollection I was thus admitted Clerk Assistant in December 1710 when Mr (Culverwell) Needler and Myself had agreed, (he being disabled by palsie) Mr. (Paul) Jodrell and he waited on Mr. Bromley (then Speaker) and acquainted him therewith, and Mr. Jodrell proposing me to succeed Needler, Mr. Bromley asked who he

---

[1] See below, pp. 53–55.   [2] See below, pp. 61–62.

[3] *R. Comm. Hist. MSS. 11th Report*, Appendix, pt. 4, p. 143.

[4] 20 C.J. 544. Two months later Jodrell fell ill and Stables took his place, while Aiskew acted as Clerk Assistant (ibid., p. 641).

thought he was to name the Clerk-Assistant, Mr. Jodrell insisted, himself, as his Clerk; Mr. Bromley denied that, as not being Clerk to the
Clerk, but a distinct and proper Clerk of the House, to be appointed
by the House, as their Clerk-Assistant and a check upon the Clerk of
the House appointed by the Crown, and that, at most, Mr. Jodrell
could only propose, but that the nomination, or approbation, was in
the House, and that no such officer could be admitted without a question; and this was the opinion of Sir John Trevor, the Mar. of the Rolls:
(In conversation).

I had the good fortune to be well spoken of to Mr. Bromley and he
received me in the most generous, and ready manner, he acquainted the
House with Mr. Needler's disability, and that a proper person had been
considered of to succeed him (according to his goodness, which I was
alwaies very sensible of) he put the question for calling me in, which
was done, without more ado; but Mr. Jodrell entred nothing of this
upon the Journal.

Give me leave, Sir, to conclude with my humble thanks also for your
great indulgence to me, on this occasion, for time to recover my health,
which I hope will be very soon, and I hope I shall alwaies make use of
it to testify, with as gratefull a heart as ever filled mortal breast, the
greatest duty to your honor most justly owing from—Sir—your—
Honors most obliged and most obedient humble servt.

E. Stables.

The main interest of the above letter, apart from the exact
narration of the circumstances, lies in the light which it throws on
the respective positions of the Clerk and Clerk Assistant. Speaker
Bromley's view, as described in this letter, that the Clerk Assistant,
once appointed, was no longer simply an underling of the Clerk
who (in fact) chose him, but a servant of the whole House, and
even a check on the Clerk, was obviously not accepted by Jodrell,
who avoided making any entry in the *Journal* that a question had
been put for the admission of Stables in Needler's place. Yet
Arthur Onslow, the great Speaker who sat in the chair from
January 1727/8 to March 1761, clearly held a similar view: for
Hatsell says that, according to Speaker Onslow, the Clerk Assistant
was called the 'Speaker's Clerk', and records that, when he himself
was named Clerk Assistant in 1760, Onslow said: 'The Clerk has
appointed you to be his Clerk Assistant, but now you are ap-

pointed you are the Clerk of the House, you are my clerk.' But the formula, Hatsell says, was not used subsequently, when Clerks Assistant were appointed:[1] and there is no record that the Clerk Assistant kept a vigilant eye upon his master and colleague, or demurred to any of his actions. Indeed, it is fair to presume that, but for Arthur Onslow's very long tenure of the Speakership, this earlier tradition would hardly have survived so late as 1760: yet we should not have known of its existence in all its rigour but for the preservation of Stables's letter, which was written only a year before he formally succeeded to the Clerkship of the House.

I have already mentioned the under-clerks whose appointments by Jodrell were an innovation.[2] About Zachary Hamlyn there is not much more to be told. He appears to have often received and given acquittance for the Clerk's fees on private bills, and in the return of his fees which the Speaker made to the committee on fees of 1731, it appears that Hamlyn was then the clerk who collected and paid over the Speaker's fees on private bills and those of the Clerk Assistant for attendance at the Committee of Elections.[3] Yet, in spite of his long service, Hamlyn never reached a principal post under the Clerk, or saw his name printed as clerk of the papers in the *Court and City Register*. We do not know when his long and useful services to the House and to the Clerk ended; we have only one specimen of his handwriting and signature preserved among the Hardwicke papers.[4] Except for the one instance where the account of the Solicitor to the Treasury showed money paid to Hamlyn for Jodrell,[5] Zachary Hamlyn's name does not appear on the Treasury books.

In Jodrell's day a far more important addition was made to the

---

[1] See Hatsell, ii. 256–7. However, Abbot recorded in his manuscript diary on 23 July 1814 (P.R.O. 30/9/35) that on Rickman's being called in on his appointment by Hatsell as 2nd Clerk Assistant, he said to him standing at the bar: 'The Clerk has appointed you to be his Second Clerk Assistant, and now that you are appointed by him you are a Clerk of the House.'

[2] See above, pp. 40, 42, 49, 50, and nn. 1 and 2 on p. 40.

[3] See Appendix IV, p. 307.

[4] Addl. MSS. 35692, fol. 166. It is an undated letter to the first earl of Hardwicke recommending Hamlyn's nephew, John Whitlocke, to succeed one Thomas Downe as collector of the earl's fee-farm rents in the west of England.

[5] See p. 40, n. 2 above.

Clerk's permanent staff namely, the 'four under-clerks without doors attending the House of Commons', whose position was quite different from Hamlyn's. It is from the Treasury books that we first learn their names, what they received from the Treasury, and the services for which (ostensibly) they were paid. The earliest entry is a warrant dated 15 June 1696[1] 'by virtue of His Majesty's general Letters Patent dormant bearing the date 8th April 1689 to pay John Hookes, George Coles, James Courthope and Hicks Borough, four under-clerks attending the House of Commons, the sum of £110 in reward and satisfaction for their services and pains in writing, copying and ingrossing several bills, writings and other papers for His Majesty's Service'. This quartet, of whom the second was properly called Cole and the fourth Burrough, continued, as the Treasury records show, unchanged till 1718 when John Hookes dropped out, to be followed in 1720 by Cole and Courthope: yet, except for the *Journal* entry recording Mr. Cole's attendance to assist in the House on 15 December 1694 when Jodrell was ill, their names do not appear in the records of the House. That their office was created by Jodrell, and that they were appointed by him, I have little doubt, though the exact date of their appointments and the question whether they in fact received any payment from public funds before 1696 must remain obscure. Jodrell, in his will, mentions that he had made his son Edward one of 'my' clerks without doors in the House of Commons: but since he also refers to Stables as 'my Clerk Assistant', this is not conclusive evidence for his creation of these four posts. More conclusive is the first petition (made in 1698) of these four under-clerks as recorded in the Treasury books. This is clearly a plaint by men who had been disappointed in their expectations, which they could hardly have been if they had had predecessors. Their incomes, they said, were barely sufficient to support them during the sessions, and in the intervals they had to live on their private fortunes. They prayed for some employment to support them. The Treasury drily minuted that there were never four places vacant at a time, but that they were to have the same allowance this year as they had the last; and this minute, in itself, prompts the

---

[1] T. 53/13, fol. 141.

supposition that the payment was not long established. Their second petition,[1] made in 1701 to the House and resulting in a humble address on behalf of the clerks, had the effect of getting their annual salaries from the Civil List raised to £50 apiece, or £200 for the four, at which figure it remained till 1833, when the posts of principal clerks without doors were abolished,[2] it being by then regarded as an 'ancient payment from the Exchequer' and a very small part of their emoluments. This petition of 1701 stated that the four under-clerks were dependent on the King's bounty for public business, and that in the present session the 'profits arising from private business' had not afforded them £30 apiece. There was, however, nothing to show in what these profits precisely consisted at that date. It is clear enough from the clerks' memorial of 1709–11 that they received fees for attendance on private bill committees, such fees being paid by the parties promoting and opposing the bill: yet the Treasury rubric for their payment quoted above made no mention of attendance on committees, but stated that they were paid for writing, copying, and ingrossing bills and other papers for the King's service.

Thus, there were left open the questions, at what time did clerks begin regularly to attend select committees appointed by the House, and whether the four under-clerks were originally appointed as writing and ingrossing clerks or were, from the outset, regular committee clerks. To the first of these questions it is probably impossible, for want of evidence, to give a precise answer; but the second is conclusively settled by the minute book of James Courthope—one of this first quartet of under-clerks—which is among the Rawlinson manuscripts in the Bodleian.[3] This manuscript, unique among parliamentary archives, is a folio minute book, bound in vellum on boards, which was kept by James Courthope during the two sessions December 1697–July 1698 and December 1698–May 1699, which period is exactly covered by volume 12 of the Commons *Journals*. It contains the minutes of proceedings, seldom quite complete, of 64 select committees, of

---

[1] See Appendix II, p. 285.
[2] See chapter 11, pp. 256–57.
[3] Bodleian, MSS. Rawl. A. 86. See p. 53 and my introduction to *Courthope*.

which 16 were on matters of public interest, 14 on public bills, 31 on private bills, 2 of the remaining 3 being committees appointed to draw up reasons for disagreeing to Lords amendments to Commons bills, and the other being a committee appointed to draft an address in answer to a speech from the King. This document establishes the fact that the duty of John Hookes and his three colleagues, from the first, was to attend committees on public and private bills and public matters. Therefore, the Treasury formula for their services was, like many other such, a fiction of the Treasury clerks; and it persisted in the Treasury books long after their memorial of 1709–11 had clearly shown their occupation as committee clerks. Yet this persistent fiction is surprising, seeing that the table of fees in the House of Commons included fees payable to clerks attending private bill committees certainly by 1695, and probably by 1690. At all events, while leaving the general subject of committees and the Committee Office to a later chapter, we can safely regard Hookes, Cole, Courthope, and Burrough as the forefathers of that office, who did the work of committee clerks themselves, without deputies, and were far from being the sinecurists, taking the bulk of the fees and doing no work, which their successors eventually became.

On the other hand, it is unlikely that they were ever employed on copying and ingrossing in their spare time, for not only is there no allusion to emoluments from such work in their memorial, but also they were of a different class from the scriveners or stationers' clerks such as were employed at piece rates to do work of that kind. Like Zachary Hamlyn, who is given the description of 'gentleman' in Jodrell's will, they were gentlemen—a description which in those days had a definite connotation of status. John Hookes, according to the historian of Dorsetshire, was descended from a very ancient family seated at Aberconway and built a house at Gaunts in the parish of Hinton Martel, Dorset, which, 'though small was a neat one, and has always been admired for the disposition and commodiousness of its apartments'. His son, John Hookes junior, married the daughter of the owner of the manor of Gaunts which descended to her, and here in 1760 he died, having been a scholar of Trinity College, Cambridge, in 1704, and in his turn, one of the four under-clerks without doors from 1720 to 1758.[1] Of George Cole, the second member of the quartet, I have been unable to find any biographical details; but James Courthope, the third member and compiler of the minute book, was almost certainly the son of George Courthope of the Middle Temple and of Moseham in Wadhurst, Sussex, 1613–91, by his wife Anne Bryan, and was himself sometime of Wharton Court, near Chancery Lane, and afterwards of St. Dunstan's in the West. Administration of his goods was granted to his widow on 31 January 1721.[2] Finally, of Hicks Burrough, the last of the quartet, little can be said except that he was the youngest of them, became the senior under-clerk in 1721, and remained in office till he died on 4 June 1733. His will,[3] which is dated 9 October 1729, shows him to have been of the parish of St. Andrew's, Holborn, and that he was able to make but a 'small provision' for his wife and son. An obituary notice in the year of his death[4] states, no doubt correctly, that he was also ingrossing clerk of the House of Commons, which meant that he supervised the ingrossing clerks and drew a proportion of the fees for ingrossments.[5]

The clerks' memorial of 1709–11 gives such clear details of the emoluments of the four under-clerks that further comment here is almost unnecessary. Their prime complaint was that they had lost a good deal in the way of fees by the passing of the General Naturalization Act of 1709, which considerably reduced the number of private naturalization bills introduced, on each of which fees would have been payable to the committee clerk. Other subsidiary losses, they claimed, were due to the reduction in the number of certain kinds of private bills introduced in the Commons

---

[1] Hutchins, *History of Dorset*, iii. 245; Venn, *Alumni Cantabrigienses*, pt. i.

[2] Admin. Acts Book (Pinfold, 1721, fol. 11). See reference on p. 54, n. 3 above for further details of Courthope.

[3] P.C.C. Price, Middx. June, fol. 170 (1733).

[4] *Gentleman's Magazine*, iii. 326.

[5] See chapter 10, pp. 227–34, for the Ingrossing Office in general. This is the earliest allusion that I know to the existence of an official ingrossing clerk of the House of Commons. With reference to Hicks Burrough, see also *Cal. T.P. 1714–19*, pp. 51, 463, his petition for some employment for his son-in-law, Christopher Thornton, who had lost a position in the Customs at Wells in Norfolk through the return of the former holder.

owing to the making of a certain standing order in the Lords with regard to estate bills and the passing of an act enabling infants to make conveyance of their estates. The Treasury recognized the validity of the prime complaint by granting all the officers concerned, except the Clerk of the House, a whole year's salary in compensation. The estimates of losses and of actual emoluments included in this memorial give a clear picture of the clerks' financial position in Queen Anne's reign. Though it was better than in 1701, it was not brilliant. A committee clerk's salary was then £50 a year, and his estimated profits from private bills averaged £90 a year until the Naturalization Act lopped £40 off this sum. It is not surprising that they looked for supplementary earnings where they could find them, as did James Courthope in the Lottery Transfer Office.[1]

The senior of the four under-clerks, it will be observed from the estimates accompanying this memorial, enjoyed larger profits than his three colleagues from private bill fees and suffered larger losses through the reduction in the number of private bills. This was because, besides being a committee clerk, he was the collector and distributor of all the fees on private bills and, as such, was paid 10s. on every private bill introduced, as the 1701 table of fees provided. Since the earlier tables of 1690 and 1695 have not survived, it is not possible to say at what date this collectorship was instituted: but this could hardly have occurred until Jodrell had established the four under-clerks without doors. By thus appointing an officer to collect and account for the fees on private bills Paul Jodrell laid the foundation of what eventually became one of the principal offices in the Clerk's department.

Just as Zachary Hamlyn was the forerunner of the Journal Office,

---

[1] Paul Jodrell, in his will, mentions that his son Edward, whom he appointed one of the four under-clerks on the death of John Hookes in 1718, also had some employment in Westminster. Certain manuscript accounts of the City Remembrancer for expenses incurred in attending to the parliamentary business of the City of London, preserved in manuscript in the Corporation of London Record Office, show payments to Courthope in 1708, 1711, and 1712, either for 'written Votes' or (in 1711) for 'his trouble in this affair', i.e. the passing of an Act promoted by the City. This shows that the four under-clerks without doors could earn rewards from corporations and other parties for special work done in addition to committee fees.

and the four under-clerks were the forerunners of the Committee Office, so the senior under-clerk who collected the fees was the forerunner of the Fees Office which, as we shall see, became the Public Bill Office. These developments will be dealt with separately and extensively in later chapters: but, in justice to the memory of Paul Jodrell they must be emphasized here. Not only was he the first of the modern Clerks of the House, but also, with his orderly solicitor's mind, he framed an organization for his department which proved to be permanent, in that it was capable of expansion without violent change, during the century after his retirement, to meet all the exigencies of an ever-increasing volume of parliamentary business. He received a gold medal on the accession of William III and another at the Peace of Utrecht:[1] but his forty years of service to the House should bring him more recognition from parliamentary posterity than he has ever received. As it was, he retired without the thanks of the House an old, sick man, the Treasury owing him a large sum of money for legitimate dues.

---

[1] *Cal. T.P.* ix. 80; P.R.O. Queen's Warrant Book XXX, fol. 423.

4

BIOGRAPHICAL
(1727–68)

(I)

THE point has now been reached at which the expansion of the Clerk's department, already begun, becomes a steady process, and the developing functions of his subordinates assume greater importance, while the body of available information about them increases. Of this information some is purely biographical, but the greater part is on the functional side. I have therefore thought it advisable, from this point onwards, to avoid confusing these two aspects of my subject (as would have been inevitable, had I tried to maintain a purely chronological record), and to separate the purely biographical from the functional. The interest of the former lies in its revelation, so far as it goes, of the origins, standing, connexions, nature, and life's course of various men who served the House of Commons as clerks: that of the latter lies in its illustration of the increasing complexity of the parliamentary machinery during the eighteenth century. It lays bare some of the cog-wheels upon which depended the work of the House, and their relations, in some instances, with other cog-wheels —notably those of the Treasury—outside the House. Human nature and human failings come, sometimes strikingly, into this picture of functional development, giving it an internal motion and a *chiaroscuro* which far remove it from being a bare diagram or a cold model made to scale. But these intrusions of humanity into the functional picture were not dependent on social circumstance, genealogy, dwelling-place, and so forth. It is circumstances and facts of that kind, in themselves by no means negligible or un-illuminating, that I propose to segregate in this and the following chapter, the aim of which is simply to make known what kind of men were the individuals whose names will recur as agents in the functional development. The present chapter will cover the period of some forty years, during which Edward Stables, Nicholas Hardinge, Jeremiah Dyson, and Thomas Tyrwhitt were successively Clerks of the House: and it will deal biographically, not only with these, but also with the Clerks Assistant and other principal clerks who served under them.[1]

Of Edward Stables, Clerk Assistant 1710–26, I have already spoken in the preceding chapter. He succeeded to the Clerkship of the House on Jodrell's retirement, and died in office on 11 or 12 December 1731.[2] Very little is to be gathered about him. He was admitted of Lincoln's Inn in October 1705, but was not called till July 1727 when he was already Clerk of the House. In the Lincoln's Inn Register he is described as 'of Battersea, Surrey', and he died at Wandsworth. The well-known picture of the House of Commons in 1730, with Walpole standing beside Arthur Onslow, the great Speaker who occupied the chair from 1727 to 1760, also depicts Stables and Michael Aiskew, the Clerk Assistant, sitting at the table of the House.[3] Whether the likenesses were anything more than conventional, it is impossible to judge: yet that picture, by a stroke of chance, has preserved the images of two of the least remarkable occupants of those seats at the table, while of the aspect of Jodrell, Dyson, and Tyrwhitt, and of their Clerks Assistant, in the same seats, there is no pictorial record.

No doubt Stables was an excellent Clerk, but he made small impression on history—that of Walpole's prime—during his five years of office. The only remarkable fact associated with his official life is that vouched for by a royal sign manual dated 5 February 1728/9,[4] of which the effective passage runs as follows:

Our will and pleasure is that by virtue of our General Letters of Privy Seal bearing date the 26th day of June 1727 you issue and pay or cause

[1] See Appendix I for a complete list with dates.

[2] See *Cal. T.P. 1731–34*, p. 322, Treasury warrant to his executors for £4. 13s. 1d. —his salary due from 24 June 1731 to 12 Dec., the day of his death. The epitaph quoted on p. 61 dates this event on 11 Dec.

[3] The original painting by Hogarth and Thornhill is in the possession of the earl of Onslow. A print of the engraving by A. Fogg, which has been reproduced in many books about Parliament, is in the collection 'Groups' in the Print Room, Brit. Mus.

[4] The sign manual is copied into King's Warrant Book XXIX, fol. 269 in the P.R.O., and is summarized in *Cal. T.P. 1729–30*, p. 185.

to be paid out of any monies arisen or to arise into the Receipt of our Exchequer of or for the Civil List revenues of the King our late Royal father unto our trusty and well-beloved Edward Stables Esq. or to his assigns the sum of four thousand two hundred pounds without account, the same being in lieu and satisfaction of the like sum expended by him for his said late Majesty's especial service.

The sign manual bears the signatures 'R. Walpole, C. Turner, G. Oxenden, Wm. Clayton', and the warrant for payment was issued on the following day. How the Clerk Assistant of the House could have afforded to expend £4,200 for George I's special service, and what that service was, I have been unable to discover. Indeed, the obscurity which shrouds Stables's acts in life make it all the more due to his memory to quote at length the epitaph which was 'designed to be inscribed on a monument intended to be erected in Wandsworth church'. The monument was not erected, and the epitaph was only preserved from oblivion by its inclusion in Hackett's *Epitaphs*.[1] It is typical, perhaps, that the composer of the epitaph did not know Stables's age.

Here lies interred the Body of
Edward Stables, Esq;

Some Time Clerk of the Hon. House of Commons;
Who exchanged this mortal Life for a better,
Dec. 11

A.D. 1731
In the　　　　　Year of his Age.
His indefatigable Application to the Duties of his
Office,
And too great Neglect of himself,
Brought him into an ill State of Health;
Which his chearful Spirit endeavoured in vain to
overcome;
For, alas!
The Strength of his Body bore no Proportion to that
of his Mind!
His Station made him generally known;

[1] John Hackett, *Select and Remarkable Epitaphs on Illustrious and Other Persons* (1757), vol. ii.

And his Qualities as generally beloved;
Yet veiled by a Modesty inseparable from true Merit,
Superficial Eyes discovered not half his Perfections.
His entire Mastery of the Methods of Business in the
House of Commons
Was supported and adorned
By a perfect Knowledge of the Laws of his Country.
The Soundness and Perspicuity of his Judgment,
Enliven'd by chearful and inoffensive Wit,
The natural Sweetness of his Temper,
Improv'd by a Knowledge of Men and Manners,
His noble Contempt of Riches,
All these great Qualities,
Which made him a second self to everyone,
Interested ev'ry one in his Welfare,
And made his Death both a public and private Loss.

Nicholas Hardinge, who was appointed Clerk on the death of Stables,[1] was a man of entirely different calibre.[2] Scholar of Eton, fellow of King's, member of the Middle Temple, a brilliant classic, and considered the most elegant composer of Latin verse of his day, he took his seat as Clerk of the House at the age of thirty-two without any previous parliamentary experience. He had already distinguished himself at Cambridge by a disquisition on the legal powers of a visitor; and, for want of any precise indications, one

---

[1] L.P. 5 Geo. II, pt. 1, no. 4.

[2] The article on Hardinge in the *D.N.B.* is mainly based on Nichols, *Literary Anecdotes*, v. 338–46, but through not taking into account the passage in vol. viii, p. 514 of that work, in which George Hardinge, his son, the judge and author, corrected certain misstatements in the earlier passage, it perpetuates these errors, e.g. that he was Clerk till 1752 and became joint secretary to the Treasury on the death of James West. Nicholas Hardinge was the grandfather of Lord Hardinge of Lahore and of the distinguished naval captain, George Nicholas Hardinge. A collection of his *Poems, Latin and Greek*, which includes his essay upon government in England during the King's minority and a fragment of a biography in Latin by his son, was published by Nichols in 1818. In his *Literary Anecdotes* Nichols repeats from Coxe's *Life of Walpole* the story of his deciding in the House on 11 Feb. 1741 a bet of a guinea between Walpole and Pulteney as to the correctness of a quotation from Horace made by Walpole. Pulteney won, and, catching the guinea thrown to him, exclaimed: 'It is the only money I have received from the Treasury for many years, and it shall be the last.' An engraving of his portrait by Ramsay is reproduced in Nichols, *Illustrations of Literature*, and in his edition of the poems.

must presume that Walpole, then at the height of his power, chose him to be appointed Clerk on the strength of his attainments.[1] In 1732 he was made law reader to the duke of Cumberland at a salary of £100 a year, and later became his attorney-general. In 1738 he married the daughter of Sir John Pratt, a lord chief justice, and thus became the brother-in-law of Charles Pratt, the future Lord Camden. He resigned the Clerkship in favour of Jeremiah Dyson in 1747, to which event reference will be made in due course,[2] in order to enter politics. He was member for Eye in Suffolk from 1748 to 1758, and in 1752 became joint secretary to the Treasury with James West, which meant that he had become one of the duke of Newcastle's followers.[3] He became seriously ill in 1758 and unable to attend to his duties:[4] he died before the end of that year.

His most notable service to the House was rendered in connexion with the first printing of the *Journals*, which will be considered in a later chapter,[5] as will the fact that he was the first Clerk of the House to receive a regular salary from the Civil List in addition to the £10 a year granted by his letters patent.[6] However, what is no less striking to the historian is that, with his appointment, the purely professional atmosphere surrounding Clerks such as the excellent solicitor, Jodrell, and the meritorious Stables suddenly changed to an aura of elegance, literary grace, and scholarship, which lasted until, with Hatsell, the professional element re-entered for good. In Hardinge's social entourage there was ease and brilliance; Latin sapphics and alcaics or polished verse in English dappled with personifications and classical allusions were freely

---

[1] This presumption is strengthened by the fact that Nichols, in telling the story of the bet given in the preceding note, observes that Hardinge 'decided against his patron'.

[2] See below, pp. 64–65.

[3] A letter of Hardinge's addressed to the duke from his country seat, Knoll Hills in Derbyshire, is preserved among the Newcastle papers (Addl. MSS. 32873). It is dated 28 Aug. 1757 and speaks of his having just returned from Buxton much benefited in health, but needing another fortnight's rest.

[4] See Addl. MSS. 32879, fol. 120 (Newcastle papers), a minute from Hardinge Stracey to James West, endorsed 'recd. 9 April 1758', stating that Hardinge was very ill and unable to write to him.

[5] See chapter 9, pp. 199–201. [6] See chapter 6, p. 108.

exchanged; a visit of hounds to a lady's garden provoked a copy of mock-heroics;[1] false quantities and false concords in Latin were worse than peccadillos. The grime of Chancery Lane and the rusticity of Battersea was dispelled from the table of the House, where now, particularly after Michael Aiskew's retirement, the aromas of more genteel London and of country seats, or else of college courts, could be breathed; one was on terms with the bench and the bishops, with the doctors of divinity and the cultivated ladies; and to have been a scholar of Eton and a fellow of King's was a certain recommendation to preferment. Such, clearly, were the recommendations of John Naylor and John Read[2] for appointments under the Clerk that must have gratified the combination room of King's College. Whether any money changed hands at these and other appointments it might have been indelicate to inquire; nor was it stated, till Hatsell blurted out the fact in retrospect, that Jeremiah Dyson bought out Nicholas Hardinge for £6,000.[3] Indeed, it has lately been discovered that, for all his elegance, Hardinge was not an entire paragon where money was concerned, for, though well and promptly paid himself for the printing of twenty-three volumes of the *Journals*, he was extremely dilatory in paying his debts to Samuel Richardson, the printer and the novelist, putting him off with repeated promises to pay and, on the last occasion, only brought to discharge his debt by the firm

---

[1] Hardinge's own proficiency in these refined diversions is fully illustrated in the collection of poems published by Nichols in 1818 (see p. 62, n. 2 above). Also, in Nichols, *Illustrations of Literature*, i. 647–55, there is reproduced a poem in praise of Knoll Hills, which Hardinge bought in 1734, by Dr. Sneyd Davies, afterwards canon of Lichfield, another much admired versifier of the day, and two versions of verses by Hardinge himself on the charms of his country seat. The memoir of Sneyd Davies by George Hardinge in which these occur also contains one or two letters from Hardinge to Sneyd Davies and several allusions to him and his circle of friends in letters to the same gentleman from Charles Pratt, the later Lord Camden—the whole bearing witness to the existence of a cheerful and highly cultivated Eton and King's *côterie*.

[2] See pp. 68–69.

[3] Hatsell, ii. 256–7, where the author remarks of the Clerk's right to appoint his subordinate clerks: 'formerly the appointment to these offices made a considerable part of the Clerk's income, as it was the usual practice to sell them'. George Hardinge, in a communication to the *Gentleman's Magazine* (lxxxiv (pt. 2), 355) on the subject of Dr. Akenside politely referred to this transaction as a 'contract'.

intervention of Arthur Onslow, the Speaker.[1] Indeed, Dyson, a man of obscure origin with no halo of scholarship around him, perhaps showed an elegance of spirit greater than his predecessor's elegance of mind in determining, once he had bought the Clerkship, never to sell a place himself—which example his successors felt bound to follow.[2]

When, on 15 February 1747/8, five days after the Speaker had announced Hardinge's resignation, a young man of twenty-six was called in to take the Clerk's place at the table, the atmosphere indeed was changed, but not so greatly as might have appeared. Jeremiah Dyson's birth was obscure, but he was not unknown, especially in the literary world, for he was already the friend and benefactor of Akenside, doctor and poet, whom he had first known as a student at Leyden where he had become learned in the history of law. He was a man of means, and certainly of ambition, besides being a very advanced radical. He had held a subordinate post[3] under Hardinge, who was also a friend of Akenside; and it must be supposed that he bought Hardinge's place in order to gain a thorough knowledge of parliamentary procedure and institutions before entering, as he also did, upon a political career. In this aim he was so successful that he became a mine of parliamentary knowledge, and was reputed, while a member of Parliament, to know the *Journals* by heart. He held the Clerkship till 1762 when he resigned in his turn, to be succeeded by the great scholar, Thomas Tyrwhitt. His biography[4] is almost wholly concerned with his generosity to Akenside, whom he defended against Bishop Warburton's criticism and whose sole legatee he became, with his change of political faith from youthful radicalism to enrolment in the party which supported the administration during the first twenty years of George III's reign, and his active and successful, if

---

[1] See William M. Sale jun., *Samuel Richardson, Master Printer* (Cornell University Press, 1950), p. 82, and Victoria and Albert Museum, Forster MSS. xiii, fols. 101–2; xiv. 4, fol. 38.

[2] Hatsell, loc. cit., on p. 64, n. 3 above.

[3] I have found no trace of his being a junior clerk, but that is not surprising, since in those days junior clerks, who received no payment from the government, would not figure in any official records or publications.

[4] See the *D.N.B.* and many allusions in Nichols, *Literary Anecdotes*.

not particularly distinguished, political career.[1] His tenure of the Clerkship of the House is mainly notable for his memorandum of 1751 which finally regulated the system by which fees on private bills were calculated, and for his contriving to obtain an official residence for the Clerk of the House in the precincts of the Palace of Westminster.[2]

This is not the place to enlarge upon his political career as member, successively, for Yarmouth (Isle of Wight), Weymouth and Melcombe Regis, Horsham, and again Weymouth. Like other supporters of the King's administration he earned considerable obloquy from his opponents and frequent appearance in satirical prints. Yet, though his acceptance of a pension on the Irish list in 1770 was too much even for the House of Commons of the day, so that the grant was rescinded, the warm tribute which Hatsell paid him[3] deserves to be remembered. It is true that Dyson had appointed Hatsell Clerk Assistant in 1760 without any fee, though he might (says Hatsell)[4] have asked £3,000, so that Hatsell had every cause for gratitude. Yet anyone who had read, as I have, all Hatsell's unpublished letters would be convinced that his tribute to Dyson's integrity was absolutely sincere; and Hatsell, himself a man of the highest principle, was no bad judge of other men. We may therefore believe him when, in the introduction to the first volume of his *Precedents of Proceedings*, published in 1776 (when Dyson was dying) and inscribed to him, after mentioning his universal knowledge upon all subjects relating to the history of Parliament, he says:

The public character of that gentleman, his comprehensive knowledge, his acuteness of understanding and inflexible integrity are sufficiently known and acknowledged by all the world: but it is only within the circle of a small acquaintance that he is admired as a man of polite learning and erudition, a most excellent father, and a most valuable friend.

[1] He was obviously a very tireless, faithful, and useful factotum of the party, thus earning the nickname of Mungo (a negro Figaro of contemporary comedy) and many offices. He ended as cofferer of the royal household and privy councillor.

[2] See as regards fees Appendix III, pp. 303–4; and as regards Cotton Garden, the Clerk's house, see chapter 6, p. 113–14.

[3] Hatsell, i, introd. p. ix.　　　　　　[4] Hatsell, ii. 257.

These words would have been impossible if the universal venality and corruption attributed to the 'King's friends' had been facts. Thanks to the work of Sir Lewis Namier,[1] we can now make a juster estimate of the King's party, but the mud has stuck for a long time, and some may still be clinging, to their reputation. Hatsell's praise of the derided 'Mungo' may therefore well be kept in mind.

Thomas Tyrwhitt[2] succeeded Dyson when the latter retired in 1762. He was born in 1730, the eldest son of the rector of St. James's, Westminster, was educated at Eton 1741–7 and Queen's College, and became a fellow of Merton in 1755. He was a student of the Middle Temple, and in 1756 was appointed deputy secretary at war: but he seems to have spent most of his time at Oxford. There is no evidence to show why this great scholar was chosen, at the age of thirty-two, to be Clerk of the House of Commons with no previous experience, or who was really responsible for the choice, since the Newcastle patronage had come to an end with Bute's appointment as the King's first minister. His short tenure of the Clerkship calls for no comment, except to remark that during it he found time to publish anonymously his *Observations and Conjectures on some Passages in Shakespeare* (1766). He resigned in May 1768, and was succeeded by John Hatsell, already Clerk Assistant, and, though Hatsell was a diligent reader of the Greek and Latin classics, it may be said that, with Tyrwhitt, the Muses departed from the Clerk's seat.

(2)

The Clerks Assistant during this period were Michael Aiskew (1727–40), John Naylor (1740–4), John Read (1744–60), and John Hatsell (1760–8). With the exception of the last, they can be quite briefly remembered. Michael Aiskew, of whose origins nothing seems to be known, is first heard of in the *Journal* in 1726. On

---

[1] Notably in *The Structure of Politics at the Accession of George III* (London, 1929), and *England in the Age of the American Revolution* (London, 1930).

[2] L.P. 2 Geo. III, pt. 3, no. 12, 10 Aug. 1762. See *D.N.B.* for an account of his contributions to scholarship and literature.

17 March of that year the Speaker read a letter from Jodrell pleading old age and indisposition to excuse his absence and begging
the indulgence of the House 'to permit Mr. Aiskew, who has
attended the Table already this session, to assist in the business of
the House'.[1] This was agreed to, Aiskew was admitted, and Stables
the Clerk Assistant, for whom Aiskew had deputized in the same
year[2] when he was disabled by rheumatism, took the Clerk's chair.
How long Aiskew had held an appointment under the Clerk it is
impossible to say. He was never one of the four clerks without
doors. He became Clerk Assistant the following year when Stables
was appointed Clerk; and the only noteworthy fact about his
career as such is that in the early part of every year, as the *Journal*
faithfully recorded, he was disabled from attendance by gout,[3]
while another clerk—William Hester till 1734 and thereafter John
Naylor—took his place. It is not surprising that he resigned[4] in
1740.

John Naylor, who succeeded him as Clerk Assistant, was one of
Hardinge's appointments, a scholar of Eton and King's and a
fellow of King's (1730). He was born in 1709 at St. Martin's in
Cornwall to one Fermor Naylor, also a King's man. He was
originally appointed one of the four clerks without doors
on the death of Hicks Burrough, and as such attended select committees. Although the junior of the four clerks, Hardinge appointed him Clerk Assistant in 1740. He did not hold the office
long, for in October 1744 he retired to take holy orders—wherein
he is unique among the Commons clerks—and at the end of the
following November was chosen Vice-Provost of King's. He became rector of Orton near Peterborough, a doctor of divinity at
Cambridge in 1749, and subsequently prebendary of Exeter.[5] He
was an intimate friend of Hardinge, Charles Pratt, and others of

---

[1] 20 C.J. 641.

[2] Ibid., p. 544.

[3] 21 C.J. 24, 111, 462, 761; 22 C.J. 281, 401, 614, 745; 23 C.J. 23, 265, 411.

[4] *Gentleman's Magazine*, x. 525.

[5] See *Eton College Register*; Venn, *Alumni Cantabrigienses*, pt. i, 3. 234. I am also
indebted for certain details to an extract from Anthony Allen's manuscript *Catalogue of the Provosts, Fellows and Scholars of King's*, iv. 2191, kindly communicated
by the Librarian of the college.

their circle, and is frequently referred to in letters from Pratt to Sneyd Davies recorded by Nichols.[1]

John Read[2] was another Eton and King's man, and son of the rector of Shilling Okeford, Dorset, born in 1721. Scholar of Eton and King's, and elected fellow of King's in 1742, he was at the age of twenty-three appointed by Hardinge Clerk Assistant on Naylor's retirement. In 1749 he was also appointed clerk of the committee of privileges and elections on the death of John Grover. He died in March 1760 while still in office, though he had relinquished the clerkship to the committee of elections in 1757. On Dr. Akenside's recommendation Hatsell was appointed by Jeremiah Dyson to succeed him as Clerk Assistant.[3]

As regards the various under-clerks whose names appear in my Appendix I as holders of definite offices under the Clerk of the House, it must be remembered that, apart from the Treasury books, in which the four clerks without doors were regularly named from 1696 onwards, information about them is chancy and often conjectural. Moreover, although from 1743 onwards the *Court and City Register* printed annually the names of the principal officers of both Houses including, for the House of Commons, others than the four clerks without doors, there is no means of knowing in what year these officers first entered the service of the House as junior clerks, if they were not immediately appointed to one of the principal offices, as many of them were in the earlier days. Edward Jodrell, for instance, as we know from Paul Jodrell's will, was directly appointed one of the four clerks without doors; and so, in all probability, were John Hookes the younger, William Hester, and Newdigate Poyntz. I have mentioned the younger Hookes, who was admitted to Trinity College, Cambridge, in 1703, in connexion with his father,[4] as I have mentioned Edward

---

[1] Nichols, *Illustrations of Literature*, i. 643, 646, 656. The last of these references is a passage in a letter from Charles Pratt to Dr. Sneyd Davies dated 28 Feb. 1744/5, i.e. just after Naylor had taken orders and retired from the position of Clerk Assistant: 'Jack Naylor is in town, after preferment, but I fear he will dance attendance for some time longer'—a prophecy which proved true.

[2] Spelt 'Reade' in the *Eton College Register*, and 'Reid' by Hatsell (ii. 257), but 'Read' in Venn, op. cit., pt. i, 3. 433 and in the King's College manuscript referred to in p. 68, n. 5 above.

[3] Hatsell, ii. 257.   [4] See p. 55.

Jodrell. The younger Hookes, who can only have been eighteen when appointed, retired in 1758 and died in 1760 at Gaunts in Dorset: Edward Jodrell died in 1742. Of William Hester, one of the four clerks without doors from 1720 till his death in 1754, we know nothing but what can be gathered from his will.[1] This tells us that he lived in Shire Lane in the liberty of the Rolls in the parish of St. Dunstan's in the West, and owned the manor of Campions in Epping, which he had inherited in 1748 from his cousin of the same name, of the court of Common Pleas.[2] He possessed money and various government and other securities. One of the two executors named in his will was his colleague John Burman of Maiden Lane, who became one of the four clerks without doors in 1742. But of Burman we know from the Civil List accounts—and we know little else, except that he died in 1763[3]—that he attended a select committee in 1732,[4] so that he, at least, served an apprenticeship before becoming a principal.

It is improbable that the same can be said of Newdigate Poyntz,[5] scholar of Eton in 1727, and admitted of the Inner Temple in 1736, who was appointed one of the four clerks without doors on John Naylor's elevation to be Clerk Assistant in 1740. He was the senior of the four clerks when he died in 1772. His name will be met with in various connexions later on: but, on the purely biographical side, the details are that he was son of Robert Poyntz, distiller, by Sarah Taverner of Hexton, Herts., and was baptized at St. Martin's in-the-Fields on 17 August 1715. He was descended from the ancient family of Poyntz of Iron Acton, into which the name of Newdigate came through the marriage in the sixteenth century of William Poyntz to Elizabeth, daughter and co-heir of Thomas Newdigate of Newdigate. A Newdigate Poyntz of Gray's Inn, barrister, was buried at Hexton, Herts., in 1701; but it was his namesake, clerk in the House of Commons, who bought the manor of Hexton in 1764—a manor which had belonged to his

---

[1] P.C.C. Pinfold (1754), fol. 10.   [2] W. Bartlett, *History of Essex* (1835).
[3] *Gentleman's Magazine*, xxxiii. 98.
[4] See chapter 7, p. 138, and Appendix IX, p. 331.
[5] *Eton College Register*; John Burke, *History of the Commoners*, iii. 539; Gray's Inn, Middle Temple and Inner Temple *Registers*; *Victoria County History, Herts.*, ii. 353.

wife's family, the Taverners, during most of the seventeenth century. His will[1] shows that he died a man of some substance, since he could charge his estates with cash legacies amounting to £6,800 and leave the use of his four best coach-horses and two best saddle-horses to his wife during her lifetime. One of the witnesses of his will was William Evatt, who ended as a deputy committee clerk in 1802.

In contrast to these fortunate men who obtained salaried positions as principal clerks very early in life, there are some of their known contemporaries who never reached these positions. The first of these was Zachary Hamlyn, Jodrell's own personal clerk,[2] who, though he was employed to keep the papers of the House in good order, and is known to have served the House from 1709 to 1742, and probably much longer, never rose even to be clerk of the papers. How early that official post was created it is impossible to say, but its first known occupant was Samuel Littlemore, according to the *Court and City Register* of 1743. However, among the Sloane MSS. in the British Museum there is a letter[3] from Littlemore to Dr. Birch, the historian, dated from the House of Commons, 1 February 1741/2, confessing that he had lost or mislaid the abstract of the Spanish papers which Dr. Birch had given him, and asking for another copy: from this I conjecture that Littlemore was then already clerk of the papers. His will[4] shows that he was of Exeter Street in the parish of St. Paul, Covent Garden, and that he possessed lands, hereditaments, money, plate, jewels, and stock in the public funds. He died on 14 February 1756[5] as clerk of the journals and papers. We shall, however, come across his name and that of John Grover, in connexion with payments made by the Treasury to clerks for attendance on certain select committees.[6] John Grover was appointed clerk of ingrossments probably in

---

[1] P.C.C. Taverner (1772).   [2] See chapter 3, p. 40.

[3] Brit. Mus. MSS. Sloane 4312, fol. 152. The name is wrongly spelt 'Littlemove' in the catalogue.

[4] The will was found at Somerset House lying loose in the Westminster file of the papers of the dean and chapter of Westminster under date 2 Apr. 1756. The date of the will is 24 June 1748.

[5] *Gentleman's Magazine*, xxvi. 150.

[6] See chapter 7, p. 139, and Appendix IX, pp. 331–32.

1733 and became also clerk of elections in 1740. His biographical interest, however, is that Samuel Richardson, as printer to the House, came to conceive a great affection for him. In a letter[1] to his friend Dr. Young of Wellwyn he described the occasion of Grover's premature death in 1749 from a violent fever in words which showed his attachment to Grover and the kindness of his heart:

Poor Mr Grover! You have doubtless read in the paper that poor Mr Grover is no more; a violent, a malignant, fever, brought on by an obliging overheating walk to Ember Court, and to carelessness of himself when hot and fatigued, the occasion. He will be greatly missed by a whole House of Commons. It was not easy to find out so much as one half of his merits. I knew not of his illness till he was in danger. I have all his very greatly disordered affairs likely to be upon me. He was the support of a maiden sister, as he had been of a decayed father, mother, and family. I have got her (a worthy creature) to N. End to my good wife. He was too much regardless of money *to leave* her very happy in that respect. I am endeavouring to get those who valued him to be kind to her.

Richardson left mourning rings to the clerks Jeremiah Dyson, Newdigate Poyntz, John Burman, Robert Yeates, Osborn Barwell, and Hatsell in his will.[2] Of Robert Yeates there will be a good deal to say when the relations of the Treasury with certain of the clerks come to be discussed. He first appears as one of the clerks of ingrossment in 1750, became one of the four clerks without doors in 1754, and while still continuing as such was also a principal clerk in the Treasury from 1759 till he died in 1769. In view of this remarkable duplicity of office, it is disappointing that the only biographical details available about him are those to be found in his will.[3] He lived in Abingdon Buildings,[4] Westminster, and was apparently a bachelor. He speaks of Jeremiah Dyson as his 'kind and generous patron and friend', from which we may

[1] *Monthly Magazine*, xxxvii (1814), 329 where this letter was printed. See also William M. Sale jun., op. cit., on p. 65, n. 1, pp. 78, 79.

[2] *Notes and Queries*, 12th ser., xi. 385.

[3] P.C.C. Bogg, 1769, fol. 239.

[4] Several clerks lived there at one time or another. It was a block of chambers on a site now occupied by the north end of the Victoria Gardens.

presume that Dyson first appointed him to the service of the House; and he left £1,000 apiece to Dyson's son and daughter. He also left £1,500 to John Rosier, his deputy in the Committee Clerks' Office, and (as we shall see) his successor as Treasury agent in the House of Commons; £200 to Robert Gunnell, then second clerk of ingrossments, and £500 to John Dorington junior, son of John Dorington senior by Yeates's late cousin Roberta, and he made John Dorington senior one of his residuary legatees. This family connexion with the Doringtons is interesting, since John Dorington junior, to whom Yeates left £500, eventually became clerk of the fees in the House of Commons, being succeeded as such by his son John E. Dorington, both of whom will figure largely in later chapters. It was no doubt owing to this connexion that the Doringtons came into the service of the House. However, of Yeates's own provenance I have been unable to find any trace, though he must have been an able man and well known in administrative circles. Some few of his extant letters, all official, which will be quoted in their due place, show that he was a faithful servant of Newcastle; and one, written in 1763 to Charles Jenkinson, then a newly appointed joint secretary to the Treasury, refers to a prospective meeting between Jenkinson and Dr. Johnson.[1]

The remaining clerk to whom Richardson left a mourning ring was 'Mr. Barwell'. This was certainly Osborn Barwell, clerk of the papers from 1748 to 1754, in which capacity he would have come into contact with Richardson, the printer to the House. Osborn Barwell and his brothers, Nathaniel and Edward, all served the House of Commons in clerkly capacities and died in office, the two latter at a good old age, but none of them—to judge by Osborn Barwell's will[2]—in any state of affluence. Osborn himself became second clerk of ingrossments in 1754 and one of the four clerks without doors in 1758. He disappears from their number in 1774, in which year he probably died, his will being dated 7 May of that year. That he must then have been quite elderly is shown

---

[1] See Addl. MSS. 36201, fol. 157 quoted in *The Jenkinson Papers, 1760–66*, ed. Ninetta S. Jucker (London, 1949). It is dated 5 Oct. 1763 from Abingdon Buildings.

[2] Admin. Acts Book, 1721, fol. 11.

by a letter dated 12 July 1772[1] in which Hatsell, with unusual
levity, suggested to John Ley that, if illness or any other accident
were to prevent Ley from attending a prorogation, 'why should
we not dress up old Barwell?' (i.e. as Clerk Assistant for the nonce).
Nathaniel, who in another letter of Hatsell's to John Ley written
in the same year[2] is mentioned as having 'only lately joined' though
older than Edward, was a deputy committee clerk till 1789 and
in that year, at seventy years of age, was appointed joint clerk of
elections with George White the younger, and so continued till
1793 when he died. His obituary stated that he was then in his
75th year and also was one of the paymasters of Exchequer bills.[3]
Edward, who was appointed first clerk of ingrossments in 1758,
became one of the four clerks without doors in 1772 and died as
the senior of them in 1799. There was a fourth brother, Godfrey,
who died in 1790 as under-doorkeeper of the House,[4] towards the
purchase of which place Osborn had lent him £200, but in his will
remitted half of that sum still owing to him.

A slight genealogical difficulty as regards these brothers Barwell
is caused by an entry in the register of the Inner Temple that
Edward Barwell, son of William Barwell of Chertsey Abbey, was
admitted in 1751. If the attribution in the register is correct, this
cannot have been the Edward Barwell who was a clerk in the
House of Commons, which means that none of the Barwell
brothers who served the House were sons of William Barwell.
The reason for this argument is that William Barwell, a governor
of the East India Company and father of Richard Barwell, M.P.,

[1] In the Ley MSS.

[2] Given in full in the next chapter, pp. 87–88.

[3] *Gentleman's Magazine*, lxiii (pt. 1), 380. The Exchequer Bill Office after 1770
was in the stone building in St. Margaret's Street.

[4] The two doorkeepers and the four messengers held from the earliest times
official positions and received small official salaries. They were, and still are,
officers in the department of the Serjeant at Arms, whose patent gave him the
right of appointing them, and for such appointments he charged a heavy fee until
this practice was prohibited by the Act of 1812 (52 Geo. III, c. 11). The posts were
the source of a considerable income from the sale of parliamentary papers and
customary fees from members of the House; see the report of the Select Committee
of 1833 on the House of Commons Offices and the returns of emoluments in the
first appendix to the report (H.C. (1833), 648).

who also figured largely in East Indian affairs, was only sixty-four when he died in 1769,[1] so that he was not born till 1705, whereas Nathaniel Barwell must have been born in 1718 or 1719, and Osborn Barwell some years earlier. Osborn, who very affectionately refers to his brothers in his will, makes no reference to Richard Barwell: moreover, he and his brothers lived in Westminster, and there is no evidence that they had any connexion with Chertsey Abbey which was bought by William Barwell in 1751.[2] A younger Osborn Barwell, son of the first, became a deputy committee clerk in 1796, but seems to have retired on his uncle Edward's death in 1799.

There will be many allusions in subsequent chapters to Hardinge Stracey and to his nephew Edward Hardinge Stracey, afterwards the second baronet of his line. Hardinge Stracey, who matriculated at Hertford College in 1752 and was a student of the Middle Temple, was the eldest son of Sir John Stracey, Recorder of the City of London, by Mary, the sister of Nicholas Hardinge—a connexion which obviously facilitated his appointment by Jeremiah Dyson to a position in the service of the House of Commons. His brother Edward, the third son of Sir John, became the first baronet, and was the father of Edward Stracey. Hardinge Stracey appears in 1756/7 as clerk of elections in succession to John Read, then also Clerk Assistant; he was one of the four clerks without doors from 1763 to 1789, besides being first clerk of ingrossments 1774–88. He retired in 1789 to his country estate of Denne Hill near Canterbury where Hatsell stayed with him at least on one occasion, and where he died in 1807.

One rather remarkable action of his as a private individual deserves to be chronicled, for the documents relating to it have never yet been made public. They are to be found among the Liverpool papers[3] in the British Museum. In October 1786, while still a clerk in the House of Commons, he was moved to write a long anonymous encomium to Charles Jenkinson (afterwards the first earl of

---

[1] Foster, *Oxford Men and their Colleges* (London, 1893); Nichols, *Illustrations of Literature*, iii. 4; vi. 642.

[2] See Manning and Bray, *History and Antiquities of Surrey*, iii. 219, 237; *The Victoria County History, Surrey*, iii. 408.

[3] Addl. MSS. 38220, fols. 173–75, 200–1, 258, 344, 361.

Liverpool) who had just become president of the Council for Trade and Plantations and Chancellor of the Duchy of Lancaster, and had been created Baron Hawkesbury. In this, over the signature 'A.B.C.' Stracey announced himself as disgusted with recent scurrilous attacks on Jenkinson in the press, and eulogized his virtues throughout his career, especially in his attempt to prevent the repeal of the Stamp Act, and in his great services during the previous session in the matters of the Greenland fishery, southern whale fishery, and Newfoundland trade. In a postscript he said he would be glad of any signification in the *Morning Herald* that X.Y.Z. had received the letter signed A.B.C. dated 14 October 1786. It cannot have been customary, even in the eighteenth century, for officers of the House to send anonymous praises to members of the government; and one might have thought that Jenkinson would have ignored this anonymous flattery. But not at all: A.B.C.'s letter was duly acknowledged by X.Y.Z., and a second letter dated 21 October followed remembering another merit of Jenkinson's, his responsibility for the new gold coinage, and assuring him that, except for his lordship, the writer scarce knew

a man from the President of the Council down to the lower Departments in office, who seems to have any inclination to step forward or do anything, but merely to reap the profits of office which they have obtained by Party, with very few other pretensions whatsoever—

and this with William Pitt as Prime Minister. Lord Hawkesbury acknowledged receipt of this in the *Morning Herald* of 26 October, and on 31 October Stracey wrote two more folio sheets of eulogy, disclaiming all desire to flatter, but hinting that, when he came to reside in London in the winter, he would disclose himself to his lordship in person. He followed this on 18 November by a letter over his own signature from Denne Hill in which he revealed himself and assured Hawkesbury that his sole motive for troubling him arose from his knowledge of Hawkesbury's real services and his indignation at the abuse to which he was subjected, and that possibly there were many independent individuals who felt the same. He (Stracey) for one was convinced that the noble lord had 'passed through the Temple of Virtue (that is of public toil and labour) in his way to the Temple of Honour'. Hawkesbury had apparently replied with much gratification, and, in a final flourish of laudatory trumpet, Stracey announced in a letter of 25 November that he would pay his personal respects, remarking that 'your Lordship (all flattery whatever apart) always appeared to me in the light . . . of one of the best informed and the ablest official men in every department of the State, and the most uniformly faithful servant of the Publick, that I know of in my time'. Thus in 1786 did the senior committee clerk of the House soothe the breast of the Chancellor of the Duchy, who had indeed come in for a good deal of unfair obloquy as the hidden power in the governmental concert of George III and Lord North.

The George Whites, father and son, fill a considerable place in the functional history of the clerks. The elder George White we find clerk of the journals and papers in 1756, though his first appointment was probably earlier. He became one of the four clerks without doors in 1770 and died in his 70th year on 20 January 1789 at Newington House, near Wallingford, which he had acquired and which he modernized in 1777.[1] He was clerk of the secret committees of 1772 and 1781, on East Indian affairs, and, as clerk of election committees, he was the first to hold that office under the new system for trying controverted elections introduced by the Grenville Act of 1770.[2] His son of the same name was born in 1748, first appears as a deputy committee clerk in 1775, and was clerk of elections from 1789 to 1813, when he died at Newington House in his 65th year. He was the first of the clerks to found a really large business as a parliamentary agent.[3] His brother, John White, was clerk to the committee of managers at the trial of Warren Hastings. Other younger members of this family became clerks in the House. With the Leys and the Whites the connexion between the clerks and Westminster School became very strong.

Lastly, John Rosier, Robert Yeates's deputy and the executor of his will, is important for his connexion with the Treasury and for becoming the first official clerk of the fees. Biographical

[1] *Gentleman's Magazine*, lxviii. 809, gives a view of this country house, which descended to his son, the younger George White.
[2] See chapter 10, pp. 221–24; also chapter 7, pp. 143–44.
[3] See chapter 8, pp. 181–85.

information about him, unfortunately, is very scanty, though his official career was successful and, as clerk of the fees from 1775 to 1796, he was in a position of considerable influence. He died at Southrop, Gloucestershire, on 13 August 1796,[1] but does not appear to have lived there. According to his will,[2] he was of the parish of St. Margaret's, Westminster, was unmarried, and had reached no such prosperity as the Whites; he expressed a wish to be buried in the parish where he should happen to die 'with as little expense as decency will permit', and seems to have had no landed property. As he was only a principal committee clerk (one of the four clerks without doors) for the last seven years of his life, he had insufficient time to profit by the vastly increased revenue from private bill fees which was then coming in to those officers of the House who were fortunate enough to share them. Rosier's will was witnessed by John Benson, who was then clerk of the journals, and Henry Gunnell, then a deputy committee clerk. John Benson, Arthur his son, the Whittams, the Doringtons, and the numerous Gunnell family will appear in various connexions, but do not call for any particular biographical comment,[3] since they all belonged to the definitely professional element, being appointed as young men and working their way to the top, like any clerk of today. By Hatsell's time the sudden appearance in principal posts of distinguished university scholars or scions of the landed gentry was a thing of the past, the one exception being Edward Stracey, whom the judicious Hatsell appointed to a principal clerkship at the age of twenty-one and whose extraordinary case will be dealt with in a later chapter.[4]

[1] *Gentleman's Magazine*, vol. lxvi.

[2] P.C.C. Harris, 1796, fol. 426. He directed his executors to purchase sufficient 3 per cent. consolidated annuities to produce £100 a year, and the residue of his estate was to be divided into four equal shares, for brothers and sisters.

[3] In Peterborough Cathedral there is a mural inscription recording John Benson's death in 1827 as the 'oldest Committee Clerk at the House of Commons'. He retired from the position of clerk of the journals in 1797, and thus enjoyed the sinecure position of a principal committee clerk (see chapter 7) for thirty years.

[4] See pp. 155–58.

5

BIOGRAPHICAL: JOHN HATSELL, THE LEYS
JOHN RICKMAN

(1)

THE period 1768–1850 is marked by very long tenures of office. There were only two Clerks of the House—Hatsell 1768–1820 and John Henry Ley 1820–50. John Ley was Clerk Assistant from 1768 to 1797 when Hatsell, retiring from his duties at the table of the House, appointed him his deputy, while Jeremiah Dyson, son of the former Clerk, became Clerk Assistant. John Ley died in 1814, and Dyson became Hatsell's deputy till Hatsell's patent expired on its holder's death in 1820. Meanwhile, John Henry Ley had been appointed in 1801 the first 2nd Clerk Assistant, became Clerk Assistant in 1814, and Clerk of the House in 1820. John Rickman, formerly secretary to Speaker Abbot, became 2nd Clerk Assistant in 1814, and Clerk Assistant in 1820, in which appointment he died in 1840. Then, for ten years, all three clerks' seats at the table were occupied by members of the Ley family. This chapter, then, is mainly concerned with Hatsell, the Ley family, and John Rickman in their biographical aspect in so far as that aspect can be separated from their official functions and careers.

John Hatsell was born on 22 December 1733.[1] He was the elder

---

[1] Not in 1743 as stated in the *D.N.B.* following an error in the obituary notice which appeared in the *Gentleman's Magazine*, xc (pt. 2), 372–3 and said that Hatsell died in his 78th year. The correct date of his birth was recorded on the memorial tablet in the Temple Church, as I was informed by the Librarian and Keeper of the Records of the Middle Temple. Hatsell therefore died in his 87th year, a fact which is confirmed by Luke Hansard's letter to his son on Hatsell's death quoted in J. C. Trewin and E. M. King, *Printer to the House* (London, 1952), p. 135. In that work there are frequent references to Hatsell, who became a firm friend of Luke Hansard and, with Rickman, a staunch defender of Hansard against the attacks of the economists and the Stationery Office. Luke Hansard was one of the witnesses of Hatsell's will (Reference Book Kent, 1820, 574).

son of Henry Hatsell of the Middle Temple, and grandson of Sir Henry Hatsell (1641–1714), a baron of the Exchequer. His mother was Penelope, daughter of Sir James Robinson, bart., of Cranford Hall, near Kettering, which accounts for his very strong attachment to Northamptonshire. His correspondence shows that he paid a visit to Cranford almost annually, and that he had a large circle of friends in the county, including Nathaniel Ryder (later the first Lord Harrowby) of Sandon Hall, with whom he travelled on the Continent in 1769, the Blencowes of Dallington, and the Powyses of Lilford Hall. Many of his letters are dated from Cranford, Dallington, or Sandon. This Northamptonshire connexion is also illustrated by his marriage in 1778 to the widow of Major Newton Barton, of Irthlingborough, whose first name marked his descent from the family of Sir Isaac Newton. Mrs. Hatsell, who was two years younger than Hatsell, and died in 1804, was herself a native of Northamptonshire, her father being the Rev. Jeffery Ekins, rector of Barton Seagrave, whose two sons Jeffery and John became respectively deans of Carlisle and Salisbury. The Hatsells visited Newton Tony, the country residence of the dean of Salisbury, annually in their regular tour of friends' country houses, and affectionately befriended Mrs. Hatsell's nieces, the daughters of both deans. Hatsell also took an extremely fatherly interest in the two sons of his wife by her first marriage, John and Newton Barton. The former took holy orders, married a Northamptonshire woman, had livings at Sonning and Chiddingfold, was Speaker's chaplain in 1801 and 1802, and died in the following year shortly after preferment to a canonry of Canterbury. His widow acted as Hatsell's chatelaine after Mrs. Hatsell's death, and her attentions received very handsome and substantial acknowledgement in his will. Newton Barton, through Hatsell's influence,[1] obtained a post in what would now be called the Civil Service. He became secretary to Addington in 1801—'Newton writes to us from Downing Street almost every day', wrote Hatsell to Ley in July of that year—but his career was cut short in 1808 when he was drowned.

---

[1] In a letter dated 1 Nov. 1793 (Addl. MSS. 34452, fol. 189) Hatsell solicited Auckland to find Newton Barton a place in the administration.

About Hatsell's youth we know little. He was admitted in 1750 of the Middle Temple, of which society he became a master of the bench in 1789 and treasurer in 1802. His appointment as Clerk Assistant on the death of John Read in 1760 was due, as he himself recorded,[1] to the recommendation made to Jeremiah Dyson by Dr. Akenside. It appears to have been thought in some quarters that, when Dyson resigned at the end of the session 1761–2, Hatsell would succeed him as Clerk, leaving the Clerk Assistant's place vacant; for on 20 June 1762 John Robinson, who was then agent to Sir James Lowther, wrote to Jenkinson, who was then member for Appleby, one of the many boroughs in Lowther's gift, to say that Sir James approved of the purchase of the Clerk Assistant's place by one Garforth, a London solicitor who was also one of Lowther's agents, and of Jenkinson's giving any assistance in his power.[2] However, the scholar Thomas Tyrwhitt became Clerk in 1762, and it was not till 1768 that he resigned in Hatsell's favour. Hatsell's letters patent[3] bear the date of 3 June of that year: he exercised their powers till his death in October 1820, firstly by appointing a deputy from 1797 onwards, secondly by surrendering none of the (by then) very large emoluments of his office,[4] which he divided with his deputy, John Ley, and thirdly by continuing as titular Clerk of the House, after resigning his duties at the table, and in that capacity continuing to exercise some authority in the direction of the Clerk's department. Also, he remained until his death in possession of the Clerk's official residence, the house called Cotton Garden, which adjoined St. Stephen's on the river-

---

[1] Hatsell, ii. 257; and see above, p. 69.

[2] Addl. MSS. 36198, fol. 258, quoted in *The Jenkinson Papers, 1760–66*, ed. Ninetta S. Jucker (London, 1949), p. 35. The relevant passage runs: 'He (Lowther) approves of Garforth's having and purchasing the Assistant Clerk's place of the House of Commons if an opportunity, and of your giving him any assistance in your power in forwarding it, as he wd. be glad to get it. I am certain he will be found sufficiently qualified for yt place, and execute it not only with the greatest care but fidelity.' It looks as if the idea had been Jenkinson's, he then being joint secretary to the Treasury and about to become the leader of the 'King's Friends' to join whom Dyson had just resigned the Clerkship.

[3] L.P. 8 Geo. III, no. 7.

[4] Thus delaying for eight years the coming into force of the act 52 Geo. III, c. 11, under which the Clerk's fees were to be paid into a fee fund.

side.[1] He was, in fact, Clerk of the House for fifty-two years and one of its officers for fifty-eight years. In spite of the terms of his letter[2] asking the leave of the House in July 1797 to 'retire from any further execution of the duties of my office', and to appoint John Ley as his deputy, he still considered himself 'in the House of Commons', witness his statement in a letter dated 11 November 1809[3] to Lord Auckland: 'I am now more than half way thro' my year of Jubilee, as on the 6th of next May, I shall have been 50 years in the House of Commons.' Moreover, John Henry Ley, when giving evidence in 1826 before a select committee[4] with regard to the Clerk's house, said: 'Hatsell superintended the office; he never gave up command over the office, but most of his duties were exercised by deputy.' References to Hatsell, therefore, which make out that he entirely retired from the Clerkship of the House in 1797 are incorrect.

In outward circumstance Hatsell's life was uneventful, though he sat at the table of the House during an epoch of unparalleled parliamentary brilliance, with Burke thundering, Fox denouncing, Sheridan sparkling, and Pitt inspiring within a few feet of his dutifully impassive countenance. From the first he threw himself into an intense study of the *Journals* upon which, in the main, were based the four volumes of his great work, *Precedents of Proceedings in the House of Commons*,[5] a work that then commanded as much respect as Erskine May's among later generations, not only in England but also in the newly established Congress of the United States. He was generally reputed the leading authority on parliamentary procedure.

These things are well known; but, with the information now available, Hatsell can be presented as a far more interesting person

[1] See chapter 6, pp. 113–14.

[2] Read by the Speaker and entered in the *Journal* on 15 July 1797.

[3] *Journal and Correspondence of Lord Auckland*, iv. 333–4.

[4] *Report* of the Select Committee on Committee Rooms and Printed Papers (H.C. (1826) 403, p. 26).

[5] The first volume, a collection of cases relating to privilege, appeared in 1776; the second, dealing with procedure, order, the Speaker, and the Clerk, in 1781; the third, dealing with relations between Lords and Commons, in 1794; and the fourth, mainly about impeachments, in 1796. The whole was reissued in 1818, with a new index compiled by Rickman.

than would appear from the very inadequate notice of him in the *Dictionary of National Biography* and its reference to Nichols's obituary[1] wherein he is described as 'a perfect gentleman of the old school', in manners mild and conciliating, abounding in stories of public men and events during the latter half of the eighteenth century, who read his Greek and Latin classics till the end, and was carried off by an apoplectic stroke early on a Sunday morning after reading prayers to his household in his country mansion the night before. This was well enough for Nichols writing in 1820 about a near-nonagenarian, but in the light of Hatsell's correspondence,[2] in the main still unpublished, a very different person emerges—a man of great zest for foreign travel and social contacts, of firm and sound views on contemporary politics and politicians, a close friend of eminent statesmen, including Addington (afterwards Lord Sidmouth), who confided to him his closest secrets, a welcome guest in many country houses, a generous host in his own, a fluent and lively correspondent, and of his own department a judicious and assiduous controller. It would be out of place in the present work to attempt more than to illustrate, by a few quotations, the varied features of Hatsell as revealed by contemporary documents.

To begin with, Hatsell's relations with leading politicians show that he attracted their confidence by his sympathetic understanding, though he was no sycophant of those in power. He had a contemptuous opinion of North and his fellow ministers who were responsible for the loss of America, which he expressed to Ley in 1778 as follows:[3]

I have for some months convinc'd myself that the return of America to the Dependency of this Country, I mean, such a Dependency as it must now necessarily be, would be our immediate ruin; the Expences it would bring with it, & the enormous increase of Patronage to the Crown, without any adequate advantages, would soon overwhelm us; & therefore, though I cannot say I expected what is call'd a favourable

[1] See p. 79, n. 1.
[2] See Introduction, p. xv, for a brief description of the Ley MSS. containing nearly 100 letters from Hatsell to John Ley and of the other collections in which unpublished letters from Hatsell exist.
[3] Ley MSS. Hatsell to Ley, 28 Aug. 1778.

answer from the Congress, yet I almost dreaded it, considering how advantageous the terms were that were offer'd to them, & how absurd, & full of difficulty with respect to us. I am therefore satisfied that this loss of America, as it is call'd, is a fresh instance of the Divine interposition in favour of the preservation of the Liberty & Independence of this Island, & that to bring about this gracious purpose, Providence, by means of George ye 3rd, chose out the only set of Men, that could be found in the Nation, for Ministers, by whose blunders, & inattention, & want of foresight, this blessing could have been dispensed.

Nevertheless, when North's administration was finally tottering, Jenkinson, North's Secretary at War, wrote to Hatsell:[1]

Dear Sir, I have just received the favour of your letter and am much obliged to you, for having communicated to Lord John Cavendish what I said to you at the Speaker's concerning my own future situation. I shall be happy if any good arises & any proper arrangement can be found out of what passed last night between the King and Lord Shelburne. Believe me when I assure you that I have nothing at Heart but the Prosperity of the Publick, and that I will contribute to it by every means in my power.

Similarly, when Pitt's ministry was cracking asunder in 1801, Auckland sent Hatsell a private letter[2] in which he said that the unhappy business mentioned in a previous letter was ending in a schism among the ministers, and in the retiring of several of the most efficient, that he was more grieved than he could describe by the divergences (the actual word is not legible) which would take place among many who have been accustomed to live and act together with friendship and entire affection, that he hoped a respectable government might yet be found, and that all this was, of course, for Hatsell's secret information till he learned it in detail from better authority. The 'better authority' was undoubtedly Addington, Hatsell's confidential relation to whom is strikingly exemplified by three distinguished witnesses when Addington was breaking with Pitt in 1804 and when, after reconciliation, he was persuaded the following year to accept a peerage. Abbot, then Speaker, in recording[3] a long conversation between himself and

---

[1] Addl. MSS. (Liverpool Papers) 38309, fol. 47b.

[2] Addl. MSS. (Auckland Papers) 34460, fol. 170.

[3] Colchester, i. 530. Abbot in his summary of his House of Commons' friend-

Addington after the latter's resignation in October 1804, wrote:
'Mr. Addington had not as yet mentioned his own proposed line
of conduct to anybody, except to Hatsell, on his way down to
me.' Lord Hawkesbury (Jenkinson), reporting to Pitt his negotiations for Addington's return to the administration on 12 December
1804, said that Addington had promised to communicate what had
passed to nobody except to Vansittart, Hatsell, and possibly Lord
Ellenborough.[1] Thomas Grenville, on 8 January 1805, reported to
Lord Grenville a conversation[2] with Hatsell about the prospect of
Addington's getting a peerage on reconciliation with Pitt, in
which the following occurs:

Upon my saying that I knew the peerage at least was settled; he said,
'then they have overcome Mr. Addington, for I know his letter to Pitt
of Saturday was to urge Mr. P. to leave him in the House of Commons
without office, though in the Cabinet, in order by being in the Cabinet
to shew his entire concurrence.' And why, said I, did Mr. Pitt press
him so vehemently to be a peer against his wish; to which he answered
'because he wanted his help in the House of Lords, *for I suppose I must
not be allowed to say that he wanted him out of the House of Commons*.' This
language in a person so confidential to Addington cannot be mistaken.

Many examples of Hatsell's political acumen might be brought
up from the long series of his letters to Auckland, notably some
very shrewd observations made in 1806 on the change of attitude
towards the employment of slaves that he had lived to see, and a
series of letters on taxation written in 1798 when Auckland, then
one of the Postmasters General, was engaged in drafting Pitt's
income-tax bill. The same correspondence also amply illustrates
Hatsell's love of social intercourse and entertainment, his geniality
and his habit of life at his country abodes. But these things, and
above all his love of travel and his *joie de vivre*, stand out still more
vividly in the correspondence with John Ley.

ships (MS. diary (P.R.O. 30/9/31), 'Notes on my parliamentary life') wrote:
'Hatsell, by Mr. Addington's means, also became tho' slowly my cordial and fast
friend, and we maintained an unreserved and confidential intercourse, from the
period of his retirement in 1797.' They frequently rode together in Hyde Park at
least up to 1812.

[1] P.R.O. Chatham Corr., bundle 143.
[2] *R. Comm. Hist. MSS. Fortescue MSS.* vi. 92.

When Hatsell became Clerk of the House in 1765 he appointed as his Clerk Assistant John Ley[1] of Trehill, near Exeter, his exact contemporary, also of the Middle Temple where both were called to the Bar in the same year. Thus began a long association only terminated by Ley's death, still in harness as Deputy Clerk, in 1814, his 82nd year.[2] It is sad that their long friendship was broken two years earlier by the dispute recorded in my next chapter.

John Hatsell and John Ley sat next to one another at the table of the House for nearly thirty years, and saw each other daily during the session: but during the long recesses when Hatsell was careering about the Continent, enjoying the waters and society of Cheltenham or Bath, or staying, as was his habit, at the country houses of the nobility and gentry, while Ley was sedately farming at Trehill, these two friends corresponded—Hatsell an inveterate and fluent letter-writer, lavish of news and views when he had any, and greedy for news when he was cut off from them, and Ley less fluent, with a much less graceful pen, but most conscientious in answering Hatsell's questions and in compiling chronicles for him when, during the five years before he married, he was travelling abroad. It was Ley who kept the letters, and it is therefore natural that little of his own contribution to the correspondence was preserved: what he did preserve were drafts or copies of long news-letters which he sent to Hatsell abroad—four in 1769, two in 1770, one in 1771, and three in 1772. In 1778 Hatsell married Mrs. Barton, who did not share her second husband's passion for foreign travel, so that, after his marriage, Hatsell's travels in the recess were from one country house to another, to Cheltenham, or to Bath where he spent many winters. The correspondence with Ley begins in 1768, between which year and the end of 1772 there are thirty letters including all of Ley's to Hatsell, continues somewhat occasionally between 1773 and 1796, and from that year till it ends in 1802 it becomes plentiful again, with a good

---

[1] See below, pp. 90–92. Among the Ley MSS. there is a letter from Mr. (afterward Baron) Maseres to John Ley approving of his accepting the appointment, but saying that, in his opinion, Ley would have become very distinguished at the Bar.

[2] *Gentleman's Magazine*, lxxxiv (pt. 1), 700. This, if correct, fixes the year of John Ley's birth as 1733.

deal about Pitt's taxes, the preparations for the French invasion, and finally about the preparations and adjustments necessitated by the union with Ireland and the advent of 100 new members at St. Stephen's. In 1769, while Ley was collecting all news of the agitation due to the expulsion of John Wilkes and of the City elections, Hatsell visited Paris, Compiègne (where he attended the royal hunt and saw Madame Dubarry), Nancy, Strassburg, the Rhine up to Basle, Schaffhausen, Zürich, Lucerne, Bern, and the lake of Geneva. In 1770 he stayed at Bern with our consul and with him rode on horseback—in all a squadron of fifteen horse—over the St. Gotthard, thence he went to Milan and returned to Basle over the Splügen. In 1771 he toured the Orléannais, and in 1772 his route was Spa, Geneva, Marseilles, Toulouse, Bordeaux, and Paris. While in Geneva he paid a call on Voltaire, of which he sent Ley an account, followed in the same letter by an outline of the promotions he meant to make if Newdigate Poyntz, reported by Ley to be very ill, were to die and leave a vacancy among the four clerks without doors (it will be observed that by 1772 Hatsell refers to them as the 'four Chief Clerks'). I shall quote this letter entire, since it illustrates Hatsell's personality more vividly than all four volumes of his rather ponderous book, although comments on the latter part must be postponed.

Geneva
Aug 27th (1772)

I am much oblig'd to you for yours of the 14th, which I found here on my arrival yesterday; we made a tour hither thro' the most beautiful scenes that Nature can possibly exhibit; it is difficult to say which are most to be admir'd, the rich & fertile provinces of Lorraine & Franche-Comté, the calm and happy possessions of the Swiss, or the most sublime mountains of Savoy, among which I paid a second visit to my friends, the Glacieres: it was not an unpleasing circumstance to me, that Ellison was in raptures with these stupendous Alps, at least it was flattering to have my own taste so thoroughly coincide with his. We shall stay here about a week, as I have a pretty large acquaintance; we sent a note this morning to desire leave to pay our complts to Voltaire, to wch we receiv'd the following answr.

'Le Vieux Malade de Ferney, est plus malade que jamais: s'il n'est pas mort demain, il aura l'honneur de voir un moment les Messieurs. S'il est mort, Est ultima linea rerum.' Whether we shall see him or no, is still a problem as he grows every day more odd & capricious.

Our route from hence, is by Lyons, Grenoble, Valence, Avignon, Aix, Toulon, Nismes, Montpellier, Toulouse to Bourdeaux where we calculate to arrive about the 6th Octobr. If therefore you will write by the post of Tuesday 29th Septr. the day of the prorogation, directed to me, *Gentilhomme Anglais* à la Poste Restante à Bourdeaux, it will arrive there in time.

If anything fatal should happen to poor Poyntz, I should wish to have your opinion on the following plan; my present idea is, to offer his place to Edwd Barwell as the senior Clerk not one of the four Chief; this will vacate one of the Ingrossing Clerks, & Stracey's Deputy; as to the latter, I should be glad to consult Stracey's inclinations, wth respect to the former I think it would be right to advance Jones to it, who has been ingrossing night & day since the year 1752: I know Stracey's wishes coincide with mine in doing something for Parker, but he could not chuse to put him out of his present seat, where his accuracy & attention is very materially interesting to us all; if Jones was also to be his Deputy, wch is about 150£ per ann. I see no objection to appointing him to both, on condition on his paying Parker 50 or 60£ a year, till Parker has something better. Nathl. Barwell, Rosier & Gunnell will, I know, be all disappointed at this arrangement; as to the latter, he is very well provided for, considering his abilities, & that his son is in the Office, and will rise in his turn: I should not wish to remove Rosier into anything but one of the Chief Clerks & to this Ed. Barwell has certainly a prior claim: Nathl. Barwell is but [lately c]ome in & cannot reasonably complain, [if his yo]unger brother takes the lead of him: [but I sh]all not decide upon any thing without your advice, for which I should be oblig'd to you, if the event of poor Poyntz's death should make it necessary: I should be glad you would not give the least hint to any one of this part of ye letter. If however this accident should happen, I have no objection to your writing to Stracey, to consult him in my name, about his Deputy & what should be done for Parker, desiring however that he will not communicate to any one anything that passes between you. Ellison desires his complts to you. As I shall be continually in motion, I have left directions at my house for all letters put in before the 29th Septr. or on that day to be directed to Bourdeaux.

Your's mt sincerely.   J. H.

In a letter of 6 September from Lyons Hatsell, among other

matters, completed his account of the visit to Voltaire in the following passage:

We spent ten days most agreably at Geneva; in consequence of his note, we had an audience *pour un moment* of M. de Voltaire, for, tho' he had put on his full-bottom'd wig, & brocaded waist-coat to receive us, he thought himself oblig'd to act the *Vieux Malade* he had painted the day before; &, tho' he walked as well as when I saw him three years ago, his whole conversation, of *two minutes*, consisted only of apologies in being prevented by his state of health from doing the honours of his house.

He told Mr. Neville the other day, that his greatest wish was, before he died, to see Mr. Garrick at Ferney; & that after his death, the world would see from his remarks in his edition of Shakespeare the estimation in which he held that author, from the numberless beauties he had pointed out.

For the rest, Hatsell's letters to Ley are dated from Lord Harrowby's at Norton or Sandon Hall, Sir George Robinson's at Cranford near Kettering, the bishop of Salisbury's palace, the dean of Salisbury's at Newton Tony, or Mr. Ellis's at Paultons near Romsey, or else from Bath, of which they describe the society and the pleasures—balls, concerts, and plays—during the winter season, or (when not from Cotton Garden) from his own country houses, Bradburne Place[1] near Sevenoaks which he gleefully described to Ley in July 1792, dwelling on its profusion of distinguished neighbours, and after 1799 Marden Park[2] when, in the autumn of 1801, as he told Ley, the house-party had seldom been fewer than a dozen, including at one time or another such guests as the bishop of London, Addington who had just become Prime Minister, and Lord Frederick Campbell. Political events are frequently canvassed in these letters, one of the most remarkable of which, written in April 1784, first expresses Hatsell's personal detachment from

[1] From Bradburne he wrote in August of the same year that the ministers Pitt and Dundas had been in the neighbourhood for two or three days at Lord Frederick Campbell's house, Combe Bank: 'I dined with them twice, and very jolly they were. . . . They came over here, and admired this place very much.' (Ley MSS.)

[2] Near Godstone in Surrey. This house is twice referred to in Evelyn's diary, on 12 Oct. 1677 and 13 July 1700. Sir Robert Clayton had bought the estate from Sir John Evelyn and turned 'a despicable farmhouse into a fine seat'. Wilberforce lived there at one time.

party politics and then gives an extremely shrewd forecast of Pitt's victory at the polls, with an estimate of the difficulties he would have to contend with as head of the administration—a somewhat pessimistic estimate, proved wrong by events, and ending with the words:

And to add to his misfortunes, his popularity has return'd him a Parliamt *personally* devoted to him; which will have the immediate effect of estranging from him *that support*, without which no Man can conduct the Affairs of this Country with firmness & Success.

Yet social events are equally prominent, the execution of Louis XVI receiving only cursory notice compared with that of happenings in England. Hatsell's letters in fine, including those to Lord Auckland, provide a body of evidence as to events and personalities of the day which it would be a pity to leave in complete oblivion.

It is strange that no letter refers to his coming retirement from the table in 1797; but on 4 January 1798 a very lively letter to Ley from Bath contains this passage:

I could not help smiling, tho' alone, to think how differently I was employed last night, about 11 o'clock, than if I had been sitting near you. I was just finishing Mrs Crespigny's novel 'The Pavillon'.

His other, and not infrequent, allusions to matters affecting the Clerk's department will be noticed in the appropriate places. In the present chapter I have only attempted to give an idea of Hatsell's variety of interests, liveliness of mind, great social intercourse, and established position in the high political world, of which, but for his letters, there would be no evidence. When he died at a great age he was the senior bencher of the Middle Temple, and his remains were interred in the Temple Church.

(2)

John Ley, elder son of John Ley of Trehill, Devon, was the first of that family to enter the service of the House of Commons and in so doing began a connexion between the Ley family and the House which lasted till within living memory. His brother, Henry Ley, who seems also to have lived at Trehill all his life and became town clerk of Exeter, was the father of John Henry Ley, appointed 2nd Clerk Assistant in 1801 and Clerk of the House 1820–50. John Ley had no direct descendants, since he remained a bachelor, but Henry Ley's second son, William, also became a clerk in the House ending as Clerk Assistant, and maintained another family connexion by marrying as his first wife Frances, daughter of James Hatsell, John Hatsell's brother.[1] John Henry Ley in 1809 married Lady Dorothy Hay, sixth daughter of George, 7th marquis of Tweeddale, by whom he had many children. His second son, Henry, eventually became 2nd Clerk Assistant, and two other sons, George and Edward, were clerks in the House. The last representative of the family in that service was William Ley, grandson of John Henry by his son Henry, who became clerk of the journals and died in 1919.

There is a well-known story of John Ley.[2] He was on one occasion so much disturbed by William Pitt's condition in the House that he had been unable to sleep all night for thinking of it. On hearing this Pitt exclaimed: 'Could there possibly have been a fairer division? I had the wine, and the Clerk, poor man, had the headache.' Hickel's painting of the House of Commons in 1793, in the National Portrait Gallery, shows Pitt orating at the table at which are sitting Hatsell and Ley, whose faces, in the picture, have a remarkable similarity which betrays an obvious want of observation on the artist's part. John Ley was a very different man from Hatsell: he was able and orderly in all his dealings, but, unlike his colleague was reserved, very limited in his interests, not particularly fond of society, and wrapped up in Trehill and its demesne, in local and in family affairs. He resisted Hatsell's efforts to tempt him abroad, and he paid no visits to other country houses. When not compelled to be at Westminster,[3] he remained solidly at Trehill, managing the farms of the estate jointly with his brother. Among the Ley manuscripts there is a diary kept by John Ley

[1] See chapter 6, pp. 103–5. This alliance complicated the quarrel between Hatsell and Ley.

[2] I take it from A. I. Dasent, *The Speakers of the House of Commons* (London, 1911), p. 291. On the next page of that book is reproduced a sketch by Gillray of Addington speaking, with Abbot in the chair and Ley at the table.

[3] For his places of residence there, see p. 121 and footnotes.

during the years 1808 and 1809 which, with its close, angular script, its carefully entered cash accounts (in themselves highly interesting), its bald records of calls made and received, dinners, church-goings, and financial affairs, and its complete absence of liveliness and emotional content, well illustrates his somewhat cold, business-like, and austere temperament, not least in its very matter-of-fact description of his nephew's engagement and marriage to a nobleman's daughter—an event of no small moment in those days—and its account of his connexion with the notorious Boringdon divorce case.[1] There is little more, on the purely biographical side, to be said of John Ley, except that, during the period 1792 to 1800, he was employed by the Treasury, jointly with two masters in Chancery, to tax the bills of costs of Messrs. Wallis and Troward, the government's solicitors in the long-drawn-out trial of Warren Hastings. The Treasury books show that this extra business brought him quite a respectable sum.[2] The subject of John Ley's emoluments in general, particularly the large increase in the Clerk Assistant's salary made during his tenure of that office, will be dealt with in another chapter.[3]

Of Jeremiah Dyson, the son of the former Clerk of the House, who succeeded John Ley as Clerk Assistant in 1797 and was Deputy Clerk from 1814 to 1820, when he was retired on a pension of £2,500 a year, there is little that needs to be said. He was born in 1757,

[1] As appears from this diary, John Ley acted as legal agent, at a small annual salary, to Lord Boringdon, a Devonshire magnate, the elopement of whose wife, Lady Augusta (*née* Fane), with Sir Arthur Paget in May 1808 was one of the great scandals of the year. Lord Boringdon brought an action for divorce and was awarded £10,000 damages. On 20 May, as recorded in Ley's diary, he was sent for by Lord Morpeth to consult as to the solicitor and counsel to be engaged for this action, and heard from his lips, and later from Lord Boringdon's, the detailed story—the whole business, in sedate, dry language, occupying several pages of the diary. See G. E. C., *The Complete Peerage*, ix. 233 n., where the reputed connexion between Lady Paget and the story of Mrs. Henry Wood's *East Lynne* is mentioned.

[2] The first reference is a Treasury letter (T. 27/43, fol. 72) dated 14 Dec. 1792 transmitting a bill of charges and desiring Ley to call on Masters Walker and Sprang to assist him in reporting their opinion what allowances were fit to be made. Similar letters were sent in 1794 and 1795 (T. 27/45, fols. 117, 328), and the C.L. Accts. for 1797–8 show a payment of £1,350. 1s. 6d. made the previous year to John Ley and others for examining and taxing Wallis and Troward's bills of expense.

[3] See chapter 6, pp. 119–21.

educated at Eton and Christ Church, and was a student of Lincoln's Inn in 1777. He died in 1835.[1] As for John Henry Ley, his name will often appear in the sequel in various connexions. His evidence given before several select committees from 1824 onwards shows that he must have been like his uncle, a solid, business-like and determined man, of conservative temperament and tenaciously held views. He was born in 1777, educated at Westminster and Christ Church, where he matriculated in 1795, and was called to the Bar at the Middle Temple in 1803, becoming bencher of his Inn in 1843. He died in August 1850 very soon after he retired. He was studying for the Bar when, in July 1801, the newly created post of 2nd Clerk Assistant was offered to him by his uncle, with the approval of Hatsell and Addington, then Speaker; and he was formally introduced at the beginning of the following session. He was the first of the clerks at the table whose salary was rigidly fixed by Act of Parliament and who did not participate in the revenue from fees.

(3)

There remains John Rickman, F.R.S., the originator of the census in Great Britain and the supervisor of the population returns of 1811, 1821, and 1831, the associate of Telford as secretary to the commissions on the Caledonian Canal and for building roads and bridges in the Highlands, the friend of Coleridge and Charles Lamb, and the lifelong friend and adviser of Robert Southey. He was a man of indefatigable energy and of far greater distinction than any of his colleagues at the table of the House, although his reserved character and dislike of any notoriety, however gratifying, prevented his receiving due recognition in his lifetime. Fortunately for the balance of this chapter—with all humility be it said—his biography, based on the large volume of correspondence, mainly with Southey, which survived him, was written many years ago by a then young clerk in the House of Commons, the author of this book.[2] Those who wish to know what kind of

---

[1] A letter praising his virtues was printed in 1820 in the *Gentleman's Magazine*, xc (pt. 2), 482.

[2] O. C. Williams, *The Life and Letters of John Rickman* (Constable, 1912). The

a man Rickman was, what his relations were with men as dissimilar to himself as Coleridge and Lamb, the nature of his domestic life, the colour of his politics, and his views of men and things may be referred to that biography, and in particular to the introduction, which is in the nature of a summary. Here it will be sufficient to give the salient facts of his life.

John Rickman was born in 1771, the only son of the Rev. Thomas Rickman, then vicar of Newburn in Northumberland, who came of a very ancient Somersetshire family, and whose father had for a time become prosperous as the contractor for the provisioning of the Spanish prisoners captured in the war that began in 1739. John Rickman was educated at Guildford Grammar School, Magdalen Hall, and Lincoln College. He first met Southey at Christchurch in Hampshire in 1797. They were both young men, violently anti-ministerial and full of desires to ameliorate society. On Rickman's side this urge was tempered by a hardheaded practicality, which led him always to look for definite means and measures to remedy observed defects. Thus, throughout his life, what would now be called social science was the only subject to which he thought it worth while to devote his whole energy, attention, and—one might even say—passion. Southey made him known to George Dyer, that estimable man who was Lamb's prime absurdity, and through Dyer he came into Lamb's circle at 27 Southampton Buildings in 1780, to figure immediately in one of Lamb's most famous letters. Rickman was then conducting *The Commercial, Agricultural, and Manufacturers' Magazine* for a publisher named Griffiths in which he was able to employ much material already amassed from reading and reflection on economics and kindred subjects. His paper on 'The Utility and Facility of a general Enumeration of the People of the British Empire'—this early use of the word 'Empire' is interesting—had found its way into the hands of another tireless worker and practical reformer, Charles Abbot, member for Helston and Clerk of the Rules of the King's Bench. Hence Abbot's Population Act of 1800 and the offer to Rickman of the supervision of the returns: and it is worth while

book has long been out of print, but is to be found in many libraries. The account of Rickman in the *D.N.B.* was, of course, still earlier.

to observe the words in which Rickman apprized Southey of this new occupation which was to involve him in immense and not at all adequately rewarded labour for much of the rest of his life, and for which, although it gained him the Fellowship of the Royal Society and much honour among European statisticians, he has never received sufficient credit from writers on this topic. This neglect is partly due to his own preference for anonymity and his refusal to make any public claims for recognition; but it makes his claim, in his letter to Southey, that the Population Act was passed at his suggestion all the more convincing. In the long letter dated 27 December 1800 he wrote:

I have another occupation offered me: of which this is the history. At my suggestion, they have passed an Act of Parliament for ascertaining the population of Great Britain, and as a compliment (of course) have proposed to me to superintend the execution of it. Next March the returns will be made, and I shall be busy enough for a short time, I suppose. I suspect all this attention (it is more immediately from G. Rose) is intended as a decent bribe: which I shall reject, by doing the business well, and taking no more remuneration, than I judge exactly adequate to the trouble. It is a task of national benefit, and I should be fanciful to reject it, because offered by rogues. As they well *know* me for their foe, I cannot suspect them of magnanimity enough to notice me with any good intention. At all events, I shall go *strait forward*.

Since Abbot, in an unpublished entry in his diary, recorded that it was at his suggestion that George Rose, then secretary to the Treasury, offered Rickman the superintendence of the returns, it seems unlikely that it was meant as a bribe to a young man of violently anti-ministerial views: nor is it likely that Rickman himself foresaw that he would draft the Acts and supervise the returns in 1811, 1821, and 1831 and would be drafting the Act for the census of 1841 and abstracting returns of births, marriages, and deaths from 1570 to 1750 from early parish registers during his last year of life. For all this the remuneration, as it turned out, was not even adequate to the trouble.[1]

---

[1] See my *Life and Letters of John Rickman*, pp. 36–38, where the letter to Southey is printed in full, and pp. 40–43, where a full summary is given of Rickman's work on the population returns, including his authoritative prefaces to the volumes of

In 1801, when Abbot was appointed Chief Secretary in Ireland, he took Rickman to Dublin as his private secretary and chief representative in his absence. The following year Abbot became Speaker, and Rickman, glad to leave Ireland though financially a loser by the change, was appointed Speaker's Secretary, in which capacity he occupied a small house just off New Palace Yard next door to the Speaker.[1] He now had a close enough view of the House to colour, by first-hand observation, the violently expressed letters on the politics and politicians of the day which he sent to Southey: and the view became closer still when, from 1814 onwards, he was a Clerk at the table. His animosity increased as Catholic emancipation and parliamentary reform came nearer and nearer, until, from 1830 to 1832, when the reform movement reached its climax and Rickman was planning with Southey a series of 'Colloquies' which were to be the bugle-call for all true patriots to withstand what he called 'mobocracy', his almost daily letters from the House to Southey achieve a tragic virulence, with scathing references to all the chief actors in the political drama.[2] The 'Colloquies' never saw the light owing to the dilatoriness and financial difficulties of Murray the publisher, and the Reform Act was passed. Thereafter Rickman became apathetic about politics, and, after an abortive attempt to retire on a pension in 1830, and the loss of his house in the fire of 1834, he died in harness in 1840 from an affection of the throat.

Rickman's appointment in 1814 to be 2nd Clerk Assistant was a unique event: no other Speaker's Secretary had previously, or has since, received a similar appointment. Unpublished entries in Speaker Abbot's diaries for 4 July 1808 and 16 February 1812[3] show that he twice unsuccessfully applied to the political head of the government to give Rickman a post as a reward for his services:

1832 and 1833; and Rickman's own statement, made in a letter to the Home Office in 1840, that on the whole he was a financial loser by this work is noted.

[1] See chapter 6, p. 121 and n. 3 to that page; for fuller discussion of the Clerk Assistants' successive residences up to 1834, see my monograph referred to in my introduction, pp. xvi–xvii.

[2] See my *Life and Letters of John Rickman*, pp. 249–98. Rickman's letters, there given, fiercely Tory in tone, and his suggestions for the 'Colloquies', are a valuable counterbalance to Whig memoirs of the period.

[3] P.R.O. 30/9/34 and 30/9/35 at the dates given.

in 1808 he only got obliging promises from Lord Portland, and in 1812, when Rickman had suggested an application from Abbot for his appointment to the vacant post of Register of Excise Appeals, Perceval made excuses which amounted to a refusal. In fact, Rickman's appointment to the table on John Ley's death in 1814 was an unforeseen sequel to the dispute between Hatsell and Ley over the right to make such appointments—a dispute in which Speaker Abbot took a very decided line and which will be recounted in the next chapter.

As a Clerk at the table Rickman was extremely efficient, but it is clear from his letters to Southey that his parliamentary duties did not really interest him. His official business was to him little more than so much tiresome routine; but he was never lax in its performance, and was always prepared to do such extra work as came his way, such as contriving and supervising a new index to the *Journals* from 1801 to 1812, indexing the 1818 edition of Hatsell's *Precedents of Proceedings*, instituting and supervising a new and more expeditious system of compiling the *Votes*,[1] or supplying information for a select committee. However, when in 1828 old Luke Hansard, the printer to the House, had to face a strong attack on his methods and charges before the Select Committee on Printing Done for the House, Rickman defended him in evidence at length and with much warmth: and his defence, which was partly a biographical summary of Hansard's merits and remarkable services to the House and which became the substance of the obituary notice of Hansard by Rickman in the *Gentleman's Magazine* in December of the same year, won the marked approval of Lord Colchester.[2] In this, one may suspect, he was prompted less by benevolence than by indignation at the injustice of certain reformers. In general, Rickman was an uncompromising man, outwardly severe, intolerant of other people's weaknesses, and a somewhat cool comforter in their sorrows. As Southey wrote to W. S. Landor in 1809:

[1] See chapter 9, pp. 209-12.
[2] For a full account of the struggle of the house of Hansard against the reformers, the Stationery Office, and jealous competitors, see J. C. Trewin and E. M. King, *Printer to the House* (London, 1952), pp. 154–58, 166–67, 171–72, 176–82, 190–6.

His manners are stoical; they are like the husk of a cocoanut, but his inner nature is like the milk within its kernel. When I go to London I am always his guest. He gives me but half his hand when he welcomes me at the door, but I have his whole heart.[1]

All those who knew Rickman well, or had occasion to benefit by his fundamental generosity, or enjoyed in intimacy his robust manner of conversation—Coleridge, Lamb, Dyer, Talfourd, Hazlitt—praised him in the warmest terms. He offered to lend Lamb all the money necessary for the publication of his play *John Woodvil*, and spared no pains to devil for Southey when one of his *Quarterly* articles was on the stocks: Rickman, indeed, wrote almost the whole of one of them, on the poor laws, with the strictest injunctions that his authorship should be concealed, even from the editor. He measured activities solely by their utility, his taste for poetry was small, and his literary style dry; yet his name is for ever associated with the annals of literature and poetry, for the services he rendered, the friendships he made, and the letters he inspired, no less than with the history of sociological inquiry. And when, on 3 February 1841, Lord John Russell moved a resolution recording the House's high sense of his services, even Joseph Hume, whose views Rickman detested, spoke warmly of Rickman's assistance to himself in parliamentary matters. 'I have never known', he said, 'a public officer so modest, so unassuming, possessed of such varied knowledge respecting the affairs of Parliament, and yet so ready to afford every information to others.'

[1] *Life and Correspondence of Robert Southey*, ed. C. C. Southey (1849), iii. 215.

6

THE CLERKS AT THE TABLE

(1)

Having disposed of pure biography in the two preceding chapters, we can now consider, under appropriate headings, the functions and organization of the Clerk's department as they developed during the period—nearly a century—between Jodrell's retirement (1726) and Hatsell's death (1820). We begin, as is natural and proper, with the Clerk of the House and his colleagues at the table.

It is worth noticing, perhaps, that during the century of placemen the Clerk's office never became a 'place', that is, an office with emoluments, often a sinecure, to which appointments were made by the government, or by the minister exercising the government patronage, as a price for political adherence and support.[1] We do not know, it is true, upon what understanding or for what precise reason Nicholas Hardinge was appointed Clerk on the death of Stables; but it is fair to assume that Walpole chose him for his already proved ability and his very high reputation at Cambridge.[2] Moreover, the Clerkship of the House had already become a highly responsible position; and it is most unlikely that the House would have tolerated the appointment of a typical placeman who took the bulk of the emoluments and left the duties to be performed by an underpaid deputy. Hatsell had been Clerk for nearly thirty years before he appointed Ley his deputy; and Ley had been Clerk Assistant for the same length of time. Also, it is unlikely that the House would have accepted as Clerk a man notoriously

---

[1] It is true that the *Gentleman's Magazine* (x. 525) in 1740 announcing John Naylor's appointment as Clerk Assistant remarked that it was 'a place of £500 a year'; but, since the appointment was wholly in the hands of the Clerk, it was not a piece of government patronage.

[2] See above, pp. 62–63.

bound by ties of political party: and, even if it had, it would have
been very difficult for such a Clerk to do any marked service to
his party while he sat at the table. In that respect the Clerkship of
the House was different from the position of Clerk of the Parliaments, tenure of which was compatible with membership of the
House of Commons and a ministerial post.[1] The Clerkship of
the House was never held as a sinecure nor was it compatible with
marked political activity: those who yearned for political life, as
did Hardinge and Dyson, left the table and went to the hustings.
It was, in fact, an office which no minister would have ventured
to turn into a place, even if the opportunity had occurred.

After Hardinge's appointment there was not even the opportunity, since the Clerk's place was never again vacant until Hatsell
died, having passed by voluntary cession from one Clerk to another. Seeing that every Clerk of the House has held his office by
royal letters patent, this process of voluntary cession was somewhat extraordinary. The letters patent granted the office only for
life, with power to exercise it by deputy: yet Hardinge did not
appoint Dyson his deputy, nor Dyson Tyrwhitt, nor Tyrwhitt
Hatsell. Moreover, Dyson paid Hardinge £6,000[2] to cede the
Clerk's office, which he would not have done had he been in any
doubt that new letters patent would be made out to himself. How
this certainty as to the transference of royal patronage was attained,
there is nothing to show. What is certain is that, by an instrument[3]
enrolled in Chancery and dated 9 February 1747/8, Nicholas
Hardinge surrendered his office to Jeremiah Dyson, whose letters
patent, reciting that instrument, were dated four days later. Similarly, Tyrwhitt's letters patent dated 10 August 1762 set out a surrender made to him by Dyson dated 22 July of the same year; and
Hatsell's letters patent dated 3 June 1768 set out a surrender made

---

[1] As instanced by the career of George Rose (1744–1818), an able politician but
a notorious pluralist (see *D.N.B.*). He received the reversion of the post of Clerk
of the Parliaments about 1783 and succeeded to it in 1788, already having a sinecure
in the Court of the Exchequer. He was secretary to the Treasury in 1784 and later
treasurer of the Navy. See his evidence in 1810 before the Select Committee on
Sinecure Offices (H.C. (1810) 362, p. 41) on the office of Clerk of the Parliaments.

[2] Hatsell, ii. 257.

[3] King's Warrant Book (T. 52/44, fols. 378–79).

by Tyrwhitt on 28 May previously. Moreover, by further letters patent dated 18 June 1768 the reversion for life of the Clerk's office after the death of Hatsell was granted to Tyrwhitt, so that in the event of Hatsell's premature death the tenure and all the advantages of the office would revert to Tyrwhitt. Tyrwhitt died in 1786, and Hatsell remained very much alive: but when Hatsell retired from the table and appointed John Ley his deputy in July 1797, he had already secured that Ley should be granted the reversion of the Clerkship after his death.[1]

Since Hatsell outlived John Ley, the latter's reversion to the Clerkship of the House had no effect; and when John Ley died in June 1814 Jeremiah Dyson the younger, who was then Clerk Assistant, and was prevailed upon by Hatsell to become his deputy in Ley's place, did not receive a reversionary grant,[2] so that, when Hatsell died in 1820, the Clerkship of the House was vacant for the first time since 1732 when Stables died in office. Dyson then retired on a pension, and John Henry Ley was appointed by the Crown to the Clerkship, since which time no reversions of the post have been granted, and fresh appointments, when necessary, have been made by the Crown on the advice of the Prime Minister then in office. However, the ancient form of the Clerk's patent has never been changed, except that since Hatsell's day it has not given the Clerk the right to exercise his office by deputy. Hatsell's long exercise of this right has no parallel in the history of the clerks.

[1] See respectively L.P. 21 Geo. II, pt. 3, no. 14; 2 Geo. III, pt. 3, no. 12; 8 Geo. III, no. 7; 8 Geo. III, no. 16; and 37 Geo. III, pt. 9, no. 3. Soon after Tyrwhitt's death John Ley obviously became anxious lest Pitt should grant the reversion of the Clerk's place to some other person than himself. He clearly made representations to Pitt through Lord Sydney, for there is among the Ley MSS. a letter to Ley from the latter, dated 14 June 1787, in which the writer reassures Ley and says that Pitt had no such thoughts. Ley replied thanking Lord Sydney on 16 June.

[2] Entries in Abbot's manuscript diary (P.R.O. 30/9/35) at this time show that Dyson wished to retire or to remain Clerk Assistant while J. H. Ley became Deputy Clerk, if Hatsell would appoint his son 2nd Clerk Assistant. My narrative which follows in the text explains why Hatsell could not entertain the suggestion. Also, Dyson professed to Abbot 'apprehensions of unfitness' for the administrative duties of the position; this was probably the reason why on 16 July he told Abbot that 'he was not desirous of a reversionary grant, conceiving it to be equally secure without it'. When Hatsell died, Dyson evaded the responsibility of succeeding to the position by retiring.

John Ley was his deputy from 1797 to 1814, there was a large income to share between them,[1] and the arrangement worked very
well until a short time before death ended it. Unfortunately, a
serious disagreement occurred in 1811 and developed into a permanent estrangement of the two old friends. The subject of dispute
was the Deputy Clerk's rights of appointment to subordinate
clerkships, including appointments to the table; and we should
know nothing of it but for certain entries (unpublished) in Abbot's
diaries which tell the whole story and show that Abbot took a
very decided line on Hatsell's side.

The trouble arose in the summer of 1811 when John Ley, whose
health was beginning to fail, proposed to appoint his nephew
William Ley, John Henry's brother, then aged twenty-seven, as
a supernumerary clerk at the table to attend there should he himself not feel well enough to come up to London, and of course to
succeed to the next vacancy as 2nd Clerk Assistant. On Hatsell's
refusal to consent to this proposal, they had an altercation, Ley
alleging, and Hatsell stoutly denying, that, when Hatsell gave up
his duties at the table and appointed Ley his deputy, he had assured
him that all the patronage should belong to Ley. During a morning
ride with Speaker Abbot on 1 July[2] Hatsell confided this dispute
to him, saying that it had never entered his head that Ley should
do more than arrange routine promotions among the clerks and
appoint boys as new entrants at the bottom of the establishment,
but not 'bring new people into the head situations'. It appeared,
however, as Hatsell wrote to Abbot later in the day, that there
had been no written agreement as to Ley's powers. Ley had undoubtedly exercised some powers of appointment since 1797, and
John Henry even claimed that he had been appointed 2nd Clerk
Assistant in 1801 by his uncle; but that appointment had been made
with Hatsell's full approbation, and, since Hatsell alone held the
patent of Clerk of the House, no appointment could be made
without his consent. He had withheld his consent once before, he

---

[1] See pp. 105, 107, 111–12.

[2] I here condense the entries in Abbot's manuscript diaries (P.R.O. 30/9/35) for
1, 18, 19, and 22 July 1811, 15 and 17 Feb., 14 and 15 Mar., and 14 Apr. 1812,
14 July 1813, and 23 Jan., 2 and 21 Mar., 13, 15, 17, 18, 22, and 30 June 1814.

told Abbot, when Ley had proposed to appoint his brother as clerk of ingrossments, and had threatened to appeal to the House if Ley persisted. Besides his outrage at Ley's presumption, Hatsell had another reason for rejecting Ley's proposal. It was that in 1807[1] he had voluntarily given Abbot an assurance that, on any vacancy at the table, he would appoint no person but such as the Speaker would approve or recommend. To this assurance he adhered, conceiving it to be his duty to give the Speaker, in effect, the opportunity of nominating to the next place at the table. Ley, he said, thought otherwise, but 'his idea was to make hay while the sun shone and mind nothing else': incidentally, to illustrate this remark, Hatsell recalled that in 1808, when he had decided that the Clerk's 'copy money' must be limited to a fixed annual sum,[2] Ley had strenuously resisted this self-denying decision. On his part, Abbot noted two reasons for agreeing with Hatsell's view—firstly, that Ley had no right to appoint a deputy to himself, and secondly, that to have two clerks of the same family at the table, thus making a majority, would 'render the control of the Speaker less effectual'. When, therefore, Ley himself made the same proposal to the Speaker later in the month, the latter declared his 'express disapproval' and said that, during any occasional absence of the Deputy Clerk, one of the experienced clerks without doors must be called in, as had always been the custom in the past. A new appointment could only be made when a vacancy arose, and that must wait on the event. From this time onwards it is obvious from Abbot's entries that no love was lost between him and John Ley.

In spite of this ruling by the Speaker the matter was raised again the following year, with an additional complication. William Ley, in fact, had made an offer of marriage to Hatsell's niece Frances, daughter of his brother James, and both families approved of the match. On 15 February 1812 Abbot entered in his diary:

Mr Hatsell to state Mr William Ley's offer of marriage to Mr Hatsell's unmarried niece, his own objection only on the score of his having no profession or situation in life, his further determination not to place

---

[1] Abbot had recorded this in his diary on 9 Apr. 1807 (P.R.O. 30/9/34).
[2] See pp. 111–12 and Appendix VII.

him 3rd at the table if Mr Ley should now retire, his determination also to take my recommendation for that place, but his inclination to appoint Mr William Ley a *supernumerary clerk* to supply occasional absence of either of the three Table Clerks, with an eventual succession of one of the present clerks at the table, and such 3rd clerk to be appointed by me.

Abbot also noted that he offered to relieve Hatsell of his previous undertaking to himself, so that no prior engagement should stand in the way of his providing for his niece's marriage, but this 'he positively [twice underlined] refused'. Two days later, during a morning ride, Hatsell reported that John Henry Ley had entered the field, and that they had had a clearly unpleasant interview. John Henry had claimed, and Hatsell peremptorily denied, that the appointment to a clerk's place at the table belonged to his uncle; he also claimed, and Hatsell peremptorily refused, that if William Ley were appointed a supernumerary clerk at the table, his salary of £500 a year should be borne equally by Hatsell and John Ley. Hatsell had then stated his previous undertaking to Abbot. On 14 March Hatsell reported to the Speaker a similar interview, ending in even sharper disagreement, with J. H. Ley; and he desired the Speaker on the following day to declare his disapprobation of introducing William Ley to the table on any absence of John Ley. He suggested that the Speaker should see J. H. Ley on the matter, but the Speaker wholly declined. On 15 March Abbot noted in his diary with vigorous underlinings what he had then declared to Hatsell: firstly, that the arrangement proposed 'would destroy the comfort of my official life, and that of any subsequent Speaker, since, upon principle, two of a family at the table were objectionable, and upon personal grounds the objection would be much increased in the present circumstances'; secondly, that on any absence from the table of John Ley, his place must be taken by an established senior clerk, and that the House 'would not suffer the Deputy of a Deputy'; and thirdly that, thankful as he would be for the opportunity to recommend a person for the post of 2nd Clerk Assistant on a vacancy, even if that vacancy did not occur, his opinion of the inconvenience and impropriety of the proposed introduction at this time of a supernumerary clerk would remain unaltered. Hatsell had replied that he was not sorry for the Speaker's determination, and had aired the possibility of William Ley's succeeding George White who was clerk of the Committee of Privileges and Elections.[1]

A month later, on 14 April, Hatsell reported an awkward interview with Henry Ley, John Ley's brother and William's father, at which he had been obliged to tell him that, though the Speaker had left him complete freedom of action, he (the Speaker) had stated objections to the proposed arrangement against which he (Hatsell) could not act. Hatsell had refused to enter into these objections, and had declined to see John Ley again, since there was nothing more to be said on the matter, they had not parted very good friends previously, and 'it might be worse next time'. Henry Ley had said that nothing, he was sure, would induce his brother to enter on the subject with the Speaker. 'And so', wrote Abbot, 'the business ended.' But an interesting passage follows these words:

Hatsell told me that he had out of curiosity cast up the amount of money which he had turned over to Ley since 1797, and it amounted to £84,000, out of which he thought Mr Ley might very well make some provision for his nephew answerable to the fortune which he Hatsell had given to his own niece.

William Ley duly married Frances Hatsell in July, in spite of the acrimony and of his having no settled situation. However, George White having died in December 1813, John Ley and young William formally applied to Hatsell requesting the latter's appointment to that situation, 'with allusions by Mr William Ley to his future advancement to the table'. These Hatsell forwarded to Abbot, who noted that he repeated his former objections to the latter point. Hatsell duly appointed William Ley to the position vacated by George White's death, and Abbot recorded in his diary an obviously very chilly occasion when William Ley was brought along by his uncle and formally introduced to the Speaker. The atmosphere of hostility between Abbot and the Leys is illustrated by Abbot's entry for 21 March 1814:

I did not meet the Clerks, as heretofore, in my Secretary's room,

[1] See pp. 77, 220.

Mr Ley no longer being able or ready to give any useful information. Mr Dyson and Mr John Ley not necessary to my despatch of the daily business. And except on special occurrences I mean to discontinue these meetings.

As regards the appointment of a new 2nd Clerk Assistant when —as would obviously occur before very long—John Ley died or had to retire, Speaker Abbot had already made up his mind the previous year. He would hold Hatsell to his previous undertaking and would recommend his own secretary, for whom he twice unsuccessfully tried to find promotion. On 14 July 1813 he wrote in his diary: 'Acquainted Rickman with my intention of recommending him to Hatsell for a seat at the Clerks' Table in the event of old Ley's death or retirement.' But this decision was not divulged to anybody else. John Ley died in June of the following year, whereupon the Speaker, in the course of a letter to Hatsell about appointing a new deputy, reminded him of his undertaking which he had repeated in 1812, refusing the Speaker's offer of release, and said that he had felt himself at liberty to hold out the expectation to another person. Hatsell replied agreeing to appoint 'the Speaker's friend' to the position, whereupon Abbot named Rickman. This, of course, upset Dyson's hope of securing the place for his son on the condition of his own retirement or of ceding to John Henry the Deputy Clerk's place: Hatsell, therefore, could persuade him to accept the Deputy Clerk's position and thus free him (Hatsell) from the disagreeable alternative of appointing John Henry Ley his deputy. The latter became Clerk Assistant, and Hatsell was able to tell Abbot that Rickman's appointment was perfectly agreeable to Dyson and J. H. Ley.

Thus Rickman came to the table of the House, and remained there till he died in 1840: but the Ley family got their way in the end. When Hatsell died and Jeremiah Dyson retired on a pension, John Henry Ley immediately appointed his brother William to be 2nd Clerk Assistant: and, when Rickman died, William Ley became Clerk Assistant, and John Henry Ley appointed his son Henry to the third place at the table. Thus, for ten years, 1840–50, three Leys sat at the table; and if the comfort of the Speaker's official life was thereby destroyed, there is no record of any such

disaster. However, the family conglomeration was thought sufficiently undesirable to be avoided in future; and Lord John Russell,
on J. H. Ley's retirement in 1850, put in a man of his own, Denis
Le Marchant, as Clerk of the House, to the strongly expressed
displeasure of Joseph Hume.[1]

(2)

As will be seen from the itemized return of his emoluments in
1809 which Hatsell made to the Select Committee on Public Expenditure in 1810, and is reproduced in full below, Hatsell exactly
divided with John Ley, his deputy, the Clerk's net income after
all taxes and other incidental payments had been deducted. If,
therefore, he 'turned over' some £84,000 to Ley between 1797
and 1812, as he told Abbot, his own net income for those years
must have amounted to the same total. This means that the Clerk's
average income for those years amounted to £11,200. Abbot
noted in his diary that in 1803 it was above £12,000, and in 1809
Hatsell returned it as £13,827 net. When it is remembered that
Speaker Bromley, reporting to the Treasury in 1713 on the clerks'
memorial of 1709–11,[2] estimated Paul Jodrell's income from his
office at between £300 and £400 a year, the enormous increase
in the Clerk's emoluments during the succeeding century is at
once evident, and necessitates some further attention. When
Stables died in 1732, the Clerk's sources of income were the same
as those mentioned in the clerks' memorial above-mentioned—
namely, his ancient salary of £10 a year from the Exchequer and
fees on private bills and on various proceedings payable at the rates
laid down in the table of fees. The report of the Select Committee on the Fees and Salaries of the Officers of the House who
reported in February 1731/2[3]—a month after Hardinge's appointment as Clerk—appears not to have contained in its appendixes
any estimate by Hardinge of his own income from fees: yet there

---

[1] See Williams, i. 96, 97 and footnote. Lord John Russell at the same time had
decided to abolish the office of Speaker's Counsel and to attach its duties to those
of the Clerk, but had to reverse his decision after the report of a select committee
on the subject in 1851.

[2] See chapter 3, p. 45, and Appendix II, p. 293.

[3] See Appendix IV.

is some indication from the Speaker's return of his receipts from private bill fees given in the appendixes, that in the twenty years since the date of the clerks' memorial the Clerk's income from private bill fees had risen. The Speaker received, under the table of fees, £5 on every single-fee bill, whereas the Clerk not only received £5. 5s. but also the bulk of the ingrossing fees: so that, since the Speaker's fees rose in the four sessions 1727–31 from £400 in the first session to £545 in the last, the Clerk's fees must have been about double.

Yet the report of that committee, to whom Hardinge repre-sented that his only fixed salary was £10 a year, was probably responsible for a new departure. The Treasury money books for 1732 contain a warrant to pay Nicholas Hardinge the sum of £200 'in reward and consideration for his extraordinary service, pains, care and attendance on the House of Commons as Clerk during the session 13 January to 1st June 1732'.[1] In the following year the same sum, under the same rubric, was included in the Civil List payments to the officers of the House of Commons, the total of which rose thereafter from £470 annually to £770.[2] This salary, moreover, like the salaries already awarded to the Clerk Assistant and the four clerks without doors, the housekeeper and messengers, was sessional, not annual: in years when two sessions occurred (e.g. 1727, 1754/5, 1760, 1768, and 1784) all these salaries were doubled. Thus, in 1732 the Clerk for the first time received a sessional salary from the Treasury in addition to his £10 annually from the Exchequer: and this continued till 1833, though by then paid into the fee fund, its origin being already lost in the mists of antiquity.[3] Hatsell continued to receive it when the Clerk's yearly income from fees was averaging over £9,000; but in Hardinge's day an addition from the government to the Clerk's very modest remuneration was suitable enough, and in fact overdue.

[1] T. 53/36, fol. 327. The word 'extraordinary' in these books has no particular significance: it was applied in respect of any extra payment.

[2] This increase of £300 included £100 to a clerk of the Treasury—a matter dealt with in chapter 8.

[3] See the return of emoluments made in 1833 to the Select Committee on the House of Commons Offices by John Henry Ley, the Clerk (H.C. (1833) 648, p. 225). 'Emoluments paid by the Treasury—Beside the ancient Salary of £10 a

Apart, however, from what he could make from the sale of sub-ordinate places (until Dyson ended this practice) and one or two smaller items of profit, such as lavish stationery and the half-guinea for each day's *Vote*,[1] it was from his fees that the Clerk obtained most of his profits. These came from three main sources all authorized by the table of fees: (*a*) fees payable on every private bill and multiplied[2] by the number of parties benefited and of different objects for which powers were sought; (*b*) fees for ingrossment of all bills, public or private; and (*c*) fees for copies of papers, bills, reports, &c., laid upon the table. All these sources would increase as the number of bills increased, and (*c*) would increase as the business of the House and its committees increased. For want of definite figures, which only become available for a certain period at the end of the eighteenth century, it would be futile and wearisome to indulge in elaborate calculations of the exact rate at which these different sources increased, or of the sums which Hardinge, Dyson, Tyrwhitt, and even Hatsell on his first appointment, received in any particular year. A rough guide to the increasing richness of source (*a*) is to be found in the statute book. The yield of source (*b*), since it depended on the length of the bills, could similarly with great labour be calculated from the statute book. Source (*c*) would be quite incalculable, since it entirely depended on the demand, until the practice of printing these papers and reports became so general as to reduce to a minimum the need for manuscript transcription. Then the system of 'copy money', already in force, by which the Clerk, in compensation for loss of fees, received one-

---

year, the Treasury had been accustomed to pay £200 a session to the Clerk. This is still paid, and carried to the fee fund.'

[1] This payment was mentioned in the Speaker's return of his profit from the sale of the *Votes* made to the committee of 1731/2 (Appendix IV, pp. 308–9), and continued at least till 1810. This must originally have been a sort of 'copy money' justified by the printing of the *Votes*. Also, the Treasury minute books from 1783–94 show annual orders to pay Hatsell sums varying from £5 to £10. 16s. for 'making out the minutes of the House for his Majesty last session': cf. p. 42 above for a similar payment to Jodrell at the rate of 8s. a week.

[2] See Appendix III, p. 301. Single fees (£14) on a private bill brought the Speaker £5 and the Clerk £5. 5s. When a bill incurred double, triple, two-double, and even higher multiple fees, both profited in proportion, as did other officers of the House.

half of the total cost of printing these papers, &c., became extremely profitable, as will appear later in this chapter.

Sources (*a*) and (*b*), private bill and ingrossing fees respectively, fluctuated more or less on parallel curves, though it must be remembered that fees were payable for ingrossing public (governmental) bills as well as for ingrossing local or private bills, the Treasury paying the former, and the promoting parties the latter, fees. Also, a private bill such as an estate bill was much shorter than a bill of the 'local bill' type, and consequently much less costly to ingross. In Jodrell's day bills of the type classed as 'local' in the statute book from 1798 onward were extremely few: it was only after 1750 that this type of bill—mainly for road improvements at that date—began rapidly to increase, and with the progress of the industrial revolution continued to increase at such a rate as almost to nullify the normal effect of war in sharply reducing expenditure on private bill legislation. From the figures given in Appendix VI it will be seen that there was a marked slump in the number of local and private bills at the end of the War of American Independence, whereas the figures (except for the year 1804) kept a steady but rising level all through the war against Napoleon, only dropping during the economic stresses of the years immediately after Waterloo. All in all, if we accept the Speaker's report to the Treasury in 1713 that Jodrell's whole income was between £300 and £400 a year, at a time when between forty-five and fifty private Acts found their way annually on to the statute book, it is unlikely that the Clerk's income from fees was anything but moderate before 1750, soon after Dyson succeeded Hardinge. The fact that Dyson valued the Clerk's place at no more than £6,000 corroborates the view that the annual income of the Clerk was not large in 1748. Twenty years later, when Hatsell became Clerk, the number of bills attracting fees had about quadrupled, and at the peak years 1809 and 1810 the number was six times what it had been in 1750.

The return of the Clerk's income from fees and emoluments (not including salary) for the years 1790-9 inclusive given in Appendix VI, shows that the average income was some £7,900 in spite of a much less than average total in 1790. It does not, however, show the Clerk's total income, because, though it obviously included the ingrossing fees, it did not include the 'copy money'. This is made evident by a return of his whole income for 1809 made by Hatsell in 1810 to the Select Committee on Public Expenditure.[1] In this he stated his receipts (less various deductions) under three heads—salary, fees, other emoluments—and then combined all three in a statement of total (less taxes). The three separate heads, stated briefly, were as follows:

		£	s.	d.
Salary.	£210 less fees at the Exchequer	183	2	4
Fees.	Ingrossing fees	7,200	12	0
	Other fees from private bills	4,831	9	4
	Copies of papers and inspections	125	0	4
		12,157	1	8
	Charged for writing the account	332	14	7½
		11,824	7	0½
Other Emoluments.	Paid by printers of the *Votes* at 10s. 6d. a sitting day	51	19	0
	Copy money (less deductions) . .	3,295	15	6
	From the Stationery Office in lieu of trunks formerly supplied[2]	10	10	0
		3,358	4	6

The total account is as follows:

	£	s.	d.
Salary and ancient fee	183	2	4
Fees	11,824	7	0½
Emoluments	3,358	4	6
	15,365	13	10½

deduct	£	s.	d.			
Land tax on office	18	0	4			
Paid to servants of the House . . .	7	6	6			
Property tax	1,512	13	6			
				1,538	0	4
				13,827	13	6½
Paid Mr. Ley moiety				6,913	16	9
Other moiety retained by me				6,913	16	9

2 March 1810

John Hatsell

[1] 9th *Report* of the Committee (H.C. (1810) 373, pp. 200–1).
[2] Hatsell's description of this item in his emoluments was incorrect. The account

The sum entered for copy money does not quite tally with his description of the deductions from the annual sum of £4,300—at which this payment had by then been fixed—in his long note which follows the account.[1] There he says that it was liable to a 5 per cent. fee at the Exchequer (£218 in 1809) and to a deduction of a sum (£785 in 1809) paid to the clerk of the journals and clerks in his office, both of which deductions are made in the account, and also of another sum (£207 in 1809) paid to the clerk of the journals for copies of papers, which deduction is not shown in the account. These three articles, he says, reduced the sum of £4,300 to £3,090, on which property tax (10 per cent. = £309) was payable, reducing the net sum divisible between him and his deputy, John Ley, to £2,781. As Hatsell was then nearly seventy-seven years old, this discrepancy between his statement and his account is understandable: and, in any case, the further deduction would only have reduced the total by some £200, so that Ley and he would each have received, after all deduction including taxes, just over £6,800. The following year, when the total of local and private bills on the statute book was 314, against 304 in 1809, they must have received slightly more.

Hatsell's account also clearly shows how large were the ingrossing fees in comparison with the Clerk's fees on private bills. Bills were drafted at great length in those days, so that a large bill might

put in to the committee by Mr. Wharton of the Treasury, which is Appendix 16 to the 9th *Report*, shows that this sum of £10. 10s. paid to Hatsell was for signing bills of stationery under the authority of Treasury letters. Moreover, it is clear from a letter in the Ley MSS. dated 7 Nov. 1810 that up to that date the trunks were regularly sent down to the Clerk and Clerk Assistant at their homes. This and other letters in the Ley MSS. show that after the 9th *Report* of this committee the Treasury issued some new regulations as to stationery and the practice of selling it to outsiders, in consequence of which Ley instructed George Whittam, the clerk of the journals, that it would be improper henceforth to dispose of the annual set of statutes, the prayer books, and the trunks, which had for a long time been the Clerk's perquisite, and which he had regularly sold for cash. The draft of Ley's letter on the subject, dated 9 Nov. 1810, shows that the trunks were red and were placed on the table of the House, being replaced by new ones at the opening of each session, the old ones going to the Clerk and Clerk Assistant.

[1] See Appendix VII for further details relating to the Clerk's copy money and the cost of printing reports and papers in the eighteenth century, of which it was a fixed proportion.

cost £200 to ingross; and the Clerk took 84 per cent. of all the charges for ingrossment, leaving 16 per cent. to be divided between two minor sinecurists and the actual ingrosser.[1] The account, moreover, clearly reveals the fact that out of his huge income from official sources Hatsell paid less than £1,000 to his subordinate clerks, and that sum only out of the 'copy money' to those in the Journal Office who did the work of preparing the copy of reports and papers for press and of correcting the proofs.

One more emolument of the Clerk remains to be mentioned—his official house. Before 1760 there was no such thing. Up to that date the Clerks of the House lived in their private dwellings—Jodrell, we know, in Chancery Lane, but Stables, Hardinge, and Dyson we know not where—and they received no allowance in lieu of a house. It was Dyson who got the house built. In 1758 he sent a memo. to the Treasury, which was referred by them to the Board of Works, asking for the erection of an additional building for the Clerk of the House on a vacant piece of ground adjoining the 'building allotted him called Cotton Yard'.[2] The site was on part of the site of Sir Robert Cotton's house (hence its name 'Cotton Garden') which lay between the eastern end of St. Stephen's and the Painted Chamber. The plea was successful. On 15 August plans and elevations were passed for the intended house, on 22 August an estimate amounting to £3,159. 4s. was sent to the Treasury, the Treasury fiat was received on 3 October, and eighteen months later, on 11 March 1760, the Board reported to the Treasury that Mr. Dyson's house was finished.[3] It was a plain square box[4] on unsound foundations, which was occupied by successive Clerks of the House, though its existence was threatened by the Surveyor General from 1795 onwards[5] until it was destroyed

---

[1] See below, pp. 228, 230.

[2] P.R.O. Works 4/12 under date 1 Aug. 1758.

[3] Ibid., under the respective dates.

[4] Two drawings by William Capon of the Painted Chamber (Brit. Mus. Crace Collection P. XV, 16 and 17) also show the Clerk's house very clearly.

[5] See the report of a select committee in 1789 (44 C.J. 549) and Sir John Soane's statement before the Select Committee on Committee Rooms in 1825 (H.C. (1825) 515) that the house had been condemned in 1795, when he was Surveyor General.

by the fire of 1834. John Henry Ley[1] described its accommodation
as consisting of a library, a dining-room, and a small store-room
on the ground floor, three rooms on the first floor, and three rooms
with garrets on the second floor. It faced the river on a frontage
of 44 feet, and adjoined the clerks' offices abutting on the south
wall of the Chamber.

(3)

Thus, from the beginning of the nineteenth century till he died,
Hatsell shared with his deputy an income more than double the
Speaker's, almost wholly derived from fees which, though originally justified, had grown fantastically productive. This was an
anomaly long before Hatsell's death. The fee system prevailing
throughout the official services had come under increasingly sharp
criticism from 1780 onwards, with resulting inquiries into abuses
and legislation which was not always calculated to increase efficiency.[2] The Speaker's emoluments had been limited in 1790 by
the Act 30 Geo. III, c. 110 to £6,000 a year; and Abbot, when pro-
testing in his diary that they were insufficient to meet his expenses,
ruefully referred to Hatsell's return in 1810, mentioned above, of
an income more than twice as large for an office involving far less
labour than the Speaker's. Yet the Clerk's office and emoluments
had twice been the subject of legislation, in 1800 and 1812,[3] before
Hatsell died; but neither Act had affected him, because neither was
to come into force as regards the Clerk's fees till the patents of
Hatsell and of Ley, the reversioner, lapsed. Ley died before Hatsell,
but Hatsell's long life delayed the enacted reforms for eight years,
so far as the Clerk was concerned, though they had already been
applied to the Serjeant at Arms and his department. The Act of
1800 created the Commissioners for the House of Commons
Offices, to whom the fees were to be paid; the salary of the Clerk

---

[1] In evidence before the Select Committee on Rebuilding the Houses of Parliament (H.C. (1835) 262). In his return to the 1833 Committee (see p. 108, n. 3,
above) he estimated its pecuniary value at £500 a year.

[2] See Emmeline W. Cohen, *The Growth of the British Civil Service* (London,
1941), pp. 36 sqq.

[3] 39 & 40 Geo. III, c. 92, and 52 Geo. III, c. 11.

was to be £3,000 a year rising after five years to £3,500, the salaries of the Clerk Assistant and the Serjeant were also fixed, and plans were to be prepared for applying the surplus fees to the payment of the officers of the House and providing pensions. The Act of 1812 created a fee fund into which all the fees of the principal officers were to be paid, raised the salary of the Clerk Assistant, provided a salary for the 2nd Clerk Assistant, and maintained the salary of the Clerk at the sums named in the former Act. Abbot in his diary stated that Addington, when Speaker, was the originator of the former Act:[1] what he did not specifically state, but is clearly to be inferred from unpublished passages of the diary, is that both Addington and Abbot, who proposed the motion for the bill at Addington's desire, were moved by a sense of indignation at the sad case of Samuel Gunnell, a committee clerk. The facts of this case[2] must here be related, because they illustrate the position of the lesser clerks at that period, and confirm that Hatsell felt no obligation to supplement, from his own fees, any deficiencies in the earnings of his subordinates, except for certain deductions from the 'copy money' which went to the clerk of the journals and his office more or less of right.[3]

On 2 July 1799 Samuel Gunnell, who was acting as clerk to the Select Committee on Improvements to the Port of London of which Abbot was chairman, put into his hands a letter couched in the correct tone of unctuous humility with which in those days inferiors were expected to address their superiors, begging Abbot as a humane man to take his distressing case into consideration and recommend him to the Chancellor of the Exchequer for temporary relief. He had served twenty-three years, he wrote, as a clerk, yet his emoluments were the same as when he entered; his juniors of less than eight years' service were now on the same footing as himself; his salary was £20, and the advantages otherwise arising from his office were considerably smaller than formerly, mainly because printing had taken the place of copies written by clerks and paid for; also, from the 'greater despatch now used in private business'

---

[1] Colchester, i. 200, 203, 206.
[2] They are to be found in the manuscript diary for 1799 (P.R.O. 30/9/32).
[3] See above, pp. 112–13.

committee work brought in less than before, because the deputy committee clerks now had time to do almost the whole of the business which was formerly done for them by the junior clerks;[1] if sick, he got nothing but his salary; his income had not exceeded £100 for several years past nor would it be more in the current year, the greater part arising from attending public committees for one of the deputy committee clerks, and he did not expect payment for nearly a twelvemonth to come; he had a large family, six children with one more on the way, and had been compelled to sell his small property until all that his father had left for their support had gone, the father having been a clerk for over fifty years. He had applied to Hatsell at different times, but Hatsell had not had it in his power by any official situation to afford Gunnell relief, and 'had expressed his concern that he had been unable to do so'.

This sad tale clearly moved Abbot to inform Addington immediately, for the latter wrote on 3 July asking Abbot to see him on the matter. The House rose and nothing was done, but the case had not gone out of mind. On 3 September Addington wrote from his country house, Woodley, to Abbot professing his anxiety to ease Gunnell's suspense, but saying that the difficulty was to decide the plea upon which assistance was to be founded 'so as to avoid inconveniences from other quarters', i.e. claims from other persons for similar assistance. This letter shows that Addington had already consulted Pitt, who was both Prime Minister and Chancellor of the Exchequer. Another appealing missive from Gunnell, saying that he had no resources left, reached Abbot at the beginning of October. He forwarded it to the Speaker, who replied on the 14th saying that Pitt had kindly interested himself upon it 'even when the torturing intelligence [from Holland] was fresh in his mind'. The upshot was that if the approaching payment to Gunnell—i.e. of the sums accrued to him for his year's committee work—were insufficient to relieve his present needs, and if his allowance could not be augmented without producing inconvenience from the claims of others, Pitt would direct something to be advanced to him out of the King's Bounty. On 9 November Abbot noted in his diary that he had given Gunnell £20 to relieve his immediate

[1] See chapter 7, pp. 141, 153, and 12, p. 246.

wants and attached a sheet of paper inscribed: 'from Mr Abbot's most grateful and most obliged humble servant, Samuel Gunnell'.

Thus, at a time of great national emergency, the Speaker and the Prime Minister had both been exercised by the unfortunate situation of a humble clerk. The following year Gunnell was clerk to Abbot's great committee on the state of the public records, which earned him altogether some £350[1] and no doubt eased his situation: also, when Abbot returned from Ireland to become Speaker, he continued to befriend Gunnell in a way which all but brought him into sharp conflict with Hatsell, as we shall see. The matter was satisfactorily settled, and at the end of 1802 Gunnell reached the safe position of a deputy committee clerk. Yet it is hardly conceivable that this episode, and its reflection upon Hatsell's attitude, was without effect on Addington's resolve in 1800 to propose a measure to limit the fees of the Clerk of the House when the existing patents expired, to which Abbot bore witness in the following entry for 6 May of that year:

The Speaker (in a committee on the Inclosure Bills) opened his plan for limiting the emoluments of the Clerk and Clerk Assistant after the expiration of the interest of the present patentee and reversioner (Hatsell and Ley) and appropriating the surplus to defray the extra allowances of the Speaker and other officers of the House and to improve the situation of the inferior clerks.

On the following day Abbot moved the motion for the bill in the form drafted by Addington. As regards the act of 1812, for which the immediate reason seems to have been a vacancy in the post of Serjeant at Arms, Abbot only noted that the bill was brought in by Perceval at his suggestion. At all events, this was the Act which, on Hatsell's death in 1820, came into operation as regards the Clerk's emoluments; and, though it held small immediate benefit for the junior clerks, it did secure that the surplus of the Clerk's fees, after deducting the Clerk's salary, was appropriated in aid of other clerks' salaries including those of the two Clerks Assistant to which, before that date, Hatsell's fees had not contributed a penny.

[1] See Appendix IX, pp. 329–30.

(4)

The Acts of 1800 and 1812, already referred to, for regulating the House of Commons Offices also fixed the salary of the Clerk Assistant, but in his case, unlike that of the Clerk, this involved no curtailment of his previous revenues which, in fact, did not reach the sum specified in either Act. His income from fees on private bills was never very large, being less than one-fifth of the Clerk's income from the same source, and he had no share in the ingrossing fees or copy money. This is plainly revealed in the striking contrast between the Clerk's and the Clerk Assistant's emoluments for the years 1790–9.[1] Until the middle of the eighteenth century the Clerk Assistant was but meagrely rewarded. Michael Aiskew[2] told the committee on fees and salaries of 1731/2 that, besides his £100 a year from the government, his fees for the last five years had averaged £121. 4s. 3d. excluding fees for attending the committee of elections. These latter, of course, varied very considerably, being largest in the first session of a new Parliament when election petitions were many, and dwindling in subsequent sessions; but there are no data for this period from which these fees can be estimated. John Naylor, Clerk Assistant 1740–4, was not appointed clerk of elections, the post having been given to John Grover on Aiskew's retirement; and it was not until Grover's death in 1749 that John Read, Naylor's successor as Clerk Assistant, received the additional appointment. He held it till the end of 1756, after which date it was never again held by the Clerk Assistant. Leaving this source of income out of consideration, we see that the Clerk Assistant's income was solely made up of the sessional salary of £100 awarded in 1701[3] and his fees on private bills. The *Gentleman's Magazine* on Naylor's appointment called it a place of £500 a year, which was probably an excessive estimate. It was not till 1757 that the government and the House of Commons began to

---

[1] Appendix VI, p. 319. The Clerk Assistant seems to have occasionally received a little copy money. A letter from the clerk of the fees to John Ley, dated 30 Sept. 1788 (Ley MSS.), states that he has received £38. 18s. 6d. copy money from Hughs the printer on Ley's account.

[2] Appendix IV, p. 306.

[3] See chapter 3 p. 48, and Appendix II, p. 292.

be more generous, partly, no doubt, as a consideration for John Read's relinquishing in that same year the clerkship of elections. On 12 May 1757,[1] 'notice being taken in the House that the Clerk Assistant, who has faithfully discharged his duty in the execution of his office, has not had an adequate recompense by the provision already made for him', it was resolved to present a humble address that His Majesty be graciously pleased to order such further provision to be made for the Clerk Assistant as His Majesty should think proper. The result of this was a royal warrant dated 18 May 1758 granting John Read a yearly sum of £200 over and above any existing provision, to commence from the date of the humble address, 12 May 1757. This payment was annual, not sessional, and ran strictly from May to May. On 7 February 1761 a similar warrant was issued granting to Hatsell, who succeeded Read in 1760, £200 a year to be paid quarterly from 9 March 1760.[2]

In 1766 the Clerk Assistant's salary was again increased in consequence of a humble address resolved on 30 May of that year[3] recommending further compensation to John Hatsell. Another £400 per annum was awarded, the payment of which ran from 10 October to the same date the following year, whereas the previously added £200 ran from 9 June to 9 June, thus complicating the Civil List payments.[4] When Hatsell became Clerk in 1768, however, John Ley, his Clerk Assistant, only received the £100+ £200 until in 1772 he was awarded the additional £400 after a humble address.[5] For another twenty years the Clerk Assistant's salary remained at £100 sessional plus £600 annual: in fact, this was the basic salary till 1800. Jeremiah Dyson the younger, who

---

[1] 27 C.J. 888.
[2] T. 52/49, fol. 57, and T. 52/51, fol. 422.   [3] 30 C.J. 839.
[4] Thus, for 1766 the C.L. Accts. show payments to Hatsell of his sessional £100, his annual £200 (one year to 9 June), and £147. 10s. being a quarter and 39 days up to 10 Oct. 1766 of his £400: and for 1788—a year in which there were two sessions—Hatsell as Clerk Assistant till the end of May received £200 double sessional payment, £199. 14s. 5d. for a half-year+177 days on his annual £200, and £264. 9s. 7¼d. for a half-year+59 days on his annual £400. The payments on the two annual salaries were not synchronized till 1784/5 by further Treasury adjustments involving halfpennies.
[5] 33 C.J. 948. The Ley MSS. contain a congratulatory letter on this event from Beaumont Hotham to John Ley, dated 5 June 1772.

became Clerk Assistant in 1797, began on £700 and had no increase till three years later. So that John Henry Ley, giving evidence in 1833, was not far wrong in saying that the average total emoluments of the Clerk Assistant from 1790 to 1800 were £1,100 a year.[1] But John Ley received a considerable bonus towards the end of his service as Clerk Assistant. On 17 May 1792 Mr. Pelham brought his situation before the House and moved an address to provide further recompense.[2] As the result of this he was awarded another £550 that year; and in the following year there was another humble address[3] to continue the allowance of the previous session and to give Ley 'such compensation as his Majesty may think equivalent to an annual allowance of the like amount'. As a result of this recommendation Ley received his additional £550 for two years more, and then a lump sum of £5,814[4] in 1794, after which his basic salary reverted to £700.

Methods changed in 1800 when, by the Act to regulate the House of Commons Offices already mentioned, the Clerk Assistant's salary was fixed at £1,500, rising after five years to £2,000. The method then adopted by the House was to present annually a humble address to issue to the Clerk Assistant such sum as, together with all fees and emoluments, would amount to the clear sum of £1,500.[5] The required sum varied, was reported to the House the following year, and also appears, not in the Civil List Accounts, but in the Treasury Disposition books[6] up to 1813/14.

---

[1] *Report* of the Select Committee on House of Commons Offices (H.C. (1833) 648, qn. 3070). However, if £700 is added to the figures for the Clerk Assistant's fees during that decade given in the return (Appendix VI, p. 319), the average total is more nearly £1,200.

[2] 47 C.J. 802, 804. That the mover was Mr. Pelham was stated by J. H. Ley in the evidence above referred to.

[3] 48 C.J. 993. The Ley MSS. contain a warm letter, dated 7 Aug. (1792 or 1793), from F. Montagu to John Ley referring to this further reward, the proceedings in the committee having been kept secret from Ley.

[4] Shown in 50 C.J. 240 (the account of moneys issued pursuant to addresses) but not in the C.L. Accts.

[5] For the first such address, see 55 C.J. 790, and for its sequel 56 C.J. 774 reporting the issue of £385. 2s. to make up the Clerk Assistant's total to £1,500. This method had already been employed to make the Speaker's salary up to £6,000, at which it had been fixed by the Act 30 Geo. III, c. 110.

[6] The series T. 61/– at the P.R.O.

After five years from 1797 Dyson's salary rose to £2,000, and by the Act of 1812, superseding that of 1800, it rose again to £2,500, but the method of humble address to make up the deficiency continued till 1818.[1]

After 1788 the Clerk Assistant had a source of extra emolument peculiar to himself, namely, as one of the examiners of recognizances and taxers of costs relating to election petitions appointed by the Speaker under Wynn's Act.[2] His fees in this capacity were not large, though they varied with the number of election petitions. A note to the return of Clerk's and Clerk Assistant's fees made in 1799 said that during the whole period 1790–9 the Clerk Assistant's fees from this source amounted to £242. 11s.—an average of less than £25 a year.

The Clerk Assistant was first provided with an official residence in 1780, when John Ley, who had previously lived somewhere in New Palace Yard,[3] was given a ground floor residence in the (then) new stone building in St. Margaret's Street.[4]

The 2nd Clerk Assistant was appointed in 1801 as one of the measures to cope with the addition of 100 new members to the House and the consequential increase of business due to the union with Ireland. Hatsell's letters to John Ley, then his deputy, in 1801 make several allusions to the appointment of Ley's nephew, John Henry, to this post, and to the problem of finding room for him at the table.[5] Until the Act of 1812 came into force in 1820 the 2nd

[1] The variation of the deficiency indicates the variation in the receipts from private bill fees. A table could be drawn up showing this fluctuation for the years 1800–18, but it seemed unnecessary to add to the figures already given in relation to the Clerk's income.

[2] 28 Geo. III, c. 52, which amended and added to Grenville's Act (10 Geo. III, c. 16). See chapter 10, pp. 221–25.

[3] As we know by the addresses of Ley's letters to Hatsell 1769–72 in the Ley MSS. The house was in the north-east corner of New Palace Yard, near the old Stationery Office, as appears from the Westminster Rate Books. An entry in Abbot's manuscript diary for 3 May 1810 bears witness to Hatsell's abode when he first became Clerk Assistant: 'Hatsell told me that when he lodged at Payne's near the Mews Gate, he always saw Mr Onslow's state coach pass at 12 o'clock punctually through the Mews, and he Hatsell immediately followed in a chair.' This must have been in 1760–1, the last session in which Onslow was Speaker.   [4] See chapter 5, p. 96, n. 1.

[5] e.g. 12 July 1801: 'I am glad to hear that your nephew had so pleasant a recep-

Clerk Assistant's salary was provided by a humble address each session for the payment of a clear sum (i.e. not subject to the deduction of fees at the Exchequer). J. H. Ley received £1,000 a year 1801–6, £1,500 1807–10, and £2,000 1810–14. Since the Act of 1812 fixed the salary at £1,500 rising after five years to £2,000, John Rickman in 1814 began at £1,500. John Henry Ley, as 2nd Clerk Assistant, had no official residence; but Rickman, who had been provided with a house as Speaker's Secretary, remained in that house as 2nd Clerk Assistant from 1814–20. His successors in that office had no official residence.

(5)

In conclusion of this chapter, a word must be said of the Clerk's functions and of any developments in the composition of his department as a whole. The only new duty imposed upon him during the period 1726–1820 was the printing of the *Journals*, a matter which will be dealt with in a subsequent chapter. Hatsell, describing the Clerk's duties in the second volume of his *Precedents of Proceedings*,[1] says that they are summed up in the words of his oath, that he shall 'make true entries, remembrances, and journals of the things done and passed in the House of Commons'. This, he added, comprehended his being attentive to the other clerks under him, that they were exact in making the proper entries of the proceedings of committees on the door of the House. He said the Clerk Assistant took note of orders and proceedings of the House in minute books, from which the *Votes* were compiled under the direction of the Speaker. At the end of the session it was the Clerk's duty to see that the *Journal* of the session was properly made out and fairly transcribed from the minute books, the printed *Votes*, and the original papers that had been laid before the House, which was commonly done during the summer recess. The Clerk signed addresses, orders, and bills. As for the Clerk

tion from Mr Addington, and that everything has been settled so much to your and his satisfaction. . . . It rests with you to find a place for him at the Table, where he may be of use, and yet in nobody's way; *this* appears to me a matter of some difficulty.' 26 July 1801: 'I am glad to hear that the Speaker and you have settled the size and shape of the Table to both your satisfactions' (Ley MSS.).

[1] Hatsell, ii. 255 sqq.

Assistant, it had 'always been the practice for the Clerk Assistant, and not the Clerk, to officiate' in committee of the whole House, whence the office of Clerk Assistant was 'much the most laborious of the two, as the principal business of the House of Commons, particularly all inquiries into matters of trade, the state of any colonies, the East India Company, etc. is generally carried on in Committees'. The Clerk Assistant's duty was to make out the reports from these committees.

All in all, if Hatsell's statement be compared with the description of the Clerk's duties in any recent edition of Erskine May, it will be seen that there is little difference, except for the comparatively modern addition that the Clerk is the accounting officer for the House of Commons. One might say, indeed, that, except for supervision of the printed *Journal*, the Clerk's Office had reached its full stature by the time of Jodrell's retirement, and that any further development was no more than that of keeping pace with changes in the proceedings and practices of the House. To be learned in the *Journals* was the Clerk's one essential attribute, in which Jeremiah Dyson, by common repute, and Hatsell, as his great work shows, excelled.

The Clerk's department, according to Hatsell's account,[1] consisted of a clerk of the committees of privileges and elections, with deputies for the latter, four principal clerks without doors to attend committees, each with a deputy, two clerks directing the Ingrossing Office, with writing clerks under them, a clerk to collect and distribute fees, and a clerk who had custody of the journals and papers, with several writing clerks under him. Apart from the clerk of elections, whose activities had been multiplied and whose deputies necessitated by Grenville's Act of 1770,[2] this account gives a total of only twelve clerks, of whom eight attended committees, with an indefinite number of writing clerks attached to the Ingrossing Office and the Journal Office; and it divides them into four offices, namely, the Committee Office, the Ingrossing Office, the Fees Office, and the Journal Office. In subsequent chapters each of these will be investigated: and it will be seen that, had Hatsell written his account any time after 1800, the total would

---

[1] Ibid., pp. 274–75.   [2] See chapter 10, pp. 221–25.

have been considerably enlarged, that he was singularly uninformative about the Fees Office even in 1781, and that there was a considerable difference between the writing clerks attached to the Ingrossing Office, who were purely scribes, and those attached to the Journal Office, who were what would now be called 'on the establishment'. On the other hand, if the account had been written by Nicholas Hardinge, the total might have been smaller. From the available information, however, it is almost impossible to tell when, in the earlier part of this period, changes and increases occurred. For instance, it is only in 1775 that the *Court and City Register* gives the names of the four deputies to the principal clerks without doors: yet we know from Robert Yeates's will in 1769 that John Rosier was then his deputy.[1] And it is only from 1796 onwards that this annual publication gives the names of the 'other clerks', some twelve in number, who held no definite office, though evidence of other kinds show that many of them were clerks long before that date. Again, it is inconceivable that, even in 1781, the clerk of the fees had no assistants, or that the clerk of the journals had not already at least one experienced assistant, destined to become his successor.

It is evident from Hatsell's letter to Ley in 1772[2] that he kept a close eye upon his staff, their deserts and their capabilities: and the conclusion to which I am driven is that the account of his staff in his *Precedents of Proceedings* was somewhat perfunctory. By 1811, when the clerks named in the *Court and City Register*, excluding the Clerks Assistant, numbered twenty-seven (but including two separate sinecures held by one person), the Speaker was satisfied that the establishment was sufficient and adequately paid, as can be seen from the following quotation from Lord Colchester's *Diary*:[3]

Sir James Graham came by appointment to state the general dissatisfaction amongst Members attending Committees upon Private Bills for the want of a sufficient number of *competent* clerks; complaining of

[1] See above, chapter 4, p. 73.
[2] See above, p. 88.
[3] Op. cit. ii. 324–25. The list of clerks given on the verso of this entry in the manuscript diary is in P.R.O. 30/9/35.

the inadequacy of the establishment and of their inadequate pay towards encouraging a succession of qualified persons.

As to *number*, I satisfied him that the number now actually in attendance was equal to the average demand of Committees sitting upon any one day for the largest number of Bills, viz. at this time seven shorthand writers and eleven clerks, of which latter four were *extra* hands brought for the occasion out of other branches of the clerks' offices, but that I had expressed my opinion that the establishment did now require to have four such clerks added for constant Committee service, instead of resorting to extra hands taken from offices where their services were also wanted.

As to *pay*, I showed him my abstract of the returns made to the Committee of public expenditure last year; exhibiting a graduated succession of pay from the junior rank to the highest, beginning with boys at £35 and £70, to lads at £100, and grown men from £200 to £700 a year, with four retiring sinecure offices of each £800 a year nett, for such as leave off usually between fifty and sixty years of age; and three great situations, viz. the Journal Office, Election Committees, and Clerk of Fees, which in emoluments fixed, or almost necessarily incident to their situation, cannot be less than £1500 to £3500 a year.

Upon this view he expressed his surprise and satisfaction, and his determination to assure Mr Ley that he would be no party to giving him any trouble upon the subject, hoping at the same time that before another session such addition would be made to the permanent establishment.

The abstract of returns made to the committee of the previous year to which this passage alludes is fortunately preserved in the manuscript diary, the returns themselves not having been printed in the reports of the committee. I therefore give it in full as showing the size of the Clerk's department in 1811, although I shall defer most of my comment upon it until later chapters which deal with the various offices in the department. It is on the verso of the entry quoted above for 10 April 1811:

Income 1809.	Hatsell and Ley between them	£15,214[1]
	Dyson	2,078
	J. H. Ley	1,509

[1] Hatsell's return (see above, p. 111) put the gross income at £15,365 odd.

1 Clerk of Fees (besides Private Business and
   custody of whole Fees)   1,665
1 Clerk of Elections   average unknown
1 Clerk of the Journals (besides house)   1,278
4 Sinecure Committee Clerks   each   863
2 Clerks Ingrossing Office, each   711
4 Dep. Committee Clerks from   £621 to £518 each
1 Acting Dep. Cee Clerk   482
6 Clerks to Clerk of the Journals,   £534, 232, 213,
                                          169, 149, 102
2 Clerks in Ingrossing Office   456 & 251
2 Clerks to Clerk of Fees   £71, £35.

2 others newly appointed and profits not settled, viz. one
to Clk. Fees and one to Election Cee Clerk but paid out
of the private business of their employers

N.B. Private Bill Office established 1811. First Clerk
£800, second 300, third 150, guaranteed at the above
sums but probably will be more.

N.B.N.B. Afterwards were paid more for this year's
services.

The facts which will be adduced in the succeeding chapters will
show that Abbot's complacency as to adequate and well-regulated
pay was misplaced: the truth being that it was ill regulated and
inadequate except for clerks in the higher positions. Also, as will
be seen, most of the pay of the clerks came from piece-work remunerated in a variety of ways, and very often necessitating unreasonable hours of work. And the subordinates of the well-paid
Hatsell had, it appears, no prescriptive right to a holiday in the
long summer recess. A letter in the Ley MSS. from George
Whittam, clerk of the journals, to John Ley, dated 18 October
1803, describes a review in Hyde Park of the brigade of which the
Bloomsbury Corps of Volunteers, in which many of the clerks
were enrolled, formed part; and, after recording the satisfaction
expressed by General the earl of Harrington at the behaviour of
the brigade, he continues:

The military engagements of the clerks, during the recess, have certainly taken up some of their time, but, as far as I can judge, not more
than would have been necessarily appropriated to moderate recreation,

and I really believe it has been the means of preventing interruptions to business from other causes, and also induced some to remain in town all the summer, who would otherwise have asked for a temporary leave of absence, which from the reasonableness of the request could hardly have been denied.

7

THE COMMITTEE CLERKS

(1)

THE Committee Office is undoubtedly the oldest of the five offices which together make up the department of the Clerk of the House. The account of that department's growth and organization, therefore, rightly begins with the committee clerks who were the first under-clerks to receive denomination as regular officers of the House. We must go back, for a moment, to the 'four under-clerks without doors', John Hookes, George Cole, James Courthope, and Hicks Burrough, whose names first appear in the Treasury books in 1696 and to whom some attention was paid in an earlier chapter,[1] in order to obtain a measure of later developments. James Courthope's minute book, as I pointed out in that chapter, proves that from the beginning they were committee clerks. They received a salary from the Civil List for attending committees on public business, and fees for attending those on private bills. Neither source of income was large, as their petitions for larger recompense show; and they can hardly have conceived how greatly, in a hundred years, the importance and emoluments of their positions would grow, so that by 1772 the Clerk of the House would refer to them[2] as the 'Chief Clerks', and by the end of the century two-thirds of the committee fees on private bills would provide each of them— by then a sinecurist in retirement—a quite comfortable income. Still less could they have imagined the Committee Office of today, organized, paid, and pensioned like a branch of any other civil department, with a telephone on every desk, a staff of shorthand-typists, a body of the most highly skilled shorthand note-takers at hand to take down evidence verbatim, and the printing-press of the Stationery Office ready to print evidence and reports with

---

[1] See pp. 49, 52–57.   [2] See Hatsell's letter to Ley on p. 88.

great speed and accuracy—an office in constant touch with many government departments, involving a large correspondence and the amassing and filing of much information, and one upon whose members now devolve, as a matter of course, duties of which James Courthope would not have dreamed, such as the writing of memoranda and précis, the drafting of a chairman's draft report on any subject referred to a select committee, the conducting of correspondence in the chairman's name, or even the planning of tours of investigation.

However, it is of less importance to consider the differences between the situation of Jodrell's four under-clerks and their successors of today than clearly to grasp, from such evidence as we have, the duties and resources of the former. Any conclusions arrived at will hold good, at least, up to 1730. The emoluments of the four clerks without doors, as I shall now call them, have already been dealt with for Jodrell's day, and need little more than brief recapitulation. John Hookes and his three colleagues received from the Civil List at first 100 guineas between them, and after 1700 this sessional payment was raised to £200, beyond which it never rose. Only on one occasion, in 1713, did the Treasury make a concession, which took the form of an extra session's salary to compensate them for the loss of fees on private naturalization bills 1709–11 while the General Naturalization Act of 1709 remained in force. Their other income was derived from the committee clerks' fees, as fixed by the table of fees, for attendance on private bill committees. In respect of any particular bill these fees varied mainly with the number of sittings of the committee; but at the beginning of the eighteenth century, before certain types of local bill became hotly contested and committee proceedings upon them long drawn-out, the committee clerk seldom earned above £3 on a single bill, and usually less. This can be seen from the early bills of costs quoted in Appendix V. Thus, the Commons committee clerk's fees on the Balliol College Act, 1695, amounted to £2. 17s. including the gratuity called 'expedition'; those on the Farington Estate Act, 1698, to £2. 0s. 2d., and those on Lady North's Naturalization Act, 1706, to £1. 7s. 6d. The Corporation of London were always generous with their gratuities: the City

Remembrancer's bills of costs in 1712 and 1718 show that they paid Jodrell about 50 per cent. more than the normal fees on a private bill, and their payments to the committee clerk on those two occasions were £4. 6s. 8d. and £7. 5s. respectively, while James Courthope got another two guineas for extra trouble.

I have made a conjectural estimate from Courthope's minute book of the fees that he would have received for attending thirteen private bill committees in the session 1698–9, and it amounts to £20. In the preceding session, when he attended eighteen such committees, his fees would hardly have reached £30—the very sum which, in their petition of 1701, the four clerks without doors mentioned as the limit of their earnings from private business. In the next twenty years private business increased, but only slightly: and, if the normal yearly earnings of a committee clerk from fees were £90 in 1709, as the clerks' memorial alleged, it is not likely that they averaged much above £100 by 1730. In this connexion, it should be noted that select committees on public bills and matters of public interest were, at that time, slightly more numerous than those on private bills. This is clearly shown by Courthope's minute book. On a rough computation from the *Journals*, Courthope attended about a quarter of the total number of committees appointed—sixty-four in all for the two sessions. In the session 1697–8 his committees on public bills or matters totalled twenty-two against eighteen on private bills; and in the session 1698–9 the proportion was eleven to thirteen. Moreover, some of the committees on public matters lasted much longer than those on private bills, and involved considerably more work.[1] Yet, for attending these, John Hookes and his colleagues received no more than their sessional salary. John Hookes alone, as senior of the four clerks without doors, derived an additional 10s. out of every private bill fee as collector and distributor of the fees. This collection of fees was still the privilege of the senior of the four clerks without doors

[1] e.g. the committees of 1698 attended by Courthope on Claims on Lottery Tickets and on Hammered Money (an inquiry into all the mints), and those of 1699 on Exportation of Wool and on Newfoundland Trade. The very long report (12 C.J. 210–34) of the committee on Foreign Lustrings and Clandestine Trade, which Courthope did not attend, shows that a committee clerk did a good deal of work for his salary (at that date) of 25 guineas.

in 1732,[1] and it may have continued till a separate collector of fees was appointed in 1775.[2]

What can we gather about the other resources of the four clerks without doors and the manner in which they carried out their duties? The only discoverable resource was the sessional allowance of stationery,[3] which was ample enough, including as it did a quire of paper daily, a serge bag, unlimited wax, wafers and pens, though only one pencil. Stationery was in those days, and long after, a valuable perquisite, so that the allowance was drawn to the full, and the surplus sold at the end of the session.[4] It is therefore a little surprising to find that James Courthope made his minute book last for two sessions, whereas he could have had a new one in 1698: probably at that period the stationery allowance was not so lavish as in 1732. Be that as it may, the question remains where the four clerks without doors kept their standishes, pens, wax, wafers, and sand, for they could hardly have carried them about all day in the serge bag. In other words, had they an office where each had a desk? So far as evidence goes, they had no office even in 1730: but, since they must have sat somewhere, the possible alternatives are either that they still sat at a table in the outer lobby, as did the Elizabethan under-clerks, or that they had some cubby-hole in the outer wall of St. Stephen's of which there is no record. Various indications in Courthope's minute book prove that his committees all met in the Speaker's Chamber, as, presumably, did those

[1] See Appendix IV, p. 310.

[2] The destruction of all the fee records in the fire of 1834 makes it impossible to be certain of this. Even in 1732 Zachary Hamlyn received and paid out the Speaker's fees and those of the clerk to the Committee of Elections (see Appendix IV). Hamlyn (see pp. 39-40, 52) was clerk of the papers, though not officially so designated; and it is significant that John Rosier was clerk of the journals when he was translated to the post of collector of fees. It may be that, at some time between 1732 and 1775, the collection of all fees passed from the senior of the four clerks to the clerk of the journals and papers. In 1746 (see Appendix IX) money was paid by the Treasury to Samuel Littlemore, then clerk of the papers, for distribution among several clerks and other officers in respect of a select committee.

[3] Appendix IV, p. 310.

[4] Cf. the remarks on this head in the 9th *Report* of the Select Committee on Public Expenditure of 1810 (H.C. (1810) 373, p. 187) and the evidence of the clerk of the fees as to the universal practice of selling surplus stores (ibid., pp. 214, 215, and Appendixes 17 and 19).

attended by his three colleagues; and it is a matter of conjecture how all the select committees managed to dovetail during the session in the occupation of this single committee room.

Judged by modern standards, James Courthope's minute book was not a mirror of good arrangement and accuracy. He wrote, except when hurried, in a very legible round hand, so neat and well aligned as a rule that he must have copied his minutes from a rough draft. The dates were not always accurately entered, and sometimes no date was entered at all. He frequently omitted to enter the chairman's name and the presentation of, and formal agreement to, the committee's report: only in two instances out of sixty-four possible did he record the choosing of the chairman, and there is no entry of questions being formally put or of any vote in committee. Nevertheless, this minute book shows that, especially as regards private bills, select committees, even as early as 1697, were conducted with a considerable degree of formality and precision. One of the most interesting features of this minute book, from a historical point of view, is that it contains rough notes of evidence[1] given by witnesses which were not reported to the House and minutes of certain committees from whom no report was entered in the *Journal*, which it thus supplements. This feature also reveals that a committee clerk of that time assumed it as part of his duty to note down the gist of a witness's evidence, and of counsel's speeches in a contested private bill, and that normally there was nobody else to perform those functions which, eventually, became the business of the official shorthand-writer to the House and his staff. Yet, owing to the very fact that none of this evidence noted by Courthope was reported to the House, and that during the two years covered by his minute book he did not attend a committee who reported their evidence at some length, of which the twelfth volume of the *Journals* contains several instances,[2] a doubt may well be entertained whether a select committee of that time, engaged in an inquiry which necessitated the

---

[1] See *Courthope*, 28–32, 37–40, 44–47, 53, 59–63, 68, 69, 71, 75–77, 80–83.

[2] See 12 C.J. 210–34, 257–58, 275–76; and for earlier *Journal* entries of long and detailed reports of committees see 10 C.J. 113–16 Prideaux's claim, 156–60 Grievances of the City; 11 C.J. 545–49 Halfpence and Farthings, 511–14 Highway Laws, 675–80 Abuses of Prisons.

hearing of many witnesses, relied only upon their clerk to write down and reduce to an ordered précis voluminous and important evidence which they had determined to report. Without assistance such a task would have been impossible to carry out: the question is whether the chairman and other members of the committee themselves took down witnesses' examinations in writing, or whether other occasional clerks were employed for the purpose.

Some light is thrown upon this question by MS. Stowe 373 in the British Museum which has never been printed or edited, and of which I give a précis in Appendix VIII, it being a document of some importance for the history of procedure. It contains the minutes of proceedings of the Select Committee on the State of the Gaols in their inquiry into the charges made to the committee against Sir Robert Eyre, the lord chief justice of common pleas, in 1730, as recorded by L. Kenn, who attended the committee at their command to take down the examination of witnesses and the proceedings of the committee (including speeches) in shorthand. The manuscript is by Kenn, and is a far fuller record of a select committee than in any minutes of Courthope. There is, in fact, no document resembling it till the minutes of proceedings of select committees began to be published with the evidence after 1852.

So far as the committee clerks and committee practice in 1730 are concerned, the salient points to be gathered from this record are the following:

(*a*) Three different clerks attended this committee, Parker, Kenn, and Edwards, only one of whom (Kenn) is known from any list of clerks or other documents. It appears that Parker was the official clerk to the committee, who took down the names of members attending and kept the official minutes; Kenn, being a shorthand-writer, was called in for the occasion, but Edwards had attended some time before and had drawn up the final versions of examinations of witnesses;

(*b*) The shorthand clerk attended at the command of the committee, and apparently supplanted the official clerk till this particular inquiry was completed and the report agreed to;

(*c*) The chairman took a deposition of a witness as a justice of the bench, and then read it to the committee;

(*d*) The examination of witnesses at the committee, before Kenn was called in, had been taken down by several members, and from their notes a final draft was dictated by a member to one of the clerks. This final draft was signed by the witness before being read to the committee;

(*e*) The dictation of a note of a witness's examination took place in the committee room while another witness was being examined by the chairman;

(*f*) The draft report was prepared, not by the chairman, but by a sub-committee appointed, after debate, for this purpose;

(*g*) The speeches made at this debate in the committee were taken down verbatim;

(*h*) On one occasion the committee not only sat in the House itself (which was a not unusual proceeding on the part of a large committee in an afternoon, when the House was not sitting), but sat there in the morning, having moved the House the night before to adjourn for that express purpose over the next day. It does not appear in the *Journal* for 29 April 1730 that any formal motion was made to this effect;

(*i*) A long-hand account of all these proceedings was produced by Kenn, and it is to be wondered, on what authority, and whether this manuscript was the only copy made, or whether each member of the committee received one.

Some of these points are extremely striking, particularly the method employed for taking the examination of a witness before a shorthand-writer was called in: this resembles the proceeding in a court where civil law prevailed, rather than that of the common law or of a parliamentary committee. Presumably the committee had employed the same method in their inquiries into the state of the gaols; and it was probably the usual method at that time when a committee's inquiry was of a judicial nature, since many appendixes to reports of committees printed in the *Journal* contain depositions signed by the witness. There is no trace of this method in Courthope's minutes, even when the inquiry was into a charge found to be baseless.[1]

[1] As in the case of Robert Barton's petition against forestallers of corn whose complaint against him was found to be malicious and groundless (*Courthope*,

(2)

So far as the committee clerks themselves are concerned, this manuscript poses a problem. Courthope's minute-book proves conclusively that at its date (1697–99) select committees of inquiry into matters of public interest were attended by one of the four 'under-clerks without doors', as they were then styled; and, so far as official records show, these officers of the House received no additional allowances from the Treasury for such attendances or for any expenses incurred, nor were any other persons named as having performed, or having been paid for, similar services for similar committees. Now, the names of these four under-clerks, styled later the 'Chief Clerks without Doors attending committees', can be given with certainty for every year from 1696 onwards, as my Appendix I shows; and the names of Parker, Kenn, and Edwards who attended the Gaols Committee in 1730 never appear among them. I do not believe that the four under-clerks had any regular deputies so early as 1730, for reasons which will appear;[1] and, if these three men had been regular deputies, they would have almost certainly have succeeded, as did the later deputies, to higher and identifiable positions on the establishment. It is strange, in any case, that of the four under-clerks of 1730— Hicks Burrough, Edward Jodrell, John Hookes the younger, and William Hester—not one attended the important committee

80–81). Courthope's minutes for 17 Apr. 1699 record evidence given before the committee. But see 20 C.J. 84, 88: when the chairman of the committee appointed to inquire into the Harburg Lottery reported that a witness had much prevaricated and asked for power to examine witnesses in the most solemn manner, the House ordered that members of the committee who were justices of the peace for the county of Middlesex should examine in the most solemn manner such witnesses as they thought fit. It would appear that this solemn examination by members of a committee who were justices of the peace was equivalent to examination upon oath, a process which (except in election committees under Grenville's Act of 1770) the House of Commons had no power to exercise till the passing of the Parliamentary Witnesses Act, 1858 (21 & 22 Vic., c. 78) which empowered private bill committees in the Commons to hear evidence on oath, and of the Parliamentary Witnesses' Oaths Act, 1871 (34 & 35 Vic., c. 83) which gave that power to all committees.

[1] See pp. 141–42 below. The Thomas Parker who was a deputy committee clerk and died in 1806, and who was mentioned in Hatsell's letter to Ley of 1772, cannot have been Kenn's colleague in 1730.

whose proceedings on the charge against Sir Robert Eyre are described in Kenn's manuscript: instead, three other clerks appear performing various functions in the committee's service, and thereafter disappear from history's view.

What status, then, had Parker, Kenn, and Edwards? What happened to them later? Was there, at that time, a body of unattached clerks, including shorthand-writers like Kenn, available to the House for various purposes, especially for inquiries of a judicial kind? If so, who paid them, since neither the House nor the Clerk of the House had any funds for that purpose? On these questions another manuscript document, and a series of entries in the King's Warrant Books[1] and other records which confirm it, must now be brought up. The evidence thus provided, though it does not answer all the questions, enables me to show, in general, the development through the eighteenth century of the arrangements for clerical services to select committees on public matters. The document, which I reproduce with certain additions in Appendix IX, is among the Colchester papers in the Public Record Office. It is a list of precedents for the payment of allowances to clerks and other persons for attendance on important select committees of inquiry between 1721 and 1789, which was obviously supplied by the Treasury to Charles Abbot (later Speaker) when he was chairman of the Select Committee on the State of the Public Records in 1800. As can be seen, I have verified all its references and, in footnotes to the Appendix, have given the necessary facts about the respective committees therein referred to.[2]

Assuming that the first payment authorized on this list of precedents was the earliest which the Treasury could discover, we see that from 1721 onwards special allowances were from time to time sanctioned by the Treasury Board for the expenses and inci-

[1] The series T. 52/– in the P.R.O.
[2] I had collected a good deal of this evidence from the Treasury books and the C.L. Accts. before I discovered this valuable document which I should, in any case, have had to check by the Treasury records. It provided some cases which I had missed, but my independent researches enabled me to supply others which the Treasury compiler of the document had himself missed. Incidentally, it is connected with the case of Samuel Gunnell with which I dealt in the preceding chapter, pp. 115–17.

dents attending the service of certain select committees of the
House. The entries up to and including that of 1748 show that,
with one exception, the subjects of inquiry were either notorious
public scandals or the conduct of persons whom it was desired to
impeach, which involved the taking of copious evidence, written
and oral, the summoning of officials as witnesses, and much clerical
work. The general form of the warrant, as copied into the Treasury
Books, was an authorization to pay Mr. X the sum of £Y without
account 'to defray the whole charge of clerks, officers and incidents attending the service of the Committee appointed to . . . in
such manner and according to such orders as the said X shall receive from Z Chairman of the Committee'. The warrant to John
Burman in respect of the committee of inquiry into Lord Orford's
conduct in 1742 mentions 'house rent and other incidents'. In one
or two instances there was a variant form by which the issue was
stated to be intended 'to recompense the clerks and other officers
who have attended the service of the Committee appointed to . . .
and for defraying the necessary expenses of such clerks and officers'.
The chairman of the committee gave directions for the distribution of the money, which no doubt the committee had already
approved, and it was on his application that the Treasury Board
considered and, if they thought fit, sanctioned the allowance.[1]
This system of lump-sum payment to cover all expenses of a committee was out of date by 1800, as will be seen, but it was employed
in that year for the special case of the Select Committee on the
State of the Public Records, and Abbot's account of his disbursements in the Colchester papers (see Appendix IX) shows that the
expenses included sums amounting to £93. 10s. 6d. for fees and
stamps at the Treasury and Exchequer[2] and to £650 for payments
to persons other than the committee clerk.

[1] There are many instances of such applications in the Treasury books at later
dates, but the earliest is in *Cal. T.P. 1729–30*, p. 67, recording the receipt of a letter
from James Oglethorpe, chairman of the Gaols Committee, to Sir Robert Walpole
desiring the payment of £700 to Alderman Child for the pay of clerks and officers
who attended that committee. See also n. 1, p. 138.

[2] So that the issue, in this instance, was not 'without account', a phrase which
implied exemption from all these fees. Where a round sum was intended to be received, the probable amount of the fees was added to the sum to be issued. The
House voted £1,000 to Abbot for the expenses of this committee (55 C. J. 790). But

As regards the payees of the sums named in these warrants, the
early practice clearly varied. Lucas Kenn, the earliest recorded, was
undoubtedly a clerk by profession, and that is all I can learn about
him, since he disappears from view after 1730 when he wrote his
above-mentioned account of the Gaols Committee's proceedings,
and presumably received some remuneration from the £1,100
which was paid to Alderman Child for the service of this committee.[1] Some of the other payees were of a wholly different
category. Francis Child, the younger of that name, was a banker
(afterwards Lord Mayor and knight) and one of the members for
Middlesex. Joseph Tudor was a legal official of the Exchequer
Court and of the Excise and Customs of Scotland,[2] and John
Sharpe was Solicitor to the Treasury. It is understandable that legal
officers should have been employed to draw up articles of impeachment, and Tudor's connexion with the Scottish Customs explains his association with the Select Committee on Frauds in the
Customs whose inquiry preceded the introduction of Walpole's
unpopular Excise Bill. On the other hand, John Burman, the
payee of the money sanctioned in 1732 for the services of the committee who inquired into the affairs of the Charitable Corporation,
though not then in an identifiable position as a Commons clerk,
became one of the four under-clerks without doors in 1742;[3] and
after 1733 all the names of payees on the list, with the exception of

---

this did not cover the huge expense of printing: Hansard was paid £3,913. 8s. 1d.
for the engravings alone (T. 29/77, fol. 125, dated 12 Nov. 1800).

[1] In Kenn's account he stated that he was employed by the committee as a shorthand-writer. Also, in *Cal. T.P. 1720–28*, p. 215, a Treasury minute is recorded on
the application of the chairman of the committee on the project commonly called
the Harburg Lottery and of three other committees recommending the clerk,
Mr. Lucas Kenn, for recompense for attendance on the committee. The minute,
dated 17 June 1723, runs: 'My Lords cannot encrease the charge of clks beyond
w^t it has hitherto been.' There is nothing to show what it had 'hitherto been'.
However, the bounty of £150 to Kenn in 1725 for unspecified services may signify
that the Treasury relented. For the committee on the Harburg Lottery, which
they stigmatized in their report as an 'infamous and fraudulent undertaking', see
20 C.J. 34, 88, 114–25 (report), 135, 141.

[2] See *Cal. T.P. 1735–38*, p. 459, Tudor's appointment as secretary to the Customs
and Salt Commissioners, Scotland, on relinquishing the post of agent for the
Scottish Exchequer Court and Commissioners for Excise and Customs.

[3] See p. 70.

John Sharpe, are those of Commons clerks already holding definite offices. John Grover was almost certainly ingrossing clerk in 1733 and afterwards became clerk to the Committee of Privileges and Elections; Samuel Littlemore was clerk of the papers, Newdigate Poyntz and Robert Yeates[1] were among the four clerks; and all the later names on the list are similarly identifiable. Unfortunately, except for Abbot's account of disbursements in 1800, no document exists to show how these lump sums were expended, or how much the committee clerk himself received in particular instances. It is curious, too, that, whereas the regular committee clerks must have contemporaneously been attending committees on public matters without any extra remuneration, individual colleagues could receive these additional advantages.

However, a more striking instance of this inequality is the payment to John Naylor in 1737, when he was already one of the four clerks without doors, of £50 for his own service in attending two select committees of the session.[2] This was a different type of payment, being a reward to a committee clerk personally for services in attending a committee. The payments to Poyntz in 1746 and 1755 were similar in kind, and he too was at the time one of the four clerks. As we shall see, this type of payment became the more usual until it developed into a regular practice with a fixed rate: but in 1737 it was unusual, and has no counterpart till 1746, nor have I discovered any Treasury minutes or letters giving the reason for this new departure. It is not till the second payment of £50 to Poyntz, in 1755, that we find the reason for this payment, which was that several members of the House of Commons had made a representation desiring that a 'gratuity' be given to Poyntz as clerk of the committee.[3] On the other hand, the payments to Poyntz in respect of the Militia Acts and to Yeates in 1755 for preparing sundry bills were for services of a wholly different kind, which will be discussed in my next chapter where I deal with the

[1] See respectively pp. 70–71, 72–73.
[2] For Naylor, who afterwards became Clerk Assistant and subsequently a D.D. and Vice-Provost of King's College, Cambridge, see pp. 68–69 and Appendix IX, p. 331.
[3] The marginal note to this entry in Appendix IX gives the reference to the Treasury minute.

Treasury's employment of Commons clerks as its agents in the House.

Before continuing my study of the system of paying clerks for attendance on committees on public matters, it will be convenient to consider, in the light of the above evidence, what light it throws upon the development of what became the Committee Office, or Committee Clerks' Office. It is clear that during the time of Walpole's long administration some change must have taken place in the conditions to which James Courthope's minute-book and the clerks' memorial of 1709–11 bear witness. The memorial makes no mention of any other clerks attending committees beyond the four under-clerks, nor does the return attached to the report of the Select Committee on Fees and Salaries in 1732.[1] None the less, Lucas Kenn was the payee of the allowance granted for the service of the South Sea Committee in 1721, he was clerk of several select committees, including that on the Harburg Lottery—a complicated inquiry—in 1723, and in 1730 he attended the Gaols Committee at one of their four inquiries, for which function he was not appointed by the Clerk of the House but, as he says, 'commanded by the committee', the appointed clerks being Edwards and Parker of whom, but for his account, we should have heard nothing. Thanks to Kenn's account we know what clerks must have received recompense out of the £1,100 paid to Alderman Child for the expenses of this committee. Similar knowledge, in the cases of the impeachments of Lord Macclesfield and Lord Lovat and of the committee on Frauds in the Customs, is denied to us: nor do we know whom, if any, of his clerkly colleagues John Burman recompensed out of the large sums paid to him in 1732 and 1742. What cannot be determined, moreover, is whether Kenn, Edwards, and Parker, and even Burman himself before 1742 when he first became one of the four clerks, were in any sense regular members of the Clerk's department, appointed by the Clerk himself as deputies to the four clerks. It is obvious that, at least up to 1760, for twelve years after which year there is no record of any special allowance for attending a select committee, active duties were performed by some of the four—Naylor, Poyntz, and Yeates—so that these posi-

[1] See Appendix IV.

tions had not yet become, as they eventually did, sinecures for senior clerks in what amounted to retirement. There is unfortunately no counterpart to Courthope's minute-book in later years; but I am inclined to suppose that, during the period 1720–50, there was a body of unattached clerks available for the occasional service of the House, but not for that exclusively, and that at some date in the middle of the century the position was regularized in the House of Commons by the appointment of regular deputies to the four clerks by the Clerk of the House. It was the existence of these deputies, to whom early in the next century assistant deputies were added, which made possible the later fixed organization of the Committee Clerks' Office with its four 'desks', each with its hierarchy of three clerks and the differential allotment of fees so thoroughly explored by the committee on the House of Commons Offices in 1833.[1]

But when were deputy committee clerks first appointed? There is no certain answer to this question. Deputies to each of the four clerks without doors were first named in the *Court and City Register* for 1775. We know, however, from Yeates's will (mentioning Rosier as his deputy in 1767) and Hatsell's letter to Ley in 1772 about promotions consequent on the prospective death of Poyntz,[2] that recognized deputies existed earlier. In that letter Hatsell put the average value of a deputy's position at £150 a year, presumably from committee fees on private and local bills.[3] It is, in any case, quite safe to say that, with the exception of George White senior, none of the four clerks without doors attended a select committee on a public matter after 1772: such attendance was left entirely to deputies and assistant deputies.[4] From about the same time most, though not all of the principal committee clerks, whom Hatsell referred to as the 'four Chief', became entirely inactive; and after John Rosier's death in 1796 all exceptions to this inactivity ceased.

---

[1] See pp. 151–55 below and chapter 11, pp. 246–50.

[2] See p. 88.

[3] An average of 180 local and private bills reached the statute-book annually at that period. By 1833 the value of a deputy committee clerk's position had trebled.

[4] Assistant deputies were not officially recognized in the *Court and City Register* till 1812, and their regular appointment seems to have been due to an intervention by Speaker Abbot early in that year; see below, pp. 152–53.

Hatsell's letter also shows that by 1772 the senior clerk not already one of the four great ones had a right to promotion to that position on a vacancy. That senior clerk was, at the time, Edward Barwell, who was senior ingrossing clerk—probably a sinecure post by that time—and also acting as deputy to Poyntz. Barwell was to be promoted if Poyntz died, and the problem was to settle who should succeed to Barwell's place as ingrossing clerk and who should become a deputy. Poyntz, after a brief recovery, died in November. *The Court and City Register* for 1773 duly shows Edward Barwell as the last of the four clerks without doors and David Jones 'who had been ingrossing day and night since 1752' as second ingrossing clerk; and, since the same publication for 1775 shows Parker as Stracey's deputy, it is likely that this appointment was also made on Poyntz's death.

(3)

We must now revert to the financial aspect of these special payments for the expenses of select committees and for the remuneration of individual clerks. Most of these payments sanctioned by the Treasury up to 1772 eventually appeared in the Civil List Accounts, but there was no settled procedure for obtaining the authorization of the House or even for reporting them to the House. As the list of precedents (Appendix IX) shows, the East India committees of 1772–4 occasioned a new departure: a humble address for such a payment, moved in the House by a responsible member of the government, took the place of Treasury sanction on the application of a select committee's chairman. However, practice did not attain regularity until the very end of the century. The general outline of the development is that, from 1773 onwards, the large and miscellaneous expenses of certain committees were sanctioned by humble addresses, and after 1782, when Burke's Act was passed and greater financial regularity became the rule, the sanction of Parliament for payments to committee clerks was obtained in most, though not in all, cases. Then came a period 1788–94 when this sanction does not seem to have been formally obtained; from 1795 to 1800 it was obtained either by resolutions in Committee of Supply or by presentation of the Civil List

Account; and finally, from 1801 onwards, the regular practice
was instituted by which at the end of each session a humble address
for payment of a lump sum for clerks attending committees on
public matters was moved and resolved.

Thus, for the two East India committees of 1772–4 the House,
by humble address, voted in all £2,700—namely, £1,300 for
various clerks of the East India House, £950 to George White
senior, and £450 to his son George. Of the committees on Indian
affairs who sat between 1782 and 1784 the principal were the two
very costly ones on the causes of war in the Carnatic and on
the administration of justice in Bengal, Bihar, and Orissa.[1] Their
clerks, George White and William Evatt,[2] received advances,
usually sanctioned by humble address and then applied for by
memo. to the Treasury,[3] of £1,000 or £500 to White and of £500
to Evatt plus occasional odd sums; and in 1784, on the final reports,
the balances of £920. 0s. 9d. due to White and of £1,779. 13s. due
to Evatt were voted in Supply and paid.[4] George White junior
was at the same time voted £116. 16s. 6d. for attendance on the
select committee appointed to consider the reports of the Court of
Directors of the East India Company. The expenses of Indian inquiries did not end here. In 1786 John White, a younger son of the
elder George White, became clerk to the committee of managers
for the long-drawn-out trial of Warren Hastings, but the occasional payments to him were not the subject of a humble address
nor do they appear in the Civil List Accounts. In 1788 he put in
to the Treasury an account of expenses incurred amounting to
£314. 2s. 6d.: this, after reference to Edmund Burke, chairman of
the managers, was paid. Further payments of £82. 16s. 5d. and
£154. 11s. 6d. certified by Burke were made in 1790 and 1794
respectively. Finally, in 1794, Burke informed the Treasury that,

---

[1] See Appendix IX and p. 334, nn. 1, 3, and 4, to the same.

[2] George White sen. died in Jan. 1789, but he was still active in 1782, so that,
in the absence of any qualification, it must be presumed that the payments were
made to him. William Evatt had been a clerk at least since 1772, and became a
deputy committee clerk in 1799. It seems curious that, after being clerk to so
important a committee, he had to wait so long for promotion.

[3] T. 29/50, fols. 285–6; T. 29/52, fols. 290–91; T. 29/54, fols. 215, 254.

[4] 40 C.J. 395, 397–98, 408.

in the opinion of the committee of managers, the proper remuneration to be made to Mr. White, their late clerk, would be £700, on which a Treasury warrant for that sum was ordered; and finally in the Civil List Accounts 1795–96 we find a payment of £906. 16s. 6d. to John White for trouble and expenses as clerk to the committee of managers—this sum presumably including the £700 for himself and a final bill of expense.[1] All the above-mentioned payments, except the specific allowance to John White, were of the same nature as those to clerks attending committees engaged in prolonged inquiry which have already been mentioned for earlier dates. The clerk acted as general cashier for defraying all expenses incurred or ordered by the committee, and reclaimed these from the Treasury from time to time or at the conclusion of the inquiry. One would like to know whether, in these arrangements, the clerk was expected to supply cash in advance out of his own pocket, or whether, as is more probable, nobody got any money until the Treasury warrant had at last been turned into cash at the Exchequer.

Concurrently, however, with payments of this kind to committee clerks, smaller payments were made, at first only occasionally, to clerks attending public committees simply as a reward for their attendance; and this was only just, since, not being principal clerks, they received no salary at all, and no committee fees were payable on public business. The list of precedents (Appendix IX) shows three such payments (each of £50) previous to 1773, all of which were sanctioned by the Treasury and duly recorded in the Civil List Accounts. Between that year and 1784 similar payments were made by the Treasury on the recommendation of the committee's chairman, but were not recorded in any parliamentary vote or in the Civil List Accounts. Besides those mentioned at the end of the list, in 1782 Arthur Benson was paid £25 or £30, on the recommendation of the Attorney-General, for his assistance on the Insolvent Debtors Bill,[2] and in 1783 the Lord Mayor, chairman of the committee on the Corn Laws, recommended £150 to

---

[1] T. 29/59, fols. 317, 332; T. 29/62 for 2 July 1790; and T. 29/67, fols. 16, 42.

[2] For the release of those arrested for debt before 7 June 1780. Several petitions from imprisoned debtors praying for extension of time were received and referred to the committee of the whole House. Previously John White had been paid £98. 8s. 6d., his bill of expense, transmitted by Lord Beauchamp, for examining

White junior for trouble and expenses. It is true that the payments in 1785 and 1786 for attendance on the committee on British Fisheries recorded in the list were sanctioned by humble address; but following this relapse into orthodoxy by the Treasury, there ensued a period of about seven years during which memorials to the Treasury for repayment of expenses and some allowance for their trouble came in regularly from clerks attending public committees, and these were minuted 'Mr Cotton to pay', not 'prepare a warrant'; but no entry for any such payment occurs in the Civil List Accounts till 1795–6. Among other committees in respect of which this occurred were those to examine the King's Physicians (1789), on the Slave Trade (1790 and 1791), on the State of the Public Revenue (1791), on Approaches to the Houses of Parliament, and on the State of Commercial Credit (1794), and the Committee of Secrecy of the same year. It would be tedious to enumerate them all with references in each case. It is more interesting to record that the personal allowance asked for by the clerks tended to crystallize at a rate of two guineas for each sitting of the committee; and also that in 1792 the Lords of the Treasury began to feel a little uneasy on the subject.

On 4 July in that year an application by three of the clerks for various comparatively small sums for these services was minuted as follows:[1]

On considering the number of applications from the Clerks of the House of Commons for attending Committees, My Lds are of opinion the compensation to be made to them should be submitted to the consideration of the House next session. Mr. Chinnery to pay the actual amount of the expenses.

Nothing more was done, however, and the claims of the unlucky clerks remained unpaid for another two years. Then, on 10 May 1794, the Treasury Lords resumed their consideration of the same memorials and others received since, and decided to refer them to Hatsell and John Ley for their opinion. This was

---

returns of the number of persons confined for debt (T. 29/50, fols. 286, 402); for the Corn Laws committee, see T. 29/54, fol. 282.

[1] T. 29/64, fol. 486.

done in a letter from Charles Long, secretary to the Treasury, dated 29 May 1794.[1] Hatsell and Ley replied, their letter was read at a meeting of the Treasury Board on 31 July, and a very long minute was made, a copy of which was transmitted by letter to Hatsell on 19 August.[2] This minute can be summarized as follows:

Letter from Mr. Hatsell and Mr. Ley in reply to Mr. Long's letter of 29th May read. Hatsell and Ley state that 'the application from clerks for gratuities for attending committees being attended with certain inconveniences, it was proposed some few years since to allow in cases of public committees two guineas a day, or some certain sum for the clerk for his attendance, and that a plan of this sort, if properly regulated, may be attended with less expense to the public, considering the very large sums which have been advanced on the occasions before referred;' and they submit that the allowance should be made only in cases of some importance and when the committee sat for more than

days[3] and only for those days on which the committee actually did sit, that no clerk attending a public committee should apply for any further recompense, and that certain other regulations should be observed as regards the payment of such allowances, the drawing up of minutes and reports of committees, and the writing and sending of letters to summon members.

My Lords approve of the suggestion and direct that an allowance at the rate of two guineas a day be paid to clerks attending public committees, subject to the suggested regulations, such allowance to commence in all cases after the first 3 days of sitting, and be paid only on the days when the committee did business. Hatsell to be acquainted and desired to communicate these regulations to clerks and chairmen of committees. Hatsell and Ley to state what sums the memorialists were entitled to receive under these arrangements. Future memorials from committee clerks would be referred to Hatsell and Ley to certify claims for allowances and expenses actually paid. The clerks to be informed that these allowances would only be made for committees *really* of a *public* nature.

Thus, a proper arrangement was finally come to between the Clerk of the House and the Treasury as to the remuneration of

---

[1] T. 29/66, fol. 442, and T. 27/44, fols. 318–19.
[2] T. 29/67, fols. 114–16, and T. 27/44, fols. 435–36.
[3] This blank is left in the minute.

clerks for attending public committees. The outstanding claims were paid up without deductions,[1] and thenceforward the accounts of clerks attending public committees were transmitted to the Treasury, with a certificate of examination, by John Ley. For a time, moreover, as is shown by Treasury out-letters of 1801 and 1802,[2] the money was paid to one of the deputy clerks with instructions how it was to be distributed. The total payments were shown in the Civil List Accounts, and were sanctioned by Supply resolutions based on accounts of moneys advanced. Finally, from 1801 onwards, they were covered by a humble address at the end of the session.

Since the allowance of 2 guineas a day for attendance on public committees remained in force up till 1833, it is unnecessary to enter into further detail (which is amply available in the Treasury minutes) of the sums paid to particular clerks for particular committees. The payment was now stabilized and invariable. One or two incidentals of the early years of this arrangement are, perhaps, worth mentioning. In 1797 Ley recommended an additional allowance on the grounds that attendance on a certain committee had been long and arduous, whereupon the Treasury granted £10 extra; but in 1804 they refused a similar recommendation made by the chairman of a committee and forwarded with his account by Ley.[3] In 1799 Ley was informed that the Treasury would not in future make any allowance unless the chairman of the committee had reported satisfactory performance of duty by the clerk:[4] and in the same year the clerk of the fees was directed that the charges of porters carrying messages sent by committees were to be more carefully checked and an account of them for each committee was to be signed by the chairman.[5] Also, it is curious to find among the Treasury minutes that in 1797 a House of Commons clerk attended a secret committee of the House of Lords for which

---

[1] They are to be seen in 51 C.J. 187, 653 (account of moneys advanced out of the Civil List and Supply resolution to make good).

[2] e.g. T. 27/52, fol. 514; T. 27/54, fol. 58; T. 27/55, fol. 144.

[3] See respectively Treasury minute in T. 29/71, fols. 392–93, and Treasury letter signed by Huskisson in T. 27/56, dated 18 Aug. 1804, following a minute of 10 Aug. (T. 29/83, fol. 337).

[4] T. 27/50, fol. 359.   [5] T. 27/51, fol. 243.

Lord Chatham recommended a payment to him of 60 guineas, which was made.[1]

By the time of the union with Ireland and the merging of the Irish Parliament with that of Britain in 1801, just over a hundred years had passed since the first four clerks without doors made their appearance at Westminster and in the Treasury pay books. The transition, during that century, from the conditions under which James Courthope kept his minute-book to those of the busy Committee Clerks' Office which functioned under Hatsell and John Ley was gradual, with a marked acceleration towards the end of the eighteenth, and at the beginning of the nineteenth, centuries. The movement of House of Commons procedure had been similar, no less in that of committees than in that of the House itself: and to trace all the developments would entail a prolonged analysis of the *Journals* and other documents which would be outside the scope of this work. The great increase of private legislation owing to the industrial revolution, the inclosure movement and the immense prosperity of the country at the outbreak of the war with revolutionary France, meant a parallel increase in the work of attending private bill committees, as well as in the fees which accrued therefrom: and the making of many standing orders from 1774 onwards for regulating the introduction of, and proceedings on, private bills added to the complexity, as well as to the expense, of private bill procedure, of which the committee on the petition for a bill and the committee on the bill itself formed a large part. These matters, however, have been amply treated elsewhere.[2] The cost of promoting any private bill which was extensively opposed, as were all bills for what are generally called 'works', mounted progressively as the precautionary standing orders were made, compliance with which was at first an extremely cumbrous

---

[1] T. 29/71, fol. 134. The clerk was J. Goodiff. The committee in question must have been the second secret committee of the Lords that year appointed to inquire into the causes of the Order in Council of 26 Feb. limiting cash payments by the Bank of England. They sat on 28 days and reported at length on 28 April (41 L.J. 186–262). A similar secret committee of the Commons was sitting simultaneously, attended as clerk by Henry Gunnell.

[2] Especially F. Clifford, *History of Private Bill Legislation*, and the early chapters of Williams.

and expensive process. Proof of consents from owners and occupiers of land to be acquired under a private bill was a particularly heavy item of cost—a fact which lends point to the following letter written by Hatsell to Ley in 1801 or 1802,[1] which shows his watchfulness over his department even after he had retired from his duties at the table:

It appears to me, that Ld Romney's unqualified assertion, 'That a Clerk of the He of Cs did, to His knowledge, receive £150 for business, which did not occupy an hour' ought, for the credit of the Office to be explain'd. If it is not *true*, it should be retracted; if it is true, it is, after being so broadly stated, *our duty*, in my opinion, to enquire, who the Clerk is, that is so publicly charg'd; & the grounds on which so large a demand was made. If this demand from the Clerk (whoever he may be) cannot be justified under the Table of Fees, some further proceeding should be had; but if it can, this should be so represented to Ld Romney; & His Lordship should then be desired to make this explanation as publick, as He made His charge. I suspect, if there is any foundation for this assertion, that it arises, from a construction, which has, I believe, obtain'd in the Office, of charging for every *consent* to a Bill, as a *Witness*, tho' the consents were all prov'd by one Person. If so, this too may be worth enquiring into, & explain'd. At all events, I am of opinion clearly, that Ld Romney's assertion ought not to rest unnotic'd; & I will beg the favour of You, to show this Note to Mr. Addington, & to the Speaker, & to take Their opinion upon what I have said.

It is particularly necessary to be attentive, that no charges should be made beyond what are allow'd by the Table of Fees; & more particularly important, for the credit of the Office, that no unfounded reports of the rapacity of the Clerks, should go unexplain'd or unanswer'd.

Hatsell, indeed, was highly concerned about many things at the time of the union with Ireland, and not only about the accommodation of the 2nd Clerk Assistant at the table or the inadequate number of committee rooms.[2] Another letter to Ley, dated

[1] Ley MSS. The letter is not dated, but the allusions to Addington and the Speaker (either Mitford or Abbot) prove it to have been written between 1801 and 1803. I have not been able to trace Lord Romney's assertion to which the letter refers.

[2] Hatsell wrote from the country to Ley (Ley MSS.) on 16 July 1801: 'But all these great manœuvres I leave, as I do matters of higher import, to the Gods, who *must* make Peace, or continue the War, and *must* find a new set of Committee

24 October 1801, makes an interesting comment on the conduct of committees in general. Hatsell wrote:

As there are to be *Three* at the Table, I should, in your case, retire in long nights of debate, and leave the conclusion of the sitting, to the two Young Men.[1] Will the present *Clerks* and *Messengers* be sufficient in number to attend all the additional committees? I wish the Speaker and you could suggest some regulations for the better conduct of business at *these* Committees. I should suppose Nominated Chairmen, like Ld. W.[2] in the Hse. of Lds. might be of service, who should be responsible to the House, for the regular and orderly management of business there.

Both Hatsell and Abbot[3] seem to have been unduly apprehensive as to the confusion and congestion which would be caused at Westminster by the addition of Irish legislation and committees to the business of the House of Commons. Committees, as a matter of fact, did not immediately increase, nor did private bill legislation. However, an incident arose out of Abbot's apprehension which deserves to be reported here, since it affected the Committee Clerks' Office and brought Hatsell firmly on to his hind legs. Abbot, about to return from the Chief Secretaryship of Ireland to become Speaker, had, it seems, intimated to John Ley that he wished to appoint a certain clerk in the House of Commons principal clerk of Irish committees. This was no less than Samuel Gunnell, the member of that assiduous, prolific, and clerkly family, Abbot's patronage of whom has already been referred to.[4] Abbot took John Rickman to Westminster as Speaker's Secretary, and no doubt wished similarly to reward Gunnell who had served

Rooms.' So far as committee rooms are concerned, the critical date is 1770 when the 'new and commodious approach' to the House of Commons was completed, as the south-west front to the 'stone building in St Margaret's Street', of which the accurate history is traced in my monograph, *The Topography of the Old House of Commons* (see p. xvi). This construction, though its facilities were not all at once utilized, provided for the first time a proper set of committee rooms. None the less, from 1810 onwards accommodation for committees was insufficient and congested. More committee rooms were provided when the new Library was built in 1827, to last only for seven years.

[1] i.e. Dyson and John Henry Ley, the Clerks Assistant.
[2] Walsingham, Chairman of Committees in the Lords.
[3] See Colchester, i. 326–30.
[4] See chapter 6, pp. 115–17, and Appendix IX, pp. 329–30.

him well. When Hatsell heard of this intention from Ley, he straightway wrote from his country home as follows:[1]

Marden Park. Nov. 7th 1801.

With regard to Mr. Abbott, I think it will be right, to break ground before He comes, or begins to act; & to state your apprehensions, both to the Speaker, & to Mr. Addington. It is impossible, & inconsistent with the establish'd practice of the House, & consequently an infringement of my *Patent* Rights, for any person whatever to attend, as a Clerk in the Office, who is not appointed by the Principal Clerk. I don't know, that there can be any objection, to permit Mr. Abbott, to select out of the Clerks, Sam Gunnell to be at the head of that Office, or to be appointed *by me*, Clerk of the Irish Committees; but *I* must also direct, who shall act under him; & you may tell Mr. Abbott, & Mr. Addington, & the Speaker, that if any attempt is made, to interfere with what I think the rights of my Office, I shall think it my duty to state it to The House, & take their Opinion upon it. But if you prepare Mr. A. & the Speaker, I am persuaded, that nothing of this sort need to happen.

This firm stand was obviously effective, since nothing further was heard of a clerk of Irish committees. Instead, Gunnell was appointed parliamentary agent to the Irish Office[2] and was promoted to be a deputy committee clerk in 1802. Ley must have dealt tactfully with the situation, for, on 14 November 1802, Hatsell wrote: 'I am glad to hear that Saml. Gunnell's business is settled without difficulty. The less puddled Waters are stirr'd, the better.' And in the Ley manuscripts there is an almost servile letter of thanks dated 18 November 1802, from Gunnell to Ley, desiring thanks also to Hatsell for his approval of the 'appointment you were pleased this morning to honour me with'. Thus ended the incident; and Gunnell remained parliamentary agent for Irish business until 1833, his position as such being strongly disapproved of by John Henry Ley, who, as we shall see, lost no opportunity of expressing his opinions on the matter.

(4)

Although the question of providing additional committee rooms and offices was referred to a select committee during the first

---

[1] Ley MSS. [2] See chapter 8, pp. 179–80.

session of the first Parliament of Great Britain,[1] it was not till 1811, as Lord Colchester's diary shows, that the sufficiency of both committee rooms and committee clerks was questioned. At the end of the preceding chapter Abbot's account of his interview with Sir James Graham on this matter was quoted and followed by the abstract giving the state of the Clerk's establishment and average emoluments,[2] which is only to be found in the manuscript of the diary. This entry, though the abstract refers to the year 1809 and was apparently laid before the Select Committee on Public Expenditure of 1810, is dated 10 April 1811. Twelve days later it is followed by another long entry[3] setting forth certain new arrangements for expediting the very numerous private bill committees, of which forty-eight had been set down for a single day. The gist of the arrangement, which was issued as a printed paper, was that three committee rooms, including the Long Gallery, were to be reserved for committees in which no material contest was expected; the committees were divided into five geographical groups, and the clerk assigned to each room was to remain in his place from twelve o'clock until the meeting of the House, and the committees were to proceed one after the other. Six other committee clerks and ten shorthand-writers were left to attend committees on opposed private bills and on public matters, and such committees were to meet in the 'committee rooms more distant from the House, or in the Courts in Westminster Hall and rooms adjoining'. Also, it appears that in June of the same year Speaker Abbot made representations[4] which resulted in the fitting up of five more committee rooms: but, since there was no additional building, they must have been found in the existing accommodation, it is impossible to say where. In the following January the improvement of the organization of the Committee Clerk's Office was tackled. Abbot's entry in his manuscript diary for 14 January 1812 runs as follows:

Mr Ley and Mr J. H. Ley submitted to me their scheme for providing

---

[1] The report of this committee (57 C.J. 647–48) mentions a plan, but this was lost with all the other papers in the fire of 1834, and without it the precise recommendations made must remain unknown.

[2] See pp. 124–26.   [3] P.R.O. 30/9/35, 22 April 1811.

[4] Ibid., 21 and 25 June 1811.

a sufficient number of Committee Clerks for a permanent arrangement, viz. the 4 deputy Committee Clerks to be made efficient, 4 assistant Clerks to be always in rota for the same sort of attendance, and 5 more extra Committee Clerks to be always in readiness to be called upon, total 13, besides any number of shorthand writers who may be wanted. The *Scale of Salaries* to be made up by cross-payments between the Clerks (according to the established usage of the office) so as to leave the 2 oldest of the dep. C^{ee} Clks in possession of their £800 a year, the 3rd to have £600 and the 4th to have £500 a year. One of the four dep. C^{ee} Clks, Henry Gunnell, to be put wholly upon the Private Bill Office, and Goodiff to be called Dep. Clk of the Fees, he being already in fact conducting the whole of *Mr Dorington's* duties as Clk of the Fees.

Abbot's summary of the year 1812 says that this new arrangement was in respect of clerks attending public committees; and what he meant by making the deputy committee clerks 'efficient' was making them effective, i.e. not engaged in other duties while nominally committee clerks. In view of my later chapter in which the conditions prevailing in the various offices, as revealed in the evidence given before the 1833 committee on the House of Commons Offices, are fully described, it would be superfluous at this point to comment at any length on the implications of Abbot's account of this reorganization. Its effect can be seen by comparing the list of officers of the House of Commons given in the *Court and City Register* for 1812 with that for 1813. The latter duly shows Goodiff as assistant clerk of the fees, and no longer a deputy committee clerk, the single assistant deputy committee clerk of 1812 (J. Robe) becomes a deputy, four clerks already on the establishment are designated assistant deputies, and two new names appear at the end of the list of 'other clerks'. So, in fact, Speaker Abbot with the two Leys set the Committee Clerks' Office on the lines which still prevailed in 1833, the one other momentous change made during his Speakership being the introduction, in 1813, of shorthand note-takers under Mr. Gurney for taking down evidence given before committees.[1]

Abbot resigned the Speakership in 1817, and Hatsell died in 1820, to be succeeded as Clerk of the House by J. H. Ley: but a

---

[1] See pp. 224–25 and page 225, n. 1.

new epoch did not immediately open, as I point out at the begining of Chapter 11. The growth of the agitation for parliamentary reform, its successful issue in the passing of the first Reform
Act, and the subsequent election of a new House of Commons
were necessary preliminaries to any further radical change in the
machinery of the House or in the organization of its Offices.
For the time being, however, we may take a farewell glimpse of
the Committee Clerks' Office through the eyes of the Select Committee on the Table of Fees which sat the year after Hatsell's
death and made various, not very precise recommendations, none
of which were then carried out. In paragraphs 4 and 5 of
their report[1] they advert to the committee clerks with a slight
tartness:

The four Clerks without doors, who from the designation of their
offices, might be supposed to be in constant attendance on Committees,
do not, in point of fact, ever attend on committees at all, and in this
respect their offices are become complete sinecures. It is obviously improper that such a system of nominal office, unaccompanied by any
duty, should be continued: and perhaps the same observation might
apply to the Clerkship of Ingrossments. Your Committee therefore
recommend that when the opportunity of any future appointment
occurs, the emoluments of these offices should be investigated, and that
in the event of their being found too large, they should be reduced, but
that at all events these offices should be *invariably* given, as they have
heretofore *usually* been, to some individual most distinguished by his
services in the subordinate situation, avoiding in general all accumulation of offices on the same person. . . .

Incidentally, in future no assistant clerk should be appointed who is
not moderately capable of writing shorthand, which has lately grown
into such general use on committees as to throw a considerable annual
charge upon the public, *while the Committee Clerks are of little or no use
where a shorthand writer is employed; and are frequently not even in attendance upon a committee to which they are nominally appointed.*

The suggestion contained in the latter of these paragraphs was
not at all a sound one, and fortunately it had no effect. No doubt,
at that period, when each committee clerk might be in attendance
on a public committee and two or three private bill committees

[1] *Reports of Committees* (1821), iv. 49, also in Appendix of the *Journal* (1821).

sitting simultaneously, the clerk was bound to be absent from any particular committee very frequently; and if that committee were hearing evidence or listening to speeches by counsel, no great harm would have been done. Yet, if the suggestion had been carried out, and the additional duty of taking shorthand notes of evidence had been imposed on the committee clerks, the result would have been disastrous. The staff of clerks would have needed to be uneconomically trebled, and, with only a 'moderate' capacity for shorthand, their transcripts of evidence would have been highly inaccurate. Anybody who has been associated, as I have been for many years, with the work of the official shorthand-writer's staff, knows that their astonishing accuracy is only attained after a long and arduous apprenticeship and by an effort of extreme concentration during the performance of their duties, with which no additional function would be compatible. Equally, even if it were possible, the addition of note-taking duties to a committee clerk's functions would be destructive of his efficiency as a clerk, at all events, today: even in 1821, the attempt to carry out this suggestion would inevitably have defeated its aims.

The first paragraph is of a different nature. It comments on the position of the four clerks without doors, as it appeared to the Committee in 1821. The four clerks in 1821 were Edward Stracey, John Benson, Arthur Benson, and John Dorington. Both the Bensons had been clerks of the journals and had been retired on their sinecure. John Dorington was still clerk of the fees, and as such very well paid, but he was undoubtedly senior to any other possible candidate when, in 1817, he had become one of the four clerks. He was certainly a pluralist, but a very active one. Edward Stracey was also a pluralist, but, so far as the House of Commons was concerned, a sleeping pluralist. He was the senior of the four clerks without doors and senior clerk of ingrossments. Reading between the lines of the 1821 committee's report above-quoted, it is not difficult to see that, without mentioning names, they were aiming, though ineffectually, at Stracey, to whom brief reference was made in a previous chapter.[1]

In 1789 Hardinge Stracey, Edward Stracey's uncle, retired,

[1] Chapter 4, p. 75.

having been one of the four clerks since 1763 and senior clerk of ingrossments since 1774. At all events in his earlier years, Hardinge Stracey was an active member of the Clerk's department as clerk to the Committee of Privileges and Elections. He was also a friend of Hatsell, who stayed with him at his country seat in 1786.[1] It can only be supposed that Hatsell, who had never sold any appointment in his gift, agreed out of pure friendship to invest Hardinge Stracey's nephew, Edward Hardinge John Stracey, on his attaining his majority, with his uncle's offices—both sinecures—if the uncle retired. Hardinge Stracey accordingly retired in 1789, and lived nearly twenty years longer: Edward Stracey, then twenty-one years old and still an undergraduate at Christ Church, was made, for life, one of the four clerks without doors and one of the ingrossing clerks. He never held a subordinate position in the House of Commons, but contentedly drew the salary of one sinecure, and the fees of both sinecures for forty-four years. Moreover, he also drew another £100 a year from the Civil List which had been originally granted to Hardinge Stracey in 1758 for 'assisting in drafting several bills of supply', but which for many years had obviously entailed no duties at all. Thus endowed with a life-income of well over £1,000 a year, to which he added by agency for private bills, he finally found a salaried employment, which was not a sinecure, as Counsel to the Chairman of Committees in the House of Lords. From 1804 to 1808 his salary in this capacity was £750, and in 1809, after a humble address from the Lords, it was doubled.[2]

This was a position of considerable responsibility, for it involved advising the Lords Chairman of Committees in his supervision of private bills—a function which was entrusted to him long before the Commons followed suit and entrusted similar duties to the Chairman of Ways and Means assisted by the Speaker's Counsel.[3] There is no reason to suppose that Edward Stracey was not com-

[1] For Hardinge Stracey, see chapter 4, pp. 75–77, and chapter 8, pp. 164–67.

[2] His salary first appears in the Treasury Disposition Books for 1805 and 1806 (T. 61/68, fol. 542, and T. 61/69, fol. 44). From 1806 onwards his salary was voted annually in the Committee of Supply. For evidence that he acted as a parliamentary agent, see chapter 8, p. 183, n. 1.

[3] See Williams, i. 55–56, 92–103 for the history and nature of this important development, also for the autocratic methods of Lord Shaftesbury.

petent to advise the Lords Chairman: indeed, since he acted as Counsel to the Lords Chairman under the redoubtable Lord Shaftesbury, he must have known his business. However, in view of the facts set out above, there is a comic element in the discovery that, in 1804 and again in 1806, Abbot remonstrated violently at this appointment. The entries in his manuscript diary[1] show that he stopped the proceeding for a time by stating his objections directly to Pitt, and also remonstrated with Lord Walsingham, the Lords Chairman of Committees, and that he repeated his objections to Lord Grenville in 1806, besides repeating them to Lord Walsingham during a morning ride and telling Stracey himself that his position as a subordinate clerk in the House of Commons was incompatible with that of Counsel to the Lords Chairman. But these remonstrances were not of the slightest avail. Stracey held his post: and it is to be observed that Abbot had not the slightest objection to his being a sinecurist in the House of Commons, but, as his diary-entries show, the improprieties of which he complained were (*a*) his appointment by Lord Walsingham without his (Abbot's) approbation; (*b*) the advantage Stracey would obtain over his fellow-clerks in the Commons as regards agency for private bills, since he would be able, in the Lords, to make difficulties for bills solicited by his colleagues; and (*c*) that he received fees, as Abbot put it, 'from the parties for settling their bills, which he was afterwards to approve, exercising, of course, not a very impartial judgment on such bills as were not previously submitted to him and paid for'. On 23 May 1806 Abbot records that Stracey came to see him and promised to relinquish all fees immediately, but that was the only satisfaction which Abbot received in the matter. It was not till the great probe of 1833 that Stracey, by then a baronet, resigned the clerkship of ingrossments in the Commons and the position of Counsel to the Lords Chairman. The four chief clerkships without doors were then abolished, but in that respect Stracey received a pension of £800 a year which he continued to enjoy for some time longer.[2] The survival

---

[1] P.R.O. 30/9/33, entry for Sunday, 29 May 1804, and the summary for 1804; P.R.O. 30/9/34, entries for 22 and 23 May and 1 July 1806.

[2] See Dean Pellew, *Life and Correspondence of Lord Sidmouth*, i. 326, and footnote,

of this curious relic of eighteenth-century practices until after the first Reform Act is certainly incongruous: but, when his two sinecures were first conferred on him by Hatsell, it was a last 'blot', as J. H. Ley described it,[1] and even then had no parallel in the Clerk's department.

where the author notes that at the time of writing (1847) Sir Edward Stracey, then all but eighty, was 'enjoying a cheerful and tranquil retirement . . . beloved by his friends, respected by his dependants, and surrounded by a happy peasantry, for whom his care and liberality provide education in childhood, employment in health, and assistance in old age'.

[1] In evidence before the 1833 Committee (H.C. (1833) 648, qn. 3075) he said that the appointment was a blot, but that it had been perpetrated before he came to Westminster.

8

CLERKS EMPLOYED AS AGENTS FOR TREASURY BUSINESS IN THE HOUSE. THE CLERK OF THE FEES. THE RISE OF PROFESSIONAL PARLIAMENTARY AGENCY

(1)

FROM the strictly chronological point of view, the Office of the Journals and Papers came next in seniority to the Committee Clerks' Office, and should therefore be the subject of this chapter. However, since it was the committee clerks who were, at the beginning, chiefly concerned in the development of the relations with the Treasury which eventually resulted in the institution of the Public Bill Office, I have chosen to follow the preceding chapter with an account of the growth of these relations, so far as this can be traced from existing documents. These, unfortunately, are scanty at the outset, and leave much unexplained. Nevertheless, the attainable facts make up a somewhat remarkable story, which has never yet been told. Even Hatsell, who must have known the facts, made not the slightest allusion to them in his *Precedents of Proceedings* when enumerating the 'other clerks' and their functions. The salient fact, which comprehends all the others, is that, in the middle of the eighteenth century, the Treasury set up and paid an agency of its own in the Clerk's department.

Allusion has already been made to the relations of William Goldesbrough and Paul Jodrell with the Treasury,[1] as revealed in their petitions for payment and in the descriptions of the services for which payments were made or claimed. Goldesbrough claimed to have had 'charge' of money bills and other public matters, and the Exchequer paid him for 'attending, preparing and ingrossing

---

[1] pp. 26–28, 43–45.

of divers large bills upon public concern': Jodrell was paid for his care and pains in 'soliciting' a certain bill, and later for 'the despatch of several money bills'. While it is uncertain what these terms connoted, there can be little doubt that they implied some form of agency in regard to money bills. However, since the payment to Jodrell of £50 a year as gratuity ceased after 1699, and there is no record of any similar payments to the Clerk of the House thereafter, it would seem that from Queen Anne's accession onwards that particular relation ceased. The Treasury always paid for services rendered and described their nature in its books. When a salary of £200 a session was first awarded in 1732 to the Clerk of the House, in the person of Nicholas Hardinge, this was described[1] as being 'in reward and consideration of his extraordinary service, care, pains and attendance on the House of Commons'. There was nothing said about soliciting, preparing, or taking charge of money bills for the Treasury. If Hardinge, while Clerk of the House, performed any services of that kind, there is no evidence to show it. I am therefore obliged to assume that there was a break in the continuity of the Treasury's relations with the Clerk since Jodrell's gratuity ceased to be paid, and that certain events, now to be described, were a new departure. At the same time, it is worth bearing in mind that Hardinge, after he had given up the Clerk's seat, became joint secretary to the Treasury from 1752 till his death in 1758. It was during his six years at the Treasury that this new departure began.

A preliminary move, however, had taken place some twenty years earlier. In the year 1733 the annual sum ordered by Treasury warrant to be paid to the officers of the House of Commons (excluding the salaries of the Speaker and the Serjeant at Arms) was increased from £470, at which it had stood since 1723, to £770. This increase of £300 was accounted for by the salary of £200 first awarded to the Clerk of the House in the preceding year and by £100 now for the first time paid to one of the clerks of Treasury.[2] The Treasury evidently considered that this increase was a matter of some importance, since the entry in the money book for

---

[1] In the Treasury warrant (T. 53/36, fol. 327).
[2] See chapter 6, p. 108, and T. 53/37, fol. 62, dated 20 June 1733.

1733 is made at quite unusual length, quoting the date of the letters patent in virtue of which the order for payment was to be made, the names of the payees (as usual) and the description of the services for which they were paid. Thus, Hardinge, the Clerk, and Aiskew, the Clerk Assistant, were paid for 'extraordinary pains and service' during the session 16 January 1732/3 to 13 June 1733, the four under-clerks (under the old and entirely inaccurate rubric) in reward for their services in 'copying and ingrossing several bills and other papers for his Majesty's Service', and the Serjeant at Arms for distribution among the messengers, door-keepers, and other persons who delivered out *Votes*. Finally there appears

Christopher Lowe one of the Clerks of the Treasury for his extraordinary care and pains in preparing for the House of Commons as well the Bills for raising the Supply granted to his Majesty as all other public Bills relating to the revenues, making breviates thereof for the use of the Speaker and other services, £100.

Christopher Lowe first appears in the year 1721 as one of the six Treasury clerks drawing a salary of £50 a year;[1] and by 1733 he was half-way up the list. Thenceforward for twenty-two years he drew another £100 per session on the salary list of the officers of the House of Commons for the services described above. In his case the description was probably accurate, since it was a new appointment; but it is unfortunate that no Treasury minute of the year throws any light on the reasons for making it.

So far as parliamentary formalities went, as could be exemplified from innumerable entries in the *Journal*, the preparation of money bills after resolutions in Supply was, and always had been, entrusted to certain members of the House who were either Law Officers or officers of the Treasury.[2] Indeed, the House could not

---

[1] See T. 53/29, fol. 153, showing the payment of a quarter of his salary to Michaelmas 1721. These Treasury clerks drew other and more considerable emoluments from fees and new year's gratuities.

[2] See Doris M. Gill, 'The Treasury 1660–1714', in *Eng. Hist. Rev.* xvi. 621–22, in which she shows that the drafting of money bills based on a resolution in Committee of Ways and Means was usually entrusted to the Attorney-General, the Solicitor-General, and William Lowndes (secretary to the Treasury 1695–1724). Generally a breviate was first prepared, then the law officers drew the bill at full length, and this draft was sent by the Treasury to the various offices concerned

entrust the preparation and presentation of a bill to any but its members. Yet, even in the great Lowndes's day, a Treasury clerk probably assisted his official superior in this parliamentary process. Why, then, if the services of a Treasury clerk were without question available to members of the House entrusted with the preparation of money bills, was it thought necessary in 1733 to appoint and pay one particular Treasury clerk, as an officer of the House of Commons, for this very purpose? No answer to this question is to be found in the Treasury records: but there is a hint of a possible answer elsewhere. Among the Carlisle papers is a letter from Sir Thomas Robinson to the earl of Carlisle, dated 14 April 1733, describing the introduction of Walpole's violently opposed Excise Bill, in which he wrote:

The Bill was introduced the 4th of this month, and the first debate that day was on a point of order, whether the Bill was exactly drawn according to the resolutions of the House; and of course the debate was in very few hands, few people having the time or inclination to read the Journals.[1]

Here, I suggest, is the possible reason for Christopher Lowe's appointment—namely, that under Walpole's administration of the Treasury, when he was at the height of his power in the House, the Treasury drafting had become a little slack, and insufficient care was taken to see that the provisions of revenue bills accorded exactly with the resolutions on which they were based. If so, this would strengthen the likelihood of my assumption that the former relations between the Treasury and the Clerk of the House had

---

(e.g. Customs and Excise) for approval or comment, as shown by entries in the books of Treasury out-letters. See also *The Liverpool Tractate*, ed. Catherine Strateman (Columbia University Press, 1937), p. xli of the introduction, quoting the passage on bills of subsidy from Lambarde's tractate (Addl. MSS. 5123), and p. 63 of the text, in which the writer of the Liverpool tractate (Addl. MSS. 38456) says (*circ.* 1761) of a money bill on resolution that the Chairman of the Money Chair (i.e. Ways and Means), the Chancellor of the Exchequer, the Lords of the Treasury, their secretaries, and the Attorney-General and the Solicitor-General were commonly the persons to prepare it.

[1] *R. Comm. Hist. MSS.*, vol. 15, Appendix part vi, p. 109. This is confirmed by the *Journal* entry on this occasion, 22 C.J. 104. See also ibid., p. 93, for the members ordered to prepare and bring in the bill, one of whom was the Chancellor of the Exchequer.

ceased; since any Clerk, let alone Jodrell, to whom the 'soliciting' or 'despatch' of a money bill had been entrusted, would have taken care that it corresponded with the relative resolution. The criticisms of the newly introduced, and in Walpole's view extremely important, Excise Bill, on the ground of inaccurate drafting would naturally have been annoying to Walpole as First Lord of the Treasury, and may well have prompted him to give instructions that measures should be taken to prevent any such occurrences in the future. A clerk of the Treasury was therefore, I surmise, detailed to attend specially to the parliamentary business of the department, and his salary in respect of this duty was attached in the Civil List to the salaries of the Clerk and other officers of the House.

This, in itself, was an interesting departure, which marked a renewed sense in the Treasury of the importance of strict attention to the dispatch of Treasury business (mainly matters of revenue) in the House. Yet it did not directly affect the Clerk of the House or his subordinates. Christopher Lowe continued to appear on the salary-list of the House of Commons officers up to, and including, the Civil List year 1755–6: and in the Civil List Accounts 1756–7 and 1757–8 his place is taken by William Plaxton, also a Treasury clerk, for the same services. A change, however, was already in preparation. From Appendix IX we see that in 1755 Robert Yeates, one of the four clerks without doors, after petitioning the Treasury, was awarded £600 for special services[1] in the past five sessions, of which sum £100 was for expenses and £500 for Yeates himself; and that the Speaker, to whom Yeates's petition had been referred, had recommended the continuance of a yearly allowance of £100 to Yeates for these services.[1] This payment is recorded in the Civil List Accounts 1755–6 (p. 44) as follows:

Robert Yeates, one of the Clerks of the House of Commons, without account viz. to reimburse his expenses for clerks and other assistants in attending several committees in the five last sessions of Parliament, *and in drawing up and preparing sundry bills to be laid before the House* . . . £100. In reward for his own service therein, £500.

Yeates continued, as the Civil List Accounts show, to receive this

---

[1] See Appendix IX, p. 332, n. 5.

extra £100 a session (except for the two sessions referred to below) until his death in 1769; but this is by no means the end of the story.

It is to the words which I have italicized above that I draw attention, all the more since, in the subsequent years, this payment of £100 to Yeates is described in the accounts simply as being 'for extraordinary services performed by him this session'. The entry in the Civil List Accounts quoted above shows that for the last five sessions (i.e. from that beginning 14 November 1751 to that which ended on 25 April 1755) Robert Yeates had been drafting and preparing 'sundry' bills, although Christopher Lowe was still drawing his £100 a session for similar duties. The following session 1755–6 William Plaxton replaced Lowe, and Yeates drew his extra £100. In the session 1756–7, not only did both Plaxton and Yeates receive their £100, but a wholly new figure appeared on the scene in the person of Hardinge Stracey,[1] Nicholas Harding's nephew. By a Treasury minute dated 6 April 1757[2] it was ordered that

Hardinge Stracey who is appointed clerk of the Committee of Privileges and Elections (to which office no salary is annexed) shall receive annually for his service in that employment *and his assistance in preparing Bills* the sum of £100 to be paid out of the money annually paid to the Clerks of the House of Commons.

Again I have italicized the words that are important so far as this chapter is concerned, the award for the first time of a salary to the clerk of elections being a matter to be dealt with in a later chapter. In the following two sessions 1757–8 and 1758–9 the Civil List Accounts[3] show Hardinge Stracey in receipt of £100 as clerk of privileges and elections, and of another £100 'for preparing bills for raising the Supplies as also other public bills relative to the Revenue and making breviates thereof for the Speaker', while William Plaxton disappears from the list. In other words, a clerk of the House of Commons had taken the place of a Treasury clerk on the House of Commons officers' salary list, for performing the parliamentary duties previously assigned to the latter. Meanwhile, for the same two sessions Robert Yeates, instead of receiving his

---

[1] See chapter 4, pp. 75–77.   [2] T. 29/32, fol. 456.
[3] In these accounts the two sessions 1757–8 and 1758–9 are lumped together, each salary being doubled.

extra £100 a session, was paid, as recorded in Appendix IX,[1] £300 and £500 respectively for services and payment of other clerks in attendance on the select committee appointed to inquire into the original standards of weights and measures. It might appear from this that Hardinge Stracey had supplanted both the Treasury clerk and his own colleague Yeates in the duty of attending to the Treasury's parliamentary business and preparing revenue bills: but this was not so. Shortly after the end of the session (2 June 1759) Robert Yeates, while still continuing as one of the four clerks without doors, was admitted a principal clerk of the Treasury. This rather surprising event is recorded in two Treasury minutes:[2]

31 July 1759. Mr. Yeates admitted as principal Clerk of the Treasury. He is to write all letters (except *re* issues for services) and references according to directions given by their Lordships' minutes, and do all the parliamentary business.

4 September 1759. Mr. Yeates and Mr. Postlethwaite called in and exhorted by his Grace the Duke of Newcastle to diligence and constant attendance, and to live in harmony with their brethren.

Yeates held his two posts till he died in 1769, drawing his emoluments as one of the four clerks without doors, his additional £100 on the House of Commons list for extraordinary services, and whatever emoluments he earned as a principal clerk in the Treasury. In January 1760 he officiated at the table of the House, when John Read, the Clerk Assistant who died the same year, was absent through illness; and a month later, when Yeates himself was ill, Hardinge Stracey attended in his stead.[3]

(2)

There is a certain mystery, it must be admitted, in the facts of the above narrative. The Treasury clerk, without any question, was eliminated after 1757 and was replaced by a Commons clerk

---

[1] p. 333.
[2] In T. 29/33, fols. 218–19. I have abbreviated these and omitted the capitals. Mr. Postlethwaite was a Treasury clerk now promoted principal. 'References', in Treasury language, meant letters to other departments referring matters to them.
[3] 28 C.J. 698, 771.

to do the Treasury business in the House; but what were the relative positions of Yeates and Stracey? Were they both doing the Treasury business simultaneously, or did Stracey temporarily take Yeates's place? It seems very improbable that Stracey did any of the Treasury's business in Parliament after Yeates had been made a principal clerk of the Treasury for this purpose; yet, as the Civil List Accounts reveal, not only did Hardinge Stracey draw his sessional £100 for preparing supply bills, &c., until he retired in 1789, but he was able to hand this salary on to Edward Stracey, his nephew, when Hatsell made this young gentleman of twenty-one a sinecurist for life in his uncle's stead.[1] Edward Stracey drew this sinecure salary of £100 for preparing revenue bills until, in 1830, J. H. Ley appropriated Stracey's salaries from the Treasury for the benefit of other clerks.[2]

The mystery cannot be entirely cleared up for want of evidence, and I can only put forward the following tentative explanation. Nicholas Hardinge was the prime mover in these changes. When he became joint secretary of the Treasury with James West in 1752, he put into operation an idea which he had probably formed while Clerk of the House—namely, that a Commons clerk could look after Treasury business in the House better than a Treasury clerk, if only because he was always on the spot. He began by employing Robert Yeates, possibly on the recommendation of Jeremiah Dyson, who had originally appointed Yeates to the establishment and whom Yeates regarded as his 'kind patron', to do part of this business, at first without pay; but subsequently, when Yeates's work had proved satisfactory for five sessions, it was arranged that he should be given £100 a session for these services with effect from 1752.[3] In 1757, young Hardinge Stracey who had taken his B.A. degree in 1755, needed a job, which his uncle naturally undertook to provide. He persuaded Dyson to appoint Hardinge Stracey clerk of privileges and elections, procured an additional £200 salary for the Clerk Assistant who relinquished this office, and saw to it that a salary of £100 was

---

[1] See pp. 155–58.

[2] As he informed the 1833 committee, see chapter 11, p. 239.

[3] See above, pp. 163–64.

provided for Hardinge Stracey whom, the following year, he also substituted for the Treasury clerk, Plaxton, on the Commons officers' salary-list, thus doubling his salary. Meanwhile, Yeates was diverted to take charge of the large and important select committee on the standards of weights and measures which sat for two sessions. Nicholas Hardinge, I suggest, intended his nephew to become his permanent assistant in the Treasury for parliamentary business relating to the revenue; and I base this suggestion on a document in the Newcastle papers.[1] It is a minute without date or address, but endorsed 'rec'd April 9, 1758', written by Hardinge Stracey to West, the other joint secretary to the Treasury:

Mr. Stracey presents his compliments to Mr. West and acquaints him that Mr. Hardinge is so very ill, as not to be able to write to Him. But the fact, w[ch] Mr. Hardinge mentioned at the Treasury Board, was that the Running of Irish made Candles had greatly contributed to lessen the Revenue. And that ready made Candles had been run from other Places. And that there were Clauses prepared to put a Stop to this Evil. Sunday Morn. (i.e. 9 April 1758).

This minute may have been written at the Treasury or at the house where Nicholas Hardinge was lying ill. West, no doubt, sent it to Newcastle. It shows Hardinge Stracey's close association with his uncle in respect of the Treasury's parliamentary business, and gives a clear illustration of the nature of that business (i.e. legislation affecting the revenue). Unluckily, perhaps, for Stracey, his uncle died that year. Either West, or Newcastle himself, I suggest, thought more highly of Yeates than of Stracey. Therefore Yeates was appointed a principal clerk of the Treasury for parliamentary business, and Stracey was allowed, as a douceur, to go on drawing his £100 a session without any duties. This payment, in the eighteenth-century manner of things, then became an appanage of some clerk in the House of Commons into which nobody bothered to inquire. Yeates did all the Treasury's parliamentary work for ten years, and also, like the rest of the Treasury clerks, acted as a political factotum[2] for Newcastle until the latter's fall.

[1] Addl. MSS. 32879, fol. 120.
[2] See Addl. MSS. 32920, fol. 472, a letter dated 'Bishopston March 22, 1761' to the duke in Yeates's handwriting, signed by William Mitchell (treasurer of the Salt Duties and the duke's electoral agent in Sussex) and Yeates, saying that all the

However, unlike most of Newcastle's men, he was not deprived of his office in 1763. Charles Jenkinson, the future first earl of Liverpool, who became joint secretary to the Treasury in that year, clearly found Yeates too useful. Hence we find among the Liverpool manuscripts a copy of a letter[1] from Yeates to Jenkinson, dated 'Abingdon Building Dec. 29th 1763', which may be compared with Hardinge Stracey's minute quoted above as an illustration of the Treasury business entrusted to a Commons Clerk. In this letter Yeates says that he has seen Mr. Tod (a gentleman interested in the linen trade) as to the proposal about Russia linens, and will see Jenkinson when Tod had digested the papers; also, that he has just finished with Mr. Tyton (solicitor to the Customs) the Plantation Bill[2] of which he will send a copy to Mr. Whateley that evening.

Whatever gaps there may be in the above account, particularly as regards Hardinge Stracey who was appointed one of the four clerks without doors in 1763, the outline of the new relation between the Treasury and a clerk in the House of Commons is clear. The Treasury now employed a Commons Clerk to assist in drafting revenue clauses or revenue bills and, of course, to see that they were procedurally correct, were properly amended, passed through all their stages in the House, and were correctly ingrossed. This clerk retained whatever position he held, or rose to, in the House of Commons, with all the emoluments accruing therefrom, but was also directly paid by the Treasury out of public funds, for doing its business in Parliament.

The device of appointing the Commons Clerk to a Clerkship in the Treasury was dropped after Yeates's death in 1769. Hence-

gentlemen were agreed that his Grace's presence would be necessary the day before the election (obviously Seaford). Another letter, dated 17 Nov. 1761, from Yeates to Mr. Hurdis, the duke's chaplain (Addl. MSS. 32931, fol. 117), encloses copies of the petition relating to the Seaford election presented that day, informs him of the date fixed for hearing at the bar of the House, and says that in spite of his present ill state of health he will endeavour to obey any commands with which he might be honoured on this occasion.

[1] Addl. MSS. 36206, fol. 376. It is printed in *The Jenkinson Papers*, ed. Ninetta S. Jucker (London, 1949), p. 245.

[2] The Plantation Act, 1764. Thomas Whateley, M.P., became secretary to the Treasury in 1764.

forward the Treasury was content to pay a Commons Clerk to be its salaried parliamentary agent, and to reimburse him for all expenses incurred in carrying out its business. The arrangements to fill Yeates's place were made by the Treasury Board on 20 November 1769. The Treasury minute[1] for that date runs as follows:

My Lds are pleased to appoint Danby Pickering, Esq., to do the parliamentary business of this office performed by the late Mr. Yeates with a salary of £600 a year to be paid by Mr. Davis at the end of each session of Parliament.

My Lds likewise appoint John Rosier, Esq., to assist Mr. Pickering in the execution of the s[d] business at a salary of £100 to be paid in the same manner.

John Rosier,[2] to whom Yeates left £1,500 and who was his deputy in the Committee Clerk's Office, had just become clerk of the journals and papers[3] in succession to George White senior appointed one of the four clerks without doors on Yeates's death. Rosier remained clerk of the journals until, at least by 1774, he was made clerk of the fees, a newly created post.[4] Of what led to the creation of this post there is no indication in the Treasury books or in Hatsell's correspondence with John Ley. The fact can only be stated that, whoever of the clerks was collecting the fees before that post was created,[5] thereafter this was made the duty of a separate office under a principal clerk. It was this principal clerk who was thereafter employed to conduct the parliamentary business of the Treasury and, subsequently, of other public departments; and, as we shall see, the Fees Office eventually became the Public Bill Office.[6]

---

[1] T. 29/40, fols. 117–18. [2] See pp. 73, 77–78.

[3] The *Court and City Register* first shows him in this position in 1770; but a letter from John Ley to Hatsell (in the Ley MSS.), dated 14 Oct. 1769, says that Rosier, Couse (i.e. Kenton Couse, the architect, then clerk of the works at Westminster), and Ley were to consult the following day about the provision of the new Journal Office, or Court of Wards (see next chapter, pp. 194–96), from which it must be inferred that Rosier was already head of that office.

[4] He first appears in the *Court and City Register* for 1775 as clerk of the fees, being succeeded by John Speed as clerk of the journals; but in the report of a select committee appointed in 1774 (34 C.J. 808–9) to report on necessary alterations in the building reference is made to the clerk of the fees' office.

[5] See above, pp. 57–58, 131, n. 2.

[6] The principal clerk of this office is still the official collector of fees on private

From 1769 onwards there can be traced through the Treasury books the salary awarded to this outlying agent in the Clerk's department, and from 1777 onwards the amount of his expense account presented annually to the Treasury. These figures are an interesting measure of the ever-increasing importance to the Treasury of the clerk of the fees in the House of Commons, and of the growth of the Treasury's parliamentary business. It is noteworthy, however, that the Treasury in minutes and letters, invariably referred to him by his name, and never to his position as a clerk in the House. He was *their* paid official, and his duties to them, so far as they were concerned, had no connexion with any other duty he might perform in another capacity. This curious position was not altered till after 1833, when the Clerk of the House's department was reorganized.[1] It would be tedious and unnecessary to reproduce all the Treasury minutes relating to the salary and expense accounts from 1769 onwards of Rosier and his successor, John Dorington, but they must be summarized. Rosier started with a salary of £100, and was awarded another £100 in 1770 for his 'extraordinary trouble and diligence'; in 1772 his salary was fixed at £200 and in 1774 he was given an extra £100; in 1779 directions were given that he should be paid £100 in addition to his former allowance of £300 'in consideration of his attending to the private bills brought into the House of Commons and taking care that nothing passes therein which may be prejudicial to the interest of the Crown and the public'. In 1781 his salary was raised by £200 to £600,[2] and there it remained for the rest of his time. John Dorington, who succeeded Rosier as clerk of the fees in 1796 and was appointed by the Treasury to do the parliamentary business of the office performed by the late Rosier, began at a salary of £600. This was increased by £200 in 1812, and in 1817 a further £300 was added for Irish business,[3] thus bringing the total salary of the clerk of the fees for Treasury business to £1,100, at which figure it remained till 1833.

bills, though the actual collection and book-keeping have for over a century been the duty of the accountant.   [1] See chapter 11.

[2] For these changes, see respectively T. 29/40, fol. 267; T. 29/43, fol. 442; T. 29/48, fol. 347; and T. 29/50, fol. 308.

[3] See 69 C.J. 594 and 73 C.J. 517–18.

As a clerk in the House of Commons the clerk of the fees received no annual salary, nor did the Clerk of the House contribute a single penny from his fees for the payment of this clerk and his underlings. His emoluments, so far as the House was concerned, arose solely from the 10s. on every private bill fee which he was authorized to collect under the table of fees, and from certain advantages in the matter of stationery (see below). Any profits from private bill agency, in which John Dorington and his son engaged and which will be dealt with at the end of this chapter, were in no sense official, but were the fruits of a voluntary activity in a commercial venture. The clerk of the fees, moreover, at any rate so far as his work for the Treasury was concerned, was responsible for paying any junior clerks whom he employed. This was recognized in 1784 by the Treasury, which made an annual allowance from that year onwards for 'extraordinary trouble and attendance' to the assistants of their agent in the House. At first this allowance was 40 guineas, but in 1793 it was raised to £100,[1] which sums were included in John Rosier's, and continued for some years to be included in John Dorington's, expense accounts. But when, immediately after the Union and the consequent increase of staff in the Fees Office and the Journal Office, the Treasury began to pay an annual sum of £400 to be divided between the subordinate clerks in the two offices, the clerk of the fees no longer charged these fixed sums in his expense accounts. This continued till 1833, and even then their proportion of the annual £400 was the only permanent salary enjoyed by these clerks, who were otherwise paid solely for work done. However, it will be more convenient to consider the origin of this payment in my next chapter which deals with the Journal Office.[2]

As regards the expense accounts, I have thought it worth while to tabulate them (with a few gaps) up to 1817 as an indication of the growth of Treasury business in the House over a period of forty years; though it is a pity that the accounts themselves have been weeded out of the bundles of Treasury in-letters in the Public Record Office, so that the nature of the various items is not

[1] T. 29/56, minute dated 20 Aug. 1784, and T. 29/66, fol. 65.
[2] See next chapter, pp. 205–8.

discoverable. The amounts are taken from Treasury minutes ordering payment and, after 1812, from entries of accounts presented in the *Journal* (see opposite).

(3)

Before passing from these details of finance and organization to consider more closely the nature of the work done by the clerk of the fees for the Treasury, I mention certain minor emoluments which accrued to him. From 1788 onwards he was paid £35 a year in lieu of stationery, in consequence of a Treasury minute of that year to the effect that various allowances in lieu of stationery formerly supplied for their own use to certain officers of the two Houses previous to the establishment of the Stationery Office should be continued 'for the advantage of the public': as the minute shows, the stationery formerly supplied comprised six sets of Acts, six sets of *Votes*, and 5 guineas.[1] This allowance continued till 1833, though any memory of what it was for had long since vanished.[2] Besides this, the clerk of the fees had the duty of ordering stationery for the use of the House, and was the sole judge of the quantity required. John Dorington seems to have used this privilege with a certain liberality towards himself, for the Select Committee on Public Expenditure in their ninth report of 1810 remarked[3] that: 'Mr Dorington . . . has a strong and manifest interest in getting in larger stocks than necessary towards the end of the session, since the unconsumed stock is his perquisite. Mr Dorington states that he considers this a compensation for the want of a regular allowance.' They proceeded to make some acid comments on the practice of selling surplus stationery by which many senior officials profited. However, Dorington's plea reported by the committee emphasizes the fact that the clerk of the fees, as such, had no regular salary as a Commons Clerk. John

[1] T. 29/60, dated 20 Dec. 1788. The sale of these publications would have brought in much more than 35 guineas.

[2] John Dorington, giving evidence before the Select Committee on Public Expenditure (H.C. (1810) 373, p. 214), said that he received this £35 a year in lieu of stationery, 'but I cannot tell in lieu of, or for, what'. His predecessor Rosier had obviously not filed the Treasury minute of 1788.

[3] Ibid., p. 187.

*Expense accounts for Treasury Business in the House of Commons
1777–1817, sent in by the clerk of the fees*

Reference	Folio or page	Year	Amount			Remarks
			£	s.	d.	
T. 29/46	154	1777	190	7	3	
T. 29/47	155	1778	296	9	11	
T. 29/48	347	1779	188	12	0	
T. 29/49	284	1780	123	3	2	
T. 29/50	307	1781	129	3	0	
T. 29/52	252	1782	100	6	6	
T. 29/54	216	1783	101	13	0	
T. 29/56	21 Aug.	1784	142	15	5	plus 40 guineas for assistants.
T. 29/56	519	1785	270	18	0	including the above.
T. 29/57	476	1786	229	10	0	,, ,,
T. 29/58	351	1787	298	7	0	,, ,,
T. 29/59	367	1788	174	6	0	,, ,,
T. 29/61	25	1789	245	1	7	,, ,,
T. 29/62	73	1790	191	11	3	,, ,,
T. 29/63	199	1791	274	18	0	,, ,,
T. 29/64	438	1792	199	7	0	,, ,,
T. 29/66	65	1793	330	9	5	including £100 for assistants.
		1794	no figure			
T. 29/68	119	1795	452	5	0	,, ,,
T. 29/69	198	1796	478	13	0	,, ,,
T. 29/71	3	1797	547	10	7	,, ,,
T. 29/73	245	1798	554	16	3	,, ,,
T. 29/74	491	1799	646	8	1	,, ,,
		1800–2	no figure			From 1801 onwards the
T. 29/81	407	1803	766	7	10	former £100 ceased
T. 29/83	298	1804	722	13	2	to be included, since
T. 29/84	212	1805	727	3	3	a regular allowance to
T. 29/87	371	1806	839	8	10	be divided between
		1807	no figure			clerks in the Journal
T. 29/95	10 July	1808	1,013	4	2	Office and Fees Office
T. 29/101	30 June	1809	1,136	0	4	was paid separately by
T. 29/106	347	1810	751	17	4	the Treasury.
		1811	no figure			
68 C.J.	758	1812	1,023	10	0	
69 C.J.	594	1813	914	3	2	
70 C.J.	App. B	1814	843	14	1	
71 C.J.	956	1815	1,211	13	0	
		1816	no figure			
73 C.J.	517	1817	1,287	11	9⎫	English business.
		,,	78	6	6⎭	Irish business.

[Note: The payees were Rosier up to and including 1796 and Dorington thereafter.]

Rosier did not succeed to a place among the four clerks without doors till 1789—fifteen years after his appointment as clerk of the fees—and John Dorington, who succeeded Rosier in 1796, became one of the four clerks in 1817.[1]

As for their subordinate staff, there is little indication of what it consisted in the earlier days of the Fees Office. Hatsell, in his letter to Ley about office arrangements in 1772, mentioned the undesirability of putting one Parker 'out of his present seat, where his accuracy and attention is very materially interesting to us all'.[2] This could only mean that he was concerned in the collection of fees, as assistant to whoever at that date was the official collector (probably Rosier), in which function he is likely to have continued even after his appointment that same year as a deputy committee clerk. In 1774 the clerk of the fees was allotted only two rooms,[3] so that his staff cannot have been large, possibly amounting to one clerk on the establishment as his chief assistant and one or two junior clerks paid out of his own pocket. It is clear, at all events, that the growth of the expense accounts must have corresponded with increase in his staff. And although Abbot, in his return of the clerical establishment for 1809,[4] showed only two junior clerks at very small salaries definitely allotted to the clerk of the fees, with another one to be paid out of Dorington's private business account, we know from John Ley's negotiations with the Treasury in 1801 that the agreed number of established clerks under the clerk of the fees was to be four; and these four would share with six clerks in the Journal Office an annual salary of £400 paid by the Treasury.[5] We also know that in 1809 the deputy committee clerk, J. Goodiff, was acting as John Dorington's chief assistant in the Fees Office, and that, under new arrangements for which Abbot was largely responsible in 1812, Goodiff was then officially designated deputy

---

[1] It is noteworthy that these two clerks of the fees were allowed to retain their positions after becoming one of the four clerks without doors, i.e. holders of a sinecure principal clerkship of committees, whereas other clerks, e.g. clerks of the journals, were retired from their active posts on becoming one of the four clerks.

[2] See p. 88.

[3] See the report of a select committee in 34 C.J. 808–9, and my monograph, *The Topography of the Old House of Commons*, pp. 17, 18.

[4] See chapter 6, p. 126.

[5] See next chapter, pp. 205–8.

clerk of the fees and an effective deputy committee clerk was appointed in his place.[1] In fact, from that year onwards it is clear that the set-up of the Fees Office closely resembled that so amply revealed in evidence before the select committees of 1833–5.

Evidence as to the nature of the work done for the Treasury by their parliamentary clerk, the clerk of the fees, can be found in the books of Treasury out-letters from 1777 onwards. This evidence is somewhat sporadic, but it is a quite sufficient indication, when read in the light of the full description of these duties given by John E. Dorington, then clerk of the fees in succession to his father, to the Select Committee on the House of Commons Offices of 1833 to which I shall allude later on. I have not thought it necessary to follow these Treasury instructions in the Treasury books all the way from 1777 to 1833, and confine myself for my present purpose to giving examples of them during the period 1777–1807. One of the recurring concerns of the Treasury was with the continuance of expiring laws affecting the revenue: no other expiring laws interested the government.[2] Thus, on 30 April 1777 Rosier is acquainted by Treasury letter that it is to be proposed to Parliament that the Act relative to bounties on certain articles should continue for the periods stated—indigo for 4 years, cordage for 4 years, silks for 6 years, supply of mariners for 1 year, timber from Dominica for 5 years, oak bark for 5 years, and the Act for the registry of corn for 5 years. Rosier is ordered to prepare clauses accordingly. The following year he is directed to prepare a clause or a bill to give effect to memorials from the merchants of Poole and of

---

[1] See Goodiff's case (1809) as narrated in chapter 10, pp. 231–44. Goodiff's petition, presented to extenuate his offence in wrongly altering an ingrossed public bill, shows the intolerable pressure of work devolving upon him, as Dorington's chief assistant, at the end of a session. He gave the following statistics of the increase in public bills passed sessionally since 1760: 1760, 29; 1770, 40; 1780, 52; 1790, 46; 1800, 105; 1805, 127; 1806, 155; 1807, 129; 1808, 149 (64 C.J. 77–78). These figures can be compared with the corresponding items in the clerk of the fees' expense accounts given above. See chapter 7, p. 153, for Goodiff's official designation in 1812 as deputy clerk of the fees.

[2] Cf. Colchester, i. 112, where Abbot records that on the Chancellor's asking him in 1797 if there was not a committee for expiring laws, he told him that there was, but that, in the way in which it was conducted, it only looked to the laws of revenue.

Dartmouth praying for renewal of Acts of 14 & 16 Geo. III for permitting export of biscuit and pease to Newfoundland for the fisheries with an increase in the amount of biscuit and permission also to export a certain quantity of flour. In 1781 he receives the draft of a clause, to be offered to Parliament, proposed by the receiver-general of the Isle of Man to obviate doubts which had arisen upon the construction of the Act respecting the exportation of rum from Scotland to the Isle of Man; and in the same year the Treasury forwards a memorial from the commissioners of Customs with a list of expiring laws which are all to be continued except those granting a bounty on flax seed from Ireland and allowing the reimportation of manufactured tobacco. In 1782 we find three letters transmitting clauses sponsored by the Customs or by the Excise to be inserted in an Act or otherwise submitted to Parliament, and a similar letter in 1783.[1]

The next example is of a different kind. I quoted above[2] the Treasury minute of 1779 increasing Rosier's salary on the ground of his attending to all private bills introduced into the House, and taking care that nothing prejudicial to the Crown or the public passed therein. This became an increasingly onerous duty of the clerk of the fees, as Treasury agent, which continued till it was transferred to the Chairman of Ways and Means assisted by the Speaker's Counsel in 1848.[3] Thus, in 1793 the Treasury forward to Rosier a report on the Warwick–Birmingham Canal Bill[4] by the acting surveyor of Crown Lands desiring him to take care that it does not pass into law except on the conditions suggested by him. In 1795 they send him the draft of a bill for allowing rape seed to be imported from all countries when the price of rape seed

[1] The references from 1777 onwards are T. 27/31, fol. 563; T. 27/32, fol. 91; T. 27/33, fols. 316, 385; T. 27/34, fols. 133, 153, 220; and T. 27/35, fol. 404.

[2] p. 170.

[3] See Williams, i. 101–3, 111–12. The latter reference summarizes the evidence as to his activity in this respect given by John E. Dorington before the Select Committee on Standing Orders Revision of 1843 (H.C. 550), in which he said that he sent copies of private bills to all the principal departments, who sent him such protective clauses or amendments as they desired to be inserted in the bills. These he transmitted to the agents for the promoters.

[4] Promoted by Rosier's colleagues, George White and his son (see below, pp. 183–88).

in this country is above £20 per last, on the same terms as rape seed is allowed to be imported from Ireland, the bill having been approved by the Lords of the Committee for Trade and Plantations. It is transmitted to Rosier 'in order that you may take the necessary steps for bringing the same before the consideration of Parliament'. Similarly, in 1807, Dorington is directed to see that certain expiring laws for regulating British fisheries are revived and continued for a year; and he receives letters from the Treasury containing observations on copies of private bills forwarded by him to them, with directions in one case to see that an amendment required by the commissioners of Excise is made.[1]

It would be tedious to prolong these examples, for they differ only in detail, not in kind. What has been said above makes it sufficiently clear that from the year 1757, when a Treasury clerk disappeared from the salary list of the House of Commons officers, and one of the latter took his place at the same additional salary for the same duties, a developing Treasury agency, conducted by one of the Commons Clerks, was set up in the House of Commons, quite independent of the Clerk of the House; although no doubt it was convenient to the Clerk, as well as to the House itself, that the Treasury agent should be a member of the Clerk's staff and, from about 1774 onwards, clerk of the fees. It is curious, none the less, that Hatsell in his account of the clerks makes no allusion to the main duties of the clerk of the fees. Many members must have been aware of them, even in 1781 when Hatsell's second volume appeared. Yet the first public reference made by the Clerk of the House to these seems to be in John Henry Ley's evidence as regards office accommodation before the Select Committee on Committee Rooms and Printed Papers of 1826.[2] There he said that Dorington's duties as collector of fees were very small; that he was also private agent to the government, 'that is to say, he is the clerk of the House of Commons who, on account of the convenience of the situation of his office, transacts the business of the government', and that he had accumulated an immense quantity of private business (i.e. as parliamentary agent for private bills),

---

[1] See T. 27/43, fol. 169; T. 27/45, fol. 372; T. 27/60, 1 July 1807; and T. 27/59, 17 and 30 Apr. 1807.   [2] H.C. (1826) 403, pp. 25-27.

hence the inconvenience of his office for public business (Dorington having complained that it was too small).

Much more extensive evidence on the duties of the Fees Office was given before the select committee of 1833, which will be the subject of a later chapter; but it may be suitable here, as an indication of the final development of the departure made in 1757, to indicate how John E. Dorington then described his duties.[1] He was, he said, paid £1,100 a year by the Treasury, in relation to whose business he was 'much the same as the agent for a private bill'; he was in personal connexion with the Treasury, the Board of Trade, the solicitors to the Boards of Stamps, Excise, and other departments on the business of those offices before Parliament and any bills that might affect them; he prepared the resolutions of Supply and of Ways and Means and any other resolutions which he deemed necessary preparatory to the introduction of a bill; he took care that amendments were introduced into a government bill at the proper stage, and that it was correctly ingrossed; he drew most of the Finance Bills, and various clauses for different bills in progress; his clerks were paid for their services in work on bills, at about 3s. an hour, vouchers for which were audited by the Treasury, and the charges made to the Treasury for clerks were partly for actual labour performed, and partly for matters for which they could not specifically charge. Before the same committee J. H. Ley, the Clerk of the House, referred to the Treasury payment to the subordinate clerks as a 'kind of salary' granted a long time ago, but 'he could not say when'.[2] Again, in 1835, before the Select Committee on the Rebuilding of the Houses of Parliament,[3] J. H. Ley referred to the Fees Office as that 'in which the public business, the Treasury business, is prepared, which is the principal part of the duty'.

That the public business of the House is equivalent to the Treasury business has not, for a long time, been true; in fact, the conception of the Treasury as an outside party, conducting their, or

---

[1] H.C. (1833) 648, qns. 395–411.

[2] Ibid., qns. 144–45. It is strange that no Treasury witness was called by this committee to explain past history which the Commons clerks had forgotten, or had never known.

[3] H.C. (1835) 262.

the government's, business through the House has long been dead. In spite of the increased power of the executive and the government's almost complete control of the time of the House, the self-consciousness of the House nowadays would not tolerate any such conception: public business is the public business of the House, not of any department, and the work of the Public Bill Office is work done by servants of the House for the House, not by agents for an outside body. Nevertheless, during the whole main period covered by this book, the older conception prevailed: and it may be that, within the frame of the picture that I have given above, a new, and badly needed, study might be made of the manner in which financial legislation and its machinery developed during the eighteenth, and the first half of the nineteenth, centuries. Such a study would be outside the scope of the present work. It will be more relevant here to suggest that this picture of the developing Treasury agency in the House throws a new light upon the history of parliamentary agency in general, which has always been somewhat obscure. It has never been determined when parliamentary agency began, what functions it implied at its origin, and by whom it was conducted, whether by officers of the House or by persons outside the House. The term 'parliamentary agency' has, for a very long time, been associated purely with the promotion of, and opposition to, private bills: and it is well known that, at all events by the beginning of the nineteenth century, clerks of both Houses, either individually or in partnership, were regularly and professionally engaged in this profitable business.[1] Yet nobody has attempted to trace the origin of parliamentary agency, or considered it in relation to the agency for public business on behalf of the government which I have described above. I shall conclude this chapter by presenting a view of this matter; but I must first bring forward further facts about agency for public business.

(4)

The clerk of the fees, in his earlier days, was not the only government agent among the clerks. We have seen[2] that Speaker Abbot appointed the clerk Samuel Gunnell the agent of the Irish Office

---

[1] See Williams, i. 52–53.   [2] p. 151.

in 1801—an event which could not then have seemed strange, nor should it seem so now, in the light of his contemporary, Dorington's, much more extensive agency for the Treasury. John Henry Ley's main objection to the appointment was that it cluttered up the Committee Office where, after being turned out of two other rooms in succession, Gunnell was obliged to carry on his Irish agency. Ley also thought that all such work should be placed in one person's hands, namely Dorington's.[1] Yet Gunnell was not the only other agent for government business when he was appointed. Some other clerk or clerks annually saw to the passing of the Mutiny Act and the Naval Mutiny Act as agents of the War Office and the Admiralty respectively. J. E. Dorington, in his evidence before the 1833 committee referred to above, told them that he was then agent for both of these Acts, at a fixed fee for each of them; but that, previously to 1825, 'another gentleman' had been responsible for the Mutiny Act, but had lost the job through charging a profit on the clerical services. I confess to have been baffled in my search among War Office papers for the name of this other gentleman at any period, but one precious piece of evidence among the Liverpool papers establishes his identity in 1781. It was Nathaniel, one of the three brothers Barwell.[2] Since he was then sixty-three and was also one of the paymasters of Exchequer bills, he may have conducted the Mutiny Act through the House for some time, and have continued to do so till he died in 1793. Some other clerk must have attended to the Naval Mutiny Act, receiving a fee from the Admiralty.

Again, I must recall the considerable payments made by the

---

[1] J. H. Ley's view of Gunnell's Irish agency as 'a great nuisance', and Gunnell's complaints about office accommodation for it, were given in evidence by both of them before the Select Committee on Committee Rooms and Printed Papers of 1826 (H.C. (1826) 403).

[2] Addl. MSS. 38215, fol. 193, a letter in the third person, dated 'Abingdon Street, Sunday morning 11th Feb' (1781), from Nathaniel Barwell (as to whom, see pp. 73–74) to Charles Jenkinson who was then the Secretary at War. It says, after presenting respectful compliments, 'Mr Barwell has read the Mutiny Bill with the proposed amendments very carefully, and does not see any inaccuracy except at the conclusion of the proviso inserted in p. 91, where the words *the said Act* shd. be *this Act*; which being a manifest mistake in the transcribing Mr Barwell has altered on the Bill presented to the House of Commons'.

Treasury to Newdigate Poyntz,[1] one of the four clerks without doors, for his service and attendance while the almost annual Militia Bills were passing through the House during the Seven Years War. It seems clear from the Treasury minutes relating to these two payments of £350 each that they were not merely for attendance in committee and clerical expenses, but were also a recompense for what amounted to agency for the government in respect of those bills.

Lastly—and this will lead us to the consideration of parliamentary agency in general—certain activities of the clerks, George White and his sons in the 'seventies and 'eighties of the eighteenth century, must attract our attention. Allusion to these clerks was made in the preceding chapter[2] where their attendance on the great committees inquiring into Indian affairs at that period was recorded. The two George Whites, father and son, must have been men of great energy and capacity for organization. It was only natural that the government of the day should make the fullest use of them; and since that government was, until 1782, Lord North's, Charles Jenkinson was probably responsible for utilizing their gifts. George White was not for long allowed to be nothing but a principal committee clerk and clerk of elections. Hardly was the inquiry of 1772–4 into the East India Company's affairs completed, than George White was, by an Act of Parliament of 1776,[3] assigned the task of sending to various local officers over the whole country copies of a questionnaire relating to the state of the poor, and of collecting and abstracting the returns for the information of Parliament. A similar bill for obtaining returns of charitable donations for the benefit of the poor failed to get the royal assent in 1777. This inquiry cost £1,000, as we see from two humble addresses, each for £500 to George White towards the expenses;[4] and the abstracts were ordered to be printed. Ten years later the same thing occurred. In 1786 two Acts[5] were passed relative to the same two subjects, the state of the poor and charitable donations for

---

[1] See chapter 7, p. 139, and Appendix IX, pp. 332, 333.

[2] pp. 143–4.   [3] 16 Geo. III, c. 40.

[4] 36 C.J. 538, 996. These payments were entered in the C.L. Accts. 1777–8 and 1778–9.

[5] 26 Geo. III, cc. 56 and 58.

their benefit, containing schedules for returns by clerks of the peace, town clerks, overseers, and churchwardens. By both these Acts George White, a clerk in the House of Commons, was again, by name, directed to send out these forms of return, to collect them, and to abstract them. The abstract was very long and costly to print, and it was annexed to the report of a select committee on the subject in the following year, in which report, as well as in a second report of 1788, some idea is given of the immense clerical work involved.[1] This time the payments to White for supervising the work were larger, and again provided by humble addresses for £3,000 in 1787 and £460 in 1788.[2]

George White's work under these two Acts, which amounted to the installation of an office to deal with these statistical inquiries and the correspondence involved by them, was not precisely parliamentary agency, but it was, none the less, the utilization by statute of a clerk in the Commons to perform functions which nowadays would devolve upon a government department.[3] But some activity on the part of the Whites more nearly resembling parliamentary agency for the government is indicated by a Treasury minute[4] of 30 July 1782, viz.:

Read, the accompt of expense incurred by Messrs. White on 3 Bills brought into Parliament relating to the Poor, Houses of Correction and Vagrants, amounting to £447. 1. 1*d.*, and the certificate of Thomas Gilbert, Esq., that the business was done by his directions and under his inspection, and that the charges appear reasonable.

Mr. Pratt to pay £250 in part, My Lords to consider further of certain articles.

Bills relating to the relief of the poor, houses of correction, and rogues and vagabonds were introduced in the House of Commons by Thomas Gilbert in the session 1780/1, and Gilbert reported

---

[1] These reports are in vol. ix of *Reports of Committees, 1715–1801*.

[2] 42 C.J. 796 and 43 C.J. 650. The payments also appear in the C.L. Accts.

[3] Similarly, John Rickman performed the functions of the present Registrar-General in collating the population returns under Abbot's Population Act of 1800, and supervised the abstraction of returns as to the state of the poor made under an Act (similar to those of 1776 and 1786) passed in 1803, see O. C. Williams, *Life and Letters of John Rickman*, pp. 40–42, 80. Rickman's duties were not, however, imposed by statute, as were George White's.

[4] T. 29/52, fol. 360.

them from the committees. They failed to obtain a third reading, but were reintroduced in the following session, when two out of three of them were passed. The account presented by the Whites presumably covered work in both sessions, and it was for expense incurred on three public bills introduced by a private member, but presumably sponsored by the government. The items are, of course, not available; but, if we had them, it is highly probable that they would resemble those of a parliamentary agent soliciting a private bill: moreover, the minute refers to 'Messrs. White' as though they were a firm of parliamentary agents.

And that is precisely what, in addition to all their work as committee clerks, they were. George White junior (*ob.* 1813), according to evidence given in 1835 by the man who had managed his agency business from 1801 to 1813, 'had been in the habit of carrying more private business than any four or five agents about the House': and this assertion is borne out by an entry in Abbot's manuscript diary (P.R.O. 30/9/35) for 24 February 1812 which, in a comparative statement of the numbers of applications for private bills, shows that in 1812 White was agent for forty out of seventy-eight bills still to be presented, but Dorington only for seventeen. Moreover, an entry in Luke Hansard's own ledger for 1803 of the sums which his clients among the parliamentary agents owed him for work in 1802 shows that George White owed him over £2,149, whereas the debts next in size (those of the brothers Benson and Edward Stracey respectively) were £646 and £483.[1]

---

[1] See the evidence of Richard Jones reported by the Select Committee on Private Bill Fees (H.C. (1834) 540, qn. 336). The entry in Luke Hansard's ledger, which I was able to consult by the courtesy of Mr. John Henry Hansard, of Unilever House, E.C. 4, is on fol. 16 of the ledger—the folio previous to that reproduced in J. C. Trewin and E. M. King, *Printer to the House* (London, 1952), p. 77—and gives the one and only full statement (for 1802) of Luke Hansard's profit and loss account for income-tax purposes. It provides the only evidence that Edward Stracey (see pp. 156–58) acted as agent for private bills in a considerable way, and shows that the clerks Samuel Gunnell, David Jones, and William Evatt did so on a very small scale. Other agents, including the Doringtons, were clients of other printers. The Bensons were, of course, John Benson and his son Arthur, successive clerks of the journals (see chapter 9). At the end of his reminiscences (Trewin and King, op. cit., p. 129) old Luke Hansard recorded that they still did business for Mr. Benson, and that Ley and Jones, who carried on the business of George White after 1813, were 'our friends'. Cf. chapter 11, p. 262–63.

The Whites, in fact, were the first among the clerks to build up
a large professional business as parliamentary agents. Various items
in a bundle of Treasury in-letters for 1783 establish that already in
that year Messrs. George White and Son, House of Commons,
were acting as agents of the Calico Printers and Manufacturers of
Manchester.[1] Similarly, John Dorington told a committee of the
House of Lords in 1827 that he had been a parliamentary agent for
over forty-five years.[2] This shows that he had entered on the business about the same time as the Whites, though it was his son and
successor, John E. Dorington, who developed the firm of Dorington and Jones into a very large business: and this is confirmed by
a statement made by certain clerks, after the prohibition of parliamentary agency to officers of the House, to the committee appointed to consider compensation. They said:[3]

The Clerks of the House have enjoyed the privilege of soliciting
private bills from time immemorial. Mr Dorington's father practised
previous to 1780, and his son has carried on the business since his death,
a period altogether of more than 56 years (i.e. 1780–1836).

The collocation of 'time immemorial' with the Doringtons'
fifty-six years of professional agency was, perhaps, a little incongruous. Although for several centuries past it had been open to
any competent person, the clerks included, to solicit private bills
in Parliament, there is no evidence that any established firms of
parliamentary agents, whether clerks or outside practitioners,
existed before George White and John Dorington started about
1780 the two businesses which lived in the memory of the next
generation. No doubt individual clerks quickly followed their
initiative. The then principal committee clerk giving evidence to
the 1833 Committee said that, on his appointment in 1791, he

---

[1] T. 1/592 in the P.R.O. contains memorials and letters from the Whites in this
capacity (nos. 618 b and 778 b). From 1792 onwards the Treasury minutes frequently refer to the activities of the Whites as agents for private bills, such as their
applications for the signification of the King's consent to bills affecting Crown
property, &c.

[2] The Select Committee on Private Bill Fees (H.L. (1827) 114, qn. 39).

[3] *Report* of the Select Committee on House of Commons Officers Compensation (H.C. (1836) 249, appendix).

found all the committee clerks acting as agents: yet the Treasury books of the late eighteenth century contain no reference to any other firms but Messrs. Whites and, occasionally, John Dorington. As for 'outdoor' agents, the same evidence shows that none existed till after 1794; and among the nine agents (or firms of agents) whose outstanding debts Luke Hansard recorded in 1803, six (including Edward Stracey) were officers of the House, while three were 'outdoor' agents, and the one firm among these to have a three-figure debit was that of Clementson and Bramwell—at that time not wholly an 'outdoor' firm, since the senior partner was deputy Serjeant at Arms.[1] The point that I make is that this professional parliamentary agency was a new thing, a product of that moment in the eighteenth century when private bill legislation was enormously increasing in scope and quantity and was becoming a far more complicated and expensive process than in earlier days when the quantity was small and the procedure easy.

Clerks, indeed, were first in the field. It would have been strange if the two men, White and Dorington, who had acquired great experience in agency for the government's parliamentary business, had not turned that experience to account when, for the first time in Parliament's history, the swelling volume of contentious private business provided the opportunity of placing their experience and organization at the disposal also of private promoters. Their abler colleagues followed their example to some profit, while others were content to pick up a few crumbs of agency here and there: the 'outside' element, which began with J. Bramwell and C. T. Ellis—both men of the law who subsequently wrote treatises on private bill procedure—developed more slowly. But this state of affairs has little relation to any that can have existed previous to

---

[1] The evidence referred to was given by W. G. Rose (H.C. (1833) 648, qn. 470). As regards 'outdoor' agents, he said that about 1794 Bramwell was employed by Mr. Clementson as a parliamentary agent, that Ellis came afterwards, and that after the Union a great number of 'outdoor' practitioners were so employed. Speaker Abbot's diary-entry, referred to on p. 183, shows other committee clerks as agents for a small number of bills in 1812, and Bramwell and Ellis as agents for eight and six bills respectively. For Luke Hansard's entry, see p. 183, n. 1 above. Ellis was his client as well as Bramwell.

the last quarter of the eighteenth century when a body of regulative Standing Orders, designed to protect the public but costly and complicated to comply with, were made by the House. At the time of James Courthope's minute-book (1697–9) and even of the *Liverpool Tractate* (1760) it obviously did not exist.[1] Who, in those days, were the typical 'solicitors' or 'agents' for private bills? They were not officers of the House, as I will proceed to prove.

To begin with, the appeal of the clerks in 1836 was indeed to 'immemorial', but not to *exclusive*, privilege: but when Clifford, in his *History of Private Legislation*,[2] wrote: 'For many centuries the work of soliciting private bills in Parliament was performed by officers of each House', he was making a statement which implied *exclusive* privilege. He produced no evidence to support it, but only referred to answers given by witnesses before committees from 1810 onwards, by which time, as has been shown, professional agency by certain clerks was well established, and the number of 'outdoor' professional agents had begun to increase. The evidence which I shall now adduce as to the soliciting of private bills in Parliament in earlier days entirely controverts the implication in Clifford's statement: it shows that, on the contrary, this activity was undertaken, in general, not by clerks, and not as a speciality, but by solicitors and attorneys in the ordinary course of their practice. The various examples of bills of costs for procuring the passage of private bills through Parliament, which I have collected in Appendix V and to which I now refer the reader, seem to be conclusive on this matter.

Thus, as regards the Corporation of London, the City Remembrancer, who has always acted as their solicitor, was the agent for their private bills, as his accounts prove. In the accounts of the churchwardens of St. Martins-in-the-Fields one of the items omitted in quotation runs: 'given Capt. Cressett a Solicitor in Parliament £1', while several other items record payments to counsel.[3] Again, the account of Samuel Brewster, the solicitor

---

[1] See *Courthope passim*, and Williams, i. 28–34 (consideration of the light thrown by the *Liverpool Tractate* on private bill procedure at the date of its compilation), and i. 41–46 on the development of Standing Orders after 1774.

[2] Op. cit. ii. 878.

[3] The churchwardens' accounts for 1719 (fol. 23) include a payment of £105

who acted as agent for the Balliol College Bill of 1695, is very largely made up of charges, which I have not quoted, for his own attendance in Parliament at 13s. 4d. a time: and, at the bottom of the bill of costs for the Farington Estate Bill are the words: 'For Sollicitor . . .', the amount being left blank. Again, in the report of the committee on the petition for the Dagenham Breach Bill, 1714,[1] there is the bill of 'Expenses of James Blew, Solicitor in Parliament for the Dagenham Breach Bill', which, besides fees, includes a sum of £53. 15s. (i.e. 50 guineas), his own expenses for attending and soliciting during the session. James Blew was not, so far as I know, a clerk in the House of Commons; nor was a certain Mr. Dawson who, according to minutes of the Common Council of Liverpool, was employed in 1725 by a delegation of the Council to act as agent for a bill to repair the roads from Prescot to Liverpool and to fix turnpikes on them. Also, in 1734 Liverpool employed a solicitor as agent for their opposition to the Weaver Navigation Bill, and found his charges very extravagant.[2] In the bills of costs, of which extracts are given in Appendix V, the payments to officers of the House are solely in respect of fees and gratuities,[3] or of copying charges. In fact, the first direct evidence that I have discovered of the employment of a clerk in the House to solicit a bill is a passage in the minutes of the Board of Works for 1 June 1768[4] relating to the Act of 1767 (7 Geo. III, c. xxxii) for enabling the Commissioners for building Westminster Bridge to spend money on making better approaches and passages to the House of Commons. It runs as follows:

to Mr. Cole and Mr. Wilson, Solicitors in Parliament, their bills for fees and soliciting about the bill for rebuilding the church. Although some solicitors may have had more practice in Parliament than others, there is no reason to suppose that such firms only carried on what came to be called parliamentary agency. There was not enough business.

[1] 18 C.J. 442.

[2] I am indebted to Mr. John Ainsworth, the City Treasurer of Liverpool, for the extracts from the Council of Accounts on which these statements are based.

[3] Cf. Rep. 99 (ii), fol. 201, a report dated 12 Sept. 1695 on gratuities to various persons for soliciting the Orphans Bill followed by the words: 'We also conceive it to be very fitt and reasonable that thirty pounds be given and distributed to and amongst the servants attending the Honble House of Commons for their assistance and attendance therein.'

[4] P.R.O. Works 6/36.

The Commrs agree to pay John Speed[1] £10. 10s. in full for his trouble in soliciting the bill thro' both Houses of Parlt; and more to him for revising the sd. bill, drawing a clause, and making a fair copy for the House; drawing the Brief and a fair copy thereof, making out amendments and examining the Ingrossment, £5. 5s.

This Act, although technically a private or local Act promoted by an outside body, was in reality sponsored by the Board of Works, as the records show: it is, therefore, another example of agency for public, rather than private business, and on behalf of the government. It is hardly surprising that it was contemporaneous with the employment of Robert Yeates as agent by the Treasury.

More evidence of such a kind would be extremely welcome, but it could not possibly discredit Samuel Brewster's bill for the Balliol College Act of 1695 or the unnamed solicitor's bill for the Farington Estate Act, 1698: and it would need documentary proof to convince any reasonable person that what Samuel Brewster could do in 1695 could not have been done by his forbears a century earlier, with judicious payments to the Clerk and his man. So far as the House of Commons goes, the picture suggested by Clifford and enhanced by Sir William Holdsworth,[2] of a horde of clerks seated in the outer lobby and haughtily denying petitioners for private bills access to the House except through their agency— is slightly grotesque. The horde did not exist, in the first place; and, in the second, the member in charge of the bill could, in early days, do almost everything himself, with the necessary assistance—in reading the bill, signing the order for the committee, ingrossing the bill, and seeing that it was carried to the other House—of the Clerk of the House. In fact, there might be some justification for regarding the Clerk himself as from earliest days the universal parliamentary agent, and as such entitled to charge fees on each proceeding, and willing, moreover, to accept gratuities for expediting business. Yet the only bills which original documents show to

[1] John Speed succeeded Rosier as clerk of the journals in 1774, and died in 1776. I have been unable to discover his previous history.

[2] *The History of English Law*, 3rd ed. (London, 1945), xi. 334 and n.—a passage obviously based on Clifford's statement and on the evidence given before various committees from 1810 to 1836 which has no relevance to earlier conditions, as I have endeavoured to prove.

have been 'solicited' by the Clerk were Treasury money bills in Jodrell's day. That precedent lapsed; but its revival in the later eighteenth century, with an under-clerk substituted for the Clerk, not only determined the functions of the future Public Bill Office, but was the foundation of professional private bill agency, at first by clerks, and later by other practitioners outside the House.[1]

[1] See also, to support the view here put forward, the remarks of the Select Committee on Fees, etc., in 1731/2, Appendix IV, p. 307, which refer to extravagant payments to 'Counsel, Solicitors and other persons without doors' in distinction from the fees taken by the clerks, and make no reference to agency on their part.

9

THE OFFICE OF JOURNALS AND PAPERS

(1)

EARLY in the seventeenth century the House came to recognize, and to supervise, the Clerk's Journal book, as the official record of its proceedings. Since that time the oath taken by the Clerk on his appointment has included an undertaking to make true entries. This undertaking he has always fulfilled by keeping, with the help of his assistant or assistants at the table, manuscript minute-books of the House's proceedings; and from these minute-books are still compiled the two official records, now for a long time reproduced in print, the *Votes and Proceedings of the House*—more shortly called the *Votes*—and the *Journal*. Moreover, the custody of the House's records, and of all other papers introduced into the House in the course of its proceedings—petitions, bills, accounts presented, reports of committees, letters, returns, and so forth—has always been one of the Clerk's functions. Some of the early Clerks were more careful in its performance than others, but all were hampered by having no official repository in which to keep them. It is safe to say that Paul Jodrell was the first Clerk who had both the will and, to some extent, the means to keep the records and papers of the House intact and in good order. Reference has already been made in earlier chapters to the Clerk's performance of these functions of record-keeping and record-preserving,[1] to the loss of half the *Journals* of Elizabeth's reign, to the unsuccessful attempts by the House to obtain a room at Westminster wherein to store its records, and to Jodrell's maintenance, at his own expense, of a clerk to help keep the papers of the House in order: we have now to proceed from Jodrell onwards and to examine the development of these functions which resulted in the creation of the Journal Office. To this office, under the clerk of the journals and papers, were delegated

[1] See chapters 1, pp. 7–8, 13–14; 2, p. 32; 3, pp. 36–40.

all the above-mentioned functions of the Clerk of the House except that of compiling the Clerk's minute-book, which is necessarily done at the table of the House.[1]

The Journal Office, however, did not suddenly come into full-blown existence: like other branches of the Clerk's department, it grew from small beginnings, and the combination of its various tasks was hardly achieved by the middle of the eighteenth century. The researches of Professor J. E. Neale[2] have proved that the Elizabethan Clerks, Seymour and Onslow, preserved both their original book of notes and the fair copy of it made, presumably, by copying clerks; but the Clerks of the seventeenth century failed to continue this excellent example of having their original notes fairly copied, with the result that, from 1604 to 1685, the Commons *Journals*, now preserved in the Public Record Office, are in most cases, the original minute-books of Clerk and Clerk Assistant, often hard to decipher, and full of erasures, corrections, and interlineations.[3] After 1685 the fairly written copy becomes the rule; and the practice of producing a copied 'manuscript' *Journal* was continued for many years after the printing of the *Journal* had been established. The Speaker's tribute to Jodrell, that he had kept the *Journals* 'in a better manner than ever had been done by any of his predecessors',[4] was no doubt prompted by Jodrell's care in seeing that the *Journal* was correctly and legibly copied each year.

[1] Under modern conditions, which include the almost universal printing of documents presented to the House, and the organization of the Library, the function of custody has become very much simplified. The Clerk is still the theoretical custodian of all the House's records and papers, but the Journal Office is no longer his universal delegate in this respect. For instance, the manuscript *Journals* are now housed at the Public Record Office, the original petitions for private bills are deposited by the Private Bill Office in the Victoria Tower, minutes of evidence taken before committees but not reported to the House (and therefore, in some cases, not even set up in type) remain in the custody of the Committee Office, and certain other documents are kept by the Librarian.

[2] See chapter 1, p. 13, n. 4.

[3] See 12 C.J. 255–6, where it is recorded that Sir Rowland Gwyn, reporting in 1698 from a select committee who had had occasion to search the *Journals* said that many books of the *Journals* before 1685 were much worn, ill written, and without any indexes. This was the occasion for the order that all the *Journals* until the year 1685 should be fairly transcribed with indexes and references to the original folios. See p. 40, n. 3.

[4] See chapter 3, p. 40.

Again, in 1680, and regularly after 1682, the *Votes* were ordered to be printed, under the supervision of the Speaker, who appointed the printers. This entailed the daily production of the copy for the printer and the correction of the proofs which, unless done by Jodrell and his Clerk Assistant—as is quite possible, for the *Votes* were not very long at that date—must have been the work of some other clerk or clerks employed by him. Moreover, since Jodrell carried out, in part and unsatisfactorily, the House's order to have the earlier *Journals* up to 1685 fairly transcribed, it is clear that he had plenty of scribes at his disposal. It is extremely doubtful, however, whether he in any way associated these scriveners' functions—the preparation of the printer's copy of the *Votes* and the manuscript of the *Journal*—with the custody and arrangement of the House's records and papers, for the better execution of which task he had maintained a clerk ever since the Revolution. In his part of the clerks' memorial of 1709–11,[1] Jodrell described this clerk—who was by then Zachary Hamlyn[2]—as one 'who hath the charge and custody (under his Master) of the Journals, and Bills and proceedings thereon, with other papers laid before the House, whereby the same are kept in order and from confusion, and he is obliged to attend constantly whilst the House is sitting, and at all times on Members of the House upon searches, and otherwise when required'. In other words, Zachary Hamlyn was a kind of assistant keeper, or librarian, of the office where, by that time, the Clerk kept the *Journals* and papers; but there is no mention that he had any function in connexion with the *Votes* or the manuscript *Journal*.

The principal difficulty in reaching any definite conclusions about the earliest history of the Journal Office is the almost complete absence of record as to staff, methods, and accommodation. The custody of *Journals* and records, for instance, was mainly a question of accommodation, and on that subject there is a certain amount of evidence with which I shall deal later. The compilation and production of the *Votes* on the other hand, is not alluded to in any petition by the clerks, and we can learn little about these

---

[1] See Appendix II, p. 291, and chapter 3, pp. 39–40.
[2] See chapter 3, p. 40, n. 1.

things till the latter part of the eighteenth century. This is not so strange as it may seem, because the *Votes* were originally produced on a commercial footing by the printer, who paid all the costs of production, including the services of any of the House's clerks employed in their compilation and correction, and a fixed fee for each day's *Vote* to the Clerk of the House and the Serjeant at Arms, after the deduction of which he charged his own profit at a fixed rate and the remainder of the profit from sales went to the Speaker.[1] It was only when, owing to competition from the newspapers, the sale of the *Votes* ceased to be profitable that the Treasury took over the expense;[2] so that, until about 1780 when this transference took place, the printers' account books and correspondence, if they were extant, would be the only sources from which anything could be learned about the earlier process of issuing the *Votes*.

There is but one indication in the Treasury books for earlier years which throws a gleam of light on the matter. In the year 1723 a certain Thomas Ward was convicted of speaking treasonable words, on the accusation of Sergeant Atherton who, with Ward and two others, 'wrote the Minutes of the House of Commons'. The words used were: 'God Damn your King George, he is no King, and I am as good a man or better than he, for you don't know who is your King.' Atherton so much objected to this man's company that, when Ward was re-engaged next session, he quitted his job. Ward, on conviction, was whipped at the cart's tail from the gate of King Street near the Cockpit, Whitehall, round Palace Yard.[3] From this unfortunate episode it must be concluded that, even as late as 1723, various copyists were employed by the Clerk to transcribe his minutes, but that these in no sense constituted an office managed by a clerk on his establishment.

The first clerk publicly known as the clerk of the papers— namely, Samuel Littlemore—was certainly holding that office in 1743 and, probably, had then held it for a year or more.[4] More-

---

[1] See Appendix IV, pp. 308–9, for the Speaker's annual profit from the sale of the *Votes* for the years 1728–32. The fees of 10s. 6d. to the Clerk and 7s. to the Serjeant were still being paid by Nichols in 1828 and were charged in his account.

[2] See the evidence of J. B. Nichols given in 1822 before the Select Committee on Printing and Stationery (H.C. (1822) 607).

[3] *Cal. T.P. 1720–27*, p. 224.   [4] See chapter 4, p. 71.

over, since Zachary Hamlyn was still in the Clerk's office in 1742 when Nicholas Hardinge reported to the House on the state of the *Journals*, it is obvious that he had never held that position. It seems likely, therefore, that the creation of this post was an act of Nicholas Hardinge's, and it is one which more or less coincided with the House's decision to have the *Journals* printed under the Clerk's supervision, beginning from the earliest and, in time, bringing the publication up to date. This laborious enterprise must have entailed some office organization by the Clerk: we know, in fact, that Samuel Richardson, who was the first printer of the *Journals* and also printer to the House of Commons from 1734–61, came into close relations with several of the clerks, including Osborn Barwell who was clerk of the papers from 1748 to 1754.[1] But since John Grover, Richardson's closest friend among the clerks, who died in 1749,[2] held positions which had no ostensible connexion with the *Votes*, the *Journal*, or the printing of reports and papers, I incline to the opinion that Jeremiah Dyson, who succeeded Hardinge in 1748, was the true organizer of the Journal Office as the place where these different activities were combined. In that year the *Court and City Register* shows Samuel Littlemore, hitherto clerk of the papers, as clerk of the journals, while Osborn Barwell became clerk of the papers; and in 1754, when Barwell was made second ingrossing clerk, Littlemore combined the two positions as clerk of the journals and papers. From then down to the present that has been the proper title of the principal clerk of the Journal Office.

It is not until Hatsell's long tenure of the Clerkship of the House that we begin to get, from various sources, a closer view of the staff and working of the Journal Office, or Court of Wards, as it was still called when Hatsell first became Clerk. I shall endeavour, therefore, to compose from the various and ragged bits of evidence

---

[1] See chapter 4, p. 72.

[2] Ibid., pp. 71–72. The annual bill for printing and binding of bills, &c., was endorsed by Grover for the year 1739–40 (*Cal. T.P. 1739–41*, p. 515). Usually this was endorsed by the Clerk himself, and after 1741 the Treasury warrant for payment, previously made out to the printer, was made out to the Clerk. This shows that, under Hardinge, it was the ingrossing clerk who dealt with the printing of papers, &c., ordered by the House to be printed.

available a general picture of the Court of Wards and its activities as they were while Hatsell sat at the table. In detailing the various clerks who held office under him,[1] he mentioned:

another clerk, who has custody of the Journals and Papers, and who has several writing clerks under him. The office of the Clerk of the Papers was formerly kept in the room which was anciently the Court of Wards, whence, though this office has been frequently removed from place to place, the chamber in which it has been held, has been always, improperly stiled, the Court of Wards.

He adds in a footnote that within the last few years the proper title, the Journal Office, had been adopted and constantly used.

The original Court of Wards and Liveries—one of the prerogative courts, abolished by ordinance in 1645 and again by statute in 1660—occupied a building which, like a cork in a bottle, stopped up all direct egress from St. Stephen's Chapel to the west. It stood between the south wall of Westminster Hall and the northern end of the Court of Requests; plans show it to have been about 66 feet long and 30 feet broad; i.e. it had the same breadth as the Lobby of the House and its length equalled the breadth of Westminster Hall. It was the first part of the Palace of Westminster on to which the House of Commons extended its hold after the Restoration. In 1660 and 1661 it was occasionally used as a meeting-place for committees, and in 1674 the inner room, or Inner Court of Wards, was repaired and put into fitting condition for keeping the *Journals* and records of the House.[2] This was the room where, at the first meeting of every new Parliament from 1679 to 1768 inclusive, the members took the oath of allegiance, as the *Journal* invariably records. Also, from some uncertain date until 1768, when the Court of Wards was entirely cleared away to make a new approach to St. Stephen's from Old Palace Yard, the papers of the House were kept in the Outer Court of Wards.[3]

---

[1] Hatsell, ii. 275.   [2] 9 C.J. 295.

[3] This was stated in 1800 by the then clerk of the journals, Arthur Benson, in a return made to the Select Committee on the State of the Public Records of that year (Appendix B (2) of the *Report*). He added that in 1768 the papers were removed to the 'lumber room' above the ceiling of the House, that the outer Court of Wards was taken down, and that Alice's Coffee House (in 1800) stood on its site, i.e. in the north-east angle of Old Palace Yard.

The various moves of the office called the Court of Wards where the *Journals* were kept is too intricate a subject to be discussed here: but the correspondence between Hatsell and John Ley in 1769[1] establishes the fact that, as the result of the rebuilding which swept away the old Court of Wards, a new 'Court of Wards' had to be found, but that its site had not been determined. They discussed a plan by which it should project off the Long Gallery eastwards, parallel to the Painted Chamber, but this came to nothing; in 1770 the Court of Wards was established in a large room on the first story over the new approach; in 1774 it was moved to the room over the Long Gallery; and at some time between that date and 1794 it was moved again to the upper floors of a building—all used for clerks' offices—abutting on the south wall of St. Stephen's, and it remained there till it was destroyed by the fire of 1834.[2] Thus, between 1768, when Hatsell became Clerk of the House, and 1797, when he resigned his duties at the table and appointed John Ley his deputy, the Journal Office was to be found successively in four different places—the old room in the old Court of Wards, the room overlooking Old Palace Yard which later became Committee Room 11, the rooms over the Long Gallery, and, finally, in the upper floors of the office building just south of the Lobby. John Rosier was clerk of the journals at the time of the first move, John Speed at the time of the second, and John Benson when the third was made. Arthur Benson succeeded his father in the year when Hatsell left the table.

(2)

Taking the functions of the Journal Office separately, and beginning with the custody of the papers and records, we get a valuable glimpse from Arthur Benson's return made in 1800 to Abbot's Select Committee on the State of the Public Records.[3] He stated

[1] In the Ley MSS., letters of 24 and 31 Oct. 1769.

[2] I must ask the reader to accept these statements without the somewhat intricate discussion of evidence (including plans) which proof would entail. This is to be found in my monograph, *The Topography of the Old House of Commons* (see Introduction, p. xvi).

[3] See p. 195, n. 3 above, and the *Report* (1801) of the committee, pp. 66–67.

that he had in his custody the manuscript *Journals* from 1547 to date, the books of Clerk's minutes from 1685 onwards, and the minutes of committees of the whole House from 1688–89. Petitions, bills, reports, accounts, and papers were entered in schedule books in the Journal Office, and arranged in separate bundles under distinct heads. For the last thirty years, i.e. from 1770, these had been kept in regular order and good preservation; but those of earlier date were in a much less complete state, some papers being displaced and in great disorder. The earlier books and papers stored in presses in the Long Gallery were in no regular order, though classified lists of books and papers 1495–1737 showed that they had once been in order. Also, the 'lumber room' above the House itself contained various volumes of reports and proceedings of commissioners, several sealed bags referring to plots, secret correspondence, and Irish affairs at the time of the Revolution, besides public and private petitions from 1607 to date, public and private bills, and reports of committees of about the same period. It is obvious that search for any unpublished papers previous to 1770 would have been very difficult, and that no effort was made to arrange or catalogue the disordered papers of earlier days, once carefully scheduled, no doubt, by the long-departed Zachary Hamlyn. The next thirty years were to cause an accumulation of papers beside which that of the past was a trifle, but the danger of total loss was minimized after the Union by the then new practice of ordering all papers and reports to be printed:[1] and this was providential, seeing that all the unprinted papers were destroyed by the fire of 1834. The printing of reports and papers, and the increase in expenditure thereon from 1743 onwards, has been dealt with in relation to the Clerk's emoluments from 'copy money'.[2] The Journal Office, as well as the Clerk, derived some profit from copy money, since the clerk of the journals was allowed to charge 2*d.* a side for the copy prepared in his office for the printer, one-

---

[1] That as late as 1761 a paper presented by a minister could be lost within a week, is shown by Jeremiah Dyson's letter to Jenkinson in the Liverpool papers (Addl. MSS. 36198, fol. 35) informing him that a copy and translation of the Brunswick treaty, presented the previous week, had been taken away from the table, and could not be found anywhere, and asking him to supply a duplicate.

[2] Chapter 6, pp. 111–13, and Appendix VII.

half that sum as pure profit, and a further sum for proof correction, which went to his subordinates.[1]

The clerk of the journals also had the custody of another class of document—the stock of printed *Journals* and papers. The surplus *Votes* were immediately sold off by the printer,[2] but the process by which the *Journal* was printed and distributed was entirely different. So far as storage was concerned, various warehouses had been hired which were not weatherproof. Hatsell complained to the Board of Works in 1779 about the dampness of the warehouse floor,[3] and in the following year the Commons, by humble address on 6 July, prayed for the purchase of a convenient building for the better preservation of the *Journals* and papers. But nothing was done till 1799 when, after some negotiation, the Clerk of the House, with the Treasury's consent, took over the lease of No. 1 Abingdon Street from John Groves, the clerk of the works, and the Board of Works carried out the necessary alterations which provided, not only a warehouse, but a residence for the clerk of the journals.[4] This building survived the fire of 1834, but, unfortunately, none of the precious original papers were stored there.

Hatsell, in his book, while saying that one of the Clerk's duties was to see that the *Journal* of the session was properly made out and fairly transcribed from the minute-books, and the printed *Votes* and the original papers laid before the House, and that this was commonly done during the summer recess, made no reference to the production of the printed *Journal*. This omission is not so very extraordinary seeing that the authentic *Journal* was then the manuscript *Journal*, not the printed copy. Nevertheless, not long

[1] See the evidence of George Whittam, clerk of the journals, reported in the 9th Report of the Select Committee on Public Expenditure (H.C. (1810) 373, p. 198). He put in an exact account of the Journal Office's portion of copy money in 1809: the principle on which it was calculated must have been as old as copy money (see Appendix VII).

[2] See Whittam's evidence referred to in n. 1 above, p. 194 of the report.

[3] See Board of Works minutes in P.R.O. Works 1/5, dated 23 Dec. 1779, and Works 4/16, dated 24 Dec. 1779.

[4] See T. 29/75, fols. 211–12, 307, Board of Works minute (P.R.O. Works 4/19) for 22 Apr. 1803, and 58 C.J. 525. The cost of refitting was £1,281. 4s. 0¼d.; and the premises were described by George Whittam to the Select Committee on Committee Rooms and Printed Papers in 1825 (H.C. (1825) 515).

before the year when Hatsell became Clerk, the printing of the *Journals*, first decided upon in 1742, had come up to date, and a certain sum was voted each year for printing the *Journal* of the session. This sum included the printer's bill and the cost of clerical work performed by the Journal Office, upon which fell the three-fold task of producing the *Votes*, the manuscript *Journal*, and the printed *Journal*, of which the office kept the unissued stock. Having already referred to the custody and warehousing of this stock, I will complete the story of the *Journal* before passing to the *Votes*.

The manuscript *Journal* need not detain us long, since its production was simply a process of copying from the Clerk's minute-book and the *Votes* in a good round hand, performed by the junior clerks or, in earlier days, by hired scriveners at so much a folio of seventy-two words. The payment to these copyists was not charged against the sum voted for the printing of the *Journal*, and it can only be conjectured that the Clerk originally paid them out of his emoluments from fees.[1] Perhaps I may here, in anticipation, dismiss the subject by remarking that, after 1817, when the form of the *Votes* was drastically revised and shortened, the manuscript *Journal* was copied direct from the printed *Journal*, mainly with a view to keeping up the hands of the Journal Office clerks and giving them some paid work to do in the recess.[2] The 1833 Committee recommended the abolition of the manuscript *Journal*, and the recommendation was followed.

The House's decision to print all the existing *Journals* for the use of present and future members was taken in 1742, following the report of a select committee appointed to consider the matter.[3]

---

[1] The returns made by individual clerks of their emoluments to the 1833 Committee on the House of Commons Offices show that the copying of the manuscript *Journal* was then paid out of the fee fund. The cost varied with the length of the *Journal*.

[2] See the evidence by Whittam, clerk of the journals, before the Select Committee on the Present Method of Ingrossing Bills (H.C. (1823) 552). At that date the cost of the manuscript *Journal* was between £110 and £150 annually, and the clerks made from £20 to £30 apiece by their copying.

[3] The committee was appointed on 5 May (24 C.J. 213) and their long report of 31 May with appendixes, including Nicholas Hardinge's report on the state of the *Journals* and Samuel Richardson's estimates of the cost of printing, was entered at length in the *Journal* (ibid., pp. 262–66).

Hardinge's proposal, framed upon Richardson's estimates, was that 1,000 copies should be printed, 600 to be issued to members of the House, and the remaining 400 to be kept for issue to future members at 20*s*. or a guinea a volume, other persons who wished to purchase to be charged 30*s*. or 1½ guineas. He asked for recompense for his pains of compilation, composing prefaces, annotation, and indexing; and also for compensation for loss of fees payable to the Clerk for searches into the *Journal* and copies, which would necessarily be much diminished if printing were decided upon. As regards production, he undertook, if advanced a competent proportion of the whole expense, to contract for paper and pay such charges as were immediately necessary and upon the delivery of each volume would expect to receive a proportionable part of the remaining expense. The resolutions of the committee, agreed to by the House with one amendment, were (1) that the *Journals* now in the custody of the Clerk, commencing with *Seymour* (the earliest volume), should be printed; (2) that 1,000 copies of the said *Journals* should be printed ('for the use of the Members of this House' inserted by the House) by the appointment and under the direction of Nicholas Hardinge, Clerk of the House of Commons, the same not to exceed thirty volumes (Richardson's estimate, a correct one, was twenty-three), with a proper preface and index to each volume, a general preface, and an index to the whole; (3) that a proper recompense should be made to Hardinge for the loss of fees. This last resolution of the committee was implemented in the final resolution of the House, that a humble address should be presented to his Majesty praying that he should order a sum of £5,000 to be advanced to Nicholas Hardinge for the printing of the *Journals*, and the further sum of £1,000 as recompense for loss of fees.

It would be out of place here to enter into great detail as to the gradual printing of the *Journals* over the next twenty years, the payments made, the laborious and not very satisfactory production by several hands of the general index, and the reprints of back numbers which added to the cost: an account of these matters is available elsewhere.[1] The feature of this process to be noted, how-

---

[1] In the *Report* of the Select Committee on Publications and Debates Reports (H.C. (1915) 321), appendix, part ii, pp. 74–86.

ever, is that the printing of the *Journals* was undertaken by the Clerk as a contractor, to whom lump sums were paid from time to time, and who made his own arrangements for purchase of paper and printing;[1] also, that the contract was a personal one and did not depend on retention of the Clerk's office. Hardinge, who contracted to print the first twenty-three volumes, resigned the Clerkship in 1748 in favour of Jeremiah Dyson; but his contract continued till his death. He received the final instalment of the first £5,000 voted in 1747, by 1750 he had received another £5,000, and a third sum of £5,000 by the end of 1752, by which time Jeremiah Dyson had been Clerk for four years. Even then the first twenty-three volumes of the *Journal* were not finally paid for: in 1758 the sum of £778. 16s. 5d. was paid to Hardinge's widow 'in full satisfaction of the balance of an account for printing the Journals up to the end of the 8th Parliament of Great Britain', and the following year £3,000 was voted and paid to her 'as recompense for the pains and services of Nicholas Hardinge in preparing copies of the Journal for the press and in directing the printing'.

Meanwhile, pursuant to a resolution of the House of 26 May 1756 that the *Journals* should be printed from the beginning of the 9th Parliament of Great Britain to the end of the present session, Jeremiah Dyson became the contractor. He appears to have received, by instalments of varying amount, a total sum of £10,751, part of which was voted and paid in 1764, two years after his departure from the table. Finally, Thomas Tyrwhitt was involved in the same process for reprinting the earlier volumes of the *Journal* and 1,500 copies of *Reports not entered in the Journals*, receiving between 1767 and 1770 the sum of £17,600.[2] However, by the time that Thomas Tyrwhitt succeeded Dyson as Clerk it was

[1] See chapter 4, pp. 64–65, for Hardinge's dilatoriness in paying what he owed to Samuel Richardson on this account.

[2] All the payments mentioned in this summary were entered in the C.L. Accts. for the years in which the instalments were paid, and the total sums voted were entered in the *Journal*. I have not thought it necessary to give the many references. The chief *Journal* references are 1756 (27 C.J. 617), 1759 (28 C.J. 601), 1761 (ibid., p. 1106), 1762 (29 C.J. 200), 1763 (ibid., p. 634), 1767 (31 C.J. 412), 1769 (32 C.J. 440). For the story and cost of the general index, see the account referred to on p. 200, n. 1 above.

possible to provide for the printing of the session's *Journal* as a single sessional expense.[1] When Hatsell succeeded Tyrwhitt the annual vote for the sessional *Journal* was £600, from 1777 to 1782 it fluctuated between £700 and £800, in 1783 it was £900, in 1784–6 £1,000, in 1788–93 £1,200, and in 1794–6 £1,800.

What sums were paid, and what clerks were employed, by Hardinge and Dyson for the preparation for press of the earlier *Journals* and the correction of the proofs there is no evidence. This was part of the expense sustained by the Clerk as contractor, and there can be little doubt that the clerk of the journals and his underlings must have been employed. As soon as the sessional printing of the *Journal* was established, it is evident that the compilation, copying for press, proof-correcting and revising, as well as the sessional index, were tasks of the Journal Office performed at fixed rates by the clerks, the expense being charged against the sum voted for the sessional *Journal*. This is clear from an account giving the details of the payments to Journal Office clerks in respect of the sessional printed *Journal* for 1830 signed by John Bull, then clerk of the journals, with a note stating that it was a copy of the account formerly charged in the printing account, but last session included in the estimate for Lords and Commons Offices. This appears among the appendixes to the *Report* (1831) of the Select Committee on the King's Printer's Patent,[2] together with a table showing the cost of the *Journal* annually since 1810 and the proportion of that cost paid to the clerk of the journals. The items charged in 1830 comprise payment to the clerk of the journals for general supervision and examination, to another clerk for compiling and indexing, and to several clerks for copying, preparing for press, and correcting proofs, together with certain smaller sums for delivery, rent of warehouse and taxes in respect of the same. The total sum paid to clerks was £1,736. 6s. 10d. out of a total printer's bill amounting to £5,577. 11s. 6d., whereas the relative figures

[1] The first sessional payments shown in the C.L. Accts., also voted by the House, are £350 in 1763, £400 in 1765, £600 in 1766; the lump sum payments of the next two sessions break the sequence, but after 1768 the vote for the sessional *Journal* became invariable till the system was entirely changed in 1796 (see Appendix VII, p. 324).

[2] H.C. (1831–32) 713.

given for 1810 were £466. 13s. 10d. and £3,134. 2s. 1d. These figures combined with those given above of the sums voted for the printed *Journal* between 1768 and 1796 show the rapid rise in this item of expenditure from 1790 onwards:[1] but they also show that, at all events up to about 1817, the earnings of the Journal Office clerks from this source were far smaller than they had become by 1830, and this in spite of the fact that from 1802 till 1835 the bulk of the *Journal* was greatly increased by the inclusion of accounts, papers, and long committee reports in an appendix.[2]

The nightly production of the *Votes* was a far more arduous task for the Journal Office than that of the *Journal*: the latter was produced at leisure in the recess, but the *Votes* have always had to be prepared for press during and after the sitting of the House. Like that of the *Journal*, the cost of the *Votes* increased rapidly from the last decade of the eighteenth century onwards. Although J. B. Nichols, the printer to the House, told a select committee in 1822[3] that the account for printing the *Votes* was taken over by the Treasury in 1777, when declining sales had caused an actual loss to the printer, it appears that it was not till 1781 that, by humble

---

[1] This alarming rise in the cost of printing for the House, particularly after the Union, was considered by several select committees from 1810 onwards. It was primarily caused by the ever-increasing business of the House so that, in spite of certain economies made in 1803 and 1817 in the manner of printing the *Journals* and the *Votes*, it could not effectively be checked.

[2] By order of the House first made on 25 June 1802 (57 C.J. 659). However, see Hatsell, ii. 268, where he says that the papers proper to be inserted in this appendix had become so numerous by 1803 that it usually occupied twelve clerks for three months in copying them for that purpose. This was altered, he says, in 1804 when the Speaker directed that a schedule of the papers was to be made for the manuscript *Journal* with references to the papers, which were done up in bundles. This answered for use till each volume of the *Journal* with its appendix came in its turn to be printed. Junior clerks in the Journal Office were still being paid for making up these bundles and schedules in 1833.

[3] *Report* of the Select Committee on Printing and Stationery (H.C. (1822) 607). Nichols also said that from 1729–77 the *Votes* were printed by William Bowyer and his successor, John Nichols. Inspection of the printed *Votes* shows that this statement was by no means accurate. Bowyer first appears in association with Williamson in 1731, but from 1735–57 drops out. He reappears in 1761 in company with three other firms of printers; Nichols first appears as his partner in 1770, as sole proprietor in 1779, but not till 1794 as sole authorized printer of the *Votes*. However, in 1782 when a payment for the cost of the *Votes* first appears in the C.L. Accts., it was made to Nichols alone, and so it was thereafter continued.

address,[1] the Commons prayed that his Majesty would be pleased to defray the cost of printing the *Votes*; and from that year till the change of system in 1797 the sum charged by Nichols for printing the *Votes* was voted annually. It began at £370 in 1781, but had risen to £709. 17s. in 1786, to £1,095. 13s. in 1793, and to £1,141. 1s. 6d. in 1796, in which year an additional payment of £250 was voted to one of the Journal Office clerks for compiling an index to the *Votes*—a payment which continued, though not separately voted after 1819, and increased as the size of the *Votes* increased. However, at the time when Hatsell resigned his seat at the table to John Ley, both the labour of the clerks and their emoluments for preparing, copying, and correcting the *Votes* were considerably less than they later became, according to evidence given before various committees from 1822 onwards.

(3)

To these developments I shall have to return, but for the moment let us hold in view the Journal Office of about 1798 when Arthur Benson had just succeeded his father as clerk of the journals, and the office—it may be said with fair certainty—was already housed at the top of the building just off the Lobby, of which the Ingrossing Office occupied the lowest, and the Committee Clerks' Office the principal floor. Their premises consisted of one tolerably large room measuring 22 feet by 20 feet 6 inches,[2] and above it of two smallish attic rooms in which most of the copying was done. The warehouse in Abingdon Street with its residence for the clerk of the journals did not come into use till 1803. There were four clerks under Arthur Benson and, except for Benson himself, none of them had any but the slenderest permanent salary. Their meagre subsistence was derived mainly from their share of copying and proof correcting, whether of papers ordered to be printed, of the *Journal* or of the nightly *Votes*. John Henry Ley, giving evidence before the 1833 Committee, drew a sufficiently damning picture of this office when he said of John Bull, then clerk of the journals,

---

[1] 38 C.J. 554.

[2] See Appendix to the *Report* of the Select Committee on Rebuilding the Houses of Parliament (H.C. (1835) 262).

that he 'was taken into the office in consequence of the office being in a most inefficient state, from the system of ill-paid, half-starved clerks'.[1] This was in 1801 when Ley himself first came to the table as 2nd Clerk Assistant, and his own uncle, as Deputy Clerk, was sharing with Hatsell an income of over £10,000 a year. By this time, it is true, the Treasury was contributing a small sum by way of salary to the clerks in the Journal Office, just as it was paying £100 a year to the assistants in the Fees Office:[2] in fact, it was in 1788 that, on representations from Hatsell that the salaries of four inferior clerks in his office were 'not adequate to their support', the Treasury Board ordered their Mr. Cotton to pay Hatsell £100 to be by him distributed among inferior clerks in the Court of Wards then and at the end of every session of Parliament[3]—this in addition to the sum of £200 which they were paying annually to the clerk of the journals.[4] A quarter share in £100 was not, even in those days, a great addition to a clerk's earnings, yet the Treasury contribution had not increased ten years later, though the Treasury's annual payment to the clerk of the journals had by then risen to £300. It was not till the year of the Union that some advance was made, after correspondence between John Ley and the Treasury.

This correspondence and its sequel require attention, since here was the source of that Treasury payment of £900 a year as a 'kind of salary' to various clerks in the Journal Office and Fees Office which was frequently referred to in the evidence taken by the 1833 Committee, but of which the historical origin had been completely forgotten. The prime reason for John Ley's approach to the Treasury at the beginning of 1801 was the prospect of much increased business in the House after the Union, necessitating increase of staff, besides increased accommodation. Several letters from

[1] H.C. (1833) 648, qns. 3105–15.
[2] See preceding chapter, pp. 171, 173.
[3] See T. 29/59, fol. 81.
[4] The earliest reference to this payment in the Treasury books appears to be in 1781 (T. 29/50, fol. 307) when a minute refers to a certificate from the Clerk of the House 'stating the annual allowance to Mr. John Benson for performing the extraordinary business of the House of Commons in last session £150'; so that this payment must have originated earlier. It was not entered in the C.L. Accts., or voted by the House.

Hatsell to Ley written about this time show his anxiety in these matters; for instance, on 26 December 1800 he wrote:[1]

> You will settle the establishment of the Ct. of Wards in the manner that you think best. As we have got more Members, and more space to put them in, we shall want more hours to talk in, more clerks to attend their business, and so to patch up the Constitution of the Chair, and the Table, that they may be able to go through twice the fatigue that was requir'd of their predecessors.

Accordingly, as we learn from a Treasury minute of 10 February 1801,[2] Ley, after consulting Dorington, clerk of the fees, and Arthur Benson, clerk of the journals, and desiring them to make out reasonable estimates for their respective offices, had written to the Treasury on the previous day, to forward these estimates with his own observations. 'It appears', so runs the Treasury minute, 'that the number of clerks in both offices will be 6 in one, 4 in the other; and that the sum of £400 (which is an addition of £300 to the present allowance) will be requisite to make reasonable allowance to the respective clerks to be employed.' Ley had observed that he considered the proposed allowance proper, considering the additional business likely to arise, and the allowance to each clerk not higher than reasonable. The Treasury Lords approved, and Ley was informed of this approval by letter dated 16 February.[3] Thus, from that date, £400 a year was divided between four clerks in the Fees Office and six in the Journal Office; and, from the returns of emoluments made to the 1833 Committee, it appears that, taking seniority into consideration, the division was fair. Dorington himself, as I have shown in the preceding chapter, was enjoying a considerable salary as Treasury agent, besides his profits as a parliamentary agent for private bills; and Arthur Benson was still receiving £300 a year from the Treasury, besides his share in 'copy money' and his yearly allowance for supervising the *Journal*.[4]

---

[1] Ley MSS.   [2] T. 29/77, fol. 226.   [3] T. 27/52, fols. 291–2.

[4] He was also made one of the four principal committee clerks in 1801, besides which he undertook parliamentary agency for private bills, and in that capacity originally employed John Bull as a copyist (see the latter's statement to the 1833 Committee (H.C. 648 of that year), p. 218).

Two years later Arthur Benson memorialized the Treasury for an increase of allowance, on the ground that his duties were more than double what they were a few years ago, and had been materially added to in consequence of the Union with Ireland—a plea which was entirely justified, as can be judged from even a cursory inspection of the *Votes* and *Journals*. This occasioned a portentously long entry[1] in the Treasury Board minutes for 5 July 1803 which obviously incorporates several letters, annexed to Benson's memorial, which had passed between the late Speaker (Addington), John Ley, Benson, and George Whittam, his deputy, and set out the various and arduous duties of Benson and Whittam who (it is incidentally mentioned) had respectively thirty and twenty-five years' service as clerks. The request was that such addition should be made to their salaries and emoluments as would bring them up to £500 and £400 a year respectively. The Treasury agreed to comply with this request in the following manner: since Benson's Treasury salary of £300 and his other emoluments averaging £250 were shared between him and Whittam in the proportion of 3 to 2, and since Whittam received £60 out of the general fund in the Court of Wards (i.e. the £400 mentioned above)—making £610 in all—an additional £290 would be issued, commencing from the first session of the year 1800, to make up the total divisible emoluments to £900, of which Benson would have £500 and Whittam £400. They added that this was intended as a recompense to the two gentlemen in question for their diligent and long services, and that only half of the increase would be allowed to their successors except on the express recommendation of the Speaker and the Clerk of the House. Benson was informed of this decision by letter, and copies of the minute were forwarded to the Speaker and Ley.[2]

This sum of £900 divisible between Benson and Whittam, it is to be noted, was *not* the £900 eventually divided between the two offices, since what the Treasury referred to as the 'general fund in the Court of Wards' was still being paid to the junior clerks. Hardly had the Treasury made these arrangements than Arthur Benson retired from the clerkship of the journals and George

[1] T. 29/81, fols. 233 sqq.   [2] T. 27/55, fols. 57, 58.

Whittam succeeded him, with John Bull, with only two years' service to his credit, as his deputy. The result, in the autumn of 1804, was the transmission by the Treasury to John Ley of a memorial from Whittam asking for an additional allowance, together with a copy of the Treasury minute of 1803, and a long reply from Ley which was read at the Treasury Board on 6 November 1804. The gist of Ley's letter was that Whittam was the fittest man for the post of clerk of the journals, but that it meant some loss to him of other emoluments, and that he ought to have some addition to his income and also 'a provision for the payment of such clerk or clerks as may be employed immediately under him'—in fact, £200 of the additional £290 authorized in 1803. This was agreed to by the Treasury.[1]

Thus George Whittam received £500, of which he allotted £100 to his first clerk, Bull, while the £400 was divided as before between the remaining clerks in the Journal Office and the subordinate clerks in the Fees Office. *This* was the '£900 salary' often referred to in evidence before the 1833 Committee; and that the principle of its division had remained unchanged for nearly thirty years is shown by the detailed returns of income made to that committee by the clerks in the two offices. Thus, although the incomes of the subordinate clerks were slightly improved since 1801, it is perhaps sufficient comment on Speaker Abbot's complacent view of their position in 1811 quoted in an earlier chapter[2] to say that, just as the junior committee clerks, who had no share in the fees, made their living partly by deputizing for their seniors and partly by laborious copying of evidence at night, so the subordinate clerks in the Fees and Journal Offices, apart from a share in the £900 in no case rising above £60, derived all their subsistence from work of a semi-mechanical nature paid by the piece. The increase of business, indeed, gave them opportunities of earn-

---

[1] This account gives the gist of a Treasury letter signed by W. Huskisson of 5 Sept. 1804 (T. 27/56, fol. 196) and of a Treasury Board minute of the following day (T. 29/83, fol. 53/2). As a comment on George Whittam's finances we may note that in 1800, when Luke Hansard took over Hughs's printing business, Whittam earned his gratitude by bringing him a voluntary loan of £500, see J. C. Trewin and E. M. King, *Printer to the House* (London, 1952), p. 69.

[2] Chapter 6, pp. 124–26.

ing more than formerly by assiduity; but a man who was ill or otherwise incapacitated lost all but his small salary during his absence from the office.

(4)

During the last twenty years of Hatsell's life, that is, until 1820, when his patent expired with him and the Clerk's fees were paid to the fee fund, the changes in the methods and staffing of the Journal Office, beyond what has been chronicled above, were unimportant, except in one instance—the great reform of 1817 in the form and production of the *Votes*. In his diary Speaker Abbot ascribed the entire credit for this reform to himself, referring to it as 'my new plan'.[1] This energetic man may well have been the prime mover, but it was John Rickman, then 2nd Clerk Assistant, who put forward the whole scheme in a memorandum and for the remainder of the session stayed up three hours nightly after the rising of the House to supervise the new and far more expeditious system.[2] A footnote to the entry in Abbot's diary well describes the defects to be remedied and the success of the remedy:

Formerly the daily votes of the House of Commons, seldom or never exceeding a single sheet, were distributed regularly to each Member, and even obtained a considerable sale out of doors, as a newspaper; but as the business increased, the bulk of the votes became so much enlarged that their delivery gradually fell into arrear, till before Mr Abbot became Speaker, they were usually two or three days, sometimes even a week in arrear, and the House of Commons was besieged all the morning by the servants of Members, endeavouring to obtain for their masters information as to what business would come before the House in the evening. Mr Abbot reformed the existing system, causing the entries to be shortened, petitions to be omitted, etc., so that it was again found practicable to publish the votes at an early hour of the morning following the transaction of the business, and Members are thereby

---

[1] Colchester, ii. 603 and footnote.
[2] See *Life and Letters of John Rickman*, pp. 133–34, though the letters to Southey on which my statement was based are not printed. Abbot's manuscript diary for various dates in Feb., Mar., and Apr. 1817 (P.R.O. 30/9/35) shows that the scheme was Rickman's, but that its final form was settled by Abbot after consultations with him and many others.

enabled, before they leave their homes, to read an official account of the proceedings of the preceding evening, and have also laid before them the business which is to engage the attention of the House at the next meeting.

A less picturesque but more factual statement is to be found in the report of the select committee appointed to consider the matter.[1] This committee heard evidence from Ley, Rickman, and Whittam, clerk of the journals, which they did not report but doubtless incorporated in their statement. The trouble was that the *Votes*, which up to this time had been compiled on the same spacious model as the *Journal*, had swollen inordinately. Whereas the average number of pages in the sessional volume of the *Votes* between 1750 and 1760 was 478, for the session 1802–3 the number of pages was 2,145 in two volumes. Some space, it is true, was then saved both in the *Votes* and in the *Journals* by closer printing, fewer capitals and compression of forms,[2] so that the *Votes* of 1805 numbered only 859 pages; but the increase of bulk continued, with the result that by 1817 the *Votes* were usually four days late in appearing, while the printed *Journal* was about two years behind-hand. The new system, recommended by the committee and immediately carried out, involved a drastic compression of the entries in the *Votes* and the relegation to an appendix, to be issued separately once or twice a week, of public petitions presented to the House and ordered to be printed. The entries of each day were numbered, and for the first time there was annexed to the *Votes* a list of notices and orders for public business fixed for the next sitting, together with the titles of private bills set down for second reading that day and notice of any other arrangements to which the House might have come to regarding the next day's business. It was estimated that £2,000 a year would be saved by the new system which, moreover, would expedite the compilation of the *Journal*, since that would be issued in sheets progressively not more

---

[1] *Report* of the Select Committee on the Votes and Proceedings of the House (H.C. (1817) 156).

[2] This can easily be seen by comparing the *Votes* of 1803 with those of 1804. See also Abbot's manuscript diary for 17 May 1803 and his summary of the year 1804 (P.R.O. 30/9/33).

than one week in arrear, the appendix and index to follow before the ensuing session.

So far as the *Votes* were concerned, this was a striking reform—as can be seen by comparing the 1816 volume with its successors—and a lasting one, since to all intents and purposes the model devised by Rickman is that in use today. One result of the re-organization of the *Votes* was that the printer of the *Votes*, J. B. Nichols, was obliged to take extensive premises near the House and give up the establishment in Red Lion Passage, Fleet Street, made famous by his father. Giving evidence in 1822 to the Select Committee on Printing and Stationery,[1] Nichols said that this move, besides the cost of new premises, had caused a great loss of trade connexions and that the losses had not so far been recouped. He also said on that occasion that, owing to night work and the need for haste, printing the *Votes* was expensive in wages, of which he gave particulars, and that the weekly appendix containing the text of petitions ordered to be printed necessitated extra pay for Sunday work; when the appendix was over fifteen sheets it was difficult to get it printed at all. The size of the annual vote for the printing ordered by the House[2] does not tend to show that the expected saving in expense was realized; but the testimony of John Bull, clerk of the journals in 1828, shows that in every other way the advantages of the new system had fully realized expectations.

So far as the clerks in the Journal Office were concerned, they gained an advantage from the new system in that payment for night attendance to correct the proofs of the *Votes* was doubled, from £250 to £500 a session, divided between four clerks; but they were kept up till the small hours in order to earn it. Also, as the number of petitions increased, they made more by laborious copying. All clerical expenses for printing the *Votes* were included in Nichols's bill, the items of which in 1828 were £500 to the four clerks for compiling, £160 to the clerk who compiled a daily index to the *Votes* for the table of the House, £100 to the clerk who made a similar index for use in the Journal Office, and £457. 9s. 10d.

---

[1] H.C. (1822) 607.
[2] See Appendix VII, p. 325.

for copying and examining petitions for the appendix to the *Votes*.[1]
In the ten years subsequent to 1818 pressure of business had, no
doubt, increased; but we may well take as typical Bull's description given to a select committee in 1828 of the work entailed in
producing the *Votes* each night.[2] The Clerk's minute-book, he
said, was sent out from the table about six o'clock in the evening.
Often there were large quantities of accounts presented, which
had to be looked at and abstracts made. Also, great quantities of
petitions (sometimes 300 a night)[3] were sent to the Journal Office
in bags: all had to be sorted and arranged, and each petition looked
at carefully. He had known this part of the business occupy, not
only the clerks whose duty it was to attend to it, but every clerk
in the office, many hours, not infrequently five or six. So the work
went on through the night, and the two Clerks Assistant were
detained for an hour after the rising of the House.

One other note must here be made regarding the duties of the
clerk of the journals in Hatsell's day. He was the custodian of a
small but highly valuable collection of books, pamphlets, and other
records which eventually formed the first nucleus of the Library.
These were kept, and could be consulted by members, at the warehouse at 1 Abingdon Street; but after the first Library had been
established (in 1818) in a small room about 17 feet square, once a
committee room, this collection was taken over from the Journal
Office by the first Librarian of the House, Mr Spiller. It was transferred to the second Library which was built in 1827 to Sir John
Soane's plans and provided several new committee rooms.[4] Un-

---

[1] See the evidence given by Whittam, Bull, and J. B. Nichols reported by the
Select Committee on Printing done for the House in 1828 (H.C. 520 of that year).

[2] On p. 64 of the report referred to in the previous note. These details can be
compared with the account of the work of the Journal Office given to the 1833
Committee (see chapter 11).

[3] The increase in public petitions which marked the first half or more of the
nineteenth century (see Erskine May, *Constitutional History of England*, i. 438–44)
had now begun. Between 1811 and 1815 4,498 petitions were presented, but between 1827 and 1831 the number was 24,492. (John Bull in evidence before the
Select Committee on Public Petitions in 1832, H.C. (1831–2) 639, pp. 1–21.)

[4] Evidence of J. H. Ley reported by the Select Committee on the Present State
of the Library in 1830 (H.C. 496, pp. 10–11). The list of books with Spiller's
receipt for them dated 1820 is reproduced in the 2nd *Report* of the Select Com-

fortunately, this Library was destroyed, with all its precious contents, in the fire of 1834.

mittee on Committee Rooms and Printed Papers of 1825 (H.C. 515). For the interesting story of the planning of the second Library, and the frustration of the original design by J. H. Ley's refusal to give up his official house, I must refer readers to my *Topography of the Old House of Commons* (see Introduction, p. xvi).

10

CONTROVERTED ELECTIONS: THE CLERK OF ELECTIONS AND THE CLERK OF RECOGNIZANCES. THE INGROSSING OFFICE. THE PRIVATE BILL OFFICE

(1)

THE full title of the first of these offices was that of clerk to the Committee (or Committees) of Privileges and Elections, but in general parlance the holder came to be styled, for short, the clerk of elections—a title which was, indeed, more suitable when, after the passing of Grenville's Act (see below) in 1770, petitions complaining of undue election were referred to specially constituted committees, and no longer to a single committee appointed and nominated at the beginning of each session. The Committee of Privileges and Elections was that instrument of James I's House of Commons which, as Professor J. E. Neale says,[1] 'lacking all historical and constitutional warrant, and yet with sound sense behind its action, usurped jurisdiction over election questions'. This committee never officially became, as did the other four, a committee of the whole House, or 'Grand Committee', although after 1672 it became a committee of the whole House in fact, since it was invariably made an open committee in which all who came had voices.[2] The exclusive right of the House to determine the legality of returns and judge the conduct of returning officers was recognized by the Courts in 1674; and its claim to the exclusive right of determining whether, or what, electors had a right to vote, which was asserted after the Aylesbury election of 1704 and the famous cases of *Ashby* v. *White*

---

[1] *The Elizabethan House of Commons* (London, 1949), pp. 78–79.
[2] See Lord Campion, *An Introduction to the Procedure of the House of Commons*, 2nd ed. (London, 1947), p. 28.

and *R.* v. *Paty*, although not explicitly recognized, was never
afterwards challenged in fact.[1] Until 1770 the *Journals* of the House
increasingly abounded in entries relating to controverted elections,
in the shape either of reports of the Committee of Privileges and
Elections to the House or of proceedings in the House when a case
was heard at the bar. Yet, whereas a hearing at the bar took place
with the Speaker in the Chair and, therefore, with the Clerk of the
House in attendance, the hearing of an election petition by the
Committee of Privileges and Elections was attended by the clerk
to that committee, who earned fees by his attendance. It is, therefore, not immaterial to the history of the Commons Clerks to inquire, not only who were the clerks to the Committee of Elections
at various times, and what their emoluments, but also the proportion between the cases heard at the bar and those referred to the
Committee between 1704 and 1770.

There can be little doubt that the Clerk Assistant, at all events
after the Revolution, was also clerk to the Committee of Privileges
and Elections, on the very reasonable principle that it was, to all
intents and purposes, a committee of the whole House and, as
such, attended *ex officio* by the Clerk Assistant. The clerks' memorial of 1709–11, to which frequent reference has already been
made, mentions incidentally that, besides his losses due to the
decrease in fees on private bills, 'the Clerk Assistant is also a looser
by the new method the House hath taken to hear elections at the
Bar, and will still be so if that method should be continued'.[2]
When that memorial was first drafted and presented in 1709,
Culverwell Needler was the Clerk Assistant, and he had held that
office since 1688. We also know that, at least by 1699, the Committee of Privileges and Elections regularly met in the House
itself. This is established by the *Journal* entry for 18 January 1698/9:[3]

A complaint being made to the House, that there have of late been
such great numbers of Strangers at the Committee of Privileges and
Elections, that the Members of the House have not been able to come
into the House, and take their seats therein; and that they have had, and

---

[1] See Erskine May, *Parliamentary Practice*, 15th ed. (1951), chapter X; Coxe,
Memoirs of Robert Walpole (ed. 1816), i. 32–35; iv. 246.
[2] See Appendix II, p. 290.   [3] 12 C.J. 425.

may have, other Annoyances to the Endangering of their Healths, if
timely Care be not taken to the contrary; and there hath been such
Crouding in the Passage, by Witnesses and others, that the Witnesses
cannot have free Passage into, and out of, the Committee;
Ordered, that the Serjeant at Arms attending this House do give
Order to the Doorkeepers and Messengers of the House, constantly
to attend the Committee of Privileges and Elections, and other Committees sitting in the House; and take care, that no Persons do croud,
or sit, upon the seats of the House, either below, or above in the Gallery,
where the Members ought to sit; and that such Witnesses as shall be
examined at the said Committees do attend in the Lobby, and be called
in, one by one, and severally examined, and then withdraw, for others
to come in and be examined; and that the Passage be kept clear for
that Purpose.

There is no reason to suppose that the sitting of this committee
in the House was then an innovation: and it may, moreover, be
remarked that James Courthope's minute-book kept from 1697
to 1699[1] records no attendance by him as committee clerk upon
the Committee of Privileges and Elections. Therefore, whether
or no this committee was attended by a clerk when, during the
Restoration Parliaments, it was ordered to meet three days a week
in the Exchequer Chamber,[2] it seems more than probable that,
under Paul Jodrell, the Clerk Assistant regularly attended the
Committee of Privileges and Elections, and drew the fees which,
by the table of fees of 1701,[3] were payable to the clerk attending
that committee. Every election case heard at the bar of the House
meant a loss of fees to Needler and Stables, who succeeded him:
so that, when the House resolved on 18 February 1708 that 'all
matters that shall come in Question touching returns or Elections
shall be heard at the Bar of the House', with the result that the
election petitions arising at the end of 1708 in the new Parliament
were, all but one, ordered to be heard at the bar,[4] it is obvious that
the Clerk Assistant had a well-founded cause for complaint in

---

[1] See pp. pp. 53–54, 130–33.
[2] e.g. the order of 11 May 1661 (8 C.J. 246) setting up this committee, which
was repeated in the subsequent sessions of Charles II's first Parliament.
[3] 13 C.J. 356; see Appendix III, pp. 300, 303.
[4] Out of sixty-three petitions, sixty-two were ordered to be heard at the bar,
but only sixteen were actually heard.

1709, when the clerks' memorial was drafted. However, by the time that Stables had succeeded Needler (1710), and the clerks' memorial had been represented (1711) and had been reported on by the Speaker (1713), the cause of complaint had passed away. In fact, the House quickly abandoned its 'new method' after one experiment; and, at all events for six new Parliaments after 1708, the Committee of Privileges and Elections had far more work, in an election year, than it could possibly get through, and its clerk[1] earned his fees.

It is, perhaps, necessary to stress this point, since one or two statements in textbooks might lead the unwary to suppose that, between 1708 and 1770, election petitions were invariably heard at the bar of the House.[2] The passages quoted in my footnote do not, it is admitted, rigorously support that inference, but they hardly suggest the true state of the matter, which was very fairly put by Archdeacon Coxe in two passages, both in his *Memoirs of Robert Walpole*. In the first, speaking of the resolutions of the House consequent on the case of *Ashby* v. *White*, he says:

It was principally owing to these resolutions, that the decisions, in regard to controverted elections, were seldom regulated by the merits of the case, but became questions of personal or political expediency; nor was this abuse corrected, until the act, known by the name of Grenville's Bill, was passed in 1770. . . .[3]

---

[1] The report of the Select Committee on Fees of 1731/2 given in Appendix IV shows (pp. 306–7, 309–10) that Aiskew, the Clerk Assistant (1726–40) attended the Committee of Privileges and Elections, was in some doubt as to the proper fees to be charged, and had put in a memorial on the subject with a bill of fees for a certain case 'corrected by Mr. Stables', from which it may be inferred that Stables when Clerk Assistant (1710–26) had also attended that committee.

[2] e.g. Erskine May, op. cit., p. 184. 'Before the year 1770, controverted elections were tried and determined by the whole House of Commons, as mere party questions, upon which the strength of contending factions might be tested'; and *Constitutional History of England*, i. 302–3 where, in describing the methods of proceedings on election petitions during the eighteenth century, May wrote: 'This Committee (i.e. of Privileges and Elections) was henceforth exposed to all the evils of large and fluctuating numbers, and an irresponsible constitution; and at length, in the time of Mr. Speaker Onslow, a hearing at the bar of the House itself—which in special cases had already been occasionally resorted to—was deemed preferable to the less public and responsible judicature of the Committee.'

[3] Op. cit. i. 35.

The second occurs when he is leading up to the adverse vote on the Chippenham election petition which caused Walpole's resignation:

Ever since the Aylesbury contest . . . the decisions became a mere party business. The merits of the case were seldom considered, and the questions were almost wholly carried by personal or political interests. . . . The Opposition made it a principal object to attend, on these occasions, and it was esteemed infamous to desert a Committee of election.[1]

What does not seem to have been recognized by any of the writers quoted is that, unscrupulous and partisan as was the spirit in which questions of controverted elections were decided up to 1770, there was a marked diminution towards the middle of the century in the number of election petitions presented. The figures for new Parliaments which I have myself computed from the *Journals*, are as follows:

Parliament	Total number of petitions	Heard before C.P.E.	Heard at bar
1713/14 . . .	55	24	7
1715 . . .	85	12	17
1722 . . .	100	8	2
1727/8 . . .	63	10	3
1734/5 . . .	69	4	8
1741/2 . . .	45	3	10
1747/8 . . .	20	3	6
1754 . . .	25	3	1
1761 . . .	13	1	7
1768 . . .	38	5	10

[*Note.* The majority of petitions referred to the Committee of Privileges and Elections were either withdrawn or not heard, while, of those ordered to be heard at the bar, there were only a few which did not get a hearing or were withdrawn.]

It is clear from the above figures that, up to and including 1734/5, the bulk of the election petitions were referred, on presentation, to the Committee[2] which, according to practice was closed before

[1] Op. cit. iv. 246.
[2] For allusions to protracted and largely attended sittings of the Committee on election petitions in 1713/14 see R. *Comm. Hist. MSS. Portland*, vol. v (Harley, iii), 390, 402, 405, 412, 415, 428, 433; see also ibid., p. 577. Edward Harley's letter to Abigail Harley about the proceedings in the Committee in Jan. 1718/19 on the

the end of the session, though this practice fell hard on petitioners who had brought up their witnesses.[1] What caused a subsequent reduction in the total number of petitions presented, I cannot explain: but it will be observed that, even in the thin years, the Committee of Privileges and Elections was not entirely superseded. So that John Grover, who was clerk to that committee from 1740–9, thus breaking for some unknown reason the traditional connexion with the Clerk Assistant, which was resumed for eight more years on his death, by no means held the office as a sinecure. The petitions arising from the election of 1768 were not heard till the second session of that Parliament, and the increase in their number may be accounted for by a rise in political temperature, and party animosity. Among the petitions heard at the bar in 1769 were those relating to the notorious Middlesex and Westminster elections: it is difficult to believe that, but for the turmoil over Wilkes and Luttrell, George Grenville would have managed to get his bill through so easily in 1770, with Lord North and the King's party, including Jeremiah Dyson, strongly opposing it.[2] Incidentally, it appears that the passage from May's *Constitutional History*, quoted in a previous footnote, rests upon the report of Grenville's speech in introducing his bill. He is reported to have said:[3]

In this House Committees were constantly chosen to examine into elections; in 1672, the chancellor having claimed the right of determining contested elections, the Commons ordered a committee of two hundred for that purpose, and resolved that all who attended should have voices. The establishment of Committees has continued ever since, but during the time that the late Mr. Onslow presided in that chair, the admirable order with which he conducted business, as well as some irregularities which took place in the Committees, induced such as wished for a candid trial to be heard at the bar of the House.

However, since Arthur Onslow was Speaker from 1727 to 1760, the change alluded to cannot have taken place till half-way through

Shaftesbury petition, when the sitting candidate was defeated, 'though not only all the Germans, but the Monarch himself solicited strenuously for him'. They were kept going till 2 a.m. with speeches and divisions.

[1] See *R. Comm. Hist. MSS. Egmont MSS.* Diary of Viscount Percival, 1730–3, i. 81.

[2] See *Parl. Hist.*, vol. 16, pp. 902–26.   [3] Ibid., p. 904.

his long occupancy of the chair. There was nothing particularly 'candid' about the hearing at the bar of the Chippenham petition which caused Walpole's fall: and, taking into account the doldrums into which the House fell under Pelham and Newcastle, the figures that I have given above do not bear witness to any startling revolution.

To revert, however, to the clerks—the figures given above show that neither John Read, the Clerk Assistant, nor Hardinge Stracey, who was appointed clerk to the Committee of Privileges and Elections in 1757, with a newly granted salary of £100,[1] can have incurred much labour or gained much in fees from the sittings of that committee on election petitions.[2] The passing of Grenville's Act in 1770 entirely changed the situation, making the post of clerk to that committee increasingly arduous and profitable in an election year till, in 1811, Speaker Abbot could describe it as one of the 'great situations'.[3] And, though the Treasury continued to show the salary of £100 as paid to Hardinge Stracey till he retired in 1788, I have little doubt that the *Court and City Register* is correct in showing George White the elder as the true incumbent from 1772 onwards, he being a man of great energy and capacity for organization.[4] On his death the post was held jointly for five years by Nathaniel Barwell and George White the younger, who probably did most of the work and, after Barwell's death in 1793, remained clerk of elections for twenty-one years longer, as well as building up a practice as parliamentary agent for private bills which was by far the largest of his day.[5] Indeed, the position was particularly suitable as an adjunct to parliamentary agency, since its work was only strenuous, and its emoluments large, in the first session of a new Parliament. In other sessions the work was light and the financial reward much smaller; yet the possession of an office in the Palace of Westminster and at least one regular sub-

---

[1] See chapter 8, p. 164.

[2] This makes it, to my mind, all the more probable that Hardinge Stracey's appointment was a job of his uncle Nicholas Hardinge, then joint secretary to the Treasury.

[3] See chapter 6, p. 125.

[4] See chapters 7, pp. 143–44, 8, pp. 181–85.

[5] See chapter 8, pp. 183–84.

ordinate clerk on the establishment was a great advantage to a parliamentary agent. Both William Ley, who succeeded to the post in 1814, and Thomas Dyson,[1] who was appointed in 1820 and described his duties very fully to the Committee of 1833, were successful parliamentary agents.

Grenville's Act[2] instituted a wholly new method of appointing the tribunal of the House for the trial of controverted elections, and for the first time delegated by statute to such tribunal the House's power to decide whether the petitioners or the sitting members had been returned, or whether the election was void. It was against the delegation of final decision that Jeremiah Dyson, in speaking against the bill, made his main attack. The system set up by this act, briefly described, was that, for the trying of every petition complaining of undue election or return of a member, a separate committee of fifteen members was appointed by a somewhat elaborate process. On a day fixed beforehand, the petitioners and sitting members and their counsel or agents were required to attend the House, which could not proceed on the matter unless 100 members were present. The parties and their counsel or agents attended at the bar, the door of the House was locked, and the names of all the members present, written on slips of paper or parchment, were rolled up and put, in equal numbers, into six glasses or boxes, and shaken together. The Clerk of the House, or the Clerk Assistant, then drew names out of the six receptacles till the names of forty-nine members then present had been drawn. There were various provisos for excuses and for filling by ballot the vacancies caused by excuses. Then each party named one member present whose name had not already been drawn. The list of forty-nine was then given to the parties, who withdrew attended by the clerk of elections and alternately struck off names till the number of names had been reduced from forty-nine to thirteen.[3] The clerk of elections then delivered these thirteen names to the House,

---

[1] The founder of the firm whose name survives today in the well-known firm of parliamentary agents, Messrs. Dyson and Bell.

[2] 10 Geo. III, c. 16, made perpetual by 14 Geo. III, c. 15.

[3] If there was no opposition, or if one party had waived the right of striking out, the clerk of elections struck out alternate names: in this case the two nominated members were chosen by the thirteen members selected by ballot, &c.

and these members with the two nominated by the parties were sworn at the table well and truly to try the matter of the petition. They were constituted a select committee, ordered to meet within twenty-four hours of appointment in a convenient room adjacent to the House properly prepared for that purpose, with power to elect their chairman, to send for persons, papers, and records and to examine witnesses on oath—this last a material innovation in committees of the House of Commons. They were to sit every day except Sunday or Christmas Day, and never adjourn for longer than twenty-four hours; no member was to be absent without leave of the House, and if more than two were absent they were to adjourn.

This new system undoubtedly produced a partial improvement in the hearing of election petitions, though corruption and party spirit were not entirely overcome, since the ballot was affected by party strength, and the power of striking out opponents emasculated each committee.[1] Also, since the trials of controverted elections became stricter, the business of dealing with all the petitions of an election year was not expedited, as is shown by an interesting letter written in 1780 by the Marquis of Rockingham to a local clergyman deprecating a motion advocating annual parliaments passed in a county committee:[2]

I have examined the number of petitions on contested elections presented—on several New Parliaments. I see both before and since Mr. Greenvile's [sic] Bill, the number of petitions on undue elections, have been so great, that they have not been decided in the first session. On the General Election in 1768—prior to Mr. Greenvile's Bill—the number of petitions were 38, whereof 5 were left undecided. Many of those which were decided, were not decided till just the end of the first session.

Mr. Greenvile's Bill, rendering the trials more equitable, admits and requires more fair and strict examination into the justice of each elec-

---

[1] See May, *Constitutional History of Great Britain*, i. 303–6. He remarks that the reduction of each committee to six impartially nominated members under Peel's Act of 1839 (2 & 3 Vic., c. 38, superseded by 4 & 5 Vic., c. 58), and the subsequent reduction to five, did not wholly eliminate party. It was not till 1868 that jurisdiction in controverted elections was transferred to the courts.

[2] *R. Comm. Hist. MSS.*, vol. 13, Appendix, pt. vii (Lonsdale), p. 137.

tion, and of course the trials are more formal and take longer time in deciding. It appears on the General Election in 1774, there were 50 petitions on undue elections at the different towns, counties, etc. All the Committees who could sit could only decide 34 out of the 50 in the course of the first session of that Parliament. So that 16 remained over for another year.

In the election years 1780 and 1784, the numbers of election petitions were forty-one and fifty-two respectively; and in the latter year the number reported on was extraordinarily small, no less than forty-three being put off to another occasion, in many cases because further petitions were presented relating to an election already complained of. It became necessary for the House to find a means of deterring frivolous or vexatious petitioners. This was the object of the Act of 1788, known as Wynn's Act,[1] under the provisions of which no petition was to be proceeded with unless subscribed by the petitioner, and unless, within fourteen days after presentation, he entered into a recognizance to the Speaker in £200, and provided two sureties of £100 each, to appear and renew his petition. If the petition were found by the committee frivolous or vexatious, costs were incurred by the petitioner. Since the numbers of election petitions presented dropped to thirty-nine in 1790 and twenty-three in 1796, it must be presumed that Wynn's Act had some effect; but after the union with Ireland they rose again to fifty-one in 1802 and forty-six in 1806, and continued at about the same level in an election year well into the nineteenth century.

It will be obvious that the duties of the clerk to the Committee of Privileges and Elections were entirely changed, as regards election petitions, by Grenville's Act.[2] Instead of having only to attend quite a small number of hearings when the whole committee sat on a petition, he had to be present whenever balloting took place for a committee on an election petition, and he was responsible for advising every such committee in its proceedings, for swearing witnesses, for keeping the records of examinations and providing

---

[1] 28 Geo. III, c. 52, subsequently replaced by 53 Geo. III, c. 71.
[2] The meetings of the Committee of Privileges, from about the same time, became much rarer once the House had acquiesced in the reporting of its proceedings.

copies of evidence to the parties, and for seeing that the report was presented. All these activities involved the payment and collection of fees under the table of fees of 1731/2, and the provision of assistant clerks (paid out of the fees) to attend election committees. The clerk of elections still received the salary of £100 a year first awarded to him by the Treasury in 1757,[1] but it was from the fees that he made his main income, and these in an election year came to a very respectable total.[2] Yet, in such a year, he was a busy man, and his clerks had to sit up very late at night copying minutes of evidence for the parties. Above all, he had to have a permanent office in the building, and it was fortunate for him that the passing of Grenville's Act coincided in date with the considerable increase in office and committee-room accommodation resulting from the building, by Kenton Couse under the Office of Works, of the 'new approach' to the House of Commons. It is impossible to say where the clerk of elections' office was originally situated, but by 1825 it was in two rooms above the Long Gallery, measuring respectively 22 ft. 4 in. by 13 ft. 5 in. and 13 ft. 5 in. by 10 ft. 8 in. The rest of this floor was then occupied by the Private Bill Office and the Clerk of Recognizances' Office.[3]

It must also be mentioned that the shorthand reporting of evidence taken before select committees was first introduced in election committees, under an Act (42 Geo. III, c. 84, s. 8) sponsored by M. A. Taylor in 1802. This immediately proved effective in

[1] J. H. Ley, in evidence before the Select Committee on House of Commons Offices of 1833, said he thought that salary had been paid for at least 150 years! (H.C. (1833) 648, qn. 34.)

[2] See the *Report* with minutes of evidence of the Select Committee on Fees in Controverted Elections (H.C. (1837–8) 50), in which, among other things, is given the list of House fees chargeable to petitioners and sitting members respectively. These were additional to the clerk of elections' fees for attending the committees, being charged for proceedings in the House and including £2 from each party to the Clerk and Clerk Assistant for attending the ballot. The Journal Office also charged 6s. 8d. to each party for sending them a copy of the order requiring them to attend on a certain day. In 1835 the total House fees received amounted to £172. 3s. 4d., the Journal Office fees to £104. 13s. 4d., and the clerk of election's fees to £2,089. 9s. 0d.

[3] Certain plans made by Sir John Soane in 1825 (Soane Museum 51. 6. 16) show this. The dimensions were also given in the appendix to the *Report* of the Select Committee on Rebuilding the Houses of Parliament (H.C. (1835) 262).

reducing the number of sittings of election committees, and in 1813 W. B. Gurney, son of Joseph Gurney, the first of the family to be employed in parliamentary work,[1] was made shorthand-writer to the House, providing shorthand note-takers for all committees engaged in hearing evidence. The shorthand-writer's transcript for many decades was sent to the committee clerk, who had copies made for the parties desiring them at the rate of 1s. a folio. Counsel's speeches, however, were not regarded as part of the proceedings, and were only taken down at the request of the parties to whom they were supplied directly by Gurney.[2]

Wynn's Act of 1788 involved the appointment of a clerk of recognizances with an office, and a certain amount of work for the Clerk Assistant (and, alternatively, after 1801, for the 2nd Clerk Assistant). Under s. 6 of the Act the Speaker was empowered to appoint two persons, of whom the Clerk or Clerk Assistant was always to be one, to report to him on the sufficiency of recognizances entered into by persons presenting election petitions; and under s. 22, in a case where a petition was found to be frivolous or vexatious and costs had been awarded, the Speaker was to direct two persons, of the same categories, to tax such costs, on application by the petitioner, and report to him. In practice, the persons so appointed were the Clerk Assistant (or, after 1801, the 2nd Clerk Assistant) and one of the Masters in Chancery, and they were authorized to charge such fees for examination and taxing as should, from time to time, be fixed by any resolution of the

---

[1] See *D.N.B.* and Colchester, iii. 332. The first of these says that Gurney's first appearance in Parliament was in 1789 to report the trial of Warren Hastings; while Abbot says it was in 1786 in the House of Lords upon the slave-trade inquiries. Both are wrong. A Treasury minute of 30 July 1783 (T. 29/54, fol. 237) records a bill of £3. 16s. from Gurney for taking shorthand evidence at the bar of the House of Lords on Baynton's Divorce Bill.

[2] See the evidence reported by the 1833 Committee (H.C. 648), qns. 23, 63 (J. H. Ley), 946–59 (Gurney), 991–1014 (Chalmers). The sitting-up all night by junior clerks to copy these minutes, for committees of any kind, was abolished after 1833 and, until printing was adopted, the copying was done by law-stationers who originally only earned 2d. a folio, the clerk taking the rest; see the *Report* of the committee of 1837–8 referred to in p. 224, n. 2, above. Much the same occurred as regards evidence taken before private bill committees, and prevailed until such evidence was ordered, in 1864, to be printed at the expense of the parties; see Williams, i. 145, 147, 295.

House. The clerk of recognizances attended these officials, undertook all the office work resulting from the Speaker's appointment, in each case, of examiners, dealt with witnesses and their expenses (which he himself, in later years, seems to have taxed with the agreement of parties), and was also paid by fees. The table of fees sanctioned was as follows:

	£	s.	d.
To the examiners (or for taxing) for the first day	3	3	0
,, ,, for every subsequent day	2	2	0
To the Speaker's secretary for his trouble	1	0	0
,, ,, ,, for taxation	1	6	8
To the clerk appointed to attend the examiners, for every attendance	2	2	0

The clerk of recognizances originally appointed was W. G. Rose,[1] who held the office until it was abolished in 1839. The fees of the Clerk Assistant as examiner or taxer of costs were expressly exempted, under the Act of 1812 for regulating the House of Commons Offices, from being paid into the common fee fund, so that in an election year he might make £100 or more by this work: but, as John Rickman pointed out to the Select Committee on Election Recognizances of 1837–8, it was a somewhat irksome business, since the Master in Chancery usually appointed four o'clock in the afternoon (i.e. after the courts had risen) as the time for the examiners to meet, and when, as happened in times of pressure, there were fourteen or fifteen examinations on the same day, it was very difficult for the Clerk Assistant to absent himself so long from the table.[2] He and his colleague, William Ley, cannot, therefore, have been sorry when Peel's Act of 1839 empowered the Speaker to appoint a permanent examiner of recognizances,[3] and the clerks at the table had no longer any concern in the matter.

[1] By 1833 he was also the senior of the principal committee clerks.

[2] These and other details are to be found in the *Reports* of the Select Committee on Election Petitions and Recognizances (H.C. (1812–13) 330), of a similar committee appointed in 1828 (H.C. (1828) 529), and of the Select Committee on Election Recognizances (H.C. 441) and the Select Committee on Fees on Controverted Elections (H.C. 50) both of session 1837–8. This last report shows that in the election year 1835 the total fees of the Recognizance Office were £597. 16s. 6d. and in the subsequent year only £70. 15s. 8d.

[3] This was Mr. J. B. Booth, appointed at the same time the first Counsel to Mr. Speaker; see Williams, i. 94–95. For Peel's Act, see p. 221, n. 1, above.

(2)

The Ingrossing Office of the House of Commons, which has now been extinct for just over a century, must have been, in respect of its function, by far the oldest branch of the Clerk's department. Ingrossing—namely, the writing of matter to be recorded with a thick quill upon parchment in a special hand with equally dark up- and down-strokes—was far more ancient, and was employed for the Rolls of Parliament long before the Commons sent an ingrossed bill up to the Lords. However, from the day when the first bill passed by the Commons was ingrossed[1] and marked by the Clerk *Soit baille as Seigneurs*, the ingrossing of bills and amendments to ingrossed bills originating in the Commons became one of the regular duties of the Clerk, which in Elizabethan times was performed by the Clerk's 'man', according to Hooker, Lambarde, and later authors of tracts on procedure.[2] It was a laborious but more or less mechanical function, of which the essential was accuracy. Whether any check was kept upon the accuracy of the ingrossments in Elizabethan Parliaments there is no knowledge, but in the seventeenth century one or two *Journal* entries show that this was necessary. Thus, on 23 February 1662/3,[3] a committee was appointed, not only to peruse the *Journal* every Saturday, but 'also from time to time to examine and compare such bills as shall be hereafter ingrossed with the paper copies by which they are ingrossed, and to see that they do cohere and agree': and, on 6 May 1690,[4] a far more effective order was made 'that no ingrossed bill be brought to the Table to be read the third time, but by the Chairman of the Committee to whom that bill was committed, after he hath examined the same'. Had this order been invariably complied with, it would have been the best possible check on the ingrosser's accuracy; but we know from later evidence that it came to be disregarded as soon as it proved irksome to members, and that the examination of ingrossments, in the end, devolved upon the clerks, or, where private bills were concerned,

---

[1] If it was a public bill, this occurred some time in Henry VII's reign; if a private bill, it may have been earlier.

[2] See chapter 1, p. 11, and n. 4 to that page.

[3] 8 C.J. 439.

[4] 10 C.J. 406.

was performed by the solicitors or agents for the bill until the Private Bill Office was instituted.

It is impossible, for want of evidence, definitely to state the time when an Ingrossing Office supervised by one of the Clerk's regular subordinates first came into being, or who was the first of such subordinates to be officially styled the clerk of ingrossments. Fees, one may be sure, were paid to the Clerk of the House for ingrossments from the earliest times, for the process was expensive in labour, parchment, ink, and pens. The earliest table of fees, that of 1649,[1] included a charge of 10s. a press for ingrossing a private bill, and in the tables of fees of 1701 and later this charge was increased to 12s. 6d. 'for ingrossing bills'; but, since this was one of the dues of the Clerk himself, and not of any under-clerk, no light is thrown by any table of fees on the origin of the Ingrossing Office or upon the proportion of the ingrossing fees that the Clerk allowed to the clerk of ingrossments. We only know, from Paul Jodrell's petition of 1723[2] that, during the first nine years of George II's reign, he had paid out of his own pocket for ingrossments of public bills, some of them very long, an accurate account of which, charged according to the settled fees, he annexed to the petition. The presence of this account, itemized for each year—whereas, in the Auditor of the Exchequer's certificate of payments made to the Goldesbroughs between 1660 and 1685 (also annexed to Jodrell's petition),[3] 'attending, preparing and ingrossing divers large bills' is the generic description of the Clerk's services—leads me to suppose that it was Jodrell who first appointed an official clerk of ingrossments, just as he first appointed the four clerks without doors. And this supposition is strengthened by the fact that, the early solicitors' bills for the costs of passing private bills which I have been able to collect[4] show, in nearly all instances from 1695 onwards, payments for ingrossing separate from the Clerk's fees; and by 1718 the City Remembrancer specifically refers to the ingrossing clerk.

Who this ingrossing clerk was cannot be determined, but, since (according to the *Gentleman's Magazine*) Hicks Burrough, who

---

[1] See Appendix III.   [2] See Appendix II, pp. 295–97.
[3] Ibid., p. 297.   [4] Appendix V.

died in 1733 as the senior of the four clerks without doors, was also ingrossing clerk of the House of Commons,[1] it may fairly be presumed that one of those four clerks was also detailed to supervise the ingrossing of bills, and probably did some of the work himself. Since Hicks Burrough became the senior of the four clerks without doors in 1720, it is probable that he was ingrossing clerk at all events by that date. His successor was almost certainly John Grover, the much mourned friend of Samuel Richardson,[2] who also became clerk to the Committee of Privileges and Elections in 1740, and died of a chill in 1749. The earliest *Court and City Register* shows him as ingrossing clerk in 1743, and the parliamentary diary of Samuel Sandys (later Baron Sandys) among the Dashwood MSS. in the Bodleian contains a note of his being called in on 11 March 1739/40 to ingross a long amendment to an ingrossed bill on third reading.[3] It does not seem likely that any other ingrossing clerk was interposed between him and Hicks Burrough.

After Grover's death two clerks of ingrossment were appointed, and the office continued to be held jointly until the death of William Gunnell in 1831, when J. H. Ley, the Clerk, did not see fit to make another appointment.[4] It has already been pointed out that, at all events by 1772, the two offices of clerk of ingrossments had become sinecures to which senior clerks had an expectation of being promoted.[5] In that year Hatsell promoted to the post of 2nd clerk of ingrossments a certain David Jones who, as he said in

[1] See chapter 3, p. 56.
[2] See chapter 4, p. 71–72, and p. 72, n. 1.
[3] Bodleian MSS. d.d. Dashwood (Bucks.). The allusion to Grover is noted as a precedent for amendments made at third readings, and runs as follows: '1739 March 11. Bill to restrain horse racing read 3rd time an Amendment made so large it could not be interlined engrossing Clerk called in Grover he wrote it on parchment at the table that pin(n)ed to Bill next day Mr. Speaker proposed that press should be new writ and he and Chair Man to over looke it the House acquiesced in it.' The long amendment in question is given in 23 C.J. 496. The point was that amendments to an ingrossed bill which were not riders or provisos could not be tacked on to the bill, but had to be interlineated at the table by the ingrossing clerk or Clerk's man. N.B. in this unpunctuated entry a stop should have come after the word 'engrossing', not after 'interlined'. It would have been Jodrell who called in Grover.
[4] As he told the 1833 Committee (H.C. (1833) 648, qns. 269–72).
[5] See chapter 7, pp. 141–42, and Hatsell's letter to John Ley on p. 88.

his letter to John Ley, 'had been ingrossing night and day' since 1752; and in the same letter he discussed the possibility of Jones's also becoming a deputy committee clerk, which would not have been possible if he had had any duties as a clerk of ingrossments. This proves that, at least by 1752, there was a regular clerk in the Ingrossing Office who was engaged in actual ingrossing and presumably managed the office in exactly the same manner as William Gunnell—one of a family long connected, like the Joneses, with the office—was managing the office in 1823.[1] So that, on inspecting the list of clerks of ingrossment,[2] and bearing in mind that Robert Yeates and Osborn Barwell were soon translated to higher spheres, I conclude that, after John Grover's death in 1749, this new system came into force at the beginning of Jeremiah Dyson's tenure of the Clerkship. From that time onwards, out of the Clerk's fee of 12s. 6d. a press,[3] the two clerks of ingrossment shared 1s., the actual ingrosser (whether a clerk or a law-stationer's scribe) was paid 9d., and the rest went to the Clerk,[4] except that by 1833 the charge for ingrossing public bills was restricted to the 1s. 9d., the Clerk himself taking no fees. At what date the Clerk agreed to this self-denying ordinance I cannot say. It obviously had not been agreed to in Jodrell's day, since his petition of 1723 included an account of what he was owed for ingrossments of public bills; and the large income from ingrossing fees returned by Hatsell for 1809 could not have accrued from ingrossments of private bills only.[5] I suggest that the Clerk's renunciation of ingrossing fees on public bills took place after Hatsell's death in 1820, by arrangement with the Treasury through Dorington, the clerk of the fees and Treasury agent. However, this would not explain the reduction between

---

[1] See his evidence reported by the Select Committee on the Present Method of Ingrossing Bills (H.C. (1823) 552). William Gunnell, as he said, had been ingrossing in the office for nearly thirty years, but the bulk of the work was sent out to law-stationers through whom, at times, he employed up to 100 men. There was no accommodation for much ingrossing in the precincts of the House.

[2] See Appendix I.

[3] A sheet of parchment 27 in. by 12 in. taking about 40 lines at 25 letters a line.

[4] See chapter 6, pp. 110–13, for Hatsell's income from ingrossing fees in 1809.

[5] On this point, see Samuel Gunnell's evidence before the 1833 Committee (H.C. (1833) 648, qns. 911–12); for Jodrell's account, chapter 3, p. 40, and Appendix II, p. 296; for Hatsell's return, chapter 6, p. 111.

1809 and 1833 of the sums accruing to the two ingrossing clerks. Speaker Abbot in his return of the establishment with emoluments for 1809 entered an average income of £711 for each of the ingrossing clerks, whereas the sinecurist Sir Edward Stracey's return of emoluments to the 1833 Committee gave his income as first ingrossing clerk as £278 odd.[1] The books of the Fees Office, destroyed by fire in 1834, could alone have explained this discrepancy.

The only other emolument of the clerks of ingrossment, besides the (no doubt) immemorial gratuities for 'expedition' or for making amendments on third reading paid by solicitors or agents for private bills, was an allowance of 20 guineas paid annually by the Treasury for examining the ingrossments of public bills. Its origin is obscure, but it is recorded in the Treasury books from 1779 onwards[2] and was still being received in 1833. The need for examining the accuracy of ingrossments is obvious, and its recognition had led to the House's order of 1690 (see above) that no ingrossed bill should be read a third time till the chairman of the committee on the bill had examined it. The allowance of £21 for examining ingrossed public bills would have been well earned by the clerks in the Ingrossing Office if they had continued to perform that function: but at some time towards the end of the eighteenth century they ceased to perform it, while still duly receiving the allowance. This development, typical of its time, is revealed in the petition presented to the House in 1809 by the clerk, J. S. Goodiff,[3] in extenuation of his offence in making alterations in the ingrossed copy of the Sugar Distillery Bill after it had been passed. Briefly stated, the facts of this occurrence were that Goodiff, the senior assistant of Dorington, the clerk of the fees and Treasury agent,[4] in examining the ingrossed bill after it had been passed—whereas this should have been done before third reading—had

---

[1] See chapter 6, p. 126, for Abbot's return, and Appendix X for Stracey's (as to whom, see chapter 7, pp. 155–8).

[2] The earliest reference that I have found is a Treasury minute of 13 July 1779 in T. 29/48, fol. 347: 'Recᵈ memo from Hardinge Stracey Esq., for payment of £21 for his extraordinary trouble in attending and examining the public ingrossed bills in the last session.' Thereafter a similar entry becomes more or less regular.

[3] 64 C.J. 77–78. The minutes of evidence and the *Report* of the Select Committee appointed to consider the matter are nos. 24 and 208 of that session respectively.

[4] See chapter 8, pp. 177–78, also Chapter 7, p. 153.

made, together with some perfectly correct alterations, one incorrect alteration which had the effect of extending the bill to Scotland. This was not intended, and the mistake had to be rectified in the Lords, thus coming to light: and Goodiff had made his position worse by trying to conceal the matter from the Speaker, whereby he incurred the suspicion of having acted venally, since two gentlemen interested in the bill, one of them the clerk to the Grocers' Company, owed him money for copies of parliamentary papers and agency in an inclosure bill. Goodiff had undoubtedly been negligent and foolish, but his plea that his error was mainly due to intolerable pressure of business was accepted by the committee and the House.

Goodiff's petition, which throws light both on the Fees Office and the Ingrossing Office at that period, states that the examination of ingrossed bills was formerly the duty of the ingrossing clerks, and was done before the ingrossed bill was laid on the table for third reading. Of 'late years', however, the examination of public bills had been conducted by 'persons employed by the Treasury or other departments to prepare those bills and attend to their progress in the House' (i.e. by the Treasury agents in the House who, at that date, were the clerks in the Fees Office, as I have already shown): the examination of ingrossments of private bills was performed by the agents for the bill. The practice of agents, both public and private—the petition continues—was to furnish the ingrossing clerks with perfect copies of bills as amended at various stages. The ingrossment, with the copy, was sent to the agents for examination, and any clerical errors were minuted by the agents on a slip of paper which was sent with the ingrossed bill to the ingrossing clerks, who made the necessary alterations. These corrections were usually examined by the agents before the bill was laid on the table for third reading, and the note of them was all that the ingrossing clerks were called on to examine. It had been the uniform practice in Dorington's office, for the sake of greater accuracy, to examine the ingrossed public bills after the corrections had been made. The examination of the ingrossed bill by the chairman of the committee on the bill had from the extraordinary increase of business for a long time been found impossible: and this increase of legislation since the Union[1] had been made worse by the practice of the House in fixing the third reading of bills for the day after they had been ordered to be ingrossed, so that towards the end of the session an accumulation of bills occurred such that there was no time to examine all the ingrossments before the bill was passed. That is what had happened with the Sugar Distillery Bill, since on the day it was down for third reading seven other public bills, also only ordered to be ingrossed the day before, were down for third reading, and the ingrossments only arrived for examination after the House had met.

This incident shows that both the Ingrossing Office and the Fees Office were intolerably hard pressed at the end of the session after the Union, and that practices grew up which were unavoidable but not correct. By 1823, as William Gunnell somewhat graphically described to the Select Committee on the Present Method of Ingrossing Bills,[2] the ancient practice of amending ingrossed bills at the table had ceased because of its inconvenience. However, the incident in which the clerk Goodiff was involved had two effects. One of these was the making of an order by the House,[3] on the recommendation of the select committee on the matter, that no bill should be read a third time until a certificate was indorsed upon the paper bill, and signed by such of the clerks attending the House as the Clerk of the House should authorize for the purpose, declaring that the ingrossment thereof had been examined against the House Bill and the amendments. And this certificate of examination persists to this day, in that the copy of every bill originating in the House of Commons, as reprinted after third reading for transmission to the Lords, is certified to have been examined against the House copy by two clerks of the Public Bill Office or the Private Bill Office, according to the nature of the bill. The second effect was the insertion among the Standing Orders made

[1] See p. 175, n. 1.
[2] See p. 230, n. 1, above. He said: 'it used to be the practice to make the amendments at the table, and there I used to feel myself very much distressed; I used to unrol them, and show the different presses; but we were up to our knees in parchment, and the crackling and noise greatly interfered with the proceedings of the House.'
[3] 64 C.J. 338–9, 24 May 1809. It was repealed in 1849 when ingrossing of bills was abolished.

the following session to regulate the practice of the newly established Private Bill Office of three orders dealing with the examination of ingrossments of private bills, one of which repeated the
order made by the House in 1809 as to certificate of examination.

(3)

The Private Bill Office is the only office in the Clerk's department which came into existence fully fledged pursuant to resolutions reported by a select committee, agreed to by the House, and
made Standing Orders. The select committee was that appointed in
1810 'to consider of providing more effectually for the accuracy
and regularity of proceedings on private bills', which was a very
urgent need at a time when the output of private bill legislation had
become extremely large[1] and the number of parliamentary agents,
both 'indoor' and 'outdoor', had correspondingly increased. The
report of the committee, for whose appointment Speaker Abbot
was largely responsible,[2] consisted of sixteen resolutions and three
schedules, all of which became Standing Orders. These provided
for the establishment of an office where a register of all private
bills, showing the agents for their promoters and the stages through
which they passed, should be kept in a prescribed form; where the
bills and their breviates should be examined against the petitions
on which they were based, the bills as reprinted after committee
against the committee bill, and the ingrossed bill against the House
bill; where proper notice should be given by agents or committee
clerks of future proceedings; and from which should be issued
daily lists of committees sitting on private bills. The expenses of
the office were financed originally by a fee of 3s. 4d. for every
entry of proceedings in the House or in committee and of 10s. for
every bill or breviate for every bill or breviate certified to be
irregular. The clerks of the Private Bill Office were, from the first,
expressly prohibited from acting as agents for private bills. On

---

[1] The figures obtainable from the Statutes alone, which do not include the
numbers of unsuccessful bills, show that from 1809 to 1814 the average annual
number of local and personal acts was nearly 300.

[2] H.C. (1810) 321. In his manuscript diary for 28 May 1810 (P.R.O. 30/9/34)
Abbot wrote: 'Hatsell, Ley and I settled finally the plans and resolutions for the
Private Bill proceedings.'

them devolved the custody of all private bills, and of deposited plans,[1] and their office consisted of one large and two small rooms on the floor above the Long Gallery. The first principal clerk of the office was one of the numerous Gunnell family, Henry by name, who had been a deputy committee clerk since 1776. The establishment of this office marked a great advance in the regularization of a hitherto somewhat chaotic private bill procedure. As I wrote in a former work on this subject.[2]

It provided for the first time for a proper channel for the contact of parliamentary agents and of other persons concerned in private bills with the House, staffed by officials who were themselves debarred from parliamentary agency: it also provided a source of accurate information to any member of Parliament or of the public, as well as a sure place for the deposit and custody of petitions, notices, memorials, plans and other documents required by the House. . . . It was not until such an office had been instituted in the House itself that further regulation of proceedings by standing order was possible.

The functions of this office, naturally, expanded, and were so intimately connected with developments in private bill procedure that it would be impossible to discuss the one without the other, which would be superfluous in view of my former work. The Private Bill Office was, from the first, a successful, hard-worked and not very well paid[3] institution. It did many necessary things which previously had not been done at all, and it superseded a certain amount of private bill agency among the clerks, since outside agents now had a source of accurate information as to the progress of their bills.[4]

[1] Custody of plans deposited under Standing Orders was added in 1811, but not till 1843 was custody of the petitions for leave added.

[2] Williams, i. 47. The developing functions of the Private Bill Office are, either explicitly or implicitly, illustrated by the whole of that work; and the original regulations for its activities are, in particular, referred to in vol. ii, pp. 241–60.

[3] See chapter 6, p. 126, Abbot's note regarding the pay of the clerks in the Private Bill Office for 1811: in his manuscript diary the summary for the year 1812 (P.R.O. 30/9/35) records, however, that in 1811 the Private Bill Office produced £1,290 in fees, 'whereof the first clerk had £650 (in addition to other payments by customary contribution from other clerks), the 2nd clerk had £400 and the 3rd clerk had £240'. For the figures in 1833, see chapter 11, p. 254.

[4] See J. E. Dorington's evidence in 1833 (H.C. (1833) 648), qn. 914, and Williams, i. 52.

II

HATSELL'S DEATH. THE REFORMS RECOMMENDED BY SELECT COMMITTEES, 1833–6. PARLIAMENTARY AGENCY BY THE CLERKS FINALLY PROHIBITED

(1)

JOHN HATSELL, vigorous in mind till the last, whose latest extant letter[1] was written from a friend's country seat only five weeks before his death, was carried off in his 87th year by an apoplectic stroke on 15 October 1820 at his own residence, Marden Park in Surrey. His remains were interred in the Temple Church on 24 October. The Speaker, accompanied by William Ley, sat in the first funeral coach, and in the second were Jeremiah Dyson, John Henry Ley, John Rickman, and George Whittam, then clerk of the journals.[2] On 31 October John Henry Ley was appointed Clerk of the House, and Jeremiah Dyson went into retirement on a handsome pension which he enjoyed for another fifteen years.[3] Rickman became Clerk Assistant, William Ley succeeded him as 2nd Clerk Assistant, and Thomas Dyson became clerk of elections.

Hatsell's death marked the end of an epoch in the history of the Clerk's office, but hardly the beginning of a new epoch. How much of the eighteenth century lingered in the circumstances and emoluments of the officers of the House was revealed by the Select Committee on the House of Commons Offices of 1833 who sedulously inquired into them. This committee, and other committees of 1835 and 1836, were the fruit of parliamentary reform and

---

[1] To Lord Colchester, dated 'Paultons, Sept. 9, 1820', remarking the deplorable effect upon conversation, especially that of women, of Queen Caroline's presence in England. (Colchester, iii. 161–62.)

[2] *Gentleman's Magazine*, xc (2nd pt.), pp. 372–73.

[3] H.C. (1833) 648, qn. 136, and see chapter 6, pp. 101, 106.

Joseph Hume's relentless activity. It is then that a new epoch began, and its beginning is the subject of this chapter. During the thirteen years that elapsed between Hatsell's death and the first year of a reformed Parliament things had remained much as they were. The reforming energies of the century's first decade directed against fees and sinecures had petered out during the climax of the struggle against Napoleon and the depression which followed. Catholic emancipation and parliamentary reform were the absorbing questions of the day. At Westminster, so far as internal economy was concerned, the members of the House of Commons interested themselves in such matters as the shortage of committee rooms, the increasing congestion in private bill procedure, and the provision of a new library. The chief immediate effect of the expiry of Hatsell's long-held patent was to bring all the Clerk's fees into the fee fund established by the Act 52 Geo. III, c. 11, and therefore under the control of the Commissioners for the House of Commons Offices who were first appointed under the Act of 1800 (39 & 40 Geo. III, c. 92). Not only was the Clerk's own salary now fixed by statute at £3,000 rising after five years to £3,500, but he had to consult the Commissioners regarding any payments out of the fee fund to clerks other than the two Clerks Assistant, whose salaries were fixed by the same statute. There was no longer any occasion for the Clerk to correspond with the Treasury about salaries, although those awarded previously by the Treasury continued to be paid. The Commissioners were the Speaker, the Secretaries of State, the Master of the Rolls (who could then be a member of the House), the Chancellor of the Exchequer, the Attorney General, and the Solicitor General. Of these, by his position of close association with the work of the House and its officers, the Speaker naturally took the lead, as he does today, and his Secretary became the secretary of the Commissioners, as he still is, for which service, until he was put on a fixed salary after the 1833 Committee's report, he received a salary of £250 a year from the fee fund in addition to his other emoluments.

Unfortunately the minute-books of the Commissioners previous to 1835 have been lost, probably in the fire of 1834, so that I cannot draw upon them for information: but it is quite clear from evidence given, and returns of income made by clerks, to the 1833 Committee that the majority of the clerks received payments, some substantial and others quite small, from the Commissioners, i.e. from the fee fund, the book-keeping for which was done by the clerk of the fees. It does not seem likely that these payments and their respective amounts can have been authorized by the Clerk himself without the sanction of the Commissioners, in spite of a somewhat ambiguous statement made by J. H. Ley to the 1833 Committee. He said:[1]

I consider I am to pay all the expenses of the clerks in the office; then the nett produce of the fees of my office are to be paid over to the Commissioners, exactly in the same manner as if the fees were paid to me, as they used to be paid to Mr. Hatsell. He paid the clerks what he thought fit out of those fees, and took the surplus; I pay the clerks, and the surplus is paid to the Commissioners.

This statement is the only evidence that Hatsell ever paid any of the clerks (except some of those in the Journal Office) out of his fees: and, in view of his return of income with all deductions made to the Select Committee on Public Expenditure in 1810[2] and of J. H. Ley's emphatic remarks in 1833[3] about ill-paid clerks when he was first appointed, I feel some hesitation in accepting it. No doubt J. H. Ley, when he became Clerk, determined to remedy what he felt to be an abuse, and did in fact settle certain payments from the fee fund, particularly to the senior clerks in the Fees Office[4] for public business done for the House (see below), but he had no authority under the Act of 1812 to make payments out of the fees on his own account, however desirable they may have been; so that, whatever may have occurred in practice between 1820 and 1833, the Commissioners could not possibly have accepted the above-quoted statement in theory. They, or at all events the Speaker, must have sanctioned these payments, though a cer-

---

[1] H.C. (1833) 648, qn. 136.
[2] See chapter 6, pp. 110–13, and Appendix VII.
[3] See chapter 9, pp. 204–5.
[4] e.g. Ley said to the 1833 Committee that a certain item in the payments from the fee fund to the first clerk of the Fees Office was 'fixed' about 1827, and another item (£200) 'seven or eight years ago', see H.C. (1833) 648, qns. 131–32.

tain latitude may have been allowed to Ley in his dealings with Dorington as regards disbursements from the fee fund.[1]

Apart from the disposal of the fee fund, however, the Clerk's position after 1820 was still autocratic. He had by statute the absolute power of nominating and suspending subordinate clerks, including the Clerks Assistant; and this power is still his, except as regards the Clerks Assistant, the power to appoint whom was transferred to the Crown by the House of Commons Offices Act of 1856 (19 & 20 Vic., c. 1). Yet, whereas for the last hundred years the Clerk's exercise of this power has been confined within the bounds of a fixed establishment based on fixed salaries annually voted by Parliament, and sanctioned in the first instance by the Commissioners (which involves the agreement of the Treasury), John Henry Ley's power between 1820 and 1833 had no such bounds. He could not, it is true, award a new salary from the fee fund; but, so long as the younger clerks could pick up a livelihood by laborious copying or by deputizing for senior committee clerks who were not paid out of the fee fund, but by committee fees, the Clerk was perfectly free to appoint them. Thus, Ley appointed three extra clerks, all very young,[2] in 1823, and another in 1830, and took them on to the establishment in 1831. Again, in 1830, when one of the four principal clerkships of committees fell vacant, Ley did not fill the place, but appropriated the share of that 'desk' in the committee fees partly to pensioning off an inefficient senior clerk who would otherwise have had a claim to the appointment, partly for general purposes of the office, and partly for charitable purposes connected with the office.[3] At the same time he deprived the sinecurist Stracey of his long-received salaries from the Treasury (£150 in all) and bestowed the money on other clerks in varying proportions, including £25 apiece to the four extra clerks

---

[1] See Appendix 12 to the *Report* of the 1833 Committee, which is an account of payments into, and disbursements out of, the fee fund for the years 1830, 1831, and 1832. A lump sum was apparently issued to Ley to pay the clerks on 5 July each year.

[2] e.g. J. B. Rose, who was appointed extra clerk in 1823 and took his first public committee at the age of sixteen (qns. 3132–49 of the 1833 *Report*).

[3] See Ley's evidence before the Select Committee on Private Bill Fees of 1834 (H.C. (1834) 540, qns. 96–107).

then placed on the establishment. These changes, however, were comparatively small. To all intents and purposes, except for the Clerk's own emoluments, the set-up of his department, revealed by the extensive inquiry of 1833, was the same as it had been during the previous fifteen or twenty years: and what called for change was not so much the set-up—that is, the staffing of the various offices under the Clerk and the distribution of functions— as the antiquated methods of pay, which varied from office to office, and from clerk to clerk, rendering impossible that cohesion and unity of purpose without which no department of public servants is worthy of the name.

(2)

On 20 March 1833 a select committee was appointed 'to take into consideration the fees, salaries and emoluments received by the officers and public servants of the House of Commons, and the fees, charges and expenses of passing bills through Parliament', and was nominated of twenty-nine members including two future Speakers (Shaw-Lefevre and Denison) and the ardent reformer Joseph Hume. The chairman was Josiah Guest. The committee sat through the session, at the end of which they produced their long *Report*, with its voluminous minutes of evidence and appendixes, which dealt in the main with the first part of their order of reference. The second part—the nature and amount of fees and expenses attendant on the passing of private bills—was taken up by the Select Committee on Private Bill Fees appointed in the following session. The work of the 1833 Committee, many of whose recommendations had not been carried into effect, was continued by the Select Committee on Printed Papers of 1835 and was the subject of their third *Report*. Finally, the business was completed, for the time being, by the Select Committee on House of Commons Officers Compensation of 1836.[1] These inquiries covered all the servants of the House, not only the clerks. The 1833 Committee,

---

[1] The parliamentary papers containing the reports of these four committees are as follows: H.C. (1833) 648, (1834) 540, (1835) 606, and (1836) 249. For the remainder of this chapter I shall refer to them as 1833 Committee, &c., in the footnotes as well as in the text.

in particular, spent a great deal of time on the Serjeant at Arms' department, which included the Vote Office, the deputy house-keeper, doorkeepers, and messengers, bringing to light the extravagance and waste of public money which had grown up in the course of one and a half centuries: but, though this part of their report contains some extremely interesting and picturesque details, I must neglect it here and confine myself to those parts which refer to the clerks,[1] the fullness and frankness of whose evidence, whether given by J. H. Ley or the youngest member of his staff, provides a remarkably vivid picture of the Clerk's department at the time, its differentiation, its varied personalities, the duties and hours of work, the points of pressure, the sore places, and, above all, its motley pay-sheet.

This last subject—the payment of the staff—was the main object of the committee's inquiry, to which the question of organization and working were only incidental. This is clear from the terms of reference quoted above, and still more clear from the *Report*. It was the antiquated financial system, its extravagances, inequalities, injustices, and, most of all, its inadequacy to a more modern conception of public service and the proper method of reward, that men like Joseph Hume were anxious to expose and reform. The opening remarks of their *Report* were as follows:

The emoluments of the Clerks in the different offices under the Chief Clerk arise from various sources, and they are paid in a variety of modes, by salaries from the Fee Fund and the Treasury, by payments for labour done and for different services, and by fees and gratuities, rendering the income of each Clerk frequently dependent upon a variety of causes, and in general occasioning its amount, especially among the Junior Clerks, to vary according to the quantity of business executed by them. The present system is strongly supported by many of the Senior Clerks, as one best adapted to the peculiar nature of the business of the House of Commons, but upon mature consideration, the Committee are of opinion, that as a general rule, fixed salaries, dependent in amount upon the nature and importance of the services to be performed would, as is the case in the other Public Departments of the State, be the best mode of remuneration. With this end in

[1] My early monograph, *The Officials of the House of Commons* (J. B. Nichols, 1909), contains a summary of the whole report.

view the Committee ordered a return from all the officials of their emoluments in 1832, which forms Appendix I of the Report.

This return of emoluments, made by every officer and servant of the House from the Clerk of the House and the Serjeant at Arms down to the day porters, night watchmen, and fire-lighters, is a remarkable document which, in my monograph of 1909, was reproduced in full. Since, however, the returns of the clerks alone occupy seventeen folio pages of print in that publication, I have somewhat reluctantly decided not to republish it here. Instead, I have compiled from it a table (Appendix X) which, by showing in columnar form the various sources of emolument revealed by the returns, brings within the compass of a single glance what I have called the 'motley pay-sheet' of the clerks.

Excluding the Clerk of the House and the Clerks Assistant, and also the assistant to the clerk of elections (who was only paid by his superior out of his fees), the total staff of clerks in 1833 is seen to number thirty-two, including a sinecurist (Sir Edward Stracey) who had two principal offices, another sinecurist who had served for fifty-one years before receiving his appointment to a principal clerkship of committees, and three extra clerks (in the Journal, Private Bill, and Ingrossing Offices respectively). The strength of the respective offices can be seen in the appendix. Several families are represented in plurality: there are 4 Leys, 2 Dysons, 2 Joneses, 4 Gunnells, and 2 Whites, all of which names have appeared in previous chapters. The years of service vary from 57 years (an exception) and 42 years to 2 years. These 32 persons received, in various degrees and proportions, payments from no less than 9 sources—the Treasury (ancient salaries or for work done), the fee fund, the copy money, the sum charged to the *Journal*, the sum charged to the *Votes*, the committee fees on private bills, the Private Bill Office fees, the sums paid for attendance on public committees, and gratuities, besides the ancient Gunnell's £200 as parliamentary agent to the Irish Office. It is hardly surprising that the committee recommended, not only some drastic reductions, but a thorough simplification of this financial cat's-cradle, of which most of the strands were ancient—in particular, the Clerk's immemorial fees on private bills, the Committee Clerks' fees on the same and their salaries from the Treasury dating back at least till 1695, the salary of £100 granted in 1757 to the clerk of the Committees of Privileges and Elections, and the salary paid by the Treasury to its agent, the clerk of the fees, which originated at about the same time. They had lingered on, though all memory or record of their origin had disappeared, except from the Treasury books where nobody had looked for them. Even the Clerk of the House, though his salary was fixed, still received and paid into the fee fund the £10 a year which had accompanied his patent for 450 years and the salary of £200 first granted in 1732.

(3)

We must now, as briefly as possible, survey the various offices as they appear in the light of this inquiry.

(a) *Clerk to the Committee of Privileges and Elections.* Thomas Dyson, who was appointed to this post in 1820 when William Ley, his predecessor, became 2nd Clerk Assistant, had one assistant clerk, Richard Jones, who was on the establishment but received no emoluments in that respect except a set of public reports and papers from the Vote Office. There were two other regular clerks, Hall and Walmisley, not on the establishment, who were also paid by Dyson out of his fees. J. H. Ley informed the committee (qn. 34) that there were practically no duties in respect of the Committee of Privileges, which had only met five or six times since 1820; he added, erroneously, that the salary of £100 from the Treasury was for the clerkship to that committee and had been paid for at least 150 years past.[1] The office was only busy in the first year of a new Parliament when election petitions were many. Then Dyson had to provide a clerk for each election committee, which entailed engaging such clerks in the other offices as could be spared. The general duties in this office have already been described in the previous chapter. The shorthand minutes of each committee were brought in each day, and the clerks had then to sit up till the small hours (qn. 62) copying them for the parties, who paid at

---

[1] For the facts see chapter 8, pp. 164–67. Ley seems to have forgotten that previous to Grenville's Act of 1770 there were no separate election committees; see Chapter 10, pp. 214–25.

the rate of 1s. a folio. The variations in the business were such that the fees received by Dyson in 1829 were £29. 15s. and in 1831 £1,759. 8s. 3d.[1] He and his regular clerks were all in practice as parliamentary agents (see below), and all except Dyson himself might act as agents in an election case when not attending the committee hearing that particular case.[2]

(b) *The Fees Office* consisted of the clerk of the fees, John E. Dorington, and four clerks. J. H. Ley (qns. 87–169) and Dorington (qns. 395–437, 932–44) described the work, charges, and emoluments of this office very fully; but, in general, regarding Dorington's functions as collector of fees and as Treasury agent, little needs to be added to what has already been said in Chapter 8, including the quotation there given[3] of Dorington's description to the 1833 committee of his work as Treasury agent. Ley's evidence on this head was somewhat less precise, at first giving the impression that Dorington drafted all the government bills, but he modified this under examination to the effect that Dorington drew 'all the usual Finance Bills' but not the larger public bills, the drafts of which were prepared in the different public departments.[4] Ley further said that Dorington advised with the Treasury and all the departments on the practice of Parliament, and was the person to go between the House and the departments of government to see that they did not make any mistakes. Moreover, Dorington acted for members who introduced public bills, attending to the copying, amending, and ingrossing of the same, charging the clerical costs, mainly for copying and ingrossing, to the Treasury. Ley explained that this service to private members used to be a matter of favour, but was now done for all alike. This clerical work for the Treasury and members was charged at a more or less

[1] The House fees and shorthand writer's fees were also heavy, so that election committees were very costly to the parties, the whole expense often amounting to over £6,000. (See *Report* of the Select Committee on Controverted Election Fees (H.C. (1837–8) 50).

[2] As regards the Recognizance Office, see chapter 10, pp. 225–26, where its functions, &c., up to its abolition in 1839 are described.

[3] p. 178.

[4] This was confirmed in evidence (qn. 2491) by William Harrison, Parliamentary Counsel to the Treasury, who said that he drew all bills for the Treasury and for certain other departments.

fixed rate of 3s. an hour, and was an important item in the emoluments of the four subordinate clerks (see Appendix X). All of these, in fact, were paid for work done; and if a man was ill, said Dorington (qn. 433), he could hardly depend on anything but his small share in the £900 from the Treasury, of which £120 was divided between the four clerks in the Fees Office, whose hours of attendance were from 10 a.m. to 10 p.m. However, Dorington and two of his subordinates were in partnership as the firm of parliamentary agents with the largest business. Parliamentary agency apart, Dorington's emoluments, except for his 10s. fee, as collector of fees, on every private bill introduced, were all fixed: they consisted of his salary of £1,100[1] as Treasury agent, his £35 in lieu of stationery,[2] and the sums of 40 guineas from the War Office and 25 guineas from the Admiralty for agency in passing the Mutiny and Militia Acts and The Marine Mutiny Act.

More novel were the details given at some length by J. H. Ley of the sums paid to the subordinate clerks from the fee fund for work done for the House. The first clerk, George Dyson, did the bulk of this work for which he was paid in all £400 from the fee fund[3], namely, £200 for preparing all the business and Order Books for the table each day, £100 for compiling the proceedings of committees of the whole House, for the fair copy of the clerk's minute-book, and for correctly inserting in public bills amendments made in committee, and £100 for arranging and transcribing reports from committees of the whole House, this last duty, according to Ley's evidence (qns. 137–8), having always been performed by a clerk paid, in former days, by the Clerk Assistant. Ley said that Dyson was paid more than clerks formerly received for these duties, but in his opinion was not at all overpaid. Dyson also got 10 guineas for making out the Speaker's list of members by counties from which, under an order made in 1825,[4] committees on

---

[1] Originally £800 for British, and £300 for Irish business (see p. 170).

[2] See p. 172.

[3] The returns of income made to the 1833 Committee show that in 1832, on account of the great length of the session, the first two clerks in the Fees Office received £50 extra and the two last £25 extra. No other clerks on the establishment received extra grants.

[4] See Williams, i. 50–51.

private bills were nominated; and also £50 out of the sum voted for the expenses of the *Journal* for compiling and examining the *Journal* entries of committees of the whole House. The second clerk, Arthur Jones, besides his £30 from the Treasury and what he made by copying, &c., was only paid a fixed sum of £100 as assistant clerk of the fees; but he did most of the detail of the Treasury work (qns. 163–76) and therefore made more out of it than his colleagues. The third and fourth clerks, very recently appointed, got about £100 each from the fee fund for various duties, mainly copying, performed for the table; their total incomes, including the extra allowance for the length of the session were just under £270. The third clerk, Henry Ley, received among the many items of his emoluments 10 guineas from the *Journal* money for assisting to examine the first clerk's *Journal* entries of committee proceedings in the House. Such were the duties, pay, and organization of the Fees Office which, Ley suggested, should be called the Office for Public Bills. Appendix No. 7 to the committee's *Report* is an interesting return, put in by Dorington, of the sums paid by the Treasury during the five previous years for parliamentary agency in addition to his own salary; these include the sums paid for copying, for writing minutes for the King (between £10 and £12. 10s. a session), for public bills ingrossed outside, extra sums to the ingrossing clerks for their trouble, and payments to messengers and porters for delivering various documents and messages.

(c) *The Committee Office.* The nominal staff of this office numbered twelve—namely, the four principal clerks (originally the four 'under-clerks without doors'), four deputy committee clerks, and four assistant deputy clerks. The principal clerkships had long been sinecures, and the work was done by the deputies and assistant deputies. The main emolument was derived from the committee fees on private bills, of which the principal clerks took two-thirds and the deputies one-third. The payments from the Treasury for attendance on public committees were not shared, but went mainly to the deputies, who had to pay their juniors for any attendances or assistance that they were required to give. The origin and developments of this ancient office have already been the subject of Chapter 7, so that they need not be further examined.

J. H. Ley seems to have known very little about their history, since he could only tell the 1833 Committee (qns. 204–6) that the division of fees was very old, that there were four clerks of Parliament without doors, each having a deputy, and that these clerks of Parliament 'no doubt did the business', but that 'the clerks now seldom get to their offices (i.e. the principal clerkships) till they were too old for active employment', and that the positions were now considered a reward for past services, to which all the clerks could look forward as a pension on retirement. The 1833 Committee spent some time in hearing evidence about this curious relic of the past, and promptly recommended its abolition.

Certain slight changes, however, had been made by J. H. Ley since the report of the Select Committee on Table of Fees in 1821, with its somewhat pointed observations on the four clerks without doors.[1] The principal clerks in 1833 only numbered three, Sir Edward Stracey, W. G. Rose, and Samuel Gunnell. Since 1827, when John Dorington, then clerk of the fees, died, no clerk receiving emoluments as the head of another office had been made a principal clerk of committees; and in 1830, when another vacancy had occurred through death, J. H. Ley had not filled the fourth 'desk', as it was called. He had taken this step for the sake of economy and out of a desire to apply part of the money to other purposes. It being the rule that the oldest of all the clerks on the establishment should succeed to such a vacancy, but the individual in question being, in 1830, the ancient ingrossing clerk, David Jones, who had become inefficient, Ley had appropriated that desk's share of fees to pensioning off Jones on £500 a year and reserving the rest for general or charitable purposes of the office, or towards a superannuation fund for deserving officers—an object which had been attained in former days by obliging the new incumbent of a principal committee clerkship to pay £100 or £200 to one of his colleagues.[2] Moreover, though Stracey, the absolute

---

[1] See chapter 7, pp. 154–58, where this report is quoted and the facts about Sir Edward Stracey's sinecures are given. The Select Committee on Private Business of 1824 in their 2nd *Report* (H.C. (1824) 468) also commented on the execution of the duties of some of the officers by deputy.

[2] Ley gave these details more fully to the 1834 Committee (qns. 96–107) than to that of 1833.

sinecurist, was irremovable, having been appointed for life by Hatsell, and Samuel Gunnell had served the House long enough to deserve a sinecure, Ley had directed Rose to undertake the general direction and co-ordination of the Committee Office[1] and even to attend committees if necessary: also, he had given Stracey's £50 salary from the Treasury as a clerk of committees to another committee clerk and divided the fourth desk's £50 between junior clerks.

For the rest, the four active committee clerks were no longer called deputies, but simply committee clerks; and the four juniors, who had been appointed extra clerks in 1823 or later, had been on the establishment since 1831 as 'clerks in the Committee Clerks' Office'. According to Rose's evidence (qn. 488), before these extra clerks had been appointed, they had been obliged to employ any clerk they could get out of any other office to take a committee in times of pressure, which was very inconvenient, since they were never sure of finding the clerk who had taken the committee. The table of fees to be taken in the Committee Office and the Private Bill Office had been carefully revised in 1830—a task in which Rose said he had assisted J. H. Ley.[2] The committee fees were still distributed in the ancient way, each principal clerk's share for 1832 being £918 odd and each committee clerk's share the half of that sum, or £459 odd. Rose and the four committee clerks were also paid by the Treasury varying sums for attending committees on public matters, at the rate of 2 guineas a sitting day, the largest sum under this head being £437 odd. The committee clerks, in addition, received sums of £106. 16s., £91. 7s., £93. 12s., and £58. 16s. respectively as their share of the gratuities paid by agents for private bills. These gratuities had been paid as a matter of course for a very long time, although they were disallowed on taxation of costs; and, as Rose pointed out (qn. 467), they rewarded overtime work either at night or in the early morning.

---

[1] This laudable plan was disputed before the 1833 Committee by other senior committee clerks, and in 1835 Ley confessed that the idea had been a failure.

[2] He said (qns. 505–15) that Ley and he had worked out the old charges 'in all manner of ways to see that the committee clerks should neither gain nor lose'. These revised tables were made a Standing Order (85 C.J. 633–5) and printed as parliamentary papers (H.C. (1830) 111 and 112).

Ley explained that, owing to some dispute which had been referred to him, a new scale of gratuities, agreed to both by the clerks and the agents, had been arrived at in 1831, as follows:

Promoters

	£	s.	d.
If a committee on a bill sits three days or less . . .	1	1	0
Every subsequent sitting	0	7	0
When a report is made the same day as the committee sits	1	1	0
When bills from the Lords are amended, or reported on the same day as the committee sits	1	1	0

Opposition

	£	s.	d.
For two sittings	0	10	6
For three or four sittings	1	1	0
For five or six, and not exceeding ten sittings . . .	1	11	6
Exceeding ten sittings	2	2	0
Newspaper	1	1	0

The committee clerk Chalmers (qns. 704–16) said that they would much prefer fixed salaries instead of gratuities, which they could not otherwise abandon in justice to themselves and their successors.[1]

In all, as can be seen from Appendix X, the four committee clerks earned quite substantial incomes, considering the value of money at that time: Beeby got £984. 15s. 3d., Chalmers £807. 13s. 9d. besides £200 from the Poor Returns Office,[2] Whittam £990. 3s. 6½d., and White £793. 16s.[3] The four junior

---

[1] Ley defended these gratuities before the 1834 Committee, on the ground that they stimulated exertion, but thought that they should be acknowledged as fees for each individual committee clerk, though their payment was not optional.

[2] This was not part of the Committee Office work, as Chalmers explained to the committee, but extra work which he did during the summer recess. It consisted in superintending the sorting, examining, and abstracting the returns of poor rates made annually by all parishes and places in England. An estimate for the expenses was presented to the House, from which Vote the Treasury paid the office expenses. One of the upper committee rooms looking on St. Margaret's Street was used for this purpose.

[3] The corresponding figures for sessions 1833 and 1834, given in Appendix 14 to the *Report* of the 1835 Committee, were W. G. Rose £871 and £1,433. 13s. 3d., Beeby £917. 9s. 8d. and £1,187. 9s. 7d., Chalmers £762. 13s. 2d. and £1,201. 7s. 1d.,

clerks collected very much smaller incomes, more than half their subsistence being earned by copying evidence, &c., for the office at night; two of them had earned a little by deputizing at public committees for their seniors, and three of them derived small sums for certain official duties, such as entering adjournments of committees in a book, affixing lists of committees in the lobbies, taking charge of petitions and bills referred to committees, or keeping an index of private bills. They had to work long hours, and their salaries were not very large, but they were young: J. B. Rose, whose father was head of the office in 1833, had been appointed an extra clerk at the age of fourteen. Altogether, the Committee Clerks' Office in mid-session was a place of bustle and some confusion, with parliamentary agents crowding the dark, low-ceilinged room, divided by partitions into its four desks, and old Sam Gunnell's Irish clients adding to the noise and the closeness of the atmosphere, which became very hot and unhealthy.[1] Also, it worked under singularly little control, in spite of Rose's alleged superintendence. Each committee clerk, to whose desk bills, petitions, or other matters referred to a committee were allotted in rotation, kept his own accounts and collected his own fees from the agents or from the Treasury for public committees, often, as Ley complained (qn. 3104) causing the reports and minutes of evidence to be presented to the House in a most incomplete state for want of proper examination.

(*d*) *The Journal Office* consisted of John Bull, clerk of the journals, six clerks on the establishment, and one extra clerk. The salary of the clerk of the journals was made up from different sources, but almost all of fixed sums, viz. £400 out of the £900 paid by the Treasury, £201 (from the *Journal* account) for superintending the production and delivery of the *Journals*, £1,000 from the £4,300 copy money, and a fluctuating sum (£61. 6*s*. 4*d*. in 1832) representing one-quarter of the total fees paid for copying papers, &c., for members and the public. The other clerks' emoluments, other

with £280 from the Poor Returns Office in addition each year, and Whittam £910. 1*s*. 2*d*. and £1,057. 2*s*. 7*d*. The committee fees on private bills in 1834 were £9,412. 9*s*. 5*d*. as against £5,509. 1*s*. 7*d*. in 1832.

[1] Evidence of W. G. Rose before the Select Committee on Rebuilding the Houses of Parliament (H.C. (1835) 262, qn. 408).

than their small shares in the Treasury £900, were made up of a large number of items, charged either to the fee fund (copying for members and scheduling papers), the *Journal* account, the *Votes* account (including the £500 for attendance at night, now divided in descending proportions between the first five clerks), and the copy money (for examining the sessional printed papers). J. H. Ley, giving supplementary evidence to the 1833 Committee after perusing their draft resolutions (which recommended fixed salaries), made a stubborn defence (qns. 3105–15) of the existing system of payment for piece work, in the course of which he said that the Journal Office had the most material duties of any office, so far as the House was concerned, that it was now in a 'most perfect state', that three more clerks would have been needed if fixed salaries had been paid, and that it would be very inexpedient to make any change.[1] And John Bull in his written observations on the draft resolutions (1833 *Report*, pp. 218–19) reinforced this argument by his own experiences as a young clerk in the Bank of England at the end of the last century, where fixed salaries had been introduced, with the result that the quick workers finished their jobs quickly and went home. Fixed salaries, he said, should mean fixed hours; and that means an increase of establishment.[2]

However, both Ley and Bull had previously given evidence which emphasized the evil side of the old system. According to Bull (qns. 761–3) James Gudge, the first clerk, having broken his leg the previous autumn and being only able to attend on crutches, could not work at night and so lost his share of the £500 for night work.[3] And, in generally describing the strenuous life of the

---

[1] He continued with his description of the Journal Office as it was in 1801, with ill-paid, half-starved clerks, already quoted on pp. 204–5.

[2] As regards the whole controversy over fees and gratuities *v.* fixed salaries in the public services, which lasted about fifty years after 1780, see Emma W. Cohen, *The Growth of the British Civil Service* (London, 1941), pp. 29–44, 69. It is notorious that efficiency suffered at first by the substitution of salaries for fees. Rickman wrote Thomas Poole a strong letter about this effect in the Navy Office in 1806; and, as I have pointed out, it was Rickman who originally wrote the defence of sinecures, high salaries, and fees contained in Southey's essay 'On the Economical Reformers' published first in the *Edinburgh Annual Register* and then in Southey's *Essays, Moral and Political* of 1832. See my *Life and Letters of John Rickman*, pp. 140, 236.

[3] Figures of Journal Office emoluments in Appendix I to the report of the 1835

Journal Office, Bull said of his assistants: 'they work extremely hard, much harder than I think they ought, but they know that if they do the business they will get paid for it; they sometimes work all night.' Of a clerk who made £1,006 in 1832, though he had only been in the office ten years, he said: 'He may consider himself very fortunate, he has risen in consequence of the death of my principal assistant[1] in the office, who died at the age of 43, his medical advisers constantly warning him that such would be the case if he persisted in not relaxing from his laborious duties; when I was in his situation, I myself for a whole week had only four hours bed on the average; at last I became ill, and it was found necessary to make an alteration so as to have a change of nights.' Of other clerks he said: 'I have known them come here (to the office) at five o'clock in the morning; in fact they almost live there, and it very often happens that they do not get a walk for relaxation for a whole week together.'

The 1833 Committee took considerable interest in the Journal Office owing to the cost of printing for the House and the somewhat high level of incomes earned by the clerks, so that from their close examination of Bull and his subordinates we get a very detailed picture of the work of the office and of the basis of its costs. This picture, as might be expected, differs little from that already given in a previous chapter in the light of evidence taken before select committees of 1828 and 1831.[2] Apart from the payments to three of the younger clerks for copying out the manuscript *Journal*, amounting in all for 1832 to £183. 2s., the Journal Office salaries still depended on actual work done under six heads, (a) compiling and preparing the *Journal* for press, (b) examining the proofs of the *Journal* and its appendix, (c) nightly attendance and examining, copying, and compiling the *Votes*, (d) compiling,

Committee show that Gudge's income in 1833 dropped by £240, while that of the other clerks rose proportionately. Gudge seems to have been restored to full activity by 1834.

[1] J. H. Ley also referred in his evidence to the death in 1831 of this clerk, by name Dickinson, 'prematurely worn out by excessive attention to the business of the office'.

[2] Those on Printing done for the House (H.C. (1828) 520) and on the King's Printer's Patent (H.C. (1831–2) 713). See chapter 9, pp. 202–3, 211–12.

examining, copying, and proof-correcting of the appendix to the *Votes*,[1] (*e*) examining proofs of the sessional papers printed by J. B. Nichols, and (*f*) copying for members and the public. Heads (*a*) and (*b*) were paid out of the *Journal* account, (*c*) and (*d*) out of the *Votes* account, (*e*) out of the £4,300 copy money, and (*f*) out of the fee fund. The first clerk was also paid £300 for making an index to the sessional *Journal* and £160 for making an index to the *Votes*, and the second clerk £100 for making an index to the *Votes* for the use of the office: and the extra clerk was paid £50 from the fee fund for endorsing, folding, and making a schedule of petitions daily. The total figures under the first four heads were much the same as those given to the two previous committees above mentioned. Thus, the total cost of the *Journal*, including rent and taxes on the warehouse in Abingdon Street, but apart from Hansard's bill for printing, was £1,734. 7s. 5d. in 1832 against £1,736. 6s. 10d. in 1830, while the charge for the appendix to the *Votes* under head (*d*) was £347 odd in 1832 against £353 in 1830.

What the evidence of 1833 brought out, however, was the definite basis on which the fluctuating payments were calculated. The process of compiling the *Journal* from the *Votes*, described by the clerk Gudge (qns. 1785–1806), was long and laborious, taking from four to six hours each day and involving much copying and abstracting. Copying for the *Journal* was paid at the rate of 2d. a sheet of 36–37 words, examination of the *Journal* proof at 4s. a printed sheet of four pages (3s. a sheet for the appendix) to each examiner, and revision of the proofs at 4s. and 3s. 6d. a sheet respectively. The first clerk's fixed payment of £200 was for drawing out the proceedings and putting together all the matter prepared by other clerks (Bull, qns. 784, 786). The *Vote*, which was not sent to press as a whole till 2.45 a.m., and which entailed copying out the Clerk's minute-book, since that could not be kept long enough to compile from, was paid for at the rate of 15s. a *Vote* and 6d. per printed page for examination of proof. The appendix to the *Vote*, which involved sorting of the petitions sent out from the table in bags and a long process of abstracting, was paid for at the rate of 2d. a sheet for copying and 2s. a printed sheet of four pages for

---

[1] Containing an abstract of public petitions ordered to be printed, see pp. 210–12.

examining (qns. 1807–17, 1857–90). Finally, the examination and revision of the proofs of the sessional printed papers were paid at the rate of 16*d*. a sheet, or 4*d*. a page (Bull, qn. 754), the total cost in 1832 being just over £700, and of this item the second and third clerks shared almost the whole labour and reward. During the committee's inquiry a long wrangle occurred between Bull, the clerk of the journals, and Mr. Church, the head of the Stationery Office, as to what was involved in the final examination of printed papers, including the proof of *Journal* and *Votes*, Mr. Church claiming that it was too highly charged for. The matter was satisfactorily settled in the end, Bull having succeeded in showing that the process was not simply proof-correcting but involved careful editing. This agreement was ratified in a letter from Mr. Church (appendix 5 to the committee's *Report*) in which no amendment was made to the charges detailed above.

(*e*) *The Private Bill Office* consisted of a principal clerk, two other clerks on the establishment, and one extra clerk, this last deriving half his income (£204. 7*s*. in all) from the Poor Returns Office. The clerical expense of the office was almost wholly met from the fees which, for that very purpose, it had been authorized by Standing Order to charge from the very beginning. The scale of these fees had been revised in 1830,[1] but, so far from being lavish, their produce was meagre, so that the clerks were worse paid, for longer service, than those of the other offices. Edward Johnson, the principal clerk, had been nearly thirty-three years on the establishment, yet his income from fees in 1832 was only £731, to which Ley had added £50 from the salaries formerly paid by the Treasury to Stracey the sinecurist. Ley admitted (qn. 3099) that Johnson's salary after thirty-three years' service was less by £200 than what, on the average, a clerk might have expected. The second clerk had served for nearly twenty-three years and only received £397—a marked contrast from the income of the third clerk in the Journal Office with only ten years' service who made over £1,000. Seeing that the work of the office, though laborious, was well done, and had saved a good deal of expense to parties promoting and opposing private bills by keeping up an accurate

[1] See p. 248, n. 2, above, and chapter 10, p. 234.

register of such bills as they went through all their stages, and thus providing information which previously had been unattainable to outside persons unless they employed and paid an agent,[1] it is difficult to fathom Ley's complacency as to the inequalities among his subordinates which this state of affairs implied. The principal clerk (qns. 625 sqq.), describing the duties, said that keeping up the register meant hard work and attendance from 10 a.m. or earlier till the office closed at 8 p.m. One of the duties, also, was to examine the ingrossed bill against the committee bill, thus checking unauthorized alterations by the agents for the promoters. Fines, originally sanctioned by Speaker Abbot, were imposed for inaccuracies of ingrossment. (Johnson, before the 1834 Committee, qns. 124–30.)

(*f*) *The Ingrossing Office* consisted of three clerks, Samuel Gunnell (the younger) with twenty-one years' service being the senior: the post of clerk of ingrossments was held as a sinecure by Sir Edward Stracey, but as J. H. Ley told the committee (qns. 269–72), when the second clerk of ingrossments, also a Gunnell, died in 1831, he had not filled the post, but had only allowed the first ingrossing clerk to take the same proportion of the ingrossing fees as was taken by Stracey. In view of my description of this office, its duties and emoluments, in the previous chapter, little need here be added. The ancient Treasury allowance of £21 a year for examining ingrossments of public bills had disappeared, presumably since the revelations of the Goodiff case in 1809[2] which showed that this examination was not performed by the Ingrossing Office, but by the Fees Office. The clerks were still paid from the ingrossing fees, for actual ingrossing, by gratuities from parties to private bills and for fair copies of breviates sent up to the Lords with private bills; but, since even so their incomes had proved insufficient, they were made up by allowances, ostensibly for amending public bills on third reading, to the fixed sums of £800, £500, and £150 respectively.

(4)

Such was the general state of things in the Clerk's department as the 1833 Committee found it: their examination of the other

---

[1] J. H. Ley (qn. 289), J. Dorington (qn. 914).   [2] See pp. 231–34.

matter affecting the clerks—the right and practice of acting as parliamentary agents for promoters or opponents of private bills— will be more conveniently dealt with later on. The recommendations of this committee, only very partially carried into effect, were as follows:

The salaries of the Clerk and two Clerks Assistant to be reduced to £2,000, £1,500 and £1,000 respectively; the Clerks Assistant to have no official house.

All payments from the Treasury to cease; all fees without exception to be carried to the fee fund, and all expenses of the establishment to be paid from that fund, any deficiency to be provided by a vote of the House; the clerk of the fees to continue his double duty as Treasury agent and collector of fees, to be the receiver of all fees and paymaster of all salaries, to keep accounts to be inspected, and to deposit a security of £2,000 on appointment;

The clerkship to the Committee of Privileges to be abolished, and the duties, if any, transferred to the Committee Office; as regards election committees, the committee were inclined to recommend a similar transfer;

Fixed salaries for each of the offices; for the Public Bill and Fees Office (1 principal and 4 clerks), the Journal Office (1 principal and 7 clerks), and the Committee Office (1 principal, 5 committee clerks and 5 assistant committee clerks, the 4 principal clerkships of committees, being sinecures, to be abolished), ranging from £1,000 for principals to £100; for the Private Bill Office (1 principal and 3 clerks) from £700 to £150; and for the Ingrossing Office (1 principal and 2 clerks, the sinecure post of clerk of ingrossments to be abolished) from £600 to £150;

The manuscript *Journal* to be discontinued, but three copies to be printed on vellum to admit possible alterations.

The result of these recommendations was scanty. By the Act 4 and 5 Will. IV, c. 70, the salaries of the Clerk and Clerks Assistant (as well as those of other chief officers of the House) were fixed at the amounts recommended by the committee, but with saving clauses securing that no existent holder should suffer any reduction or salary or perquisite, or loss of house; and that the Clerks Assistant, if promoted, should enjoy the salaries laid down by the Act of 1812; the sinecure posts in the Committee Office and the

Ingrossing Office were abolished, their fees to go to the fee fund; and the Committee of Privileges was discontinued, though the clerkship to it remained with the clerk to the Committee of Elections. The 1834 Committee, though mainly concerned with the amount of the House fees on private bills, heard evidence which showed that the committee fees on private bills were still being paid by the agents to the committee clerks, the ingrossing fees to the Ingrossing Office, and the Private Bill Office's fees direct to that office (Dorington, qns. 12, 13), that the copy money was being treated exactly as before (Ley, qns. 89–94); that the committee clerks were being paid separately by the Treasury for attending public committees;[1] and that they were still receiving gratuities, which Ley again defended.[2] Then came the great fire, but it did not hinder the prosecution of this inquiry. It was the 1835 Committee, to whose findings those of the 1836 Committee were only supplementary, that for the time being secured the desired reforms and eliminated nearly all the relics of antiquity from the Clerk's department.

The findings of these two committees,[3] so far as they affected this department, can be summarized together. They heard a certain amount of evidence from officers of the House, but this, apart from figures of some individual incomes for the years 1833 and 1834, did not add much to the massive body of information collected by the 1833 Committee. It only showed the extent to which the recommendations of that committee had so far been ignored. Taking the various offices in the same order as above, the recommendations, all of which were carried out, were as follows:

(*a*) *The Clerk to the Committees of Privileges and Elections.* The clerkship to the Committee of Privileges with its salaries was to be abolished. Though the 1833 Committee had been inclined to recommend that the business of the clerk of elections should be transferred to the Committee Office, the 1835 Committee followed Ley in thinking that the office should continue separate, and that a special room should be allotted for

[1] And 'badly paid', said Ley, though very well paid for private bill committees.
[2] For a summary of the important recommendations of the 1834 Committee for lessening the cost and cumbrousness of private bill procedure, see Williams, i. 53–55, 274.
[3] See p. 236, and p. 240, n. 1 above.

the duties. The duties were to include those of the clerk of recognizances and for settling allowances for witnesses, and of clerk to the taxing officers, and the salary was to be £600. Under this head the 1835 Committee remarked: 'The present Act regarding the taxation of costs in private bills, and for examining sureties for election petitions, is not satisfactory in its operation.[1] It often interferes with the duty of the Clerks Assistant of the House, and your Committee recommend the subject for inquiry with a view to amendment in the ensuing session.'

The 1836 Committee again recommended the transference to the Committee Office of the attendance on election committees, and this transference was made.[2]

(b) *Public Bill and Fees Office.* The committee concurred in the opinion expressed in 1833 that this office should continue two duties, which, however, were to be kept separate: (A) Treasury business, for which the chief clerk was to receive a fixed salary of £1,000 chargeable only on the establishment of the House; and (B) the collection of fees, etc. All fees whatsoever were to be paid to this office, and the chief clerk was to be paid $1\frac{1}{2}$ per cent. on them, giving sufficient security on his appointment. Ley, in giving evidence, expressed the opinion that the Treasury ought to pay for the work performed, and he did not think that £1,000 a year was sufficient for a gentleman who engaged in the service of the House of Commons as a profession, and who would have the responsible duties to perform which would be imposed on the head of this office, should he not also be allowed to add to his income by engaging in private business.[3] The recommendation as to the number and salaries of the subordinate clerks was the same as in 1833.

---

[1] For the examination of recognizances and the taxing of costs in election petitions, see chapter 10, pp. 225–26. By an Act of 1825, 6 Geo. IV, c. 123, provision had been made for taxing costs in cases of private bills on application by a promoter. The Speaker, being responsible for making the reference, chose one of the Clerks Assistant as taxer, following the similar procedure under Wynn's Act. W. G. Rose, now senior clerk of committees, had acted as clerk in this respect, having been clerk of recognizances from the beginning. Rickman, giving evidence before the 1834 Committee (qns. 115–21) had enlarged on his duties in this respect and the difficulties of carrying them out for want of adequate knowledge. He had suggested that some other persons should be appointed to tax bills. However, a taxing officer was not appointed till 1847 under the Act 10 & 11 Vic., c. 69. (See F. Clifford, *History of Private Bill Legislation* (London, 1887), ii. 814–15, and Williams, i. 117, 145, 261, 273).

[2] Evidence of R. Chalmers, principal clerk of the Committee Office, before the Select Committee on Election Recognizances (H.C. (1837–38) 441, qn. 637).

[3] See below, pp. 262–63, 266.

The committee also recommended that the agency for the Irish Office should be transferred from Samuel Gunnell to this office.

(c) *The Committee Office.* The four principal clerkships of the committees having been abolished, there were only eight clerks left, and the office was in need of reorganization.[1] 'At present', the *Report* continues, 'committee clerks are appointed to public and private committees in rotation, taking the chance of the continuance of the committee for one day or more during the session. The clerks are paid according to the days each public committee may sit, but as all fees for private business are brought into one sum at the end of the session, and each of the committee clerks takes an equal share of the amount, the committee clerks have been desirous of handing over to their assistants as many of the private committees, and of retaining as many of the public committees as possible.' 'Mr. Rose, one of the principal committee clerks, was appointed some years ago to be superintendent of the committee office, but the trial was unsuccessful.' It was recommended in 1835 that, after the death or retirement of the present clerks, the office should be divided into three desks, with three clerks at each desk, receiving £800, £300, and £100 a year respectively; that the ancient allowance of £50 from the Exchequer should be discontinued; that the present senior clerks should be allowed £100 a year as compensation, and the assistants should be paid extra for copying minutes of evidence for private parties. In 1836 it was recommended that there should be four desks instead of three, one to do the work of the clerk of elections; that the salary of the assistants should be raised from £300 to £400 in lieu of profits from copying minutes, and that of juniors from £100 to £160.

(d) *The Journal Office.* The 1835 Committee recommended the payment of a fixed salary of £1,000 a year with no house or rent allowance to the clerk of the journals, John Bull having died during the session. They added: 'It is the opinion of your Committee that fixed salaries should be paid where practicable to the subordinate clerks of the establishment as well as to the Chief Clerk; but they refer on this subject to

---

[1] J. H. Ley, in describing the previous accommodation for the clerks' offices before the Select Committee on Rebuilding the Houses of Parliament in the same year (H.C. (1835) 262, qns. 1–118), had also given details about their personnel and functions. As regards the Committee Office, he said there were 4 desks of 2 clerks each, but he would have preferred 4 desks of 3 clerks each. The number of 10 clerks recommended by the 1833 Committee would not be enough if each committee had to have a clerk all the time: but, with shorthand-writers in attendance, a clerk could manage two or three committees simultaneously. This is not so today.

the evidence of Mr. Ley, who represents that remuneration by fixed salaries alone would not answer so well as the present system. . . . These allowances (the payments made in 1833 and 1834) are apportioned to the labour performed by each individual in the office; and as there is much work at night, an inducement to industry and to the speedy dispatch of the business ought to exist. Your Committee therefore concur in the opinion of the Clerk of the House (Mr. Ley) that the mode or remuneration to the clerks, except to the Chief Clerk, should continue as at present.' Thus Ley had gained his end in preserving the old system of piece-work plus a small fixed salary in the Journal Office, which he firmly considered more conducive to efficiency. The committee, while accepting this, recommended that the sums paid for copying and examination should be entered separately in the annual accounts. They did not consider the rates excessive.

(e) *Private Bill Office.* Payment by fees was to be abolished here, and the permanent salaries of the four clerks fixed at £800, £450, £350, and £150 respectively.

(f) *Ingrossing Office.* Stracey having voluntarily resigned his sinecure, there remained only the three active clerks, whose salaries were fixed at £700, £400, and £150. The Committee offered the suggestion that the system of ingrossing in black letter might be beneficially changed to the common letter then generally in use in other public offices.

(g) *Estimates.* The 1835 Committee made one recommendation which had no result. Ley (qn. 36) had explained that the money annually required to defray the cost of the House of Commons offices was voted in Supply and issued in one lump sum, from which all the clerks were paid except for those whose incomes were partly furnished by their share of private bill and ingrossing fees. The committee recommended that a more minute and detailed account than formerly should be laid before the House, and that a general estimate of the whole expense of the establishment should be laid before the House annually, which should contain an estimate of every salary and of all contingent expenses—these estimates to be presented by the Speaker as chairman of the Commissioners for the House of Commons Offices: also, that no fees should be deducted from the amount of the estimate, but that the whole estimate should be voted and the fees brought into account by the Chancellor of the Exchequer (this last recommendation was intended to apply to all public departments).

Thus, by 1837, the Clerk's department had been thoroughly

reorganized on a basis of a fixed establishment with fixed salaries (except in the Journal Office), all fees without exception being carried to the fee fund, and all allowances from the Treasury, including those for attending public committees, abolished. There were no material changes for another twelve years.[1] However, before speaking of these, mention must be made of the other important matter considered, and finally settled, by the committees of 1833–36—namely, the prohibition of parliamentary agency by the clerks.

(5)

The position and functions of parliamentary agents in respect of private bill legislation are too well understood to need any enlargement. They serve their clients, the promoters and opponents of private bills, before Parliament in much the same way as solicitors serve litigants before the court of law. Their position is now recognized, and their functions regulated, in various Standing Orders relative to private business; and for over 150 years they have done indispensable service as the medium, in this business, through which the public approaches either House and effects the representation of its wishes or contentions. They are directly remunerated by their clients, to whom they present bills of costs. Those costs can, on request, be taxed by the taxing officer of either House; but neither House has any other control over these costs which, however, have often been scrutinized by select committees appointed to consider, in general, the expense of private bill legislation.[2]

Having put forward, in a previous chapter,[3] my view that parliamentary agency as a definite profession originated during the late eighteenth century in the activities, as professional agents, of the

---

[1] Except that the present method of taking divisions by the members passing through the lobbies, their names being marked off on lists by the division clerks and the numbers counted by the Tellers, was instituted in 1836 pursuant to the report of the Select Committee on Divisions of the House (H.C. (1835) 66). This additional duty of the clerks will be referred to in connexion with the reforms of 1849–50, chapter 12, pp. 269–70.

[2] Further information on this subject is to be found in Williams and in F. Clifford, op. cit.

[3] Chapter 8, pp. 179–89.

clerks George White and John Dorington, the facts there given need not be repeated. By the beginning of the nineteenth century not only had other clerks followed their example, though on a much smaller scale, but there was sufficient business to encourage 'outdoor' firms, managed by persons who were not servants of either House, to engage successfully in the same profession. In 1827 John Dorington told a select committee of the House of Lords that there were eight firms of 'indoor' agents including his own, and ten firms of 'outdoor' agents.[1] In an appendix to the report of the 1833 Committee giving the number of bills promoted by the different agents in 1832,[2] the number of agents mentioned is smaller, viz.:

Agents	Number of bills promoted
Doringtons and Jones	34
Jones and Walmisley	26
Dyson and Hall	18
*Sherwood and Thorp	21
*Brown	18
*Bramwell, Son and Fenner	9
*Hayward	15
J. Bull	1
W. G. Rose	3
S. Gunnell	2
G. Gunnell	3
G. White	1
G. Ellicombe	1

Of these the agents marked with an asterisk were 'outdoor' firms.

The evidence on this subject given to the 1833 Committee[3] shows that the firm of Doringtons and Jones, who had much the largest business, consisted of J. E. Dorington (the clerk of the fees), his brother (not a clerk), Arthur Jones the assistant clerk of the fees, and George Ellicombe the fourth clerk in the Fees Office, the last of whom also took a few bills on his own. Their office was the

[1] See chapter 8, p. 185, and footnotes.
[2] Appendix 15 to the *Report*.
[3] Ley, qns. 69–84, 214–16; Rose, qn. 470.

Fees Office, in the two upper rooms of which three writing clerks were installed for the private business, though they were also employed by Dorington in copying for his Treasury business.[1] The two firms Jones & Walmisley and Dyson & Hall both originated from the office of the clerk of elections. Richard Jones, as Ley told the 1833 Committee and Jones himself told the 1834 Committee, had been employed as assistant and managing clerk by George White the younger who 'had more private business than any person about the House' and was clerk of elections from 1788 till he died in 1813. Jones had continued in the clerk of elections' office under William Ley with whom he carried on business as a parliamentary agent, the firm being known to Hansard as Ley and Jones; and, when Thomas Dyson succeeded William Ley in 1820, Jones had been in similar partnership with him, sharing equally the profits of election committees and private business. Recently, owing to a difference of opinion, that partnership had been dissolved. Dyson had taken on Hall, and Jones had joined with Walmisley, both Hall and Walmisley being assistant clerks employed by Dyson on election committees. Other clerks on the establishment were too busy to take more than a few bills. For instance, John Bull, the clerk of the journals, said he only did so occasionally to oblige old friends who were solicitors (qn. 788, 1833 Committee): and, of the others mentioned in the list quoted above, Rose, S. Gunnell, and White were committee clerks, and G. Gunnell the second ingrossing clerk. The practice, therefore, was by no means universal and was, in fact, mainly carried on by those clerks who had the leisure to attend on the needs of many clients and contested bills.

As regards the propriety of parliamentary agency by clerks, Ley expressed decided opinions to the 1833 Committee. He did not think (qns. 72–75) that persons in the clerk of elections' office could be better employed than in conducting private business, especially those with Richard Jones's very long experience, and, in general, he said (qns. 81–84) he thought that private business was more satisfactorily done by clerks on the establishment than by

---

[1] Dorington (qns. 339–43) in the minutes of evidence of the Select Committee on Rebuilding the Houses of Parliament (H.C. (1835) 262).

other persons, since the House ought to have persons responsible to the Speaker to inform him if the parties should attempt any irregular proceeding.[1] He would rather, however, that the clerks acting as agents should confine themselves to giving instructions to the attorneys upon the practice of Parliament, than that they should take an active part in contests and mix themselves up in them, though, even if they did, there was no inconvenience. As regards the committee clerks he said (qns. 214–16) that acting committee clerks ought not to act as party agents in any contested business,[2] certainly not when they were attending, as clerks, the committee to whom the bill for which they were acting had been referred. He thought they had enough to do without private business, but saw no objection to each having four or five bills under their supervision, if they did not neglect their other duties. The clerks of the Private Bill Office were, from the first, debarred from acting as agents; but the assistant clerks in the clerk of elections' office were not debarred from acting as agents on election committees. Dyson, the clerk of elections, said he could not forbid them to act, and it is obvious that for him to forbid assistants who might also be opposing agents to act, would have been exceedingly difficult and unpleasant. The chief objection to private business being conducted by clerks came out in the evidence of a Mr. Henry Archer, who had complained of certain action of the agents, Jones and Walmisley. It was that clerks, having an opportunity of examining all proceedings at the earliest moment, enjoyed exceptional facilities for vexatious opposition. The action of this firm, which drew sharp censure upon their heads, was to substitute, quite illegally, a document of their own for a paper deposited in the Private Bill Office. Such a proceeding would have been impossible to an outside agent. Yet complaints as to the charges or the fair dealing of these clerk-agents seem to have been very few, and

---

[1] At this time the regulative Standing Orders were far fewer than they became in the next thirty years: moreover, the Chairman of Ways and Means had not yet been invested with superintendence of private business generally, assisted by the Speaker's Counsel.

[2] A proportion of the private bills introduced in any session are, and always have been, unopposed since they do not affect the rights of other persons. Procedure on them, therefore, has always been simpler and more expeditious.

no doubt their knowledge of procedure was very useful to their clients.

However, the 1833 Committee were not impressed by Ley's opinion or by the general absence of complaint. They reported that they strongly objected to private business being done by officers of the House, but at the same time did not wish to take any drastic action. 'Feeling', they said, 'much disinclination to interfere with the interests of persons who, having been permitted for many years to devote their attention to private business, now derive considerable emoluments from this source, the Committee content themselves with recommending that the clerks in the Private Bill Office and the Committee Clerks be forthwith prohibited, and that every officer hereafter to be appointed, and who is not now so engaged, be prohibited from undertaking the solicitation of Private Bills, or engaging in the conduct of business before Election Committees.'

The result, as J. H. Ley bluntly told the Select Committee on Rebuilding the Houses of Parliament in 1835, was that this suggestion that officers of the House should not interfere in private business had not been adopted at all.[1] The 1835 Committee, i.e. the Select Committee on Printed Papers in their 3rd *Report*, then settled the matter in their first three resolutions:

1. That this Committee, adopting the principle of the Committee on the House of Commons Offices, 1833, are of opinion that no clerk or officer of the House appointed since the Session 1833 shall be henceforth permitted to transact any private business, or directly or indirectly participate in any benefit arising therefrom.
2. That the Committee Clerks and their assistants, as well as the clerks of the Private Bill Office (who are at present restricted), be henceforth prohibited from acting as agents for Private Bills, or from being concerned, either directly or indirectly, for Petitioners or sitting before Election Committees.
3. That, as regards such clerks or officers as may have been on the Establishment previous to Session 1833, such practice shall cease and determine on 1 January, 1840, unless within 12 months from

---

[1] H.C. (1835) 262, qns. 43–48. Ley also expressed to this committee the view that committee clerks ought not to transact private business at all (qns. 20–32).

the date of this Report any such clerk or officer so circumstanced shall declare his intention to surrender his public office, in which case he shall be entitled to such compensation as may be determined upon by the Lords Commissioners of His Majesty's Treasury.

The 1836 Committee was appointed solely to consider questions of compensation raised by the recommendations of the 1835 Committee. As regards parliamentary agency, they had before them the memorial[1] of the clerks, to which reference has already been made,[2] claiming that the clerks had enjoyed the privilege of soliciting private bills from time immemorial. It continued: 'Committees have repeatedly inquired into the offices of the House, but never expressed any opinion adverse to the practice; but the Committee of 1833 determined that it ought to cease with the lives of the then possessors. Those who practised then imagined they might securely calculate on the permanence of their employment; and though they could not pretend to any vested interest, still conceived they might plead a prescriptive right, and after 1833 a recognized possession.' The 1835 Committee had recommended compensation for those who resigned their public office. The memorial asked how much this would be, and stated that the clerks would rather have compensation for loss of private business, and that the amount required for that purpose would not be larger than in the opposite case. J. E. Dorington also put in an account of his emoluments from his public office for the years 1828-35,[3] with a statement that his private business was considerably increasing, and was producing annually more than the average ($\pounds$1,412) of his public office for the last eight years. His private business, he said, could not be disposed of except on very indifferent terms: it was only certain and profitable so long as he was personally engaged. He would be happy to remain on the establishment, if the committee would grant him about $\pounds$750 for the loss of it. The upshot was that he was awarded a salary of $\pounds$1,900, and resigned his private business. Thomas Dyson, on the other hand, resigned his post as clerk of elections, and received in compensation an

---

[1] Appendix 10 to the *Report*.   [2] Chapter 8, p. 184.
[3] Appendix 12 to the *Report*.

annuity of £800. Since Jones and Walmisley received no income on the establishment, and the election committee work was transferred to the Committee Office, they needed no compensation; and the other clerks, who only took occasional bills, presumably acquiesced in this slight reduction both of work and incomes. So ended parliamentary agency by the clerks, at a time when, owing to the development of railways, it was about to become more profitable than ever before. This was just as well, since the embittered and expensive contests over railway bills before committees would have made the position of clerks, had they been acting as agents, quite incompatible with their duties to the House.

12

FURTHER REFORM, 1848-50

(1)

FOR twelve years after 1836 no further changes took place in the Clerk's department. Here, as well as in the Serjeant at Arms' department, most of the antiquities—the sine-cures, the old Treasury salaries, the gratuities, and the perquisites[1]—had been swept away. The business of election committees had been transferred to the Committee Office, the head of which office, W. G. Rose, was awarded an extra £100 in 1836 for assisting the Speaker's Secretary in a session of many election petitions.[2] Rose also remained clerk of recognizances and for taxing witnesses' expenses in election cases until in 1839, as the result of Peel's Act, his office was abolished and Mr. J. B. Booth was appointed both Counsel to Mr. Speaker and examiner of recognizances.[3] He was given a special retirement allowance on the abolition of this post, in addition to the allowance of £1,000 (his full salary under the 1835 reorganization) on retiring in 1840 after fifty years' service.[4] For the rest, John Rickman had died in 1840 from a throat affection caused by having to go at night from the overheated House to the house in Duke Street, Westminster,

---

[1] In particular, the entitlement to sets of the *Votes* and parliamentary papers which could be sold by their recipients through the Vote Office. It was, however, chiefly the doorkeepers and messengers who profited thereby.

[2] Min. Comm. H.C.O.

[3] See chapter 10, p. 226, and Williams, i. 95–103.

[4] Min. Comm. H.C.O. The regular granting of retirement allowances by the Commissioners can hardly have begun till the sinecure clerkships of committee had been abolished, although (see p. 239) J. H. Ley had methods of pensioning off a clerk who failed to secure one of these. After 1835, as the minutes of the Commissioners show, the scale of the Pensions Act (3 Geo. IV, c. 113) as modified, for those who joined a service after 1829, by 4 & 5 Will. IV, c. 24 was applied by them. A clerk who had served forty years got $\frac{8}{12}$ths of his salary; but those who had served fifty years—and these were not a few—were granted their full salaries.

which he took when his old residence in New Palace Yard was pulled down; but John Henry Ley, who had moved, after the fire, to a house in Richmond Terrace, with a house allowance of £500 a year, suffered no ill effects therefrom and remained Clerk of the House. In 1842 Barry made a residence for him in the new Palace of Westminster.[1] Rickman was succeeded by William Ley, the 2nd Clerk Assistant, who was J. H. Ley's brother; and Henry Ley, his son, became 2nd Clerk Assistant, so that for ten years, 1840–50, there were three Leys at the Table of the House. Dorington remained head of the Public Bill and Fees Office; James Gudge became clerk of the journals when Bull died in 1835; and Chalmers succeeded W. G. Rose as head of the Committee Office.

The Clerk's department consisted of five offices—namely, the Public Bill and Fees, the Journal, the Committee, the Private Bill, and the Ingrossing Offices. Under the reformed organization of 1835 each of these offices had a fixed establishment of clerks, with graded salaries but no annual increments: but the scale of salaries, as between the offices, was not uniform. And one office, the Journal Office, was still, except for its principal clerk, paid partly by salary and partly, as before, by sums, fixed in some cases, varying in others, accruing from the performance of specific functions—compiling the *Journals* and *Votes* respectively, examining proofs and so forth.[2] Yet, although the emoluments of the clerks had been, on the whole, somewhat curtailed by the reforms of 1835, one new source of income had been added by the adoption in 1836, of the modern system of taking divisions in the House. An experiment in 1834, by which on a division being called, the names of those who 'went forth' were taken down as they came in again, by a clerk standing at the door, while the clerks at the table took down the names of those who stayed in, had shown that twenty-

---

[1] Min. Comm. H.C.O. for 1867 show that, though Rickman received a house allowance of £200, no provision was made in the new building for a Clerk Assistant's residence, though a residence was provided for Vardon, the Librarian, who also had to attend at night. On Vardon's death in 1867 the Commissioners allotted this to the Clerk Assistant.

[2] Appendix 4 to the *Report* of the Select Committee on Miscellaneous Estimates (H.C. (1847–48) 543) shows in detail the composition of the total incomes of each clerk in the Journal Office.

five names could be taken down in long-hand by one clerk in one minute. The Select Committee on Divisions of the House appointed the following session recommended[1] that lobbies should be built for the new House, and also for the temporary Chamber in the old Court of Requests, through which the Ayes and Noes should pass respectively, two clerks in each lobby taking down the names and two Tellers at each door counting the numbers. Originally the names were taken down in writing by the division clerks, not marked off on printed lists, as was later arranged. The extra pay for taking divisions, £1,200 in all, was unequally divided between the 2nd Clerk Assistant (who received £100 for general superintendence) and nine other clerks, three from the Fees Office, four from the Journal Office, and two from the Committee Office.[2]

Also, a body of five clerks under the supervision of the Librarians, Vardon and Erskine May, were employed, during recesses, in compiling a new general index to the *Journals*, 1547–1713, thus carrying on a good work originally organized by Rickman from 1818 onwards, whereby the general index was no longer entrusted to outside indexers. The expenses of this work were, of course, defrayed out of a special vote.[3] The appointment of the Speaker's Counsel had only affected the Clerk's department by leading to the abolition of the clerk of recognizances; but the appointment of Examiners of petitions for private bills in 1846,[4] a useful step which very materially accelerated private business, necessitated the services of clerks to attend the Examiners. Accordingly, the four clerks in the Committee Office, J. B. Rose, Pole, C. M. Gunnell, and Frere, who had been appointed extra clerks at very juvenile ages in 1823 (Frere in 1831), had had their salaries raised from £400 to £500 for this service.[5] On the other hand, the laborious copying of evidence taken before private bill committees by which

---

[1] In their *Report*, H.C. (1835) 66, in which the experiment of the previous session was described.

[2] *Report* of the 1848 Committee (see p. 269, n. 2, above), qns. 617–24. William Rose, 2nd Clerk in the Fees Office, got £350, other clerks got £130, £120, £70 (in four cases), £50, and £40.

[3] Ibid., qn. 1081.

[4] See Williams, i. 74–75.

[5] *Report* of the 1848 Committee (see p. 269, n. 2, above), qns. 1545–52.

junior committee clerks had largely earned their bread, with the result that 'they sat up all night and were fit for nothing next day',[1] had been abolished. Instead, for the benefit of parties to whom these copies were essential in conducting their cases, a copying office had been set up under Vacher, the stationer. Clerks could accept work through that office, but very few did so.[2] However, when the railway boom of 1844–46 ensued, with forty committees sitting on railway bills the same day, extra temporary clerks had had to be taken on at the rate of £1 a committee, with permission to do copying.[3] Also, the Journal Office had abandoned the examination of the proof of the printed papers to Hansard, the printer, to whom £200 a year was paid for this purpose.

Many of the above details have been taken from part of the report of the Select Committee on Miscellaneous Estimates appointed in the session of 1847–48, to which I refer as the 1848 Committee. This committee, appointed at a time of great economic stringency, went closely into the expenditure of practically all the government departments, and their long report[4] breathes a spirit of uncompromising retrenchment. The House of Commons Offices were the earliest object of their scrutiny; and they embodied their criticisms and recommendations in a series of sixteen resolutions,[5] arrived at after hearing evidence, mainly from the Clerk of the House, J. H. Ley, who put before the committee his estimate for the establishment for 1848–49, with an additional column showing the recommendations of the 1833 and 1835 Committees (Appendix 4 to the *Report*). This comparison showed that, except in the Journal Office, no serious departure had been made from these

---

[1] Ibid., qn. 568, J. H. Ley.

[2] Ibid., qns. 611–16. The Copying Office was abolished in 1864 when the House ordered that all evidence taken before private bill committees should be printed (Min. Comm. H.C.O.).

[3] Ibid., qn. 581. The congestion caused by this mass of private bills introduced was unprecedented. The Deputy Serjeant at Arms informed the Commissioners in 1846, that there had been altogether 1,336 sittings of committees that session, and frequently over 4,000 strangers attending committees each day. (Min. Comm. H.C.O., 1846.) In that year the fees collected and paid to the fee fund amounted to £223,608 odd, whereas ten years previously they had amounted to £53,263 odd. (Ibid., for the years 1836 and 1846.)

[4] H.C. (1847–48) 543.   [5] Ibid., pp. xiii–xiv.

recommendations. Nevertheless, the 1848 Committee resolved that these recommendations had not been strictly carried out; and in their own resolutions they recommended many further economies: that it might be advisable to reconsider, when vacancies occurred, the salaries of the Clerk and Clerks Assistant which were fixed by statute, and also that in the next vacancy at the table or in the office of Speaker's Counsel the necessity of the latter office should be reconsidered;[1] that £500 was a sufficient sum for equal distribution among the clerks occupied in taking division lists; that the payment of £100 to the 2nd Clerk Assistant for attending to these lists should be discontinued; that a secretary to the Principal Clerk was unnecessary;[2] that all allowances granted for extra purposes in 1846 and 1847 (due to length of session and press of business) should cease with 1848; that upon a vacancy the receiver of fees and principal clerk of the Public Bill Office should receive £1,000 per annum; that 'a graduated scale should be established in this as in other public offices, and not departed from, commencing at £100 and rising to £800, consisting of three classes, the proportions to be arranged by the Speaker and the Commissioners of the Fee Fund'; that the expenditure in respect of the Journal Office, the allowances for which exceeded the recommendations of the previous committees by £2,612. 6s., was excessive, and the mode of payment objectionable and unsatisfactory from want of principle; that in no case should the entire emoluments of any clerk in the Journal Office exceed £800 a year; that the payment of £200 to the printer for examining proofs of printed papers should cease; that, as regards payment, the same rules should be observed for the clerks in the Public Bill and Fees Office as for those of the Journal, Ingrossing, and Private Bill Offices; and that the Committee Office should be a separate branch,

---

[1] Pursuant to this recommendation Lord John Russell, the Prime Minister, arbitrarily suppressed this office when Ley resigned the clerkship in 1850: but it had to be revived the following year. See Williams, i. 97 (n.).

[2] Ley explained (qns. 504–7) that a sum of £100 to pay a personal assistant to himself had appeared on the estimates for the last two years, but that he had never drawn the money. It is interesting to state that, until very recent years when one of the assistant clerks was so appointed, no Clerk of the House had a private secretary, such as had long been allowed to the head of a public department.

into which no clerk should enter before the age of twenty-five, with a minimum salary of £250 and a maximum, only to be received by the principal clerk, of £1,000.

(2)

Another matter dealt with in these resolutions was the annual estimate of expense for the House of Commons Offices. Ever since Hatsell's death and the full application of the Act of 1812 regulating these offices, the practice had been for the Commissioners, after considering estimates of expenditure for the coming financial year prepared by the Clerk, the Serjeant at Arms, and the Speaker's Secretary (for the Speaker's department which included the Library), and approved by the Speaker, to deduct these expenses from the amount of money in the fee fund, and then, after retaining a reasonable balance in hand, to pay the surplus to the Exchequer. This practice had even received further sanction by an Act[1] of 1846 under the provisions of which all fees collected by the collector of fees were to be paid to the Bank of England to the account of the Commissioners; the money was to be applied in paying salaries and superannuation allowances; and if the moneys in the account were sufficient to defray all charges (according to the estimate submitted under the former Acts) the Commissioners, retaining enough money to cover expenses to the 1st July ensuing, were to pay the surplus to the Exchequer to the credit of the Consolidated Fund. Accordingly, the minutes of the Commissioners for 25 August 1846 showed the account thus:

A statement was laid before the Commissioners of the fees of the session which amounted to	£223,608. 16. 10
Deducted from them for next year's salaries etc.	£ 52,281. 16. 10
Estimated surplus.	£171,327. 0. 10[2]

It was resolved that £165,000 shall be paid over to the Consolidated Fund under the provision of Section 2 of the Act.

---

[1] 9 & 10 Vic., c. 77.
[2] This arithmetical inaccuracy is in the original.

Although the estimates approved by the Speaker were presented to the House, no money needed to be voted. The 1848 Committee pointed out the weak spot in this system, complaining that the Speaker's sanction to the estimates was purely nominal, and that when the fees covered the expenses this vote was practically withdrawn from the observation of Parliament. They recommended that all the fees should be paid into the Exchequer, so that the estimated cost of the House of Commons Offices for any ensuing year would have to be voted by the House, and therefore subject to scrutiny. This recommendation of the 1848 Committee was eventually put into force by an Act[1] passed in 1850, which repealed former Acts as to the application of money collected, and provided that all moneys arising from fees, and all balances, should be paid quarterly to the Consolidated Fund. The salaries of the existing Clerk, Serjeant at Arms, and other principal officers which were fixed by statute were to be paid by warrant quarterly out of the Consolidated Fund; and after the respective officers ceased to hold their offices, all provisions of Acts of Parliament directing and fixing salaries were to cease. All salaries, with the above temporary exceptions, were to be paid out of moneys from time to time provided by Parliament. From that time onwards the expenses of the House of Commons Offices have been presented as a vote of the Civil Estimates, and subjected to the same procedure as the other estimates presented by departments.[2]

As regards the establishment, the Commissioners resolved in 1848 that the Speaker should draw up during the recess a new scheme for the salaries of the officers of the House in accordance with the recommendations of the 1848 Committee, and that the Clerk should adhere to them as far as possible in making the remaining sessional and other payments for the year. In the following session a select committee was appointed to consider how far the estimates for the salaries and allowances of the clerks and officers of the House had been framed in accordance with the

---

[1] 12 & 13 Vic., c. 72.

[2] Min. Comm. H.C.O. for 5 Sept. 1848 contain the following entry: 'Resolved that the salaries and allowances of the officers of the House be paid according to the last estimate until the new estimate for 1849–50 be voted by the House.' This, however, was previous to the passing of the Act mentioned in n. 1 above.

report of the 1848 Committee and to consider any other regulations that might be necessary. The committee had before them the Clerk's estimate for 1849–50 prepared in pursuance of the Act of 1846 and the new scheme for the establishment drawn up by the Speaker (Shaw Lefevre). Both these documents were printed as appendixes to the committee's *Report*,[1] but, since the committee adopted the new scheme with small alteration, it is unnecessary to reproduce them here. The most important section of this report runs as follows:

It appears to your committee that although the plan for the future Establishment of the House of Commons offices thus proposed by Mr. Speaker does not precisely conform to the resolutions of the Committee on Miscellaneous Estimates, yet that it does substantially effect the main object which that Committee had in view, viz.: the substitution of fixed salaries for uncertain allowances, and the assimilation of the offices of the House of Commons to the other public offices, as regards promotion and a graduated scale of salaries.

Your Committee have therefore adopted the principles of the plan proposed by Mr. Speaker with some deviations.

Your Committee recommend that the future establishment of the House of Commons shall be divided into four classes; that the rise in each class shall be by seniority; but that promotion from class to class shall take place, not merely with reference to length of service, but with regard also to qualification and character.

The division into classes took this form:

1st class.	4 principal clerks.		Salary £850 rising by £25 to £1,000
2nd class.	6 senior	,,	Salary £650 rising by £15 to £800
3rd class.	12 assistant	,,	Salary £300 rising by £15 to £600
4th class.	12 junior	,,	Salary £100 rising by £10 to £250

There were also to be two accountants with salaries of £500 and £200 respectively.[2]

---

[1] H.C. (1849–50) 258.
[2] There had been an accountant since 1833, and the heavy fee-work of the 'forties had necessitated an assistant accountant.

The existing establishment contained five principal clerks and five senior clerks, but the abolition in 1850 of the Ingrossing Office would remove one principal clerk and allow another senior clerk to be appointed. There were also thirteen assistant clerks on the establishment, but this number was to be reduced to twelve on the next vacancy. All clerks were to enter at £100, except committee clerks, who would not be eligible under the age of twenty-five and would begin at a salary of £250. The Committee Office was to consist of one principal clerk, and four of each of the other classes, all to rise by seniority.

The committee did not require these new scales to be introduced by any but gradual means, and, as regards compensation, they recommended that clerks then in office should receive in addition to their salary such sums as might make their total incomes respectively equal to those which they had enjoyed on an average of the last six years, ending on 31 March 1849. This average was not to include sums taken for divisions, and the payment was to cease so soon as the person receiving it should attain a salary equal to his total emoluments.[1] It was also recommended that £500 should be paid to the Clerk of the House for remunerating the clerk who superintended divisions and for dividing the remainder among such clerks, not exceeding four in number, as might be employed in that duty; that when the excess of payment for compiling the *Votes* (in the Journal Office) should cease by vacancy, a sessional gratuity of £150 should be allowed at the discretion of the Clerk to those who discharged that duty; that expenditure for contingencies was only to be sanctioned by the Commissioners; and, finally, that the only means of effecting economy was a vote taken annually in the Committee of Supply.

This scheme of reform was immediately put into force, and, being in principle that of the Civil Service as a whole, it has remained in force with such variations as have been applied through-

---

[1] A statement (p. 6 of the *Report*) gives a list of the clerks by name and by class under the proposed scheme, showing in one column the proposed salaries under the scheme, and in another the salaries including compensation (if any) recommended for existent clerks. The Journal Office clerks, who would otherwise have lost heavily, were those who chiefly gained by compensation: in other cases tne differences between the two columns were slight.

out that Service from time to time, or as have been sanctioned by the House in Committee of Supply.[1] The last relics of the old régime are to be found in the provision made by the Commissioners of retiring allowances for one or two of the clerks who were granted compensatory salaries above the scale laid down in 1850. Thus J. E. Dorington in 1853, and Rowland and Gray of the Journal Office in 1869, received the full amounts of their higher salaries on retiring after fifty (or more) years' service.

EPILOGUE

JOHN HENRY LEY retired from the Clerkship of the House in 1850, and died the same year. He had entered the service of the House under his uncle, John Ley, while Hatsell, though in retirement, was still the Clerk, and drawing a huge income from fees. He had known the ancient régime with its sinecures, gratuities, piece-work, and inequalities, and he lived just long enough to see the completion of the new régime, which he accepted after stoutly defending, on occasion, what he considered valuable elements in the old. With his death and the reforms of 1850 I designedly bring this record to a close.

By 1850 the Clerk's Office, as regards both tenure and organization, had received the mould of modernity, which, in this last hundred years, has not changed in essentials. The Clerk of the House still holds his office by letters patent under the Great Seal, but he and all his staff are dependent for their emoluments upon an annual vote in Supply. The framework of his department, except for one or two additions, is that of a hundred (or even more) years ago. There is the Public Bill Office to manage all the routine of the public business of the House, especially on the side of financial legislation, to be in close touch with the government draughtsmen and the public departments where public bills or amendments thereto are concerned, to collect such fees as there are, and to prepare the annual estimate for the House of Commons Offices; the Journal Office produces the nightly *Vote*, the sessional *Journal* with

---

[1] Which, of course, implies the agreement of the Treasury with the Commissioners in any variation proposed by the latter.

its index and its decennial general index, is in frequent correspondence with public departments respecting papers presented to the House, and is the research department as regards past procedure; the Committee Office staffs committees on public matters;[1] and the Private Bill Office still performs the functions of managing the private business of the House and providing a medium of communication between the House and parties (or their agents) promoting or opposing private bills. The chief addition, and that quite recent, is the small Table Office which relieves the clerks at the table of the mass of work and correspondence involved by the vast development of parliamentary questions to ministers. Also, owing to the payment of members and the facilities granted them of free travel to their constituencies, the labours devolving on the accountant have enormously increased in scope and complexity. However, though the framework is the same, there have been great changes in the apparatus, in the demands made upon the Clerk and his staff, in methods of work, in the relations of the clerks to the members, and, as one may well say speaking generally, in efficiency and knowledge of procedure and its principles.

These changes and developments should, indeed, be recorded. They include the minor, but very important, improvements in machinery—telephones, one on every clerk's desk instead of a solitary machine in the wall of each office; the use of the typewriter; the advent of the female shorthand typist; the file and the filing cabinet. They also comprise major developments, of intellectual or organizational import—the imposition of competition by examination as a condition of entry; the position gained by the Clerk assisted by his colleagues as *the* authority on procedure, which is symbolized by the successive editions of 'May' produced, ever since the ninth edition, by Erskine May's successors; the development of annual select committees on finance (public accounts, national expenditure, and estimates), which has brought about a new and extremely close intercourse between the Committee Office and the officers of public departments responsible for policy

---

[1] But no longer the standing committees on public bills, that function having very recently been transferred to the Public Bill Office which, however, relies on the Committee Office to supply part of the necessary personnel.

and finance; the impact of two wars, with widely differing effect, upon the Clerk's department; and finally the part played by clerks of both Houses in the international organization of the European Assembly at Strasbourg. The parliamentary historian cannot neglect these matters; and they will be best recorded by one who, by long personal experience, has known—and, I might say, felt—them from the inside.

Nevertheless, to have continued the record beyond 1850 would have been incompatible with my aim in the present work, already long enough. That aim has been to fill a gap in parliamentary history by studying the Clerk's office during its period of emergence from the medieval to the modern form through the intermediary eighteenth-century stage of patronage, privilege, and perquisite. The Goldesbroughs petitioning the Treasury for their dues, Jodrell the Chancery solicitor giving an elementary organization to his subordinates, Hatsell the supreme enjoyer of a hitherto unpredictably advantageous position, and John Henry Ley who lived to see all those advantages removed in the interests of economy and efficiency—these are the symbolic figures of this work. As it opens with a retrospect summarizing the pre-Restoration past from Robert de Melton and John de Scardeburgh to Elsyng, Scobell, and Smythe, so it must close with a prospect from Le Marchant to Ilbert, Webster, and Campion, to which some other pen will, as I hope, do justice. This will present a different material, a richer documentation, and at the same time a narrower outline. It will need an accompanying study, far closer than was needed for this work, of changes in parliamentary procedure and machinery; it will have fewer touches, perhaps, of simple humanity at odds with circumstances, such as the assault on William Brerewood, the poverty of Samuel Gunnell, and Hatsell's quarrel with John Ley. In fine, it will be a different study, which I am not likely to see. If this work provides for it an adequate point of departure, it will have attained its end.

Table showing the successive Clerks of the House, Clerks Assistant, and other principal clerks

(1) *Clerks of the House of Commons (under-clerks of Parliament)*

1363 Robert de Melton
1385 John de Scardeburgh
1414 Thomas Haseley
1440 John Dale
1461 Thomas Bayen
1503 (?) Thomas Hylton
1510 William Underhill
1515 Richard Urmeston, or Ormeston
1548 John Seymour
1567 Fulk Onslow
1603 Ralph Ewens (d. 1611)
1613 John Wright
1640 Henry Elsyng
1649 Henry Scobell (later Clerk of the Parliament)
1658 John Smythe
1658 Thomas St. Nicholas
1660 William Jessop
1661 William Goldesbrough the elder
1678 William Goldesbrough the younger
1683 Paul Jodrell
1727 Edward Stables
1732 Nicholas Hardinge
1748 Jeremiah Dyson
1762 Thomas Tyrwhitt
1768 John Hatsell
1820 John Henry Ley

(2) *Deputy Clerks of the House*

1797 John Ley
1814 Jeremiah Dyson the younger (retired on Hatsell's death)

(3) *Clerks Assistant*

1640	John Rushworth	1688/9	Culverwell Needler
1648	Ralph Darnall	1710	Edward Stables (became
1649	John Phelpes		Clerk of the House)
1649	Ralph Darnall	1727	Michael Aiskew
1653	— Davey	1740	John Naylor
1654	Ralph Darnall	1744	John Read
1660	„ „	1760	John Hatsell (became
1661	— Sharpe		Clerk of the House)
1663	Thomas Marsh	1768	John Ley
1673	William Goldesbrough the younger (?) (became Clerk of the House)	1797	Jeremiah Dyson the younger
1678	Paul Jodrell (?) (became Clerk of the House)	1814	John Henry Ley (became Clerk of the House)
1688/9	Samuel Gwillym	1820	John Rickman
		1841	William Ley

(4) *Second Clerks Assistant*

1801	John Henry Ley	1820	William Ley
1814	John Rickman	1841	Henry Ley

(5) *The Four Clerks Without Doors (Principal Committee Clerks)*

1696	John Hookes		William Hester
	George Cole		Newdigate Poyntz
	James Courthope	1742	John Hookes
	Hicks Burrough		William Hester
1718	George Cole		N. Poyntz
	James Courthope		John Burman
	Hicks Burrough	1754	John Hookes
	Edward Jodrell		N. Poyntz
1720	Hicks Burrough		John Burman
	Edward Jodrell		Robert Yeates
	John Hookes the younger	1758	N. Poyntz
	William Hester		John Burman
1734	Edward Jodrell		Robert Yeates
	John Hookes		Osborn Barwell
	William Hester	1763	N. Poyntz
	John Naylor		Robert Yeates
1740	Edward Jodrell		Osborn Barwell
	John Hookes		Hardinge Stracey

1769	N. Poyntz		David Jones
	O. Barwell		John Benson
	Hardinge Stracey	1799	E. Stracey
	George White		D. Jones
1773	O. Barwell		J. Benson
	H. Stracey		John Roberts
	George White	1801	E. Stracey
	Edward Barwell		J. Benson
1774	H. Stracey		Arthur Benson
	G. White		Henry Coles
	E. Barwell	1817	E. Stracey
	Robert Gunnell		J. Benson
1789	E. Barwell		A. Benson
	Robert Gunnell		John Dorington
	John Rosier	1828	E. Stracey
	Edward Stracey		A. Benson
1795	E. Barwell		George Whittam
	John Rosier		Samuel Gunnell
	E. Stracey	1831	E. Stracey
	David Jones		S. Gunnell
1797	E. Barwell		W. G. Rose
	E. Stracey		— (fourth place not filled)

After 1835 these posts ceased to exist.

(6) *Clerks of the Journals and Papers*

1740	Samuel Littlemore (clerk of the papers)	1756	George White
		1770	John Rosier
1748	Samuel Littlemore (clerk of the journals)	1774	John Speed
		1776	John Benson
	Osborn Barwell (clerk of the papers)	1797	Arthur Benson
		1803	George Whittam
1754	Samuel Littlemore (clerk of the journals and papers)	1828	John Bull
		1836	James Gudge

(7) *Clerk of the Fees (eventually the principal clerk of the Public Bill Office)*

1774	John Rosier
1796	John Dorington

1828　John E. Dorington (in 1842 called principal clerk in the Public Bill Office and clerk of the fees)

(8) *Clerks of Ingrossment*

?　　Hicks Burrough (d. 1733) (date of appointment uncertain)

1733　John Grover (d. 1749) (date of appointment uncertain)

1750　George Dowdall
　　　Robert Yeates

1754　George Dowdall
　　　Osborn Barwell

1758　Edward Barwell
　　　Robert Gunnell

1772　R. Gunnell
　　　David Jones

1774　Hardinge Stracey
　　　David Jones

1788　David Jones
　　　Edward Stracey

1795　Edward Stracey
　　　John Roberts

1799　E. Stracey
　　　Thomas Parker

1806　E. Stracey
　　　David Jones the younger

1831　E. Stracey
　　　William Gunnell

1832　E. Stracey

The posts of clerks of ingrossment were abolished in 1835.

(9) *Clerk to the Committees of Privileges and Elections*

Until 1740 this office appertained to the Clerk Assistant

1740　John Grover

1749　John Read (also Clerk Assistant)

1757　Hardinge Stracey

1772　George White (according to the *Court and City Register*, though the Treasury books continue to show the salary paid to Hardinge Stracey)

1788　Nathaniel Barwell
　　　George White the younger

1793　George White the younger

1814　William Ley

1820　Thomas Dyson

The post was abolished after 1835.

(10) *Principal Clerk of the Private Bill Office*

1810　Henry Gunnell

1824　Edward Johnson

1843　William Hawes

APPENDIX II

Petitions from the Clerk and under-clerks of the House of Commons for payments due or for increases of emoluments preserved in the Public Records, with Notes of the Action taken thereon

1. *Petition of William Goldesbrough (sen.) to the Lord Treasurer (circ.* 1677) (P.R.O. 30/32, vol. 36, p. 6).

As transcribed into a Treasury Book containing entries of miscellaneous petitions, with the action taken noted in the right-hand margin, the petition runs as follows:

'Peticōn of Willm Goldsborough Clerke of the house of Comōns, Showing that he haveing from the beginning of the Rebellion served yᵉ Crowne not without losses hazards and considerable expence his Matie on his Restoraċon gave him that place, with the Sallary of 10ᵗ ₱. annᵈ which is in arreare from the time of his Grant and to have the usuall allowance for his labour care and charge of money Bills and other Publique matters, for which he never recᵈ anything but 100ᵗ in the Lord Clifford's time and what he recᵈ for Bills coppyed this last Session by Mʳ Lownds. The Petʳ haveing orders registred on the Revenue unsatisfied for former work, Praying your Lordpp to give such direċcon as shall be fitting. Yᵉ Petʳ complaines that Mʳ Barnard recᵈ money for him for Coppyes of Bills upon a suggestion to yoʳ Lordp that he had pᵈ yᵉ Petʳ, but the Petʳ never knew he had recᵈ any money for a greate while: and now he will not pay him his due. Memᵈ also that the Petʳ in his bills annexed to his Peticcon incerts those for wᶜʰ Mʳ Barnard was pᵈ soe that Yoʳ Lop may be doubly charged, if this be not taken notice of.'

In the right-hand margin is entered '200ᵗ graunted'. See below, p. 297, for the Exchequer certificate of what was paid to Goldesbrough at various times, annexed to Jodrell's petition of 1723.

2. *Petition from the four under-clerks, Hookes, Cole, Courthope, and Burrough, circ.* 11 Aug. 1698, as recorded in the Treasury books (*Cal. T.P. 1697–1701*, vol. ii, p. 190).

'They had faithfully discharged their duties, but their incomes were barely sufficient to support them during the sessions, and in the intervals they had to live on their private fortunes; they pray for a grant of some employment which would support them.'

Minuted: 'Recd. 11 Augt. 1698. There never are four places vacant at a time, but yᵉ Clerks to have yᵉ same allowance this year as they had yᵉ last.'

3. *Petition of the Clerk Assistant and the under-clerks to the House, 1701.*

This had been preceded by a humble recommendation made by the House that the Clerk of the House, Serjeant at Arms, the Clerk Assistant, other clerks and officers of the House, 'having served with great diligence and fidelity, and being but slenderly provided for' might have 'competent salaries, answerable to their trusts and services settled upon them' (13 C.J. 316, 6 April 1700). The Treasury books record (*Cal. T.P.* xv. 75) that on 7 May, the King and all the Treasury Lords being present, 'upon the address of the Clerks of the House of Commons the King resolves to do something for the Under-clerks'. Reference to the above is made in the petition of 1701 (13 C.J. 640, 24 June 1701) recorded in the *Journal* as follows:

'Petition of the Clerk Assistant and Under-clerks presented to the House and read.

'That the Clerk Assistant has been obliged to lay by most of his other business; and the said four Clerks have totally for many years quitted their employments to apply themselves to their attendance upon the House, That they have no other consideration of public business than what his Majesty shall be pleased to bestow upon them; and that the profits arising from private business is so small that this present session had not afforded the said 4 Under-clerks £30 apiece; that the House was pleased last session to recommend them to his Majesty for competent salaries, answerable to their trusts and services, to be settled upon them; that his Majesty, upon receiving such recommendations, was graciously pleased to do something for the Petitioners, the Under-clerks; but they, not having as yet received the effect of his Majesty's royal intention, pray the further consideration of the House of the premises. *Resolved*, That a humble Address be presented to his Majesty that he will be graciously pleased to take into consideration the services of the said Clerks and other servants of the House and make them allowances for the same.'

This petition and the humble address were duly brought up at the

Treasury Board (*Cal. T.P. 1697–1701*, vol. ii, p. 503) and minuted 'To be read when Mr. Lowndes is present', a schedule of the allowances made in 1701 to officers of the two Houses being entered at the foot of the page (i.e. of P.R.O. Treasury Papers, vol. 84, no. 7). This schedule, not printed in the *Cal. T.P.*, is as follows:

Serjeant at Arms House of Peers 10s. a day during the session for which he is to produce a certificate from the Speaker and will

amount for last session to about	60		
Doorkeepers of Peers	50		
	110		
Mr. Needler, Clerk Assistant of the House of Commons at 50 gns. a session . .	53. 15	= 100	
4 Underclerks of the same House . .	110	200	
Mr. Ryall for last session . . .	10	30	
Messengers and Doorkeepers . . .	40	60	
Sjt. Powell about	100		
Jos. Taylor for business relating to the impeachments	201. 8		
	515. 3		
total . .	625. 3		

On 24 July 1701 a warrant was made out to pay the officers of the Commons the increased sums noted in the right-hand column of the above schedule (T. 53/15, fol. 464).

4. *Memorial of the Clerk and other Officers of the House to the Queen, 1713, praying for compensation for losses due to the passing of the General Naturalization Act, 1709, and to other causes.*

(*Note.* The humble Address of the '12th day of April last' to which the memorial refers at its opening was that resolved to be presented on 12 April 1709 (16 C.J. 198), hence it is obvious that the memorial was originally composed in that year. This is confirmed by the fact that, in the account appended to it, Needler appears as Clerk Assistant, whereas he retired in 1710 and was succeeded by Stables, who is mentioned in the Speaker's report on the memorial made in 1713. The humble address of 1709 had no result in spite of the Queen's favourable answer,[1]

[1] The House of Lords presented a similar address on behalf of the Lords' clerks for similar reasons in 1709 (18 L.J. 712), but this had no result at the time, nor did the Lords' clerks subsequently get the compensation granted to the Commons clerks.

and it was renewed in 1711 (16 C.J. 689–90). The memorial was finally read by the Treasury (see below) in 1712, referred to the Speaker and reported on by him in 1713. Meanwhile the General Naturalization Act had been repealed in 1712.)

The Memorial (P.R.O., Treasury In Letters, T. 1/160, fols. 99–101) runs as follows:

TO THE QUEEN'S MOST EXCELLENT MAJESTY.

MAY IT PLEASE YOUR MAJESTY.

THE Honourable House of Commons on the 12th day of Aprill last taking into their consideration the great losses which had been and would for the future be Annually to the Clerk, Serjeant at Armes, Clerk Assistant and other Clerks Officers & Servants attending the Said House, by reason of the passing a Bill for a Generall Naturalization this last Session, and in respect of the late Orders made concerning the passing of Private Bills through this House and otherwise, Did then come to a Resolution Nemine Contradicente.

THAT an Humble Address Should be presented to your Majesty, That your Majesty would be Graciously pleased to take the losses which have been and will for the future be Annually to the Clerk, Serjeant at Armes, Clerk Assistant, and other Clerks, Officers and Servants Attending the Said House (by reason of the passing the Bill for a Generall Naturalization this last Session, and in respect of the late Orders made concerning the passing of Private Bills through the Said House and otherwise) into your Consideration, and to give them such Recompence & Incouragement, with respect to their Trusts, as your Majesty in your Royall Wisdome should think fitt.

WHICH Address having been presented to your Majesty, your Majesty was Graciously pleased on the 20th day of the Said Month to Say, That your Majesty would take the said Losses into your Consideration, & give such Recompence & Incouragem^t as your Majesty should think proper.

PURSUANT to which Address, and your Majestye's most Gracious Answer, The Clerk, and other Clerks, do humbly presume to represent to your Majesty, That the Office of the Clerk of the said House is a place of great Trust, and attendance in respect of the various Publick business there transacted, and of the many money and other Publick Bills begun and carried on there, and of the many Publick Papers Delivered into the said House, which are committed to his Custody & care, and which of late years have been very many by reason whereof not only the business of the house is very much Increased, but a great Deal of time after the house is arisen, is almost Daily Spent in taking care of the papers, putting them into a method and keeping them Regularly and in order, whereby almost his whole time, during the Session, is Spent in Attending the Duty of the House, and whose Sallary is only 10[li] p. Annum.

THE Clerk and other Clerks and Officers have Constantly Discharged the Trusts reposed in them with great Industry, Integrity and Fidelity, and they do humbly presume to Say to the Satisfaction and well-liking of the whole House, Since they have so Unanimously addressed your Majesty on their behalf.

THAT it may appear what great Losses have already been and will be Annually to the Clerk, and the other Clerks and Officers Attending the Said House by the passing of the Generall Naturalization Act only, They do humbly presume to lay before your Majesty an Account of the profitts that have arisen to them in respect of Naturalizations for nine years last past, That by computeing what has arisen from that Head an Estimate may be made, what in all probability would have come to them this last Session, and what would have Annually for the future arisen to them if that Act had not been made, Moreover it is Conceived, That in Times of Peace there would have been more particular Naturalizations.

A Computation of the fees which arose by Naturalizations for the nine years last past.

A Computation of the said fees as they arise to each pticular Clerk & Officer.

	No. ffees		£ s. d.
In the year 169[8]/[9] there was .	130	To Mr Jodrell Clerk by fees on such Bills, Orders Ingrossm[ts] & Swearing psons. to be naturalized.	208. 2. 6. p. ann.
178[9]/[0]* . .	38		
170[0]/[1] . .	15		
170[1]/[2] . .	41	To the Serjeant at Armes for Such fees on Such Bills & Swearing psons to be naturalized	057. 16. 3. p. ann.
170[2]/[3] this year the Bill lost.		To Mr. Needler Clerk Assistant for fees on Such Bills for reading Petiçons relating thereto	047. 0. 0. p. ann.
170[3]/[4] . .	23		
170[4]/[5] . .	9	To Mr. Hookes, Senr Clerk of the 4 Clerks attending the Comm[ees] for fees on Such Bills & Comm[ee] fees thereon to himself only	067. 16. 8. p. ann.
170[5]/[6] . .	35		
170[6]/[7] . .	23		

An error for 1699/1700.

170⁷/₈	.	.	19	To the Speaker's Secretary for fees on such Bills	018. 10. 0. p. ann.
			—		
			333		
			—	To the Housekeeper for fees on such Bills & Comm^{ee} fees	018. 10. 0. p. ann.
				To the two Doorkeepers between them on Such Bills	009. 5. 0. p. ann.
				To the 4 Messengers between them for fees	004. 12. 6. p. ann.

$$431.\ 12.\ 6.$$

The Same when divided is 37 fees Annually.

which for the future will be an Annuall loss to each particular pson upon the Head of Naturalization.

THAT the Clerk and his under Clerks most humbly further represent to your Majesty that besides the losses they shall sustain by the Generall Naturalization Bill, they have been and will be considerable Losers in respect of the Matters following viz:

1ˢᵗ IN regard of the Orders made by the House of Lords for referring Private Bills to the Judges,[1] most Bills now begining there, to avoid (as

---

[1] This complaint refers to one of five Standing Orders made by the House of Lords on 16 Feb. 1705 (18 L.J. 105–6). It ordered that: 'When a petition for a private bill shall be offered to this House, it shall be referred to two of the Judges, who are forthwith to summon all Parties before them who may be concerned in the bill; and, after hearing all the Parties, are to report to the House the state of the case, and their opinion thereupon, under their hands: the same method to be observed as to private bills that are brought up from the House of Commons, before the second reading of such bills.'

Although this Standing Order, in terms, applied to all private bills, it seems to have been intended mainly to restrict the number of estate bills, nearly a hundred of which were passed in the two sessions of 1704–6. The five Orders were made consequent on resolutions of a committee of the whole House appointed to consider 'the best means to prevent the increase of private bills in Parliament and the surprising the House in their proceeding thereupon' (18 L.J. 99, 104–5, 111) (see H.L. MSS. New Series, vi, introd. p. xxxix, where an account is given of these proceedings, with the following note: 'Previous to these Orders, Estate Bills originated in either House, but, after the new Orders came into force, it was clearly more convenient that an Estate Bill should originate in the House of Lords, and this gradually became the invariable practice.')

The complaint of the Commons clerks was, therefore, to some extent justified: on the other hand, when the Commons claimed that all private bills imposing charges not in the nature of a tax must originate in their House, the Commons officers who drew fees from private bill legislation gained a great advantage over the Persons apprehend) Such Difficultyes as might happen in the House of Commons, whereby the Clerk and his Clerks loose the fees upon Petitions for and against the Bill, and attendances thereon, and the Ingrossments thereof, also by reason of the Order for Printing of Bills before they are read, He looses the Copyes of all Bills; which two Articles used to be very considerable yearly.

TO which may be added the great losses wch will happen in the decrease of the number of Private Bills, by the Bill that past the last Session[1] to enable Infants who are siezed of Estates in Trust or by way of Mortgage to make Conveyances of such Estates and by the Great Discouragement, The House sheweth to Bills for making forreign built Shipps free.

2dly AS to the Clerk Assistant and the Senr of the four Clerks, as the number of Private Bills decrease they will likewise be loosers proportionably: And the Clerk Assistant is also a looser by the new Method the House hath taken to hear Elections at the Barr, and will still be so if that Method should be continued.[2]

THE 4 Clerks attending Comm^ees formerly had the benefit of four or five Sittings or more upon every private Bill when begun in the House of Commons and had its first enquiry and consideration and Proofs of the Allegations before the Comm^ee there, but now by reason of the preexamination by the Judges and coming Ingrost from the Lords, be such Bills never so long, a Comm^ee of the House of Commons rarely (if ever) Sits twice, and though formerly almost every one of them was attended with one or more Petitions ag^t such Bills, yet now very few such Petitions are presented (if any) because upon such preexamination all partyes concerned are heard before the Judges, and by many other Orders relating to Private Business the Profitts usually accruing to the said four Clerks formerly amounted to above ninety Pounds p. Ann̄. each, which is now reduced to forty.[3]

4^thly AS to the Speaker's Secretary, as the number of Private Bills decrease so likewise doth his profitts in proportion.

those of the House of Lords. It was not till 1858 that the Commons relaxed this claim (see Williams, i. 141–2 and footnotes).

[1] 7 Anne, c. 10.   [2] See chapter 10, pp. 215-17.

[3] See p. 288, n. 1, above. The Lords' Standing Orders of 1705 may have had this effect at first, but the effect was certainly not permanent. If only a committee clerk's minute-book of the years immediately after 1705 had survived, as did James Courthope's minute-book for the years 1697-9 (see chapter 3, p. 54, and chapter 7, pp. 129-30), we should know whether this complaint was exaggerated or not.

5^thly THE Clerk of the House hath had a Clerk under him ever since the Revolution, Publick Business so much increasing, who hath the Charge and Custody (under his Master) of the Journalls, and Bills and proceedings thereon, with other papers laid before the house, whereby the same are kept in order and from confusion, and he is obliged to attend constantly whilest the House is Sitting, and at all times on Members of the House upon Searches, & otherwise when required; Hath not any Sallary from Her Majesty & very little (if any) perquisites for so doing the same, But the Clerk is necessitated to maintain him in his house to be Constantly at hand and allow him a Considerable Sallary yearly whereby the Business of the House is much the better dispatch't.

6^thly AS to the Housekeeper who is at great Charge of keeping of Servants for Cleansing the House, and keeping the same descent, had proportionable fees on Private Bills and at the Comm^ees upon all such Bills the benefitt whereof is in a very great measure decreased by the means aforesaid.

7^thly AS to the two Doorekeepers, as the number of private Bills decrease, so likewise doth their profitts in proportion.

All which are most Humbly represented and Submitted to your Majestye's Consideration.

An Account of the Losses of the Clerks & other officers of the House of Commons by reason of the Generall Naturalization Act and otherwise and also An Account of what Sallaryes are by them received and what Augmentation may be proper to each of them if thought fitt.

Mr. Jodrell Clerk of the House	Their losses Annually	Their sallary and losses	What proper annuity if thought convenient
His losses annually by fees on the Head of Naturalization	208. 2. 6.		
and his losses by copyes of Bills, Ingross-m^ts &c. may be computed at . .	100. –. –.	308. 2. 6.	
His Sallary by his Patent		10. –. –.	260. –. –. p. Ann.
		318. 2. 6.	
Mr. Jodrell craves an allowance for his Clerk Mr. Hamlyn who looks after the Journalls and other Papers &c. to accomodate the Members			40. –. –. p. Ann.

	Their losses Annually	Their sallary and losses	What proper annuity if thought convenient
Mr. Needler the Clerk Assistant			
his losses on the Head of Naturalization	47. –. –.	67. –. –.	
His losses by other bills and proceedings	20. –. –.		150. –. –. p. Ann.
His Sallary	–. –. –.	100. –. –.	
		167. –. –.	
Mr. Hookes the Senr Clerk of the 4 Clerks attending Comm^ees who of the 4 hath only fees out of all Bills his losses on the Head of Naturalization put Estimate.	67. 16. 8		
Hee likewise is a looser in proportions on other Bills	10. –. –.	127. 16. 8.	
Hee likewise is a great looser by Comm^ees upon all private business and other Proceedings thereon as one of the said 4 Clerks which formerly was worth to them about 90^li p. ann. each and now not forty put Estimate	50. –. –.		150. –. –. p. Ann.
His Sallary as one of the said 4 Clerks		50. –. –.	
		177. 16. 8.	
The 3 other Clerks are the like loosers by Comm^ee fees and other proceedings thereon	150. –. –.	150. –. –.	
Their Sallaryes		150. –. –.	300. –. –. p. Ann.
(Mr. Cole, Mr. Courthop, Mr. Burrow) [these names in margin]		300. –. –.	
The Serjt.			
His losses on the Head of Naturalization and upon other accounts he craves an allowance of	57. –. –. / 50. –. –.	107. –. –.	100. –. –. p. Ann.
Mem^dm. he has a Sallary as Queens Serjeant			
Mr. Smith the Housekeeper			
His losses by the Naturalization Bill .	18. 10. –.	48. 10. –.	60. –. –. p. Ann.
His losses on other Bills & Comm^ees .	30. –. –.		
His Sallary		30. –. –.	
		78. 10. –.	
The Speaker's Secretary this is an office that the person is changed upon the choice of every new Speaker. The losses to his office on the Head of Naturalization	20. –. –.	20. –. –.	20. –. –. p. Ann.
The two Doorkeepers & the four Messengers and Assistants They humbly beg that their Sallaryes may be made double which amongst them is . . .	–. –. –.	100. –. –.	200. –. –. p. Ann.
Mr. Royall who delivers the Votes and has no fees his Sallary is 10^li which he hopes will be made double . . .	–. –. –.	10. –. –.	20. –. –. p. Ann.
			1300. –. –.

The Treasury endorsement on the Memorial was: 'Read 3 July 1712, Send this to Mr. Speaker. My Lord will speak to him ab^t this. My Lord thinks there should be an Acc^t of what they do receive as well as what they have lost.'

Speaker Bromley's report (ibid., fol. 97) was as follows:

To the Right hon^ble Robert Earl of Oxford and Earl Mortimer, Lord High Treasurer of Great Britain.

Yo^r Lordship having transmitted to Me, by Mr. Lowndes, the En-clos'd Memorial of the Clerks and Servants of the house of Comõns and by him Signified Yo^r pleasure, That I should report to Yo^r Lordship what I think fit to be done thereon, and particularly, That I shou'd let Yo^r Lop̄p have an Acco^t of what they receive, as well as what they have lost, I humbly report to Yo^r Lop̄p.

That upon Examination of the said Clerks and Servants they assure Me, That their yearly loss in the profits of their respective Places, by the General Naturalization Act, and otherways mention'd in the Memoriall is as therein is set forth, and what they receive to be as followeth.

Mr. Jodrell between three and four hundred pounds p. annũ, for which he gives great Attendance, Sometimes for more than Six Months together and has only 10^li per Anñ. Salary from the Crown; he finds it necessary for the Service of the house to keep a Clerk on purpose at the Expence of 40^li p. Anñ,—at the least, in Wages Diet &c.; he farther Acquaints Me That he used to have every Session a Gratuity of 50^li on Acco^t of publick Business, which for several years has been discontinued.

Mr. Stables[1] gives the same Attendance, and all the profits of his place (as far as he can Estimate them) do not exceed 120^li p. Annũ. including his Salary.

The Under Clerks are obliged to so much Attendance; and that so early and late that they can follow no other Business,—and they reckon all they receive, more than their Salaries, does not exceed 50^li p. Annũ each.

The Serjeant computes his place not worth more than 290^li p. annũ W^ch is including his Salary.

allowed And what the other Servants of the house recieve is now by bill. become very inconsiderable.

---

[1] Edward Stables succeeded Culverwell Needler as Clerk Assistant at the end of 1710, i.e. between the time when this memorial was first drafted and 1713 when the Speaker made his dilatory report to the Treasury (see chapter 3, pp. 49–51).

This is a true state of their Cases as they represent them to Me, But I cannot presume to say what is fit to be done therein; that must be humbly submitted to Your Loͤp. by

My Lord,

Your Ldhps. most obedient

& most humble Servant,

Apr. 21. 1713. ꜱᵈ W. Bromley

The Speaker's report was endorsed:

'21 Sept. 1713 prepare a Wᵗ for the usual aid.' Accordingly, in December 1713 (P.R.O., Treasury Order Book, viii. 362) a money order was made out to Edward Stables for the Clerks, &c., of the House of Commons 'for their paynes and attendance relating to the Act (7 Anne c. 5) for a General Naturalization, and for the losses sustained by them during the said Act (until repealed by 10 Anne c. 9).

£

Edward Stables & Culverwell Needler Clerks Assistant in proportion to their services 100

John Hookes, George Cole, James Courthope, and Hicks Burrough 200

The Housekeeper 30

The Messengers 110

440'

These amounts were equivalent to one session's salary of the respective officers (i.e. 'the usual aid') bestowed as a compensatory bonus.

5. *Petition of the 4 under-clerks to the Lord Treasurer Robert Harley, Earl of Oxford.*

(This petition, which is in the same Treasury bundle immediately following the preceding item (fol. 103) bears no date, but must be more or less the same date as the Memorial. It bears the signatures of the four under-clerks, but bears no endorsement of Treasury action.)

To the most honoᵇˡᵉ Robert Earl of Oxford and Earl Mortimer Lord High Treasurer of Great Britain:

The most humble Memorial of the Clerks attending the Honoᵇˡᵉ House of Commons.

Sheweth.

That the Honoᵇˡᵉ House of Commons having severall times taken into their consideration the long and faithfull Services and constant attendance of the said Clerks and humbly represented the same to her

Majesty by their Unanimous Addresses desireing her Majesty would be pleased to give them a recompence for the same, and a suitable encouragem^t therein, her Majesty in Answer to such Addresses did gratiously Assure the house She would do according to their desire.

That her Majesty having been pleased to refer the said Clerks and the State of their case to your Lordship's Consideration

> They most humbly Pray yor Lordship's favour and compassion for the Support of them and their families.

John Hookes,
Geo. Cole
James Courthope
H. Burrough.

6. *Petition of Paul Jodrell, Clerk of the House, to the Lords Commissioners of the Treasury, for payment of arrears due to him, 1723.*

(Treasury In Letters, P.R.O. T. 1/248, no. 39, fols. 164-8.)

To the Right Honble the Lords Comm^rs of the Treasury.

The humble Petition of Paul Jodrell Esqr, Clerk of the hon^ble House of Com̄ons.

Sheweth.

That yor Pet^r hath, with great Industry, Diligence and Application, Constantly attended the Duty of the said Office (The Salary whereof is only Ten pounds p. Annũ) as well before as ever since his Ma^tyes happy Accession to the Crown.

That the Fees allow'd to be taken by the respective Officers of the House for all Business done by them have been Settled by a Comm^ee appointed for that purpose.

That during his Ma^tyes Reign many Money Bills of very great Length have been Ingross'd, which have been dispatch'd with great Diligence & Expedition and with great Charge to Yo^r Pet^r, he having out of his own pocket paid for such Ingrossments, and never yet had any Allowance for the same; An Acco^t whereof is hereunto Annex'd & Charg'd according to the said Settled Fees.

That Yo^r Pet^r hath during his Ma^tyes Reign made out Copyes of Bills, Acco^ts, & other Papers for the Lords Com^rs of the Treasury, as they had Occasion & gave Directions for, and he hath had no Satisfaction for the same; An Acco^t whereof is also hereunto Annex'd.

That Yo^r Pet^r hath also every Session made out many Orders, directed to the Com^{rs} of the Customes, Excise & other publick Offices & Persons to lay Acco^{ts}, Estimates & other Papers before the House, and many other Things for the publick Service, for which Yo^r Pet^r hath not had any allowance.

That at a time when Matters had run in arrear, A Predecessor of Yo^r Pet^r had Satisfaction from the publick for such Matters as aforesaid; As by a Copy of a Certificate from Sr Robert Howard (then Aud^r of the Excheq^r) Appears.

That Yo^r Pet^r acknowledges he had the favour of his late Matie King Willm by a Lease for years of some lands & Fee Farm Rents from the Death of Queen Dowager; And also of her late Ma^{ty} by a Grant to Yo^r Pet^{rs} Eldest Son, of Yo^r Pet^{rs} Office in Reversion after Yo^r Pet^r.

Wherefore Yo^r Pet^r humbly prays, That Yo^r Loꝑps will please to take the Matters aforesaid into Consideraċon, and give such Directions touching the same as to Yo^r Loꝑps shall seem just & reasonable.

And Yo^r Pet^r Shall pray &c.

^{sd} Paul Jodrell.

Cler. Dom. Com.

Ingrossm^{ts} of Publick Bills since his Ma^{tyes} happy Accession to the Crown—Viz.

	£	s.	d.
In $17\frac{14}{15}$	265.	8.	6.
In $17\frac{15}{16}$	140.	10.	–.
In $17\frac{16}{17}$	248.	–.	–.
In $17\frac{17}{18}$	136.	10.	–.
In $17\frac{18}{19}$	187.	10.	–.
In $17\frac{19}{20}$	160.	–.	–.
In $17\frac{20}{21}$	153.	–.	–.
In $17\frac{21}{2}$	142.	10.	–.
In. $17\frac{22}{3}$	311.	10.	–.
	1744.	18.	6.

Copyes of Papers for the use of the Treasury &c. since his Ma^{tyes} happy Accession to the Crown, viz.

	£	s.	d.
In $17\frac{15}{16}$	1.	13.	–.
In $17\frac{16}{17}$	6.	10.	8.
In $17\frac{17}{18}$		7.	6.
In $17\frac{18}{19}$		10.	–.
In $17\frac{19}{20}$	6.	5.	8.
In $17\frac{20}{1}$	19.	5.	10.

In 1721	9. 16. 4.
In 17$\frac{22}{3}$	18. 12. 2.
	63. 1. 2.
Ingrossm^{ts} brought forward .	1744. 18. 6.
Totall . .	1807. 19. 8.

Copy of Sr Robt Howard's Certificate.

These are to Certify, That the several Sums amounting to 878^{li} 12^s hath been paid at the Receipt of his Ma^{ts} Exchq^r unto William Golds-brough decd. his late Ma^{tyes} Clerk in the Com̃ons House of Parliam^t, of his Ma^{tyes} Grace & Bounty for the Services hereunder express'd from the year 1660 to the 21st Novr. 1685, Viz.

£

450. –. –.   Paid 6th Oct. 1666, For attending, preparing and Ingross-ing of divers larg Bills upon Publick Concern for which he had no Allowance since the first Session of Parliam^t.

100. –. –.   Paid 10th Oct. 1673: To be distributed amongst his Under Clerks for Services.

£   s.   d.

200. –. –.   Part of 319. 15. 4. Paid 12th Novr 1677 on an Order Registred on the Law Duty dated 30th Octr 1671: for divers larg Bills on publick Concernment pass'd in that House which he Attended, prepared and Ingross'd from the 18th Sept. 1666: to the 6th of March 1670, and also for many Copyes of Bills, Reports and other Proceedings made out by him from January 1660 to the 6th March 1670. The rest remains unpaid on the Register.

128. 12. –.   Paid 21st Novr 1685. For his Labour & Pains in taking Copyes of several Bills delivered into Parliam^t begun 6th March 167^8/$_9$ And for ingrossing sev^{ll} publick Bills begun in that Parliam^t, wch last mention'd Sum of

£   s.

128. 12. was paid to his Executors.

£878. 12. –.   28th June 1686. ^{sd} Ro. Howard

The Petition was endorsed '16th Decr. 1723. Mr. Speaker is desired by my Lords of the Treasury to examine and rate these Bills & to certify thereupon'.

On the following day William Lowndes wrote accordingly to Spencer Compton, the Speaker (ibid., fol. 162).

Sir,

   Paul Jodrell Esqr, Clerk of the House of Commons, having preferred a peti͠con to My Lords of the Treasury to be paid the Sum of One Thousand Eight hundred and Seven Pounds Nineteen Shillings and Eight pence which he alledges to have been Expended by him for Ingrossments of publique Bills and for Copys of Bills Acco^{ts} and other papers for the Service of his Ma^{ts} Treasury Since his Ma^{ts} Accession to the Crown, I send the said peti͠con to you hereinclosed and am by their Lordp's Command to desire the favour of you to Examine and Rate his Bills for the said Demand and to Certifye the Same to their Lordps, I am,

Sir,

Your most faithfull
humble Servant,
^{sd} W. Lowndes.

Treasury Chambers,
17 Decr 1723.
R^t Hono^{ble} Spencer Compton Esqr.

The Speaker's reply appears to have been much delayed, for it is dated on the endorsement 17 Nov. 1724. It was as follows (ibid., fol. 160):

   To the Right Honble the Lords Comm^{rs} of his Maj^{ties} Treasury. May it please Yo^r Lordships;

Your Lordships having Signifyed to Me, by letter from William Lowndes Esqr, late Secretary to the Treasury, That Paul Jodrell Esqr, Clerk of the House of Co͠mons, had presented a Petition to Yo^r Lordships to be paid the Sum of One Thousand Eight hundred & Seven pounds, Nineteen Shillings & Eight pence, in Consideration of his Diligence & Charge in Ingrossing Publick Bills, and making out Copy's of Bills, Acco^{ts} & other Papers, for the Service of his Maties Treasury, I have Examin'd the several Allegations of the said Petition (Except what relates to the Copys deliver'd to the Treasury, which is but a small part of the Sum) and find, That they are truly Set forth; and as his Predecessor, Mr. Goldsborough, had Satisfaction made him, for the like Services in King Charles the Second's Reign, and as the Petitioner has also been recompenced for the like Services in the two last Reigns, as Set forth in his Petition; It is submited to Yo^r Lord$\bar{\text{p}}$s if it may not be reasonable to allow the Petitioner the Sum of Fifteen hundred pounds in Consideration of the Services in his Petition mention'd, and also of his keeping the Journals of the House in a better manner than ever had been done by any of his Predecessors, and for his faithful & Diligent

Discharge of his Duty, as Clerk of the House of Com̃ons, since his Maties Accession to the Throne.

All which is Submitted to Your Lordships.

^sd Sp. Compton, Speaker.

I have been unable to trace any action by the Treasury by way of further payment to Jodrell, who retired at the end of 1726.

APPENDIX III

Early tables of fees payable to the Clerks and other officers of the House

1. The Table of 1649 (6 C.J. 287).

THIS earliest Table was a list 'of fees resolved to be taken by the Clerk of the Parliament'. There was at that time, under the Cromwellian régime, only one House, of which Henry Scobell was the Clerk. On the same occasion a yearly salary of £500 was voted to him in consideration of his heavier duties consequent on the combining of two offices, and a salary of £200 to the Clerk Assistant. The Table was as follows:

	£	s.	d.
Of every private person taking benefit of any private act	2	–	–
Of any private person taking benefit of any proviso in any act public or private, and being named therein	2	–	–
Of every corporation, town, company, society, several shire or place taking benefit of any private act or of any proviso etc. (as above)	4	–	–
Of every Knight of the shire returned by certificate from the Clerk of the Crown after the first day of every session		5	–
Of every Burgess returned as above		2	6
For the entry and copy of every private order taken out by a party		6	8
For every copy of the names of a private committee taken forth for the party himself		2	6
For writing copywise, 16 lines in the sheet		1	–
For ingrossing every private bill, for every press		10	–
For every one that is to be naturalized		13	4
For the Clerk's hand, for signing business		2	–
For every discharge of a prisoner committed by this House as a delinquent		18	4
For a search in the old records before this Parliament		10	–
The under-clerks for every private bill		10	–

2. The Table of 1653 (7 C.J. 291).

This Table also was of the 'fees of the Clerk', to whom on the same occasion a salary of £400 a year was voted, out of which he was to pay all his under-clerks except the Clerk Assistant, who was to have £150 a year.

(*Note*. Where the description of the items is identical with that in the Table of 1649 it is abbreviated.)

	£	s.	d.
Of every private person taking benefit of any private act		2	—	—
Of any private person taking benefit from any proviso in any act etc.	2	—	—
Of every corporation etc. taking benefit as above, in either case	2	—	—
For the entry and copy of every private order taken out of the book		3	4
For every copy of the names of a private committee taken out by the party		2	—
For writing copywise, 16 lines to the sheet			8
For ingrossing a private bill, per press		10	—
Of every person to be naturalized, for his oath		13	4
For the Clerk's hand, for signing business		2	—
For every discharge of a person committed etc.		18	4
For search in the records, if it be 20 years before this Parliament		10	—
If within that time, and not the present Parliament		5	—
If of the present Parliament		1	—
On every private bill to the clerks to the Clerk of the Parliament		10	—

(The last item was added at a later date, 7 C.J. 333.)

3. The Table of 1700/1 (13 C.J. 356).

This Table,[1] except for certain small additions and modifications, remained in force till 1847. It was laid before the House by the Clerk, according to Order, entered in the *Journal* and referred to a committee, from whom, however, no report seems to have been made. It covered the fees payable to all the Officers of the House including the Speaker, and began with an account of the fees payable to all Officers on a private bill. Since the same Table, as printed in 1731 (see below), was arranged in clearer form, I shall only append here the account of fees on a private bill with which the Table opens.

	£	s.	d.
For Private Bills, total	13	13	4
To Mr Speaker	5	—	—
To his Secretary	10	—

[1] See pp. 16, 18, 19, 46, 57, 109–10. This table replaced previous tables of 1690 and 1695 which were not entered in the *Journal*. Hatsell, ii. 276–8, says that the table of 1690 was lost by the committee clerk, but that the table of 1695 was still preserved (i.e. in 1781).

	£	s.	d.
To the Clerk for the several readings	3	13	4
— — — for breviating, amendments, interlocutory orders, and other proceedings	1	5	—
To the Clerk Assistant	1	—	—
To the Serjeant	1	5	—
To the Chief Clerk without doors who receives the monies, and pays the several Officers of the House		10	—
To the two Doorkeepers		5	—
To the Housekeeper		5	—
For the Order of Commitment		6	8

For every enacting clause, the same as for a bill.

Where a bill concerns a county or counties, or corporation or corporations, or in such like cases, which are called double bills, double those fees.

There is a footnote to this page of the *Journal* which says that, though the total of £13. 13s. 4d. appears both in the original manuscript of the *Journal* and in the paper as put in by the Clerk, it ought to be £14. The discrepancy is obviously due to the fact that, in the *Journal*, the 6s. 8d. for the order of commitment is not included in the total. This was reasonable, because the fees had to be paid before the second reading of a bill, whereas the order of commitment could only be made after second reading, and would not be charged if the bill failed to get a second reading. This is very clearly shown by the comparison of certain solicitors' bills for expenses of promoting private bills at this period, extracts from which are given in Appendix V. Thus, in the solicitor's account for the Farington Estate Act, 1698 (Lancashire Record Office, DDF. 1301), the fees of the bill in the House of Commons, £13. 13s. 4d. are followed by 'for the Order of the Committee 6/8d.'. Whereas similar accounts for the Balliol College Act, 1695 (Balliol College Deed B. 22. 64 b), and for Lady North's Naturalization Act, 1706 (P.R.O. MSS. North. b. 17, 25 r), the fees to the House of Commons are £28 and £14 respectively, with no charge for the order of commitment. In the latter case, Lady North's solicitor seems to have given Jodrell a gratuity of £2. 7s. 6d. which is separately entered.

4. The Table of 1731/2 (21 C.J. 807 sqq.).

This Table, identical in content though not in form with that of 1700/1, was formally ratified by two resolutions of the House, after the report of a select committee appointed 'to inspect and settle the fees to be taken by all the officers and servants of the House, and to examine what salaries or allowances they have from the Government'. The two resolutions were entered in the *Journal*, but it is there mentioned that 'the Report and Appendix thereto, being too long to be conveniently inserted in this Journal, is bound up with the other papers of this session'. Consequently, they were destroyed in the fire of 1834. Fortunately, a clerk in the House of Lords made a copy of this report and an abstract of the valuable appendixes, which are printed in Appendix IV (q.v.). The two resolutions of the House were as follows:

'That all fees to be demanded or taken by any Officer or Servant of this House be fixed according to the rates of the List of Fees entered in the Journal in the year 1700, and that Tables of the same, being first perused by Mr Speaker, be printed and hung up in the Speaker's Chamber, in the Lobby, and in the Clerk's Office, and that the Clerk take care to renew such printed Tables from time to time as occasion shall require, and to preserve them always fair and legible.

'That if any Officer or Servant of the House shall presume to demand or take any greater fee than what shall be contained in the said printed Table, the House will proceed against such offender with the utmost severity.'

It was ordered that the above resolutions should be Standing Orders of the House, and be printed with the Table of Fees.

Here follows the Table, so far as the fees payable to the various clerks are concerned:

To the Clerk.

	£	s.	d.
For every Private Bill. For the several readings	3	13	4
For breviating, amendments, and other proceedings	1	5	0
For order of commitment	0	6	8
For every private enacting clause the same as for a Bill. Double fees for 'double' Bills.			
For every order upon a Motion, a Petition, or Committee, or postponement on private matters, or copies of them, or Committees on public matters taken out by any person	0	6	8
For every order for the Commitment or Discharge of any person	0	6	8
For copies of all Petitions, Reports, or other matters out of the Journals, if under 10 sheets	0	6	8
If over 10 sheets, per sheet	0	1	0
For every search in the Journals	0	6	8
For copies of Bills, per sheet	0	1	0
But if for Members	0	0	4
For engrossing Bills, per press	0	12	6
For every hearing at the Bar from each side	1	13	4
For attending a Committee of the House or Grand Committee in private concerns	0	13	4
For preparing the Report and transcribing	0	10	0

	£	s.	d.
For reading at the Table and entering in the Journal a Report on private matters, if long	0	10	0
If short	0	6	8
For swearing every Member without and within doors, filing the certificate and entering it in the return book	1	5	0
For the test by Act of Parliament at the Table	0	1	0
For swearing every person ordered to be naturalised	0	13	4

To the Clerk Assistant.

	£	s.	d.
For every Private Bill	1	0	0
For every private enacting clause the same fee as for a Bill. Double fees for 'double' Bills.			
For every hearing at the Bar, from each side	0	6	8
For attending a Committee of the whole House or Grand Committee in private concerns	0	6	8
For every order of such Committee	0	5	0
For reading every Petition in private matters	0	2	0

To the Clerk of the Committee of Elections.

	£	s.	d.
For attending to hear the merits of a cause	0	13	4
For drawing the Report	0	6	8
For a fair copy of the Report for the Chairman	0	3	4
For each exhibit	0	2	0
For examination of a witness	0	2	6
For each order of the Committee	0	5	0

To the four Clerks without Doors, attending on Committees.

	£	s.	d.
For attending to adjourn a Committee upon a Private Bill or Petition	0	3	4
For attending a sitting of the Committee on such Bill or Petition	0	6	8
For drawing and transcribing the Report for such Committee.	0	6	8
Double fees for 'double' Bills.			
For a summons for a witness to attend a Committee	0	2	6
For examining a witness, or taking the consent of a party to the passing of a Bill	0	2	6
For every deed, or other exhibit, made use of before a Committee .	0	2	6

To the Chief Clerk without Doors, who receives the Fees and pays them to the Officers of the House.

	£	s.	d.
For every Private Bill	0	10	0
Double fees for 'double' Bills.			

5. The Inquiry into fees of 1751 (26 C.J. 277–8).

This inquiry by a select committee of the House was not concerned with the table of fees as such but with the incidence of fees on private bills and the liability of parties to pay fees. It resulted in five resolutions of the House, the first of which defined what was a private bill in this connexion. The committee's report was accompanied by an account given by the Clerk of the House, Jeremiah Dyson, of the system adopted in calculating the number of fees to be charged on a particular bill. It is unnecessary here to go into the whole subject which is well treated in Clifford, *History of Private Bill Legislation*, ii, ch. 19.[1] For the purpose of the present work the importance of these resolutions of 1751 and of the practice thereafter based upon them is that they systematized the charging of multiple fees on bills which concerned more than one single interest, the principle of which had been laid down in the earliest table (i.e. double fees for bills by which a corporation or any other company or society would benefit). Moreover, when more than one object was to be attained by the bill, a fee or fees were payable for each separate object, e.g. drainage, road repair. The working of this system can be gathered from the evidence given by John Dorington, formerly clerk of the fees in the House of Commons, before the select committee of the House of Lords upon fees in 1827 (H.L. (1827) 114). Thus, in 1810 the Ely Drainage Bill incurred thirty-two fees and in 1824 the Welland Outfall Bill ten fees. This system explains in part the very large and rapid increase in the income from private bill fees earned by the Speaker, the Clerk, and other officers of the House during the latter half of the eighteenth century. It will be observed that multiplicity of fees applied also to some of the fees payable to the committee clerks, i.e. those above the words 'Double fees for double bills' in the Table of 1731/2.

In 1830 the table of the Committee Clerks' fees on private bills and the fees payable to the Private Bill Office was revised (see p. 248), but it was not till 1847 that a wholly new system of charging fees on private bill proceedings was recommended by a select committee and agreed to by the House; see Williams, ii. 273–5.

---

[1] See also Hatsell, ii. 276–8.

APPENDIX IV

The Report of the Select Committee of the House of Commons on Fees and Salaries of the Servants of the House, made on 22 February 1731/2 but not entered in the *Journal*, with abstracts of the appendixes thereto, from a manuscript copy preserved in the House of Lords Records Office

THIS valuable document, to which allusion was made in the foregoing appendix, is in the House of Lords Records and is contained in a small notebook bound in vellum on boards marked on the outside 'Reports, Fees. 1731'. The fly-leaf bears the name 'Mr Croft', and the notebook contains a transcript of the report of the Lords committee on fees of 1725 followed by a transcript, in a very good clerkly hand, of the Commons committee's report of 1731/2 on the same subject. The great interest of the document lies, not so much in the committee's report, as in the appendixes which give some extremely interesting details as to the emoluments of officers and servants of the House, from the Speaker downwards, at the date of the report. It is only to be regretted that the abstract was not fuller. In particular is to be deplored the omission of the comparative table showing the differences between the fee-tables of 1690, 1695, and 1700/1, which was the second appendix, of Aiskew's memorial relating to his fees as clerk to the Committees of Privileges and Elections and of the list of fees taken by the four committee clerks, both of which were part of the fourth appendix. Since it is treasure trove, I give this document practically *in toto*, though parts of it concern other officers than the clerks: but, seeing that it is a transcript, I have modernized the punctuation, use of capitals, abbreviations, and so forth, and I omit the preamble which appears in the *Journal* (21 C.J. 807).

The Report of the Committee

The Committee pursuant to the Order of the House bearing date the 28th of January last have searched the Journals and Papers and examined the Clerks and Servants of the House and have also examined persons of experience in the forms of business which relate to the House, and the charge which attends the same.

It doth not appear to the Committee that the fees to be taken by Officers and Servants of the House were ever fixed and settled by any Order of the House for that purpose or that a Report from any Committee appointed for that service was ever made, although Committees to consider the fees of the Officers and Servants of the House appear in the Journals to have been frequently appointed,[1] as by an abstract of the Orders for such Committees hereunto annexed No. 1 will appear.

The Committee having found a List of Fees presented to the House in the year 1695 and another list presented in the year 1700 (which list is entered in the Journal) and having compared these lists (which are the only lists that can be found) with the list lately delivered pursuant to the Order of the House bearing the date 28th of January last, do observe several differences betwixt the two former lists but more material variances betwixt the two former lists and that lately delivered, which variances do appear in a Paper no. 2 hereunto annexed, containing in three columns the said three lists.[2]

The fees taken by, and the usual allowances made to, Mr Speaker do appear in a Paper hereunto annexed, No. 3, which Paper the Chairman of the Committee received from Mr Speaker and delivered to the Committee by his order in which paper is contained an account of stores received by him for the use of himself the Chaplain and his Gentlemen.

The Committee received from Mr Hardinge, Clerk of the House, a list of Clerks of the House, and from the four Clerks without Doors attending upon Committees, a list of their fees, together with an account of their salaries and allowances, and from Mr Spence, the Serjeant at Arms, a list of the Officers and servants employed by him, together with an account of their salaries and allowances; and from Mr Felton, Secretary to Mr Speaker, an account of his fees, and stores allowed to him, the Chaplain and Mr Speaker's trainbearer, which list and account are hereunto annexed No. 4.

The Committee have inspected the original voucher for the allowances of stores delivered to Mr Speaker, the Clerk, and Serjeant at Arms, copies whereof are hereunto annexed No. 5.

Mr Hardinge did show the Committee a Patent of his Office for life with a fee of £10 p. annum.

Mr Aiskew, the Clerk Assistant, did inform the Committee that he received a salary from the Government of £100 p. annum, and that the fees belonging to his Office had been worth £121. 14. 3d. p. annum at a medium for five years last past (besides such fees as he receives for

---

[1] See Appendix III.   [2] Unfortunately these were not transcribed in this copy.

attending Committees of Privileges and Elections), which fees have been received for him by Mr Hamlyn,[1] and that he could never see a list of fees till this Committee was appointed, though he very often desired it, as by his Memorial annexed appears.

The Committee is informed that the extravagant payments for Bills which pass in Parliament to Counsel, Solicitors, and other persons without doors is equal to the charge of the fees, which in a Single Bill that passes without opposition amounts to about £60, except in Naturalization Bills, the whole charge of which amounts to about £63 and in which every person named therein pays as for a single Bill.

The Committee comprehends that the difficulty of knowing what are legal fees and what the charge of passing a Bill is of an encouragement to Clerks and Servants to demand and take unreasonable and excessive sums & to exact great fees where none are due, and it appearing to the Committee that to settle and make publicly known the fees of all these Officers and Servants of the House is the most proper method to prevent any imposition for the future, the Committee came to the following Resolution, viz.:

[Here follow the resolutions given in Appendix III, p. 302, as agreed to by the House, and the consequent Orders of the House as there mentioned]. Then follows:

An Abstract of the Papers annexed to the aforesaid Report.

NO. 1. Contains an Account of all proceedings in the House concerning fees, by appointing Committees to inspect into that matter, addressing the King etc., from July 24 13 Car. 2;

NO. 2 contains the said 3 Tables of Fees, in separate columns.

NO. 3 is an account of all fees taken by, and all allowances made from the Government to, the Speaker of the House of Commons and are the same which he was informed and does believe were taken by his predecessor in that office.

i. For every Private Bill and every enacting clause according to the list of fees delivered into the House £5, the amount of which in every session of this Parliament is contained in four papers hereunto annexed marked 1, 2, 3, 4, and are copies of what Mr Hamlyn delivered to the Speaker when he paid him those fees, he being the person who has usually received and paid the fees upon Bills.

ii. For the expenses of the Speaker's table £5 a day throughout the

---

[1] For Zachary Hamlyn, first appointed by the Clerk, Paul Jodrell, as his personal clerk, see p. 40.

year, paid out of His Majesty's Exchequer without any deduction but the common fees. He has besides two hogsheads of claret every session out of the King's cellar, and two brace of bucks and the same of does out of some of the King's forests, chases or parks.

iii. There are stores delivered to the Speaker every session the particulars whereof are included in a paper hereunto annexed marked No 5. and which is a copy of the stores delivered to the Speaker in the 1st session of this Parliament, and varies only from what has been delivered in the subsequent sessions (of which he has no copies) in the number of volumes of the Acts of Parliament and of the speeches, proclamations and addresses, and other occasional papers: in this list of stores are also included the stores delivered to the Chaplain of the House and to the Gentlemen attending the Speaker.[1]

iv. The profits of the printed Votes and other papers ordered by the House to be printed, the amount of which for every session of this Parliament is in another paper hereunto annexed marked No. 6.[2]

v. The Speaker on his entrance upon his Office had £1000 out of H.M. Exchequer for his equipage, and there was also 4000 ounces of white plate delivered to him from the Jewel Office for the use of his table.

Feb 2nd 1731/2. These profits and allowances, and no other fee, profit, salary or allowance have been received by me

Ar: Onslow, Speaker

[Then follow annexes 1–6 to the above account signed by the Speaker, viz.:]

1. The amount of private bills in the 1st session of this Parliament to the Speaker 1727/8 . . . . . Fees 80. £400
2. In the 2nd session, 1728/9 . . . . 83. £415
3. In 1729/30 . . . . 105. £525
4. In 1730/1 . . . . 109. £545.
5. The amount of the value of the stores delivered to the Speaker, 23 January 1727 . . . . £111. 11. 6

---

[1] Two bills of the stationery provided in 1671 and 1673 for Speakers Charlton and Edward Seymour respectively are to be seen in Addl. MS. 5756, fols. 10, 11. Both bills are identical in content, including 1 large Russia leather trunk, 1 small gilt trunk, 1 satin bag with gold and silk tassels, 1 Poulton's Statutes, 1 large bible in Turkey with silk strings, and 1 common prayer-book similarly bound. Total for the Speaker £27. 4s. 8d., for his gentlemen £16. 2s. 5d., for his chaplain £3. 10s. 8d. Grand total £46. 17s. 9d.

[2] For the printing and sale of the *Votes*, see p. 193. This is the only allusion that I know to the Speaker's profits from their sale. See p. 309.

Those to his Chaplain amount in value to   .   .   9. 15. –
Those to his Gentlemen amount in value to   .   .   16. 10. 6
Total £137. 17. 0.

6. The clear profit of the printed Votes to the Speaker in the first session of this Parliament, after paying the Clerk of the House half a guinea a Vote, as usual, and the Serjeant 7 shillings for the same, as usual, and after the usual allowances for the Votes,

comes to   .   .   .   .   £456. 15. –
the same in the 2nd session   .   .   .   .   .   £456. 15. –
the same in the 3rd session £471. 16. 4
the same in the 4th session £493. 12. 3

As to the other Papers printed by Order of the House, there hath been no profit on them, except on the two Reports relating to the Fleet and Marshalsea Prisons,[1] and for which the Speaker had £100, but that money was distributed by him to other persons[2] according to his discretion, as had been done in some like cases.

No. 4 (Annex) Mr Hardinge's list of Clerks and Officers of the House.

Nicholas Hardinge, Under Clerk of the Parliaments appointed to attend on the Commons of Great Britain.

Michael Aiskew, Clerk Assistant

4 Feb 1731
Edward Jodrell
John Hooks   Four Clerks without Doors[3] attending
William Hester   Committees.
Hicks Burrough
sd. N. Hardinge Cl. Dom. Com.

Mr Aiskew's Memorial relating to his fees,[4] with Mr Baron Miller's

---

[1] These reports from the select committee appointed in 1728/9 to inquire into the state of the gaols in the Kingdom, whose chairman was James Oglethorpe, were entered *in extenso* in the *Journals* (21 C.J. 274–83, 378–87). Their revelation of the horrible abuses caused a great sensation, which explains the order to print them and their profitable sale. See pp. 133–9 and Appendix VIII.

[2] It is impossible to tell who these persons were. As to the clerks' payment for attending this committee, see chapter 7, pp. 137, n. 1 and 138, and Appendix IX, p. 331.   [3] For these officers of the House, see chapter 3, pp. 53–56.

[4] A passage in the committee's report above shows that this memorial related to Aiskew's fees as clerk to the Committee of Elections, as to which office see chapter 10, pp. 214–17.

bill of fees due on hearing Petersfield Election, annexed, the same being corrected by Mr Stables[1] together with a trifling paper of fees formerly delivered Mr Aiskew as a guide.

A list of fees taken by the four clerks without doors, containing (besides the said list) an account of their salaries which are £50 p. session each, out of which they pay the sixpences towards the Civil List.[2] Their stores are:

To each of the said clerks a serge bag, 1 committee book, 1 pocket book, two penknives, 1 lead standage, 1 glass ditto, 1 sand box, 1 ruler, 1 quire of paper per diem, tape, pens, wax, wafers, sand, 1 hone, 1 pocket book almanack, 1 sheet almanack and one pencil; and each of them are rated at £10 p. annum to the land tax for their places, as an office of profit in Westmr. Hall. 7 Feb. 1731

signed by each of them.

A fee taken by a clerk without doors, who receives the fees, pays the several Officers of the House, out of every Private Bill . . 10s.

Edwd. Jodrell.

Mr Spence, the Serjeant at Arms appointed to attend the House of Commons by Letters Patent, with an allowance of £3 a day wages and 2/6d p. day board wages through the year.

(then follows an account of his fees).

The Serj[t] at Arms doth likewise appoint several Under Officers; which are as follow, viz.:

Mr Thos. Ward, Housekeeper, who hath a salary of p. annum £60 (then follows an account of his fees).

Mr Abraham Osgood who delivers out the Votes and Acts of Parliament to the Members, and hath a salary from the Government of p. annum £15. What other profits he may have arise from voluntary contributions of such Members for whom he sends the Votes or Acts of Parlt. into the country etc.

---

[1] Edward Stables, Hardinge's predecessor, was Clerk Assistant 1710–26 and Clerk of the House 1727–Dec. 1731.

[2] In 1721, when the debts on the Civil List amounted to £550,000, Walpole devised the expedient of making the Civil List discharge its own arrears, by deducting sixpence in the pound on all payments from the Crown towards raising a fund for liquidating the interest on the sum of £500,000 which the King was authorized to borrow at 5 per cent. See Coxe, *Memoirs of Robert Walpole*, ii. 56. This charge was additional to the Land Tax to which offices of profit as well as land were liable: it is referred to at the end of this return made by the four clerks without doors.

John Bradshaw, Doorkeeper to the House, at a salary from the Government of p. ann. £13.

Walter Moffatt, Doorkeeper to the Lobby, at a salary of p. ann. £13.

The Three Messengers.

Edmd. Driver, Thos. Hollingshead, and John Pope, each of them at a salary of p. ann. £13.

Feb. 4 1731/2.   Tho: Spence.

Then follows an account of their fees, after which is an account of fees taken by the Speaker's Secretary, the amount of the value of whose stores is every session .   .   .   . £6.
His salary is nil, and the whole profit of the Secretary's place at a medium for the four last years is about p. session £70.

The value of the stores to the Chaplain are £8. 8s and to the Train-bearer £6. 6s.

Feb. 7. 1731   Jon Felton

No. 5 contains an Account Of Stores delivered to the Speaker the
21 January 1730 amounting in value to   .   .   .   116. 13. 9
the amount of those delivered to his Chaplain   .   .   9. 15. –
the amount of those delivered to his gentlemen is .   .   16. 10. –
the amount of the stores delivered to Mr Stables[1] in 1730/1
comes to 506. 18. 9

[1] Then Clerk of the House, see p. 310, n. 1, above. Addl. MS. 5756, fol. 12 also contains a bill of stationery delivered to William Goldesbrough, Clerk of the House, for the use of the House (and presumably for his own) in 1673. It shows the great difference in money values of such stores between that date and 1730. It is as follows:

At the Prorogation, April 16, 1673.

	£	s.	d.
1 common prayer book Turkey gilt			
7 reams of fine paper, cut			
A large box of wafers	8	–	3
500 pens			
2 pound of hard sealing wax			
6 powder standishes			
5 bottles of best ink			
6 ink glasses with feet	004	14	02
12 pieces of carnation tape			
6 wooden sandboxes			
6 dozen presses of parchment	003	19	09
1 bag of sand			

the amount of the stores delivered to Mr Spence the Serjt
at Arms 21 Jan 1730 is . . . . . . 82. 8.
the value of King's Speeches, Lords' Addresses, Acts of
Parlt, abstracts etc. delivered to Mr Spence the Serjt in
1730/1731 there being 570 of each is . . . 831. 15. 6

[The abstract continues with a reproduction of Mr. Spence's account for disbursements during the last session, i.e. the usual account for coal and candles, mops, brooms, &c., and the sum paid to messengers for serving public orders on Commissioners of Customs, Judges, &c., at 2s. 6d. each. This last item came to £36. 16s.

Finally there follows the Table of Fees set out on pp. 302–3, which was referred to in the Report and printed in the *Journals*.]

At the Session Feb. 4 1672/3

6 Journal books folio bound in ruff leather with silk strings	
1 bible in 4° complete Turkey gilt silk strings	
1 bible in 12° blen. Turkey, gilt	008 02 06
1 service in folio bound marble fillets	
10 reams of paper cut	
2 reams fine paper cut	
10 bottles of ink	012 07 05
1 bag of sand	
1000 best pens	
2 lb. of hard sealing wax	
1 lb. of soft wax	002 18 03
6 penknives, and 6 bodkins to them	
3000 wafers in a box	
12 pieces of carnation tape	001 03 04
21 cedar pencils	

42 5 8

For the ordering of stationery for the House and the perquisites of the Clerk in that respect, see chapter 6, p. 111, n. 2, and chapter 8, p. 172. The Select Committee on Public Expenditure of 1810 made some caustic comments in their 9th *Report* (H.C. (1810) 373) on the practice under which many items of stationery were regarded as perquisites of certain higher officials, including the Clerk, and were regularly sold by them for cash. A certain Mr. Parker, who held some minor post in the House, seems to have acted as agent for these sales, which were regarded as perfectly legitimate. Even Hatsell sold his yearly set of the statutes through Parker. After 1810 new regulations by the Treasury put an end to this perquisite so far as the Clerks were concerned.

APPENDIX V

Extracts from certain solicitors' bills of costs, late seventeenth and early eighteenth centuries, showing payments made to clerks and other officers of the House which were incidental to the passing of a private Act

1660/1. (Bedford MSS. at Woburn). The account of George Collop, Receiver-General (to the Earl of Bedford).

		£	s	d
Nov. 29.	To one of the Underclerks of Parliament for copying the Act for making Covent Garden a parish parochial, By his Lordship's command.	1	10	–
Nov. 31.	To Mr Throgmorton which was for passing the said Act in the Lords' house, viz. for the Chancellor's fee £10, for the Clerk of Parliament's fee £7 and for a waiter at the Committee 10s.	17	10	–
Jan. 1.	To Stow (?) Withers, another keeper at Parliament, by his Lordship's command.	1	10	–
Jan. 17.	To Mr Throgmorton for another copy of the said Act and to his under(clerk)		5	–
Feb. 12.	To Mr James Norfolk in full for all fees for passing Covent Garden parochial Act in the House of Commons.	19	15	–

[Note. The surprising thing about the last item in this account is that James Norfolk was the Serjeant at Arms. I have no evidence that at this date the Serjeant was the general collector of the fees on private bills. It is probably to be explained by the fact that the second session of the Convention Parliament ended on 29 December 1660 and that the Clerkship was in abeyance till the restored king appointed a Clerk. This he did by letters patent dated 13 April 1661 (William Goldesbrough).]

1675. (Corporation of London Record Office: extract from Mr. Doe's (a Remembrancer's) bill, 20 December 1674–20 December 1675, loose MS.).
Paid the Clerk of the House of Commons £6

1685. (Westminster City Library. Churchwardens' accounts of St Martin's in the Fields)

Extracts from 'Charges about objecting against the Bill for dividing the Parish, and making part of it a new Parish, to be called the Parish of St James'.

	£	s	d
To the Clerk of the House of Commons for a copy of the Bill being 153 sheats at 12d. p. sheat Seaven pounds Thirteen shillgs	7	13	–
For an Order to wait on the Committee		6	8

. . . .

June 13. To the Doorkeepers at the Committee ten shillings and for coachhire and expenses that day seventeen shillings — 1 7 –

. . . .

June 17. Paid the Serjeant at Arms the same day, one pound as his fee for admitting Counsell to plead before the Committee — 1 – –

. . . .

For a copy of the Committee — 7 –

. . . .

June 23. Paid for coachhire to Westminster and wateridge from thence to the Temple to gett a copy of the Bill examined by the Speaker's clerk (several alteraĉons being made in the Bill since the copy was taken) and expended. — 10 –

To the Speaker's Clerk for his readiness to speak to his Master about it, tho' the examining of the Bill would not be granted, unless we would pay for a new copy — 2 6

1695. (Balliol College deed, B. 22.64 b.)

Extracts from the solicitor's bill of expenses in passing the Act of Parliament for St. Lawrence Jewry (Balliol College Act, 1695), showing only the fees paid in the House of Commons, the bulk of the account being for his own and other legal charges.

		£	s	d
Feb. 6	Pd for yᵉ Order upon yᵉ Petiĉon		13	4
	copy		6	8
7	fees to yᵉ house of Comͦns	28	–	–
8	pd. for yᵉ Briatt (breviate) of yᵉ Bill		5	–

		£	s	d
	copy for Mr Sayer		2	6
Feb. 11	6 copies of Briatts for the Comittee of Commons		15	–
12	pd, yᵉ housekeeper's fees		12	–

. . . .

		£	s	d
18	pd Comittee Clerks fees and exp̄.	2	17	–
	pd for ingrossing yᵉ Act & expedic̃on	2	14	–
	pd for yᵉ Order of Leave		6	8
	pd yᵉ Doorkeeper		5	–
	copy of Order		3	4

[Note. 'exp̄.' or 'expedic̃on' means a gratuity for work done quickly.]

1698.   (Lancashire County Records Office. Account in connexion with the Farington Estate Act, 1698. Document DDF. 1301.)

This is the manuscript solicitor's account for costs in both Houses. The bill originated in the Lords, so that the costs in that House, totalling £38. 1. 10, come first

In the House of Comons

	£	s	d
p the Brief for the Speaker		6	8
fees of the Bill	13	13	4
p the Order of the Comᵉᵉ		6	8
p four coppyes thereof		4	–
The Clerks Bill attending the Comᵉᵉ	2	–	2
To the Housekeeper & Doorkeepers		10	–
	——	—	——
	17	–	10

1706.   (P.R.O. MSS. North. b. 17, fols. 25 r. & v.) Papers of William, Lord North and Grey. Account relating to Lady North and Grey's Naturalization Act, 1706.

The Clerk of Comᵉᵉˢ Bill upon Lady North Naturalization

		£	s	d
Dec. 19	Attending the Comᵉᵉ		6	8
20	Do.		6	8
	One Exhibit		2	6
	Two witnesses		5	–
	Report		6	8
		——	—	—
		1	7	6

	£	s	d
For making the brief for the Speaker		5	–
The Housekeepers fees		10	–
The Messengers fees		5	–
	2	7	6
Ingr: the Bill	1	3	4
printing the Bill	1	1	6
porter to the printing office		1	–
	2	5	10
paid Mr Jodrell Clarke of yᵉ House of Com̄ons ⎫	14	–	–
p my Ladys bill ⎭	2	7	6
	18	13	6¹

1711/12.   (Corporation of London Records Office, loose MS.)

The Remembrancer's bill for business done in passing the Act to repeal part of a clause of an Act of Jas. I relating to Bankrupts.

23 Feb.   . . . .

	£	s	d
pd Serjeant at Arms his fees for introducing the Sheriffs	1	1	6
pd doorkeepers fees		15	–
pd for the Order to bring in the Bill		15	4
Breviat of Bill for the Speaker		10	–
Pd Mr Jodrell upon the Second Reading	21	10	–
for Order of commitment on second reading		15	4

		£	s	d
25	pd for copy of the Comᵉᵉ		13	4
	pd Clerks fees at the Comᵉᵉ	4	6	8
	pd Housekeepers and Messengers fees	2	5	–
28	For an Order of Leave to add Clauses		15	4

. . . .

		£	s	d
2 Mar.	Pd for ingrossing the Bill & gave	2	–	–
	the Clerk for new Breviate for the Speaker		10	–
	Gave Mr Courthope the Clerk for his trouble in this affair	2	3	–

1718.   (Corporation of London, loose MS.)

The Remembrancer's bill for business done in passing the Act for continuing an Act for settling the Assize of Bread etc.

---

¹ I have transcribed the figures into modern form: the incorrect total is in the original.

	£	s	d
Pd Clerks fees on the Com^ee of Parliament for Expiring Laws in getting the Bill reported as fitt to be continued.	2	8	8
pd Housekeepers & Messengers fees	1	10	–
Report thereupon		15	–
Pd for Order to bring in the Bill		15	6
Breviate to the Speaker and several coppys		15	–
Coppys of Bill for Members	1	10	–
Gave Mr Jodrell in full of fees	21	–	–
Pd Clerks fees on commitment (i.e. Committee fees)	7	5	–
Housekeeper & Messengers	2	3	6
pd Ingrossing Clerk	1	10	–

[There is a similar bill for business done the same year in passing the Bankrupts Act, from which I only quote the following items:]

	£	s	d
Paid fees for Second Reading	28	13	6
Pd Serjeant at Arms and other officers on commitment	4	5	–
. . . .			
Ingrossing the Bill etc.	24	12	–

APPENDIX VI

The revenue of the Clerk of the House and Clerk Assistant from fees on private bills, eighteenth and early nineteenth centuries

AFTER the return of his fees from private bills made by the Speaker to the select committee of 1731/2 (see Appendix IV, p. 308), no official figures showing the revenue from fees of any officer of the House are available until, in 1790, the clerk of the fees presented to the House an account of the fees on private bills paid to the Speaker from 10 October 1776 to 10 October 1788 (45 C.J. 251). Ten years later the clerk of the fees presented an account of the net produce of fees and emoluments of the Clerk and Clerk Assistant for the years 1790–9 inclusive (55 C.J. 523–4). I have combined these in a table to which I have added a column giving my own estimate (previous to 1798 when local acts were printed in the statute-book under a separate heading) of the number of public 'local' bills added to the number of private bills on the statute-book, and another column showing the number of single fees which the

Speaker's total—at £5 per fee—represented. This last column is of interest in showing that the average number of fees incurred by a private bill from 1776 to 1788 was between 2 and 2½, so that bills on which a large multiple of fees was charged must have been exceptions. In order to complete the picture and give a rough idea of the whole curve during the eighteenth century, I begin with a table of the number of feeable bills at five-year intervals, more or less, from 1710 to 1776. I continue column 5 of the second table down to 1820, since the figures given in column 3 for the years 1790–9 will enable the reader to form a fairly close estimate of the total Clerk's fees on private bills from 1800 to 1820.

It must be noted that the totals of the Clerk's and Clerk Assistant's fees do not include salary of any kind: also the Clerk Assistant's fees were calculated over a different period of the year from the Clerk's. I did not think it necessary to record this in detail, or to include a return of the Serjeant's fees for the same years made later in the session (55 C.J. 670). The totals for the Clerk undoubtedly include the ingrossing fees on all bills, public and private, but do not include 'copy money' (see pp. 109–13 and Appendix VII) which was not collected by the clerk of the fees, but was included in the printer's bill presented to the Treasury and paid, after deducting fees, at the Exchequer. (For the subject in general and other statistics, see H. Clifford, *History of Private Bill Legislation*, ch. xix.)

TABLE A. *Estimated total of fee-attracting bills on the statute-book 1710–76 at intervals of five years or so. This table = Table B, col. 5, for an earlier period*

Year	Number of bills	Year	Number of bills
1710	45	1750	54
1715	50	1755	94
1720	46	1756	116
1726	56	1760	97
1730	43	1765	178
1736	58	1771	180
1740	30	1775	133
1745	42	1776	167

Footnotes to TABLE B (opposite).

(a) Cf. Colchester, i. 482. '24 Feb. 1804. Last day of receiving private petitions, 172 this session. Average about 200; last year 300. The profits of the Clerk of the House last year amounted to above £12,000.'

(b) Cf. Hatsell's account of his income for 1809, chapter 6, p. 111.

TABLE B

Year	Speaker's fees	Clerk's fees	Clerk Asst.'s fees			Number of bills	Number of single fees, i.e. col. 2 divided by 5
	£	£	£	s.	d.		
1776–7	2,320	..	..			214	464
1777–8	1,845	..	..			183	369
1778–9	1,770	..	..			175	354
1779–80	1,095	..	..			108	219
1780–1	1,021	..	..			90	204
1781–2	960	..	..			80	192
1782–3	1,120	..	..			90	224
1783–4	985	..	..			75	197
1784–5	1,380	..	..			124	276
1785–6	1,510	..	..			132	302
1786–7	1,125	..	..			95	225
1787–8	1,360	..	..			121	272
1790	..	4,463	777	18	11	117	..
1791	..	6,948	537	6	5	159	..
1792	..	7,779	441	3	–	171	..
1793	..	10,912	600	1	4	220	..
1794	..	8,237	464	2	7	184	..
1795	..	8,252	451	3	7	182	..
1796	..	7,995	412	15	9	186	..
1797	..	9,613	520	4	3	219	..
1798	..	6,994	349	8	10	160	..
1799	..	7,797	463	12	4	202	..
1800	..	..	..			219	..
1801	..	..	..			277	..
1802	..	..	..			239	..
1803 (a)	..	..	..			267	..
1804	..	..	..			161	..
1805	..	..	..			224	..
1806	..	..	..			226	..
1807	..	..	..			268	..
1808	..	..	..			234	..
1809 (b)	..	..	..			304	..
1810	..	..	..			314	..
1811	..	..	..			295	..
1812	..	..	..			289	..
1813	..	..	..			295	..
1814	..	..	..			298	..
1815	..	..	..			212	..
1816	..	..	..			163	..
1817	..	..	..			140	..
1818	..	..	..			153	..
1819	..	..	..			208	..
1820	..	..	..			197	..

APPENDIX VII

The 'copy money' paid to the Clerk of the House, and the cost of printing bills, reports, and other papers ordered by the House to be printed

ALTHOUGH John Henry Ley, in his return of his emoluments to the Select Committee on House of Commons Offices in 1833 (H.C. (1833) 648, pp. 255 sqq.), gave a description of copy money, which had been fixed many years before at an annual sum of £4,300, and of the basis on which it had been charged, the fullest description—on which J. H. Ley's was obviously based—was that given in a long note by John Hatsell in 1810 to the Select Committee on Public Expenditure (H.C. (1810) 373, p. 201), to which reference is made in chapter 6, pp. 111–12. In this Appendix I give (1) a summary of Hatsell's account, followed by certain subsidiary details to be found in the Treasury books, and (2) some figures showing the vast increase in the expenditure on the printing of the House as the eighteenth century drew to its close and the nineteenth century began.

(1) According to Hatsell's account of the matter in 1810, the custom of paying to the Clerk a moiety of the printer's bill for printing reports, bills, &c., ordered by the House to be printed was the practice in Hardinge's and Dyson's time. He could not himself say when the charge originated, but he had heard from Messrs. Barwell, Yeates, and White, ancient clerks, that the origin was the fee allowed for copies of papers, &c., in the table of fees. This had formerly amounted to a considerable sum, since members and large companies or corporations, such as the East India Company, the Corporation of London, and the like, habitually ordered copies of all such papers. The sessional bills incurred by these customers for manuscript copies came to large sums. Very few papers were then printed, but the general practice, Hatsell believed, was introduced (i.e. after 1801) by Lord Newhaven and other members of the Irish Parliament, whose practice was to print all papers. The general printing of papers and reports was at first opposed by the Speaker, but was soon adopted and became general. The Clerk's copy money then became so large that Hatsell and John Ley wished to reduce it. For this purpose Hatsell had several conversations with Lord Sidmouth and Grenville (when they were respectively at the head of the Treasury)

and with the present Speaker (Abbot). The difficulty was to ascertain, as he put it, a distinct and permanent rule. At length, when Perceval was appointed Chancellor of the Exchequer, Hatsell and Ley suggested that copy money should be fixed at the average of sums paid on this head since the Union with Ireland: this average was £4,300 annually, and it was adopted.[1] By 1809 the sum paid would have been far larger if this fixed sum had not been adopted. Hatsell then set out the deductions that had to be made before the residue accrued to the Clerk (see chapter 6, p. 112). He added that when Shelburne or Portland was head of the Treasury in 1782, he had received an official letter signed by Sheridan inquiring into the grounds upon which copy money was charged, and had replied in much the same terms as his present note.

Such is the gist of Hatsell's account of the matter in his communication to the committee of 1810, when he was in his 77th year. Light can be thrown upon his account from other sources, although not upon the date when the payment of copy money in the form of a moiety of the printer's bill began. Through Speaker Arthur Onslow and Nicholas Hardinge, both friends of his, Samuel Richardson became printer to the House in 1733 and continued as such till 1761. Payments to him for 'printing, folding and stitching bills and reports' begin in the Treasury money books in 1733, his account being certified either by Nicholas Hardinge or by John Grover, one of the clerks, who became a great friend of Richardson and was deeply mourned by him on his death in 1749 (see pp. 71–72). At first the Treasury warrant was made out to Richardson himself, but from 1739 onwards (see T. 53/39, fol. 468) the warrant was made out to Hardinge. There is, however, no proof that at this date the Clerk was paid 50 per cent. of the printer's bill.[2] Mr. William M. Sale in his valuable study *Samuel Richardson, Master Printer* (Cornell University Press, 1950), says on p. 78 of that work that the Clerk of the House was paid 1s. per sheet for copying the bills and reports for press: but I suggest that this was a payment to the clerk who

---

[1] In Abbot's manuscript diary (P.R.O. 30/9/34) there is the following entry for 13 Mar. 1808: 'Hatsell to say that he and Ley meant to propose to Perceval a reduction in the rate of the Copy Money, which in 1796 was about £2000 a year, in 1800 £4000, and since the Union £6000 a year over and above the profit of the Clerk's Office.' See chapter 6, p. 103, Hatsell's statement that Ley resisted this decision.

[2] The principle of compensation to the Clerk for the loss of income by fees through the introduction of printing was, however, certainly established in 1742, when Hardinge was awarded £1,000 for loss of fees due to the decision to print the *Journals*, see chapter 9, p. 200.

actually did the work of preparing the manuscript copy and correcting the proof, and that this clerk was John Grover. Thus, the Treasury money books (T. 53/41, fols. 259–60) record on 20 July 1743 a payment of £154. 7s. to Hardinge for 'printing and other work for the said House in the session 1743 viz: for printing, folding and stitching of bills etc. and for John Grover for attending the service of the said House'. This entry may be compared with the earliest entry in the Treasury books of an itemized account for printing (T. 53/55, fols. 21–23) in the session 1779–80. This shows that the charges were for printing bills or bills with amendments, accounts ordered to be printed and the report of one select committee. The total was as follows:

	£	s.	d.
Total printer's bill	398	11	6
Copy money	199	1	6
Allowed for performing the extraordinary business of the House	150	0	0
	£747	13	0

The copy money, it will be observed, was all but half the printer's bill, but another £150 was added which clearly was paid to some officer of the House for work done. On the other hand, by 1787 the amount of copy money had become eight times as large, and there was no additional sum charged for 'performing the extraordinary business of the House'. This we know, not from the inquiry signed by Sheridan in 1782 which I have not traced, but from a Treasury minute of 21 July 1787 (T. 29/58, fol. 426). This records the receipt of a memorial from Henry Hughs (then printer to the House) praying payment of his account amounting to £4,827. 14s. 6d. including a charge of £1,609. 4s. 10d. copy money to the Clerk of the House (exactly one-third of the total, or half the cost of printing). A warrant was ordered to be prepared accordingly, but with the following addendum:

My Lords are however of opinion that allowing the Clerk of the House of Commons a moiety of the printer's bill in lieu of the advantage he had from copy money is not an advisable mode of compensating him; and will have it under their consideration to reward him in future in a less objectionable manner for the loss he sustains by the proceedings being printed.

This justifiable and dignified remonstrance by my Lords had no sequel at all, for, as already made clear, this method of paying copy money continued until the Clerk received a sum so large that even he had scruples. The variable sum was then commuted—and this in spite of even more forcible objections to the continuance of this payment expressed in the 9th *Report* (p. 181) of the public expenditure committee (1810) referred to above—for a fixed annual payment of £4,300, which almost immediately saved the public over £3,000 a year; and this payment, though after 1820 it was paid to the fee fund with deductions of about £1,000 for clerks in the Journal Office, continued till it was abolished on the report of the 1833 Committee. Incidentally, the existence and size of this addition to the Clerk's emoluments explains several references in Hatsell's letters to John Ley (Ley MSS.) to the receipt of the printing account, e.g. '13 August 1801. I have received Mr Hansard's and Benson's [clerk of the journal] accounts. When the money is paid at the Exchequer I suppose the balance due to us will be about £1,500, or rather less, including the salary'. In the following month he informs Ley regretfully that no money on this account was to be expected before 10 October, as the constantly repeated answer of Treasury to applications was 'no money, no money!'

(2) In this connexion it may be of interest to give some indication of the rate of increase in the printing account[1] of the House from the middle to the end of the eighteenth century. The most reliable guide is in the C.L. Accts., which from 1746 to 1796 give the total sums paid for this service in the year previous to the entry: these accounts are in the series T. 38—at the P.R.O., one volume for each year. After 1796 the item disappears, owing to a change of method (see below).

The sums paid to the Clerk of the House for printing charges appear quite at the end of each volume of the C.L. Accts. among various other miscellaneous charges. These entries are more trustworthy than the corresponding entries in the Treasury money books (the series T. 53/-) because the Treasury sometimes paid the printer's bill in instalments as the printer presented his memorials for payment.

After the entry in the Treasury books for 1743 quoted above, the similar entries for the next two years were for £215 and £273. 15s. respectively. The C.L. Accts. for 1746/7 then show an unusual (at that time) increase to £963. 18s. after which they returned to a fairly normal level of between £250 and £400 up till the year 1771/2. The abnormal expenditures in those years were £532. 5s. in 1749, £472. 18s. 6d. in 1753/4, £180. 17s. 6d. (low) in 1755, £586. 7s. in 1758/9, £200 odd in 1760 and 1763, and £925 in 1766/7. For the following years up to 1796 I give the amounts in columnar form:

---

[1] i.e. the printer's bill for printing reports, bills, accounts, and other papers ordered to be printed. This did not include the cost of printing the *Journal* or the *Votes*, as to which see chapter 9, pp. 200–4.

	£	s.	d.		£	s.	d.
1771/2 . .	422	7	6	1785 . . .	3,160	5	6
1772/3 . .	3,305	1	3[1]	1786 . . .	5,172	16	6
1773/4 . .	421	1	0	1787 . . .	4,827	14	6
1774/5 . .	703	15	6	1788 . . .	2,071	13	0
1775/6 . .	709	6	0	1789 . . .	3,484	18	3
1776/7 . .	1,100	3	9	1790 . . .	3,143	15	6
1777/8 . .	567	13	4	1791 . . .	2,959	18	3
1778/9 . .	502	2	6	1792 . . .	2,533	8	6
1779/80 . .	747	13	0	1793 . . .	3,521	7	3
1780/1 . .	3,337	15	3	1794 . . .	1,814	13	3
1781/2 . .	6,118	4	0	1795 . . .	1,591	8	6
1782/3 . .	4,258	10	3	1796 . . .	4,265	5	9
1783/4 . .	2,460	5	3				

In the session 1796–7 the House, in general keeping with its closer scrutiny of expenditure, changed its method of meeting the cost of printing. An estimate was presented for the total charge of printing and delivering the *Votes* and *Journals* and of printing reports and papers, and a resolution authorizing this expenditure was passed in Committee of Supply. In the ensuing session a similar resolution was passed to meet any deficiency on the previous year's vote. The individual charges, except that for the index to the *Votes*, no longer appeared in the C.L. Accts. As time went on, and the printing of the *Journal* got more in arrears, the various printing expenses came to need six or seven resolutions in Supply. Thus, in session 1819–20, they were as follows: deficiency 1819 on printing the *Votes* £1,425. 11s. 4d.; for printing *Votes* 1820, £3,500; deficiency 1819 on printing reports, &c., £8,765. 8s. 5d.; for printing reports, &c., 1820, £21,000; for reprinting *Journals*, &c., £3,000. It therefore becomes difficult after about 1810 to determine the actual cost of printing *Votes*, *Journals*, and papers respectively for any one year.

For a few years after 1796, however, there are certain indications in the Treasury Board minutes. These record the bills presented by Hughs, Hughs and Hansard (1798–9), or Hansard (1800 onwards) for the printing of reports and papers.

	£	s.	d.		£	s.	d.
1797 . . .	5,965	7	9	1799 . . .	5,137	19	0
1798 . . .	6,956	13	3	1800 . . .	7,762	3	9

[1] The reason for the sudden increase in 1772 and 1781–3 was the printing of the long reports of select committees on East Indian affairs. Similar reasons regularly operated from 1783 onwards, as Luke Hansard recorded in the recollections which he wrote for his sons, see J. C. Trewin and E. M. King, *Printer to the House* (London, 1952), pp. 67–68.

After 1800 the cost of printing reports, &c., becomes mixed with that of printing the *Journals*: but since we know, from Hatsell's statement, that the cost was steadily rising,[1] and that the average copy money for some six years after the Union was £4,300, the average cost of printing reports, &c., for the same period must have been twice that sum and the cost to the public three times that sum, or £12,900. Hatsell states that copy money for 1809, if it had been calculated on the old percentage basis, would have amounted to over £7,500. It is unnecessary to proceed further, since the amounts spent on printing no longer affected the Clerk's copy money. The report of the Select Committee on Printing done for the House (H.C. (1828) 520) opens by remarking that, whereas in 1799 the total expense (they should have said the total estimate) for printing *Journal*, *Votes*, and reports, &c., was £8,000, in 1827 the cost, exclusive of printing the *Journal*, was £46,184. This enormous increase, however, was largely caused by the immense rise in the cost of the *Votes* due to the printing in full of petitions upon public matters (particularly parliamentary reform).

APPENDIX VIII

A précis of Brit. Mus. MS. Stowe 373, being the minutes of proceedings of the Select Committee on the State of the Gaols touching the charge against Sir Robert Eyre, Lord Chief Justice of Common Pleas (1730)

Preliminary. The select committee referred to was appointed on 25 February 1728/9, on the initiative of Mr. (afterwards General) Oglethorpe who was its first chairman, to inquire into the state of the gaols of the kingdom. The committee made a long report on the Fleet prison which was entered at length in the *Journal* and ordered to be printed (21 C.J. 274–83) on 20 March of the same year; and in the following year they made a long report on the Marshalsea prison, also set out at length in the *Journal* and ordered to be printed (21 C.J. 378–87). The charge against Chief Justice Eyre was that he had personally

---

[1] See p. 112 and p. 321, n. 1 above.

visited Thomas Bambridge, late Warden of the Fleet, whilst he was a prisoner at Newgate under a commitment of the House of Commons, and had made suggestions to him calculated to defeat the ends of justice; and this charge had come by way of information to the committee who in 1730 were investigating the state of the King's Bench prison, on which they similarly made a long report, entered in the *Journal*, and ordered to be printed (21 C.J. 576–85) on 12 May 1730. Previous to making the report on the King's Bench prison they made a report on the charge against Eyre which they had taken up as a separate issue. This report, which found the charge false, malicious, and utterly groundless, was made on 5 May and was entered at length in the *Journal* (21 C.J. 567–8) but was not ordered to be printed.

The manuscript is written in a small, bound folio book containing seventy-two folios, of which seventy-one are covered on both sides. It is written throughout in a fine, clerkly hand. On fol. 1 the title is set out, namely: 'Proceedings of the Committee of the House of Commons appointed to inquire into the State of ye Gaols; and touching a Charge against Sr Robert Eyre, Kn^t, Lord Chief Justice of the Common Pleas, for personally visiting Thos Bambridge late Warden of the Fleet, whilst he was a prisoner in Newgate, under a Commitment of the House of Commons.' On fol. 2 the title is set out again, followed by the words: 'Taken by L. Kenn with ye copys of ye Several Examinations taken before, and the Several Papers produced to the said C^{ee} upon that Occasion, as also the Special Report made to the House thereupon, and the Debates touching the method of drawing the same.'

L. Kenn (see chapter 7, pp. 133–5, 138, and Appendix IX, pp. 330–1), therefore, was the author of this manuscript, and fol. 3 explains his presence at the committee. This explanation sets forth that the committee, having had the information against Sir Robert Eyre in the course of their inquiry, had thought fit to inquire into it, and had accordingly taken several examinations of witnesses—four in number, whose names are given—on various dates between 20 and 25 April, 'at which times, as well as some time before, Mr Edwards attended the said C^{ee} as Clerk'. But then the committee, finding it to be a matter of great consequence both to the Government and to the reputation of Eyre, resolved to 'enter very strictly' into such inquiry, and 'being desirous to have the Examinations upon that Occasion taken with the greatest exactness, thought fit to have them taken down in Short Hand, whereupon Mr Kenn received their commands to attend them, which he accordingly did on the 25th of April (and continued to attend y^e

said C^ee till the Report was made upon that Affair)'. Kenn goes on to explain that the minutes only take place from 25 April, but that, since the former proceedings had had to be recapitulated for many members who had not been present at them, all that was material appears in his minutes.

Fol. 4. Kenn's minute reads:

> At the Speaker's Chambers at the House of Commons:
> At the C^ee appointed to inquire into the State of the Gaols of this Kingdom.
>> Edward Hughes Esq. in the Chair.
>> Sabti 25 die Aprilis 1730.
> The Committee met, and Examined Ric^d Ackerman in the most Solemn Manner, part of which Examination was taken by Mr Edwards and part by Mr Kenn.

The minutes of this day continue by recording the absence of a witness, a woman. She was ordered to attend. The Chairman read her information taken before him as a Justice of the Bench and a letter from her. Twenty persons were ordered to attend the following Monday at 8 in the morning.

Fol. 5 gives the minutes of proceedings on Monday 27 April, when four witnesses were examined and letters were produced. All the witnesses ordered to attend on Wednesday at 8 o'clock. With fol. 6 the longer notation of proceedings begins, of which the gist will be given without exact folio numberings.

On Wednesday 29 April the committee was very full, several members being present for the first time and desiring to be informed of previous proceedings. The Chairman gave information and read letters received. The clerk Edwards, who had been appointed to attend the committee in the absence of Kenn, was then called upon to inform the committee whether he had taken any, and what, minutes of the examinations. He replied that the examinations were dictated to him by Mr. Oglethorpe and some other members of the committee, but that the minutes of the committee were kept by another clerk, one Parker.

Then Thomas Parker was asked what he had done in relation to the minutes: he said he had entered the names of the members that came, but took no minutes of the examinations. Then Edwards, being asked whether he had any of the papers out of which the examinations were extracted, said he had been employed in drawing examinations while other witnesses were being examined. Further, on a question relating to the examination of James Brown, Edwards said that the examination was drawn from the minutes of Sir Archibald Grant and Sir Humphrey Howarth, and that Sir Archibald dictated to him from those minutes, and dictated to him at the window. When asked whether during the time he was at the window the Chairman was going on with other business, he said he believed so. It appears that Sir A. Grant and Mr. Oglethorpe had both taken down minutes of Brown's examination, and that Sir Abraham Elton had also taken minutes in shorthand of the same examination. In the appendix both Grant's minutes and Ogle-thorpe's minutes are set out, followed by Edwards's minute taken from the several minutes by members. Brown had signed the minute drawn by Edwards. Similarly the evidence of Ann Jones had been taken down by Grant and Edwards, and the final minute (all set out in the appendix) was read over to her while the committee was sitting and signed by her.

Then a motion was made that the House be moved to adjourn over to Friday, that the committee might have an opportunity of sitting there, being numerous, which after some debate was agreed to.

[Note. The House did adjourn from Wednesday to the following Friday as recorded in the *Journal*, but there is no reason given for that adjournment. This manuscript alone gives the reason.]

On Thursday 30 April the committee met in the Speaker's Chamber and adjourned into the House. All the minutes and examinations, both those taken by Edwards and verbatim by Kenn were read. Certain witnesses were called and contradicted one another. It was then resolved that 'there hath been a wicked conspiracy carried on by certain infamous and profligate persons to vilify and asperse the character of Sir R. Eyre': it was also resolved that the informations given to the committee against Eyre were false, malicious, scandalous, and utterly groundless. The committee adjourned till Saturday at 8 o'clock.

On Saturday 2 May the committee met. Debate arising touching the method of drawing the report, after some time spent therein, it was referred to the Chairman, Mr. Attorney General, Mr. Solicitor General, Sir William Young, Mr. Earl, and Mr. Towers to consider of and draw up the same. The speeches made at this debate were recorded verbatim by Kenn.

On Sunday evening the Chairman, the Attorney General, the Solicitor General, Sir Abraham Elton, Mr. Towers, and Mr. Caesar met at Sir William Young's, where Kenn attended them with all the papers and examinations, and the report was drawn up. These proceedings were all taken down by Kenn and included, with the draft report, a paragraph disagreed to.

On Monday 4 May the committee met and the report was read a first time, and then paragraph by paragraph. The first five paragraphs were agreed to. The sixth and seventh paragraphs were amended. The resolutions were read, and it was ordered that the report as amended with the several resolutions be reported to the House when they would please to receive the same.

APPENDIX IX

Treasury precedents of allowances to Clerks for attendance on Select Committees, &c., of the House of Commons (Colchester Papers. P.R.O. 30/9/32)

FOR some unexplained reason, among the papers appended to Speaker Abbot's manuscript Diary at the end of the year 1798 there are many sheets relating to the payments made by the Select Committee on the State of the Public Records, which sat between February and July 1800 and reported in the latter month, to various persons including the clerk to the committee, Samuel Gunnell. They begin with the minutes of this committee on 4 July 1800 at which it was resolved:

That the Chairman be requested to confer with Mr Speaker upon the pecuniary compensation that it may be proper to make for the special services rendered to this Committee by (here follow the names of six persons, including Alexander Luders, Joseph Planta the principal librarian of the British Museum, and four officials in various legal departments), and also concerning the extra allowance which it may be proper to give to Mr Samuel Gunnell, the Clerk to the Committee, for his extraordinary trouble and unremitting attention to the daily business and extensive correspondence of this Committee, and for his expenses incurred in respect thereof, from the date of their appointment, viz. the 18 February last until this 4th day of July.

From a list of suggested rewards to persons in Abbot's handwriting it appears that he calculated on paying Gunnell

	£
120 sitting days at 2 guineas . .	252
Actual expenses	30
	282
Extra	18
	300

There is then a letter from Gunnell, dated 4 College Street 17 July 1800, referring to some accounts for the report of the committee, and inquiring if he was right in supposing that the Speaker (Addington) would promise his interception for some 'immediate relief', with profuse expressions of gratitude to Abbot. This, of course, refers to his plaint of the year before as regards his extreme poverty, with Abbot's strong interest in which I have dealt in chapter 6, pp. 115–17. This select committee, pursuant to a humble address (55 C.J. 790), was granted the sum of £1,095 to be distributed to various persons (see C.L. Accts. 1800–1, fols. 160–2, and 56 C.J. 774, also Treasury minute in T. 29/76). In Abbot's MS. diary Gunnell's letter mentioned above is followed by an account of how the sum of £1,095 was spent. This account shows that £223 was paid to Gunnell, for which he gave Abbot a receipt dated 18 Sept. 1800, and that on 22 Sept. there was remaining a balance of £127. 8s. 6d. Abbot recorded that he paid this balance to Gunnell on the following 23 Dec. Then follows the document which is the true subject of this Appendix. It is headed: 'Instances of Allowances to Clerks of the House of Commons', and it is a list of such payments, giving in each case the name of the payee, the services and the committee involved, and (in the margin) the date of the Treasury Warrant or, at later dates, the *Journal* reference for the humble address sanctioning the respective payments. I reproduce the document in full, noting (in italics) the folio reference in the Treasury books and inserting (also in italics) certain other instances which the Treasury clerk who compiled this document had overlooked. General comment on the information which it provides will be found in the text of my chapter 7, pp. 136–48.

Instances of Allowances to Clerks of the House of Commons.

Dates of the Warrants.		£
19 Jan. 1721 *T. 52/31 fol. 195.*	To Mr (*Lucas*) Kenn for recompense to the clerks attending the Committee upon the South Sea Business[1]	1200
26 Apr. 1725 26 May 1725 *T. 52/33 fol. 339 (£500) and fol. 366 (£700).*	To Mr (*Joseph*) Tudor for recompense to clerks and officers attending the Committee to prepare impeachment against Lord Macclesfield[2]	1200
26 May 1725 *T. 52/33 fol. 363.*	Bounty to Mr Kenn (*no reason stated*)	150

[1] The famous committee of 1720/1 whose report was printed in the *Journal* on 16 Feb. (19 C.J. 425–50).

[2] See 20 C.J. 408, 453–9, 478–84, 503 for the activities of the committee appointed to draw up articles of impeachment against the Earl of Macclesfield.

Dates of the Warrants		£
27 May 1729 *T. 52/36 fol. 342.*	To Mr (*Francis*) Child for recompense to clerks and officers attending service of the Committee upon State of Gaols[1]	700
27 May 1730 *T. 52/36 fol. 505.*	*To Ditto for ditto*	*400*
16 May 1732 *T. 52/37 fol. 393.*	To Mr (*John*) Burman for clerks, officers and incidents attending service of the Committee upon the petition of the creditors of the Charitable Corporation[2]	1200
13 Nov. 1733 *T. 52/38 fol. 178.*	To Mr Tudor for clerks and incidents attending service of the Committee upon Frauds in the Customs[3]	900
19 Jan. 1733 *T. 52/38 fol. 102.*	To Mr (*John*) Grover for clerks and incidents attending service of the Committee upon the petition of the creditors of the York Buildings Company[4]	350
1737. C.L. Accts. 1737–8 fol. 102 not among Treasury Warrants.	*To Mr John Naylor without account for his extraordinary service in attending Committees appointed to consider the petition relating to the manufacture of iron and to the Justices of the Peace of Middlesex[5]*	50
13 July 1742 *T. 52/42 fol. 35.*	To Mr (*John*) Burman for clerks, officers and incidents attending service of the Committee to inquire into the conduct of Lord Orford[6]	2650

[1] See Appendix VIII for this committee's reports.

[2] See 21 and 22 C.J. for several reports of this committee; also, *R. Comm. Hist. MSS. Egmont MSS.* i. 219–21, 242, 266, 271 for allusions to this committee in Viscount Percival's diary. After the debate on the committee's report on 3 May 1732 Sir Richard Sutton and Sir Archibald Grant were expelled and others were censured.

[3] The report of this committee was ordered by the House to be printed (22 C.J. 199).

[4] See 22 C.J. 145, 172–98 for the two reports of this committee: the first report was ordered to be printed, but the motion for printing the long second report was negatived.

[5] So far as I can discover, the only record of this payment is in the C.L. Accts. The committee on the petition from the manufacturing towns against the manufacture of iron in Massachusetts reported on 21 Mar. 1737/8 (23 C.J. 109–17). The committee on the petition from St. Giles's in the Fields and other parishes complaining of the misapplication of money levied for county rates by the Middlesex justices reported on 3 June 1737 (22 C.J. 894).

[6] This was the committee of secrecy on Walpole's administration of the Treasury, who reported on 13 May and 30 June 1742. The first report was ordered to be printed, but the second report, occupying with its voluminous appendixes forty-two pages of the *Journal* (24 C.J. 289–331), was not printed. This long report explains why the expenses were so large.

Dates of the Warrants		£
4 Feb. 1746 T. 52/43 fol. 496.	To Mr (*Samuel*) Littlemore for attending the Committee on the State of the Army[1]	400
Ditto.	To Mr (*Newdigate*) Poyntz for his attendance on the Committee relating to the Poor Laws[2]	50
21 Dec. 1748 T. 52/44 fol. 502.	To Mr (*John*) Sharpe[2] for Solicitor, clerks and incidents attending service of the Committee on the impeachment of Lord Lovat[4]	2000
8 Oct. 1755 T. 52/47 fol. 196.	To Mr (*Robert*) Yeates to reimburse his expenses for clerks and assistants in preparing sundry bills during the last three years[5]	600
1755. C.L. Accts. 1756–7 T. 29/32 fol. 334.	*To Mr Newdigate Poyntz to reimburse his expenses and for services to the Committee on the Lottery of 1753*[6]	50
3 Aug. 1757 C.L. Accts. 1757–8 and T. 29/32 fol. 476.	To Mr Poyntz to reimburse his expenses and in reward for his service and attendance during the time the Bill for the better ordering of the Militia Forces was preparing and depending in the House of Commons[7]	350

[1] See 25 C.J. 162, 166 (2 June 1746) for the report.

[2] A bill on this subject was brought in and referred to a committee of the whole House in 1746.

[3] Solicitor to the Treasury: he was appointed solicitor to the committee of managers for the impeachment (25 C.J. 286).

[4] See 25 C.J. 211, 213–15, 234, 241, 256, 286 for the proceedings relating to the impeachment of Lord Lovat.

[5] Yeates petitioned the Treasury on 30 July 1755 praying a compensation for money expended by him and for services performed by him in the last five sessions. The Treasury minuted that the Speaker should be desired to report what he thought proper to be allowed (T. 29/32, fol. 114). On 1 Oct. (ibid., fol. 342) Nicholas Hardinge, then joint secretary to the Treasury, reported that the Speaker was of opinion that Yeates was entitled to £100 for expenses incurred and paid by him in the last five sessions and that he well deserved the reward of £100 (*sci.* per session) for his services in the said sessions, and that the Speaker recommended the continuation of the yearly allowance to the petitioner. A warrant for £600 was ordered to be prepared accordingly. What committees Yeates attended in the five sessions cannot be determined. For Yeates's subsequent appointment as a principal clerk in the Treasury see chapter 8, pp. 164–5.

[6] See 26 C.J. 987–1001 for the long report (14 Mar. 1754) on this case of peculation.

[7] A Treasury minute (T. 29/32, fol. 476) recorded 'a representation by several members of the committee for the Militia Bill proposing that £350 be allowed to Poyntz' in reward for business done by him and for his attendance relative to the bill. There was a Militia Act passed almost every session between 1756 and 1761/2,

Dates of the Warrants		£
21 Aug. 1758 C.L. Accts. 1758–9.	To Mr (*Robert*) Yeates for his services and expenses as clerk of the Committee to consider Weights and Measures[1]	300
1759. C.L. Accts. 1759–60.	To Mr Yeates to be distributed by him to the persons mentioned in the paper signed by Lord Carysfort Chairman of the Committee to consider of Weights and Measures	500
1762. C.L. Accts. 1762–3 and T. 29/34 fol. 339.	*To Mr Poyntz for service and attendance while the Militia Bill was in progress*[2]	350
26 May 1772 by letter to 1st Lord of the Ty.	To Mr John Benson for his services and expenses in attending the Committee to inquire into the affairs of the East India Company	200
1773. By letter.	To Mr Geo. White for Dº on Dº Committee re-appointed	300

Addresses for Monies to be advanced on Account of Attendances upon Select Committees.

Journals.	
Vol. 34. 385 28 June 1773 Secrecy Cᵉᵉ £1000 950 infra ———— 1950£ (a line and arrow point from 950 to the first entry for 1774 below)	£1000 to be issued to the Chairman of the Committee of Secrecy to inquire into the state of the East India Company to be distributed to several clerks at the East India House for extraordinary trouble in attending on the Committee.
Select Cᵉᵉ £ 200 450 infra 100 infra ———— 750£ (lines and arrows point from 450 and 100 to the 2nd and 3rd entries for 1774)	£200 to the Chairman of the Committee appointed to inquire into the nature, state and condition of the East India Company to be paid to Mr Johnson one of the clerks in the East India House.

preceded in many cases by a select committee to draw up estimates. The similar payment in 1762 only appears in the C.L. Accts. after being sanctioned by the Treasury minute referred to in the margin.

[1] This committee made two reports on 26 May 1758 and 11 Apr. 1759 respectively (see *Reports of Committees, 1715–1801*, vol. ii).

[2] See footnote 7 on opposite page.

Journals.
Vol. 34. 819
21 June 1774

£950 to George White Esq. for his attendance and expenses in last session as clerk to the Committee of Secrecy (above). £450 to Geo. White Junior Esq. for attendance and expenses in last session as clerk of the Committee to inquire into the nature etc. of the East India Company.

£100 to Mr Thomas Morton one of the clerks in the East India House.[1]

36 C.J. 538
1777   £500
£1000

Geo. White for expenses incurred in business done by authority of the House relating to Inquiries into the State of the Poor[2]

1778   £500
* see below

To D° for D°.

38 C.J. 1143.
1782   £500
£1000

To Geo. White Esq. for expenses and attendance on the Committee of Secrecy—War in the Carnatic.[3]

39 C.J. 698
1783   £500

To D° for D°.

38 C.J. 1143
1782   £500
£1000

To Mr Evatt for expenses and attendance on the Select Committee appointed to inquire into the State of Administration of Justice in Bengal, Behar and Orissa.[4]

350
————
1350

[1] The sums written in the margin of this list show how the allowances issued were divided between the services of the two committees on East Indian affairs of 1772–4. The reports of these committees and of the equally important committees of 1781–3 on the same subject were all printed and are bound up in vols. v–viii of the 16-volume set of *Reports 1715–1801* produced in 1803 at Speaker Abbot's instigation. See Lucy S. Sutherland, *The East India Company in Eighteenth Century Politics* (London, 1952), on the composition, aims, and political aspect of all these committees. The two Whites had to memorialize the Treasury in 1774 to get their money (see T. 29/43, fols. 441–2).

[2] The services for which this payment was made are discussed in chapter 8, pp. 181–2. They were wholly different in kind from attendance on committees.

[3] This was the committee first set up in April 1781 and reconstituted on 30 Nov. of that year to investigate the progress, conduct, and present state of the Mahratta war and other hostilities in which the Presidency of Bengal was engaged (see 38 C.J. 430, 435, 598, 600, and Sutherland, op. cit. in footnote 1 above, pp. 362–74). It was the Government committee of which Henry Dundas was chairman and Charles Jenkinson his right-hand man. These time-to-time issues usually sanctioned by humble address and then applied for by memo. to the Treasury (see entries in T. 29/50, fols. 285–6, T. 29/52, fols. 290–1, and T. 29/54, fols. 215, 254), do not show the total cost of this committee which finally amounted to £3,263. 19s. 9d. (see 40 C.J. 397). Their last four reports were made in Feb. and Mar. 1782.

[4] See preceding note. This was the Opposition committee and the organ for Burke's powerful attack upon the East India Company. Their eleventh and last

Journals.

39 C.J. 698 (1783)	£500	To Mr Evatt for Dᵒ more.

$39\ C.J.\ 698$ $\pounds500$ To Mr Evatt for Dᵒ more.
(1783)

	£200	To one of the clerks of the East India House.
	£150	To another clerk of the East India House.
40 C.J. 1166 1785	£220	To Mr Arthur Benson for actual expenses and trouble in the attending the Committee on British Fisheries.[1]
41 C.J. 12 June 20 days 1786	£100	To Mr Henry Gunnell for attending Dᵒ.
42 *C.J. 796 1787	£3000	To Mr White towards reimbursing him for expenses for business pursuant to Acts of Session respecting the Poor (for procuring and abstracting returns).[2]
43 C.J. 650	£460	More to Dᵒ in full remuneration for Dᵒ business.
1778, by letter to the 1st Lord of Ty.		To Henry Gunnell for attendance on the Committee appointed to examine the Accounts of Extras of the Army[3] £ 150
1782, by Dᵒ. 30 days.		Committee to inquire into the Management of the Victualling Office. H. Gunnell[4] 150
1783, by Dᵒ. 20 days		Mr Samˡ Gunnell. Committee appointed upon the petition from the Inhabitants of Portsmouth[5] 105
1789		Committee[6] appointed to examine Physicians respecting the King's Health—sat twice a day 4 gⁿˢ p.d.

report was made in November 1783. The total cost of this committee was £3,549. 13s. It was first appointed to examine the petition against the Supreme Court (38 C.J. 202) in Feb. 1781, and was reconstituted in Dec. with its full terms of reference (ibid., pp. 599–600).

[1] See *Reports of Committees, 1715–1801*, vol. x.

[2] See p. 334, n. 2 above.

[3] For the appointment and report of this committee, see 36 C.J. 871, 997–8. The payment was made on the recommendation of the chairman of the committee on the Accounts of Extraordinary Services of the Army (T. 29/47, fol. 228).

[4] See T. 29/52, fol. 252, for the Treasury minute of the chairman's recommendation that the committee clerk (unnamed) should receive £150 for his trouble.

[5] This committee was appointed in two successive sessions 1783 and 1784 to inquire into frauds in the Victualling Office. On the application of the chairman, Mr. Jervoise, allowances of £105 were made to Samuel Gunnell (for 1783) and £100 (for 1784) to G. White, junior (see T. 29/54, fol. 230, T. 29/55, fol. 419, and for the reports, 39 C.J. 421, 692, 1049).

[6] This examination took place after the King's first serious breakdown: for the reports, see 44 C.J. 6–10, 47–87.

N.B.—From 1782 onwards this list is not exhaustive, but I have not thought it necessary to make it complete. I mention the omissions in chapter 7, pp. 144–5.

INDEX

Abbot, Charles, M.P. (later Baron Colchester): Speaker (1802–17), 96; and the quarrel between Hatsell and Ley, 86, 102–6; Gillray's sketch of, mentioned, 91 n. 2; his Population Act (1800), 94–95, 182 n. 3; and John Rickman, 94–97, 182 n. 3; and appointments to the table, 97, 102–6; and Jeremiah Dyson, jun., 101 n. 2; on the Speaker's income, 114; and Samuel Gunnell, 115–17, 136 n. 2, 150–1, 179–80, 329–30; and clerks and their pay, 125–6, 136–7, 174, 208, 231, 235 n. 2; and assistant deputy clerks, 141 n. 2; and additional committee rooms, 152; and committee clerks (1812), 153, 185 n. 1; and Sir Edward Stracey, 157; and committee for expiring laws, 175 n. 2; and committee on the state of the public records (1800), 136, 195, 196, 329; new form of *Votes* instituted by (1817), 209–11; and private bill proceedings, 234 n. 2, 255; and copy money, 321.

Abingdon Building, Westminster, home of Robert Yeates, 72, 168.

accountants (House of Commons), 275.

accounts and papers: custody and arrangement of (1800), 39–41, 197; Clerk's fees for copies of, 24–26, 40, 109, 111–13, 115, 295; printing of, 109, 110, 320–5; *see* copy money.

Ackerman, Richard, 327.

Acts: supply of six sets as perquisite, 172; salary, &c., of deliverer of copies to members (1731), 310.

Acts of Parliament:
All Souls College Act (1715), 40 n. 2.
Assize of Bread (1718), 316–17.
Balliol College Act (1695), 129, 187, 188, 301, 314–15.
Bankrupts (1711–12, 1718), 316, 317.
Burke's Act (1782), 142.
Covent Garden Parochial Act (1660), 313.
Expiring Laws, 175–6.
Farington Estate Act (1698), 129, 187, 188, 301, 315.
Grenville's Act (1770) (controverted

elections), 77, 121 n. 2, 123, 214, 217, 219–24, 243 n. 1.
House of Commons Offices (1800, 1812), 114–18, 120–121, 226, 237–9, 273; (1834), 256–7; (1846), 273; (1850), 274 n. 1; (1856), 239.
Marine Mutiny Act, 245.
Militia Acts, 245.
Mutiny Acts, 180, 245.
Naturalization Acts: General (1709), 45, 49, 56, 57, 129, 286, 287, 294; Lady North's (1706), 129, 301, 315–16.
Naval Mutiny Act, 180.
Parliamentary Witnesses Act (1858), 134 n. 1.
Parliamentary Witnesses' Oaths Act (1871), 134 n. 1.
Peel's Act (1839), 222 n. 1, 226, 268.
Pensions Acts, 268 n. 4.
Plantation Act (1764), 168 n. 2.
Population Acts (1800 &c.), 94–95, 182 n. 3.
Reform Acts, 96, 158.
Registration of members' parliamentary attendances (1514), 9, 10 n. 1.
Shorthand reporting of evidence in election committees (1802), 224–5.
Stamp Act, 76.
State of the Poor, 181–3.
Taxing of costs in private bills (1825), 258 n. 1.
Taxing officer in private bills (1847), 258 n. 1.
Westminster Bridge (1767), 187–8.
Wynn's Act (1788), 121, 223, 225–6, 258.

Addington, Henry, M.P. (later 1st Viscount Sidmouth), 80, 93, 121 n. 5, 207; close friend of John Hatsell, 83–85; and Charles Jenkinson, 84; at Marden Park, 89; Gillray's sketch of, 91 n. 2; and salaries of officers of the House, 115; and Samuel Gunnell, 115–17, 330.

agent: Parliamentary, *see under* Parliamentary agency; Treasury, *see under* Parliamentary agency (2).

Aiskew, Michael: Clerk Assistant (1727–40), 64, 281, 309; deputy for Edward Stables during illness, 50; picture of

Clerks (*cont.*)
clerk of the fees (*cont.*)
Treasury agent, 169–79, 244; allowance for stationery, 172; orders
stationery for the House, 172; office
accommodation, 174; salary from
Treasury till 1835, 126, 170–1, 178,
245, Appendix X; Treasury payment
abolished, 258; expense accounts of
(1777–1817), 173; fees as collector of
fees, 171, 245, Appendix X; subordinate staff and their pay, 171, 173–4,
205–9, 244–5, 258; private bill agency
conducted by, 183–5, 258, 262–3, 266;
agent for Mutiny and Naval Mutiny
Acts, 180, 245. *See also* Rosier; Dorington, J. and J. E.; Fees; Public Bill Office.
clerk of ingrossments: holders of the
office, 71, 72, 73, 74, 75, 88, 229–30, 255,
283; emoluments and fees, 154, 228,
230–1; dealt with printing of papers,
194 n. 2; post probably created by
Jodrell, 228; Treasury allowance for
examining ingrossments of public bills,
231, 255; 2nd clerk of, 73, 229; both
offices had become sinecures (1772),
154, 229–30; sinecure offices abolished
(1833), 255; subordinate ingrossing
clerks, 88, 126, 229, 255, 283. *See also*
Ingrossment; Ingrossing Office.
clerk of the journals and papers: creation
of official post, 194; chief clerk in the
Journal Office, 40, 123, 194, 282; his
office formerly in the Court of Wards,
195–6; custody and arrangement of the
Journals and papers (1800), 196–8;
emoluments, 112, 125, 126, 197, 205–9,
238, 250, 259, Appendix X; holders of
the office, 71, 77, 78, 188 n. 1, 194, 204,
250, 282; official residence in Abingdon
Street (1803–35), 198, 204; custodian of
early library, 212. *See also* Journal
Office and Clerk of the papers.
clerk of the papers, 71, 73, 193–4, 282;
origin of official post, 71; combined
with clerkship of journals (1754), 194.
See also *Journal Office*, Hamlyn.
clerk of the public bill office, *see under*
Public Bill Office and Clerk of the fees.
clerk of recognizances: accommodation,
224; duties, 225–6, 258; fees, 226;
necessitated by Wynn's Act (1788),
225; office combined with clerkship of

elections, 258; office abolished (1839),
226, 268. *See also* Rose, W. G.
clerks of the Treasury, *see* Treasury.
Clerks:
under-clerks (early): the Clerk's men or
servants, 11, 15–17, 31–32; accommodation, 15; duties, 15–19, 24, 25;
numbers, 15; personal, employed at
own charge by Jodrell, 40, 52, 291;
payments to, 16–19, 24–25, 31, 34.
See Brerewood, William; Hamlyn,
Zachary.
under-clerks (later): gratuities, salaries,
and fees, 45, 46, 48, 49–50, 57, 108,
123–6, 174–5, 293, 299; regulation of
emoluments (1812), 117–18; (1820–
33), 238–61; (1828–35), 266–7; lesser
clerks often underpaid, 115–17; salary
paid out of the fee fund after 1820,
237; need for revision of method of
pay, 240; Joseph Hume on clerks'
emoluments, 241–2; reforms of establishment after 1833, 240–77; parliamentary agency by, 179–89, 261–7;
table of emoluments (1832), 242,
Appendix X; estimates for emoluments (1835), 260; further reform
(1848–50), 268–77; retirement allowances, 268 & n. 4; pay for attending
divisions (1848), 270, 272. *See* Clerk
of the House; Committee Office;
Fees Office; Journal Office; Private
Bill Office; Parliamentary agency.
the four 'clerks (under-clerks) without
doors': the first quartet to appear in
Treasury books (1696), 53–57; Courthope's minute-book, evidence of as
to functions, 54–55, 132–3; their
salaries from Civil List, 49–50, 53–55,
57, 108, 128–9, 310; their fees in
respect of private bill committees,
54–56, 129–30, 288–9, 291–2; petitions
by, 54–57, 129–30, 135, 284–95;
special payments to for attending
select committees, 139–40, 331–2;
became the four principal committee
clerks, 57, 88, 128, 135, 154–5; biographical, 55–56, 69–78; deputies, 88,
123–4, 141; stationery allowance and
accommodation, 131, 310; rate of post
for land tax (1731), 310; senior clerk
without doors original collector of
fees, 57, 130–1, 292, 303, 310; list of,

ment of clerks under, 31; solicitor to the Court of Chancery, 35–36; his wife, 35; joint lessee of Lincoln's Inn, 36; English agent for the Earl of Meath, 26 n. 1; moved to Syon Hill, 39; his garden at Westminster, 39; maintains a clerk for keeping records of the House, 39–40, 190, 192, 291, 293; *and see* Hamlyn, Zachary; Speaker's tribute to his keeping of the *Journals*, 40, 298; his retirement (1726), 41; memorial inscription in Lewknor Church, 41; reorganization for preserving and arranging papers, 42, 190–2; and the four clerks without doors, 42, 53; first modern Clerk of the House, 42, 58; emoluments, 42–46, 107, 109 n. 1, 110, 130, 288, 295–9, 316, 317; grants from William III and Queen Anne, 43; a servant of the Crown and the House, 45; and nomination of Clerk Assistant, 50–51; gold medals, 58; his 40 years' service not fully appreciated, 58; transcription of early *Journals* under, 40 n. 3, 192; losses (1713), 291, 293.

Jodrell, Paul, jun.: eldest son of Paul Jodrell, sen., Treasurer of Lincoln's Inn, 36; reversion of the Clerkship granted by Queen Anne, 43.

Jodrell, Sir Paul, physician, 35.

Jodrell, Richard Paul, scholar, poet, and dramatist, 35.

John de Scardeburgh: Clerk (1385–1414), 3, 280; granted an aid (1388), 4; relations with Richard II, 4; and 'Anonimale Chronicle of St. Mary's, York', 4.

Johnson, Edward: principal clerk Private Bill Office (1824–43), 283; emoluments (1832), 254–5, Appendix X.

Johnson, Mr., clerk in the East India House: allowance for attending committee (1774), 333.

Johnson, Samuel, 73.

Jones, Ann, examined by Gaols committee, 327, 328.

Jones, Arthur, clerk in the fees office: emoluments and duties (1832), 246, Appendix X; private bill agent (1832, 1835), 262, 267.

Jones, David, sen.: clerk without doors (1795–1801), 282; clerk of ingrossment (1772–95), 88, 142, 242, 283.

Jones, David, jun.: clerk of ingrossment

(1806–31), 229–30, 242, 247, 283; private bill agent, 183 n. 1, 262; friend of Luke Hansard, 183 n. 1.

Jones, Richard: assistant to Thomas Dyson, clerk of elections (1820–35), 183, 243, Appendix X; parliamentary agent, 263.

Jones & Walmisley, private bill agents (1832), 262–4, 267.

Journal of the House:
general:
inception, 5, 10, 12; 'Seymour' and 'Onslow', names of first and second vols. of the printed *Journal*, 12, 200; developed from the register of bills, 13; 1584–1601 volumes missing, 13, 190; parliamentary control of contents, 13; individual speeches not to be recorded in, 13 n. 2; Scobell's surrender of, 7–8; early supervision of, by members, 13, 190; safe custody of, 14, 192, 195; part of the Clerk's luggage, 14; 1629, *Journal* written in two different hands, 15; Speaker's tribute to Jodrell's keeping of, 40, 298; transcription of, under Jodrell, 40, 41, 191 n. 3, 192; Clerk provides (for fee) copies of *Journal* entries, 26, 46, 109, 111; *see also* copy money; names of Clerk Assistants not mentioned in, 28, 30, 47, 51; kept at William Brerewood's lodgings, 32; John Evelyn borrows some volumes, 32; Jodrell recovers folios borrowed by Samuel Pepys, 37–38; unauthorized printing of, Jodrell's complaint, 37; Jodrell employs personal clerk as custodian of, 39–40, 291; *and see* Hamlyn, Zachary; table of fees (1700), entered in, 46; Jeremiah Dyson reputed to know them by heart, 65; John Hatsell's intensive studies of, 82; minutes not entered in, recorded in Courthope's minute book, 132–3; original manuscript now housed at the Public Record Office, 191 n. 1; Nicholas Hardinge's report on the state of, 40 n. 3, 194, 199 n. 3; Arthur Benson's account of arrangement of (1547–1800), 196–8; warehousing of printed stock, 198, 204, 253.
compilation:
inception and development of, 5, 10, 12; the Clerk of the House and, 11–12,

PRINTED IN
GREAT BRITAIN
AT THE
UNIVERSITY PRESS
OXFORD
BY
CHARLES BATEY
PRINTER
TO THE
UNIVERSITY